HIGH PROFITS

FROM RARE COIN INVESTMENT

THE BASIC PREMISES OF THIS BOOK:

✔ A quality collection is the best investment.

✔ Successful rare coin investment requires knowledge.

✔ This book will help you gain knowledge.

HIGH PROFITS

FROM RARE COIN INVESTMENT

Thirteenth Edition
By Q. David Bowers

Published by:
Bowers and Merena Galleries, Inc.
Box 1224, Wolfeboro, New Hampshire 03894

Other books by Q. David Bowers

Coins and Collectors, United States Half Cents 1793-1857, Early American Car Advertisements, Put Another Nickel In, Guide Book of Automatic Musical Instruments—Vol. I, Guide Book of Automatic Musical Instruments—Vol. II, How to Be a Successful Coin Dealer, Encyclopedia of Automatic Musical Instruments, How to Start a Coin Collection, Collecting Rare Coins For Profit, A Tune for a Token, Adventures With Rare Coins, The History of United States Coinage (for the Johns Hopkins University), Treasures of Mechanical Music (with Art Reblitz), The Postcards of Alphonse Mucha (with Mary Martin), Robert Robinson, American Illustrator, Harrison Fisher (with Ellen and George Budd), Common Sense Coin Investment, Official ANA Grading Standards for U.S. Coins (Introduction), United States Gold Coins: An Illustrated History, U.S. Copper Coins: An Action Guide for the Collector and Investor, U.S. Three-Cent and Five-Cent Pieces: An Action Guide For the Collector and Investor, U.S. Ten-Cent to Fifty-Cent Pieces: An Action Guide for the Collector and Investor, U.S. Coins By Design Type: An Action Guide for the Collector and Investor, An Inside View of the Coin Hobby in the 1930s: the Walter P. Nichols File, Virgil Brand: the Man and His Era—Profile of a Numismatist, The Moxie Encyclopedia, Vol. I, The Compleat Collector, Abe Kosoff: Dean of Numismatics, Muriel Ostriche: Princess of Silent Films, The Strange Career of Dr. Wilkins: A Numismatic Inquiry, Mint Marks (Introduction), Nickelodeon Theatres and Their Music, The Norweb Collection: An American Legacy (with Michael Hodder), The Numismatist's Bedside Companion, The Numismatist's Fireside Companion, The Numismatist's Lakeside Companion, Buyer's Guide to U.S. Gold Coins, A Buyer's Guide to the Rare Coin Market, The American Numismatic Association Centennial History, and Commemorative Coins of the United States: A Complete Encyclopedia.

Important Information

International Standard Book Number (ISBN): 0-943161-38-X
Library of Congress Catalogue Number 74-76711

First Edition: April 1974
Thirteenth Edition: November 1991

Copyright © 1991 by Bowers and Merena Galleries, Inc.

Bowers and Merena Galleries, Inc.
Box 1224
Wolfeboro, New Hampshire 03894
(603) 569-5095

Contents

About the Author

The author has been in numismatics since 1953 and has been a dealer since 1954. He has been an advocate of rare coins as an investment (accompanied by a collecting interest) for many years—long before coin investment was a popular subject. His great experience in the field forms the basis for the present book.

Q. David Bowers, a 1960 graduate of the Pennsylvania State University, received in 1976 the Alumni Achievement Award from that institution's College of Business Administration. He served as president of the Professional Numismatists Guild 1977-1979 and is a recipient of the PNG Founders' Award, the highest honor given by that group. A life member (No. 336) of the American Numismatic Association, he became a member of that organization's Board of Governors in 1979, served as vice-president for the 1981-1983 term, and as president from 1983 to 1985. He was a recipient (in 1987) of the ANA Medal of Merit.

His weekly column, "Numismatic Depth Study," has appeared in Coin World for many years and has earned several "Best Columnist" awards. When the 25th anniversary of Coin World was celebrated in 1985, it was noted that more of his columns had appeared in that publication than had the works of any other writer.

Another of his columns, "Coins and Collectors," appears monthly in The Numismatist, the official journal of the American Numismatic Association. In addition, his by-line has appeared in all other major numismatic periodicals, including Numismatic News, The Coin Dealer Newsletter, Coins magazine, COINage, and others. He has written the numismatic section of the Encyclopedia Americana and the investment section of the Coin World Almanac. His television appearances include NBC, ABC, CBS, Metromedia, and cable networks. He is the author of over three dozen books, many of which have received honors and distinctions and have become classics.

Of the top 10 most valuable United States coins (as evidenced by auction sale records) Q. David Bowers has catalogued and sold seven, highlighted by the $725,000 1787 Brasher doubloon which was part of the $25 million Garrett Collection sold for The Johns Hopkins University, the most valuable collection of United States coins ever auctioned. Virtually every major rarity in the book has passed through his hands, including the unique 1870-S $3 and the similarly unique 1870-S half dime, the famous 1913 Liberty Head nickel and multiple examples of the classic 1804 silver dollar, as well as various specimens of the 1894-S dime, 1884 and 1885 trade dollars, 1876-CC 20-cent piece, 1838-O half dollar, the only 1822 $5 in private hands, MCMVII Extremely High Relief double eagle, etc. The author has discovered numerous previously unknown die varieties, overdates, patterns, and other issues during several decades of numismatic research. He has acted as an advisor to the Treasury Department, the American Numismatic Association, the Smithsonian Institution, the Secret Service, and many other organizations.

Since its initial publication in 1974 the present book has gone through many editions and has been used worldwide. It has garnered favorable reviews and has proved to be a useful reference for thousands of collectors and investors. In the process it has become the most popular book on the subject ever written.

An idea of the success of Q. David Bowers in the field of coin investment can be gained by the introduction to Harry J. Forman's book, *How You Can Make Big Profits Investing in Coins*. Mr. Forman said:

"Anyone can make predictions, and if he does so in the field which he is already well known, theirs should be widely read. Moreover, by waiting until people's memories have become somewhat blurred, and then republishing only his successes, he can build up a rather good reputation for himself.

"In the numismatic field we have three kinds of forecasters. The first and most common is the person who makes predictions simply as a promotional device to help sell whatever he has on hand. I don't say that in all, or even most cases, this involves a deliberate deception. On the contrary, the very fact that a person has invested his own money to purchase one or another item would indicate a certain amount of faith in its market potential. But such predictions necessarily lack true discrimination and depend for their success, if not on luck, then on the progress of the market as a whole.

"A second type of forecaster is the non-professional numismatist who dabbles in speculation and writes books or articles on market trends. Such an individual is more serious in selections and understands that there are always widespread differences in the potentials of various issues in series. But for all that, his livelihood is not dependent on his predictions, and even if they fail he is still reimbursed by his royalties.

"The third and rarest type is the successful full-time dealer who forecasts not for promotional purposes, but simply to share his insights with the general investing public. My good friend, Q. David Bowers, is one such forecaster, having given much excellent investment advice through the *Empire Review* and more recently the *Rare Coin Review*."

Q. David Bowers was the only dealer specifically mentioned by Mr. Forman in this connection.

With Raymond N. Merena and a fine staff, the author conducts one of America's leading rare coin businesses, Bowers and Merena Galleries, Inc., Box 1224, Wolfeboro, NH 03894 and a related firm, Auctions by Bowers and Merena, Inc. Auction sales are conducted regularly in New York City and other metropolitan areas. In addition, the firm's Kingswood Galleries division holds mail bid sales at regular intervals.

Acknowledgements

 For price and market information I acknowledge the help of the following periodicals: the *Certified Coin Dealer Newsletter*, *Coin Dealer Newsletter*, *Coin World*, *Coins* magazine, COIN*age*, *Numismatic News*, *The Numismatic Scrapbook Magazine*, *The Numismatist*, and *World Coin News*.

Among reference books utilized are A *Guide Book of* U.S. *Coins*, *Auction Prices Realized* (issued yearly by Krause Publications), and the *Standard Catalog of World Coins*. In particular, I am grateful for the help provided over a long period of years by the Whitman Coin Products Division of Western Publishing Company, including Kenneth E. Bressett and Ed Metzger, as well as the late Richard S. Yeoman.

James F. Ruddy, author of *Photograde*, assisted with certain aspects of this book in its early editions.

Among Bowers and Merena Galleries staff members who worked with the latest (13th) edition, Dr. Richard A. Bagg and Andrew W. Pollock III assisted with market analyses, price studies, and the gathering of outside economic data. Cathy Dumont provided many of the photographic illustrations. Liz Arlin, John Babalis, Mark Borckardt, Chris Karstedt, and Ray Merena read all or part of the manuscript and offered suggestions. The following assisted with graphics and layout of the book: Bill Winter, Jennifer Rose, John Maltzie, Lee Lilljedahl, and Jennifer Meers.

HIGH PROFITS

FROM RARE COIN INVESTMENT

BY Q. DAVID BOWERS

Introduction to Coin Investment

Getting Started

 The field of rare coins is very large, and federal coins minted by the United States government from 1793 to date comprise thousands of varieties. Add world and ancient coins produced over the centuries, and the number climbs into the hundreds of thousands, if not far more.

"Given the size of the field, is it possible for me to invest in coins successfully?" you might ask.

The answer is an emphatic "Yes!"

Before we start, here are three quick ideas which I believe you will find to be very useful:

◆**1.** Building a *collection* is the best way to invest in coins. Over the years, by far the best investment returns have been made by those who have carefully built collections and who have held them for the long term.

◆**2.** Knowledge is necessary to effectively build a collection and to make good buys while doing so. Fortunately, now in the early 1990s there are more sources of information available than any other time in numismatic history.

◆**3.** No one has ever become an expert overnight, nor has anyone ever become an expert in all numismatic areas. However, just about anyone with a degree of ambition, dedication, and intelligence can make an excellent start by picking *one limited area* of numismatics—Morgan silver dollars 1878-1904, for example—and studying prices, offerings, market cycles, etc. in that specific area. You can do it! The knowledge gained and the strategies observed will be equally valid as you later extend them to other market areas of interest.

Opportunity

Welcome to the 13th and latest edition of my book, *High Profits From Rare Coin Investment*. Each past edition has seen its own market conditions, and over the years the text has been changed here and there to reflect what I believe to be interesting opportunities.

Today in 1991, as these words are being written, many areas of the rare coin market have seen recent sharp price declines. Nowhere is this more evident than with coins grading Mint State-65, Proof-65, or better in such series as 19th- and 20th-century "type" coins, common-date gold, commemoratives, and silver dollars of the Morgan and Peace design.

For a number of years I have been wary of the MS-65 market, and, in fact, warned readers of the last edition that better values could be found among coins in lesser grades. I believed that the market for MS-65 and better coins lay primarily with investors, not with collectors, and because of this the market was not stable. My feelings were borne out in the summer of 1990 when the market for MS-65 and higher coins, which had reached unreasonable heights, began to fall. As these words are being written a year later in the summer of 1991, market levels in some series are less than half of what they were a year ago, with selected additional downward adjustments probably still in store.

At the same time, there are many interesting opportunities which I shall discuss in the pages to follow. In addition to what I have to say, take note of this situation: If, as an investor, you thought that a given coin was worth owning at, say, $1,000 a year ago, the same coin at $500 today should be an even better buy. There is a problem, and it is one of market psychology. Investors would rather buy in a rising market or at the top of a market. Few investors have the courage to engage in contrary thinking and buy when a market is falling or is at the bottom. As strange as it seems to relate, investors don't like to buy bargains! I've seen the truth of this many times over. I hope that you can engage in independent thinking and can go against the tide.

In the 12th edition of this book, written in 1987, I noted the following:

"Such figures [as given in the Salomon Brothers index; see following commentary] are exciting to contemplate, but at the same time they can also be misleading. Not all coins have been good investments, any more than all stocks have been good investments, or that all paintings by a given old master have been financially rewarding to own.

"By selectively quoting from history, a present-day numismatic investment writer can create a record of performance which seems amazing, almost incredible. And, indeed, much of what has happened in the past *has* been incredible. However, there have been problems along the way, and in the present volume I endeavor to present the entire subject on an objective basis—to recite the good with the bad, the pleasures with the problems. When you have finished reading all I have to say, it is my hope you will be knowledgeable on coin investment and will possess an insight which should enable you to outperform the coin market as a whole. At least that is my intention."

My opinions are just that: opinions. The opinions of others may vary, and the future may prove to be different from what I expect it to be. However, my thoughts are based on what I consider to be a great deal of experience and observation, plus what I consider to be good common sense. As noted, I hope that in the pages and chapters to follow you will find many opinions and ideas that will prove to be profitable. Comments from past readers have indicated that most (in fact, no one has ever told me of any exceptions) have indeed done better financially by following my suggestions. Of course, there is this question: Will this be true of you as well? Only time will tell.

The Track Record

Why invest in coins? Different people have different reasons, of course, but there is no doubt that the proven track record of coin investments is a powerful incentive to many.

For many years a widely-read study by a leading securities firm included a section on rare coins. A year ago in its issue of July 3, 1990, *Numismatic News* reported the following:

"U.S. rare coins ranked fourth in one-year appreciation among 14 different investments in the annual investment survey conducted by Salomon Brothers. Thirteen tangible and financial assets and the government's Consumer Price Index are charted in the survey. Old Masters paintings were the biggest winner by far for 1989, as they posted a gain of 44.5%.... Chinese ceramics came in second with a one-year increase of 18%. Stocks took third place, appreciating 15.4% in the Salomon survey. U.S. coins gained 14.6%, and foreign exchange rounded out the top five with an annual return of 10.5%.

"Other investments in the survey are gold, diamonds, bonds, oil, three-month Treasury bills, housing, U.S. farmland, and silver. The metals were among the weakest performers in 1989, as gold gained 0.5% for a 12th place finish. Silver was last among the asset areas, as it fell 2.9%.

"Over the past 20 years, U.S. coins are ranked first, with a compound annual rate of return of 17.3%. Gold is in fifth place in the 20-year calculations, as it has a 12.3% average annual gain. Silver is in 13th place, appreciating at a 5.4% clip in the past two decades.

"Prices used in the most recent survey were based on certified coin values, according to Kelly Healey of Salomon Brothers. In the past, 'BU' [brilliant Uncirculated] coins were followed. Twenty coins are charted for price appreciation in the Salomon Brothers index. It is heavily weighted towards scarce and high-priced coins, according to Healey.

"Among the coins surveyed are the 1795 Draped Bust dollar, 1807 Draped Bust dime, 1873 Liberty Seated quarter with arrows, 1884-S Morgan dollar, and 1916 Standing Liberty quarter. The only copper coins in the annual investment rankings are the 1794 half cent and the 1873 two-cent piece. Type coins include an 1862 three-cent silver piece, a Liberty Seated half dime from the same year, 1866 Shield nickel with rays, an 1866 Liberty Seated dime (which had an original mintage of 8,725), and an 1886 Liberty Seated quarter.

"Four different half dollars are listed. They are Capped Bust halves dated 1815 and 1834, an 1855-O Liberty Seated, and a 1921 Liberty Walking. An 1847 Liberty Seated dollar and an 1881 trade dollar (a Proof-only issue) are also used in the survey. The only commemorative on the list is a 1928 Hawaiian half dollar. No U.S. gold coins are used in the index...."

Problems developed with the application of the Salomon Brothers survey in that certain promoters used the findings to help sell *common* coins, suggesting that such pieces would perform in step with the Salomon index. The American Numismatic Association and the Federal Trade Commission each issued warnings

Two American Silver Rarities

The 1876-CC 20-cent piece has always been one of America's most famous coins. Although Mint records show that 10,000 were coined, it is believed that nearly all were melted. Fewer than two dozen examples are known today. Most of these are in Uncirculated grade, indicating they may have been originally reserved for assay purposes. In the 1950s the author handled a group of four examples found in a Baltimore safe deposit box. The one shown above, Choice Uncirculated, was formerly owned by American composer Jerome Kern. At the Armand Champa Collection Sale, (auctioned by the author's firm in May 1972) it brought $24,000. In 1974 the writer reacquired the coin, paying a generous profit for it, advertised it for $59,000, and received four orders. The same piece crossed the auction block again in 1984 and fetched $44,000, probably a bargain price. Another specimen, that in the Emery-Nichols Collection, was sold by Auctions by Bowers and Merena, Inc. in December 1984 for $66,000. On a long term basis, nearly all great American rarities have been superb investments.

An 1884 trade dollar, one of just 10 specimens believed to have been minted of this date. The first one owned by the author was purchased for $1,000 in 1957. Today, the same piece would undoubtedly bring well over $100,000 at auction!

concerning such abuses.[1] In June 1991 Salomon Brothers announced that henceforth the annual survey would not include rare coins, but stamps would be featured instead. Unless Salomon Brothers has a change of heart, in future years their coin index will probably fade from memory.

I, for one, am sorry to see coins deleted from the index, for their inclusion drew attention to the rare coin field and along the way helped to interest many new buyers. However, many such newcomers acquired coins for the sake of investment alone and did not take time to study coins in detail. Apparently, in the view of those compiling the index the perceived abuses of the coin listing outweighed the advantages. As only a small number of rare coin dealers attempted to mislead buyers by suggesting that common coins could perform as well as rare ones, the delisting of coins is comparable to delisting stocks from the index just because some securities brokers have made misleading statements to their clients. I would bet that misleading statements in the field of securities are found much more often than misrepresentations in rare coins.

Opinions and Observations

This book is a personal one, based upon my own opinions, observations, and reflections. Books by other writers often pursue a different tack and have different opinions. I am not unbiased in that ever since the early 1950s I have been engaged in rare coins as a profession. Thus, the success of the coin hobby in the future, and the price appreciation of numismatic specimens in the future, have a direct bearing upon my own welfare.

I hope in the course of pursuing your coin investments you will do well, for nothing is more pleasurable to an author than to have a reader utilize knowledge gained in one of his books to turn a profit, to enhance his lifestyle, or to be inspired in one direction or another. Similarly, as a dealer in rare coins, it has always given me great pleasure to write a check for say, $100,000 for a group of coins which I sold the buyer 20 to 30 years ago for some tiny

[1] Beginning with the efforts of Phoebe Morse in 1987-1988, the Federal Trade Commission has taken a close look at the workings of the coin business in recent years, with the view in mind to curb abuses in the investment sector. At the 1990 convention of the American Numismatic Association, Ms. Morse and her associate, Barry J. Cutler, gave a presentation on the subject. Information concerning this can be found in my *Buyer's Guide to the Rare Coin Market* book.

fraction of that sum. Far from being an isolated incident, this sort of thing has happened many times.

In the past, selected coins have indeed been superb investments, as the Salomon Brothers study indicates (although that survey comprises just a tiny fraction of the rare coin market and is not representative of the market as a whole). Will they continue to be good investments? The future is unknown, and no one can tell. In this book I shall give you my own ideas as to which areas do offer such possibilities for gain.

Why Invest in Coins?

Why invest in coins? Financial gain is an important consideration, and that, perhaps, is why you bought this book. However, other factors are likewise important. At this point in the book it may come as a surprise to you to learn that in the field of rare coins, collectors have made more profits than investors have! In my book, A *Buyer's Guide to the Rare Coin Market*, I expand upon this to great length. I strongly suggest that you read the *Buyer's Guide* in connection with the present text.[1]

When I was president of the Professional Numismatists Guild,[2] I worked with Paul Koppenhaver, executive secretary of the PNG, to spur a campaign to acquaint the public with the benefits of coin collecting. Investment, to be sure, was an important aspect, but other such factors as art, history, and romance were likewise significant. The idea was well received, and quite a few people told me that because of it they had broadened their appreciation of numismatics. To give both sides of the story I should mention that there were those who felt that coin investment was an entity unto itself and that art, history, and romance were irrelevant.

Numismatic Art

"If I wanted art, I would buy a painting," you might say, continuing with some philosophy such as "I don't care whether a coin is ugly or beautiful, its price performance is the only thing

[1] I am not trying to sell you this or other books against your wishes; you can borrow a copy free of charge from the American Numismatic Association Library if you don't want to buy them.
[2] The Professional Numismatists Guild began in the early 1950s through the efforts of the late Abe Kosoff, and was incorporated in 1955. Since then it has grown to become the world's largest organization of professional coin dealers, each of whom has pledged to uphold the PNG Code of Ethics, and each of whom has met certain financial requirements. I served as PNG president for the 1977-1979 term.

Leading Numismatic Organizations

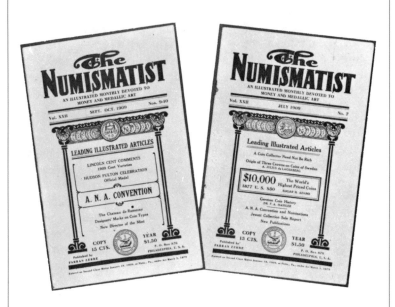

The American Numismatic Association, organized in 1891, is the world's leading non-profit organization. Q. David Bowers (ANA Life Member 336) and Ray Merena (Life Member 2440) would be pleased to send you complete membership information. *The Numismatist*, published monthly, is a source for information, offerings, and other items of interest. Two long-ago issues from 1909 are shown above.

The two leading dealers' organizations are the Professional Numismatists Guild and its worldwide counterpart, the International Association of Professional Numismatists. Dealer members are bound by a rigid code of ethics.

that counts." If you feel this way, fine. However, you are missing much of what numismatics has to offer.

The concept of art in coins costs nothing extra—it is simply a plus which adds to your enjoyment. Take, for example, the Liberty Walking half dollar. In 1916, Adolph A. Weinman, a noted sculptor and artist, created a new design for the 50-cent piece. From then until 1947, the Liberty Walking motif was seen on half dollars struck for circulation. Millions of these coins, featuring Liberty as a goddess striding forward from the sun, were made. Over the years, scarce Liberty Walking half dollars of all dates, and common dates in Uncirculated preservation, have been superb investments (although these, too, suffered in the market downturn of 1990). The beauty of the design costs nothing extra!

Then there is the well-known story of President Theodore Roosevelt and his involvement with Augustus Saint-Gaudens. Shortly after the turn of the century, Roosevelt visited the Smithsonian Institution and was impressed with the artistic quality of the ancient Greek coins he saw on display there, pieces with beautifully sculptured profiles. Considering current United States coinage to be rather bland in comparison, Roosevelt sought to improve the designs. He contacted Augustus Saint-Gaudens, a well-known sculptor who maintained his studio and residence in Cornish, New Hampshire.[1] The artist was commissioned to redesign the entire coinage spectrum from the cent through the $20 gold piece.

In 1907, designs were prepared, culminating in the Indian $10 and the beautiful MCMVII High Relief $20. The $20 piece, or double eagle, has been characterized as one of the most attractive coins ever produced for circulation. Examples with the MCMVII Roman numeral date were produced in 1907, and related low-relief pieces with regular (also known as "Arabic") numerals in the date were produced from 1907 through 1933. Examples of certain common dates within the 1907-1933 span can be obtained for little more than gold bullion value; again, the artistic element is "free."

Similarly, the "Mercury" dimes, designed by Adolph A. Weinman and produced from 1916 to 1945 and the Standing Liberty

---

[1] Today this is operated as the Saint-Gaudens National Historic Site by the National Park Service. On exhibit are models and sketches for U.S. coins. The curator in recent years, John Dryfhout, is well versed and has written extensively concerning the artist's involvement with coinage. Additional material is held by Dartmouth College in nearby Hanover, NH.

quarter dollars, created by Hermon A. MacNeil and minted from 1916 to 1930, have had a high degree of artistic appeal to many rare coin buyers.

In my opinion, if an investment can be beautiful to behold, so much the better!

Numismatic History

History forms another reason to collect coins. The finances, politics, hardships, and other aspects of the American colonies, and later the individual states, are reflected upon a wide variety of coinage produced prior to the opening of the federal Mint at Philadelphia in late 1792.[1]

Did you know, for example, that during the 1785 to 1788 era, copper coins of many different varieties were issued by such states as Connecticut, Vermont, New Jersey, and Massachusetts? The story of the still earlier Massachusetts Pine Tree shilling and related coinage, nearly all of which bear the date 1652, is fascinating to learn. For example, it was said that a Pine Tree shilling, if bent twice, was ideal for warding off witches and evil spirits, believed by many to have been prevalent in Salem and other Massachusetts communities during the late 17th century. Today, Massachusetts Pine Tree shillings with bend marks are seen with some frequency, evidence of the belief in this tale.[2] Nathaniel Hawthorne's story of a bridegroom receiving as dowry the weight of his bride in Pine Tree shillings is likewise fascinating to contemplate. Perhaps this falls in the category of romance, instead of history. In many areas the two are intertwined.

The gold and silver bullion market of the early 1800s caused all sorts of problems with coinage, for when silver or gold prices rose sharply, coins could be melted down for a profit above the face value. This bit of historical knowledge may explain why of the 17,796 $5 pieces reported minted in 1822, just three examples survive today! In my firm's sale of the Eliasberg Collection of United States Gold Coins, held in 1982, one of these crossed the auction block for a record $687,500![3]

[1] Over the years the Philadelphia Mint has occupied several different structures, each larger than the preceding one. Relocations were accomplished in 1830, 1901, and 1967. The present Philadelphia Mint is on Independence Square not far from Independence Hall and the Liberty Bell exhibit.

[2] Eric P. Newman, for one, has written about this. In recent times others have suggested that the bending seen on certain pieces is a result of the coins having been struck by rocker-type dies.

[3] The other two specimens of the 1822 $5 are held in the National Coin Collection at the Smithsonian Institution.

The Civil War is likewise reflected in our coinage, as are numerous later political and social events. After World War I ended, the Peace silver dollar, first minted in 1921, observed the truce among nations. The metallic shortages of World War II are reflected in the zinc-coated steel cent of 1943, minted in an effort to save strategic copper.

Among commemorative coins—an area popular with investors for many decades—are found numerous historical issues. Indeed, each and every coin within the series commemorates one historical event or another, some prominent and others obscure.

Among commemoratives of the half dollar denomination many diverse topics can be found, including those forming the basis of the designs for such coins as the 1936-S San Francisco—Oakland Bay Bridge, 1921 Alabama Centennial (actually the centennial was celebrated in 1919, and the half dollar was produced two years after the fact!), the 1892 and 1893 World's Columbian Exposition, and the 1928 Hawaiian Sesquicentennial half dollars.

Perhaps taking the prize for commemorating an event of strictly local interest (and there is even a question as to how great the interest was locally) is the Norfolk Bicentennial half dollar, which was produced to commemorate the 200th anniversary of the operation of Norfolk, Virginia under the borough form of government. The coin bears the dates 1636, 1682, 1736, 1845, and 1936, none of which represents the date in which the coins were struck, 1937!

Again, history, like art, is "free" as part of the coin collecting package. In my opinion, if an investment has an interesting history, so much the better!

Numismatic Romance

Closely allied with history is romance. We have all heard of pieces of eight from pirate days, but through an interest in numismatics you can actually collect such coins; and—good news—they are not particularly expensive. The Gold Rush era has among its mementos a number of privately minted gold coins, all of which are highly desired today. Each one has its own story to tell. Similarly, when the community at Salt Lake was set up by the Mormons, one of the first things they did was issue their own coins. In Oregon in 1849, private gold pieces of $5 and $10 were minted, a coinage with a fascinating history.

Federal coinage began with the inception of the Philadelphia Mint in late 1792, followed by the production of half cents and cents for circulation in 1793. By 1838 the United States had expanded westward, and a branch mint was opened in New Orleans to serve the growing commerce in the Mississippi River trading area. Gold discoveries in the Southeast prompted the opening of the Dahlonega (Georgia) and Charlotte (North Carolina) mints in the same year.

Later gold discoveries in California and the consequent population growth were responsible for the opening of the San Francisco Mint in 1854. The exploitation of Nevada's vast Comstock Lode and the silver and gold extracted there furnished cause for the opening of the Carson City Mint in 1870.[1] The Denver Mint, which produced its first coins in 1906, handled gold bullion from the Cripple Creek District and also served to mint coins in an area of rapidly expanding population.[2] Each of these mints has romantic stories connected with it. For example, during the Civil War, Louisiana troops occupied the New Orleans Mint and used government dies to create coins for its own purposes.

In my opinion, if an investment is romantic to contemplate, so much the better! Art, history, romance—the more you explore these areas, the more interesting coin collecting becomes.

Social and Psychological Benefits

Not to be overlooked are the social and psychological benefits of numismatics. Around the world, many millions of people collect coins, hundreds of thousands of whom belong to numismatic societies, subscribe to popular periodicals in the field, and attend coin shows and conventions. Much enjoyment can be gained from attending talks and educational programs, swapping stories at local coin club meetings, or attending regional or national conventions and becoming acquainted with others who share your interests.

Or, perhaps you may wish to pursue coin collecting privately; many do. When in my mind's eye I think of a numismatist, I

[1] Although the Comstock Lode, located in and near Virginia City, Nevada, is best remembered for its silver, in terms of coinage the total value of silver and gold metals used were about equal. Today, the Carson City Mint building serves as the Nevada State Museum.

[2] In 1862 the U.S. government purchased the private mint of Clark, Gruber & Co., intending to open the federal Denver Mint soon thereafter. However, this did not come to pass, and the facilities were used during the late 19th century as an assay office. Finally, when the Denver Mint was opened in 1906 the institution was housed in a new building.

The ANA Centennial Auction

1662 Massachusetts Bay Colony
Oak Tree twopence. MS-60
$4,510

1796 silver Myddelton token
Proof-63/64
$5,775

1856 Flying Eagle cent
Proof-63
$5,720

1792 half disme
EF-40
$15,400

1901-S quarter dollar
MS-65
$45,100

1916-D Mercury dime
MS-65 Full Bands
$13.090

On this page and the following are a few of the many highlights of Auctions by Bowers and Merena Inc.'s sale held with the American Numismatic Association's Centennial Convention in Chicago in August 1991.

1821 half dollar
MS-65
$12,100

1902 quarter eagle
MS-65 to 66
$10,450

1861 $5 gold
AU-55
$12,100

1889-CC Morgan dollar
MS-62 DMPL
$10,450

1858 Canadian 20-cent piece
Specimen-65
$12,650

1867 pattern $20, struck in copper
Proof-65 RB
$8,250

1851 Augustus Humbert $50
MS-64
$99,000

envision a cozy scene of a wood-paneled room, with interesting books on the shelves, glowing embers in the fireplace, a comfortable overstuffed chair, and a reading lamp. Many hours of enjoyment and freedom from care can be had by studying coins under magnification, identifying them in reference books, and beholding their beauty.

In the 1880s, T. Harrison Garrett set aside a special room in Evergreen, his mansion on North Charles Street in Baltimore, for the study and appreciation of his coin collection. One of his contemporaries, Joseph J. Mickley, a man of many intellectual pursuits, spent many evenings in his Philadelphia home exchanging coin collecting stories and adventures. Chicago brewer Virgil M. Brand, who collected coins from 1889 until his death in 1926, overdid it; family records indicate that he virtually ate, lived, and slept coins. More will be said about Brand later.

Today, appreciation is still possible in numismatics. In fact, it is more possible than ever before—what with the proliferation of excellent periodicals, interesting organizations, and valuable reference books to aid and reinforce the endeavor. Whether you live in a one-room studio apartment in Manhattan, or have a ranch or estate comprising hundreds of acres in Montana, time set aside in a cozy corner for coin collecting will make the hours pass quickly and enjoyably.

In many other fields, the aspects of art, history, romance, social involvement, and psychological satisfaction are apt to cost many thousands or even tens of thousands of dollars. Millions of people have bought expensive cars, yachts, jewelry, and other objects to satisfy these very same desires—with no hope of financial gain. Not so with coin collecting. These quintessential, intangible psychological aspects are free, a bonus, at no extra charge! When evaluating the potential of coin investments, do not overlook these other pleasures. For some, they are worth just as much as any financial gain, if not more. Curiously, the immense psychological advantages of numismatics are usually ignored!

The 1950s Revisited

A number of years ago I wrote an article on the subject of rare coin investment. A reader wrote in to say, "I enjoyed your article very much, but why didn't you give more examples of how coins have appreciated in value over the years? I like reading about such things." The late Abe Kosoff, who for years wrote a column for *Coin World*, once told me that his articles telling about "the good old days" were more popular than those on any other subject.[1]

Taking this as a cue, before progressing further, let's talk about investment successes of the past. As these words are being written, I have before me a copy of a coin catalogue I published in July 1958. Let's look through it together, observe the prices and descriptions of that time, and then compare their replacement value today.

Although there are many who ignore the fields of colonial and early American coins, for me these have always been a great area of interest. And, as an investment they have performed in a manner not to be sneezed at!

A 1773 Virginia halfpenny, described as "bright red Uncirculated" (this was in a time when the numerical grading system was not in use for series other than large cents), was offered at $13.50. The description noted, "Various attributed varieties available on request," indicating we had a number of them.[2] Today, the same coin would cost you about $750! Stated another way, this coin has increased in value about 55 times. Stated still another way, $1,000 invested in a group of these coins back in 1958 would be worth about $55,000 today!

A 1776 Continental "dollar" in Fine or slightly better grade would have cost you $95 back then. Today, the same coin catalogues for $3,000 in the 1992 edition of *A Guide Book of United States Coins*, and at that figure they are harder to find today than they were back in 1958! Another specimen was offered in Extremely Fine grade or close to it, for $160, a tiny fraction of today's $6,000 valuation.

Around 1785 a curious token appeared in circulation. The obverse consisted of the monogram USA in intertwined letters, while the reverse depicted a series of 13 parallel bars, giving rise to the name "Bar Cent." I offered an Extremely Fine coin for $42.50 in 1958. Today, if you had $2,000 to spend for one, I'm sorry to say that I couldn't find one for you easily!

Among half cents, the smallest of all American coin denominations, you could have ordered a 1793 in Fine grade for $92.50,

---

[1] Abe Kosoff began his coin dealership in 1929 and by 1937 formed the Numismatic Gallery in New York City, later enlisting Abner Kreisberg as a partner.

[2] Such coins are attributed to *Coinage For Colonial Virginia*, by Eric P. Newman, American Numismatic Society, 1957.

a minute fraction of the approximately $3,500 you would have to pay for the same piece today! Similarly, the price of $35 I charged for a Fine 1794 half cent represented a tremendous investment, especially when you consider that same piece would sell for $650 or more now. I am not picking Uncirculated or Proof examples— but instead am selecting nice collector-type coins in circulated grades. This illustrates that coin investment has rewarded buyers of such pieces, although in recent times, much publicity has been given solely to Uncirculated and Proof coins, with lesser grades being overlooked.

There were some Uncirculated and Proof coins among half cents in my 1958 list, with an 1833 Uncirculated example pegged at $25 (today it would cost about $500), a Proof 1842 with Small Berries at $150 ($3,500 now), and an Uncirculated 1855 at $8 (as opposed to $300 now).

Among one-cent pieces, a Good to Very Good 1793 Wreath variety offered for $77 then, would cost around $1,250 today, while an 1816 Uncirculated cent, priced at $25 in 1958, would run about 20 times that figure now. If you had ordered the rare Proof 1857 large cent from my 1958 catalogue for $165, and if you put it in one of my auctions now, the chances are good that it would sell for $5,000 or more! Back then, my firm had a nice stock of 1955 Doubled Die cents. If you had spent $30 for an Uncirculated example, you could cash in today for $3,250 or more! As noted earlier, these are not "theoretical" returns on investments giving prices that someone *might* have earned. These are real situations—back then I had the coins for sale, and I sold them!

Among nickel three-cent pieces you could buy an 1865 Uncirculated for $4, an 1866 in the same grade for $4.50, an 1867 Uncirculated for $4, or any one of various Proofs from 1879 to 1889 for $9 to $10 each. In the meantime, each of these has increased in value more than 50 times! Stated another way, if you had opted to spend, say, $1,000 with me on Uncirculated and Proof nickel three-cent pieces back then, you would have coins worth around $50,000 now.

The same type of return would have attended the purchase of an 1868 Uncirculated Shield nickel for $8, a 1900 Uncirculated Liberty nickel for $8.75, an Uncirculated 1902 nickel for $5.75, or a 1908 in the same grade for $5.75. On the other hand, if you had spent $250 for a specimen of an 1877 Proof—a well-known rarity

Beautiful U.S. Half Cents

1793 half cent
AU-50, $13,200

1796 No Pole half cent
F-15 to VF-20, $25,300

1796 With Pole half cent
MS-60, $25,300

1802 Reverse of 1800 half cent
F-15 to VF-20, $28,600

1811 half cent
Proof-60, $30,800

1831 Second Restrike half cent
Proof-60 to 63, $41,800

1845 Second Restrike half cent
Proof-65, $8,800

1852 Large Berries Original half cent
Proof-63, $39,600

A sampling of United States half cents from the Norweb Collection sold by Auctions by Bowers and Merena in 1987.

in the series—you would have a coin worth $2,000 or more—or a return of "only" eight times the price paid!

I should mention here that today, grading of coins is different from what it was then. Back in 1958, a coin was Uncirculated or it wasn't. Today, the simple "Uncirculated" term does not suffice. We have MS-60, MS-63, MS-65, MS-67, and many other numbers as well—all of which will be explained (to the best of my ability) in a later chapter on the subject. Thus, the 1908 Uncirculated nickel sold by me for $5.75 is worth now, about 30 years later, any one of several different figures based upon its numerical grade. A copy of *The Coin Dealer Newsletter*, a weekly report of coin valuations, informs me that if the piece is graded MS-60, it is worth about $65 on a wholesale basis, whereas an MS-63 example is priced at $95, an MS-64 coin at $245, but that an MS-65 coin will fetch $900. The return for any Uncirculated grade, MS-60 on up, is sufficiently attractive that an investment in such coins probably outper-formed anything else you can name.

If you cared to part with $8.50 in 1958 you could have purchased an Uncirculated 1832 half dime, or for $7.50 you could have acquired an 1833 in the same grade. On the other hand, an 1831 cost $10 and an 1835 cost $12. Assuming these pieces average what we would call MS-63 today, replacement cost would be about $900 each! Or, if you assume that some or all could be called MS-65 today, the valuation would be about $5,000 per coin!

In the same series, an 1853 half dime with arrows at the date would have cost you $8.50 back then. Now, an MS-60 preservation piece would cost you close to $200, while to obtain an MS-65 coin you had better be prepared to write out a check for the best part of $5,000!

In the dime series, Proof Barber pieces were available for $27.50 to $30 each for several different dates, coins which in Proof-63 preservation are worth close to $800 each and which in Proof-65 state are worth over $2,250 apiece.

An Uncirculated 1826 Capped Bust half dollar would have cost you $10. I wonder if it is as nice as a coin I saw the other day priced at $3,750? Perhaps it was even the same coin.

A Proof 1835 Capped Bust half dollar was offered to all comers for $95. Today, I doubt if $9,500 (or 100 times the investment) would secure another for you! An 1851-O half dollar could have been yours for $16. Today, it would take about $2,000 to acquire an MS-63 example and probably about $7,500 to own an MS-65 coin. I say, "probably," for such pieces are numismatic classics and cannot be obtained easily. It is often the case that catalogue values are just theoretical, and when prized rarities cross the auction block, higher figures result. Indeed, if you were to run nationwide advertisements offering to pay $20,000 each for MS-65 1851-O half dollars, this price being about three times the "theoretical" valuation, I doubt if you would buy more than two or three—and perhaps you would not buy even a single piece! This is something that should be kept in mind; a philosophy that will be discussed in later chapters.

A rare coin is rare by definition, and is hard to find. On the other hand, common coins present no such purchase difficulties. Take for example an 1881-S silver dollar, a coin which over the years has been the subject of much commotion and editorial comment. Thousands upon thousands of MS-65 examples exist, and if you are willing to pay the current price, you probably can acquire several suitcases full of them! This is not to disparage the 1881-S dollar for, unquestionably, each and every collector of Morgan silver dollars needs one. However, it does point out the difference between something that is easy to find and an issue such as the 1851-O half dollar in MS-65 grade, which is truly rare.

Among silver dollars in my 1958 catalogue you could have ordered a Proof 1865 for $67.50, a Proof 1867 for $56, a Proof 1868 for $62.50, or a Proof 1872 for $48.50. In Proof-63 grade, these coins would cost $1,750 or more to replace today, while Proof-65 pieces would be valued in the $5,000 range!

A Proof 1892 Morgan silver dollar would have cost you $45 back then, which is about 1/100th of the current price. To be dramatic I could state that $1,000 invested in such Proof Morgan dollars back then would result in coins worth about $100,000 today.

Proof trade dollars of various dates were offered from $50 to $72.50, about 1/100th of their value now. Among gold coins, an Uncirculated gold dollar, date of my choice, from 1856 to 1889, would have cost you $18.75, about 1/100th of what it would cost now. Double eagles of the Saint-Gaudens type in Uncirculated grade could be bought for $48.75, as opposed to $450 or so for a minimum MS-60 coin in 1992. Of course, MS-65 coins are worth considerably more, about $1,500 each, in fact.

The Story of the 1894-S Dime

On the cover of my 1958 catalogue was an illustration of a 10-cent piece, with the enthusiastic headline, "SECOND 1894-S DIME ACQUIRED!" Then followed a description:

"With great pleasure near the end of last year, outbidding a large field of collectors and dealers from all parts of the United States, we purchased at auction the 'Empire' specimen of the 1894-S dime. This coin is now part of one of America's finest collections.

"Fortunate, indeed, is the dealer who can offer one 1894-S dime in a lifetime. We are now proud to offer another 1894-S dime; the second specimen we have handled within a year! The specimen here offered, one of six or seven known examples remaining from the 24 coined in 1894, is the coin originally sold to James A. Stack from the collection of John Clapp. Like its predecessor, the 'Empire' coin, the piece is graded Uncirculated. Here is an opportunity to acquire one of the very rarest of United States coins—an opportunity which may not be repeated for a long time. Serious inquiries invited."

If memory serves, the coin sold for about $6,000, and the buyer was Abraham Kaufmann.

The story of this particular issue is fascinating. In 1894 at the San Francisco Mint a rarity was created: the 1894-S dime. During the preceding year, 1893, nearly 2.5 million dimes were produced at this Western mint. During the following year, 1895, the dime mintage was 1 million. What happened in 1894? Only 24 pieces—yes, just 24 in all—were struck! Thus one of America's most famous classic rarities came to be.

The reason for striking just 24 pieces is not known today. One account has it that 24 coins, amounting to $2.40 in face value, were struck in order to balance the coining account ledgers for that year.

Another theory holds that 24 impressions were struck in order to test the dies. The anticipation at that time was that many more, perhaps over a million, would be issued. When no further coinage order was forthcoming, the mintage remained at just 24 pieces.

A third theory is that San Francisco Mint Superintendent J. Daggett realized in 1894 that no dimes would be coined, even though dies for that purpose had been sent from Philadelphia (where all dies, including those for branch mints, are made).

The Famous 1894-S Dime

The famous 1894-S dime, purchased by the author for $4,750 in 1957.

Seeking to create something unusual, he had two dozen pieces struck for distribution or sale to his friends. It is said that he kept three, two of which were sold in later years to San Francisco dealer Earl Parker by his daughter, Hallie Daggett. A third coin is said to have been spent for an ice cream cone.

Of the 24 1894-S dimes believed to have been minted, only about a dozen are known to exist today.[1]

My first encounter with an 1894-S dime was in 1957. James F. Ruddy, who was to become my coin business partner in 1958, purchased on my behalf the previously noted "Empire" example for $4,750 at an auction sale conducted by Stack's. $4,750 for a dime![2] This news, sensational at the time, was quickly spread all over America by the various newspaper wire services. The result was a deluge of thousands of letters and postcards! I appeared on NBC's *Today* TV show as a result of this dime purchase. I remember that the host, Dave Garroway, had three guests that particular day—all teenagers (I was 18 or 19 at the time) who had "made good."[3]

I expected that my television appearance would bring in thousands of additional letters and postcards, but such was not to be the case. I learned an interesting lesson, one which perhaps has no relevance to the main purpose of the present book, but it does shed light on the advantages and disadvantages of certain publicity. When I appeared on television I was seen by many millions of viewers. As interesting as the purchase of a dime for $4,750 might have been, it was simply one of a series of events flashing across the screen. Few people took the time to find a pencil and paper, write down my name, and keep a record of where I could be contacted. Thus, no more than a few dozen television viewers were heard from! On the other hand, the newspaper articles could be clipped and saved—and my name and address were permanently recorded. Since then, my coin buying activities

[1] In 1958 I estimated that six or seven were known, but since that time the 1894-S dime has been the subject of intense research by Jim Johnson and others, and more have been identified. A listing of known specimens appears in the *Coin World Almanac*, 6th edition, pp. 568-569; since that listing of 12 pieces was printed it has been determined that the Connecticut State Library does not have an example, leaving a net possibility of 11 coins (one other of which is listed as "not verified").

[2] Jim Ruddy and I owned and operated the Empire Coin Co., Inc., Johnson City, N.Y., from April 1958 through 1965. Later, we were associated again in Bowers and Ruddy Galleries, Inc., in Los Angeles, the predecessor to the present Bowers and Merena Galleries, Inc. firm, which located in New Hampshire in 1983.

[3] Another guest was Sally Salve—a displaced person from Estonia (if I recall correctly), who as a teenager, had built a nice business in fabrics—I wonder what has happened to her in the decades since our paths crossed over 30 years ago.

Barber Coins

   Barber or Liberty Head coins, designed by Charles E. Barber, were produced beginning in 1892. Dimes and quarters were made from that year through 1916, while for the half dollars the terminal date was 1915. Proofs were struck of each denomination each year from 1892 to 1915.

   Among Barber dimes 1894-S is recognized as one of America's greatest rarities. Only 24 were struck! Among Barber quarters, 1896-S, 1901-S, and 1913-S are particularly desired. There are no great rarities among Barber half dollars, but certain of the branch mint pieces are elusive in higher grades.

have figured in many newspaper and television stories, and, without exception, the newspaper features have drawn by far the most letters.

What happened to the 1894-S dime which Jim Ruddy and I bought back in 1958? It was sold shortly thereafter into one of America's finest private collections, that of Ambassador and Mrs. R. Henry Norweb. In 1986, the Norweb family consigned to my firm their fabulous collection for sale at unrestricted public auction sale in 1987 and 1988. Once again this coin crossed the auction block. In November 1987 it fetched $77,000, many times what it sold for in 1958. In 1990 it crossed the auction block again, this time in Stack's sale of the Allen Lovejoy Collection, where it brought $85,000.

Although the 1894-S dime did spectacularly well for the Norwebs, its increase in value is actually less than many other coins have experienced! So, using it as an example is, if anything, conservative. It should also be noted that during the height of the market in the 1979-1980 years the same coin probably would have sold in the $125,000 range, so the 1987 valuation of $77,000 may have represented a bargain. In the market high of 1990 the James A. Stack specimen, a particularly outstanding Proof (and considerably nicer than the Norweb coin), fetched $275,000.

A second 1894-S dime came my way in 1958, as earlier mentioned, and was sold into the Kaufmann Collection, followed by a third example in 1961, the latter being part of the collection owned by Edwin Hydeman and sold by Abe Kosoff. Abe described it as follows, in part:

"Although there were supposed to have been 24 coins struck, there seem to be only seven known specimens of the 1894-S dime. All are Gems in Proof condition. The present market for rarities of this calibre should result in a runaway price with this offering. So seldom does it appear, that advanced collectors would best reach for the 1894-S now."

Jim Ruddy and I were contemplating buying the coin for our company stock. What would it bring? The last known auction record was $4,750 for the 1894-S dime we purchased in 1957. Now in 1961 it was four years later—and, as the coin market has a way of doing, prices in general had advanced. Would it bring $8,000? $10,000? We didn't know. Just before the sale we received a telephone call from a prominent New York industrialist. He *had* to own this dime—and he wanted us to buy it for him! A few hours before the sale was to take place I received my instructions in the form of a coded telegram. There was a ripple of excitement on the sale floor as the bidding progressed: past the opening bid up to $11,500, then to $11,750, then to $12,000. There was a pause, and then the advance continued: $12,150, $12,500, and on to $12,750— then the final bid to me: $13,000. The coin was mine!

The $13,000 was described as a "runaway price," and once again, the 1894-S created a sensation. However, today's "runaway price" is often tomorrow's bargain.

When contemplating my previously mentioned 1958 catalogue, or the 1961 purchase of a 1894-S dime for $13,000, or any other of the catalogues and events of years ago, one thought recurs: At the time, the market to nearly everyone seemed to be "fully priced." That is, back in 1957, when I purchased my first 1894-S dime for $4,750, I paid the highest price anyone in the world was willing to pay for it. Stated another way, I did not buy a bargain, at least not in the eyes of anyone but me.

Similarly, in 1961, when I paid $13,000 for Edward Hydeman's example of the 1894-S dime, I outbid all competition. Quality coins of proven scarcity and rarity were not cheap then, they are not cheap now, and they probably will not be cheap in the future. Virtually every first-class collection ever put together was done so by paying the going rate, by buying coins at current market value when they seem to be "fully priced."

The Eliasberg Collection

During the 1940s, Baltimore collector Louis Eliasberg frequently made newspaper and magazine headlines when he outbid the competition to acquire rarities for his fabulous collection. Eventually, he achieved what no one had ever done before: By 1950 his collection contained one of each date and mintmark known to exist—in all series from half cents through double eagles! I knew Mr. Eliasberg well, and one of my favorite memories was a week spent with him in August 1975, when he invited me to come to Baltimore to appraise his collection. He told me at the time, and his story was subsequently reiterated in a little brochure he published, that he had paid about $350,000 for his collection. By his own calculations, his collection had appreciated at an annual rate of 119% by that time!

While Mr. Eliasberg made many *good buys* by being a knowledgeable collector and studying the field intensely, in his own words he purchased few, if any, *bargains*. And yet, history shows that his logic was flawless. In 1982 my firm sold at public auction just the gold portion of his collection, from dollars to double eagles, and it brought $12.4 million. Two coins in the sale, the 1870-S $3 piece and the 1822 $5, each sold for $687,500; each of these single coins sold for *about twice the price he had paid for his entire collection*!

The experience of Harold Bareford, who paid less than $20,000 for his collection, a holding that was eventually sold by Stack's for over $1 million, was similar. Over a period of years, he carefully formed a *collection*. When the collection was sold, a wonderful profit resulted.

Some Philosophy

Apart from the countless suggestions, pieces of advice, anecdotes, and experiences given in this book, I urge you to consider two precepts, and they are as follows:

1. A fine *collection* is your best investment.

2. Successful rare coin investment requires knowledge.

Both of these precepts differ greatly from the investment advice you might find in print elsewhere. A third precept, not as universal as the others, is that this book can help you gain knowledge. I address the two primary precepts in detail, starting with the second, the one about knowledge:

Knowledge a Requirement

Successful rare coin investment requires knowledge. This is counter to the often expressed thought that the less a buyer knows, the better it is. Actually, from the standpoint of a coin seller, an uninformed buyer may be a delight—for he or she will buy anything offered. That might be fine for the coin seller, but it isn't good for the buyer. Such sayings as, "There is no substitute for knowledge," "Buy the book before the coin," and "The best investor is a knowledgeable investor" are all in the same vein. The more you know, the better you will do—whether you want to design a computer, start a real estate development in Arizona, trade in commodities, hybridize cymbidium orchids, or write a book on the Crimean War. In my own life, I have spared no effort or expense to gain as much knowledge as possible in any field of interest to me. If I could not replace it, I would not sell my numismatic library for its weight in gold.

There is good news and bad news: First, the bad news: Gaining knowledge requires work. Now, the good news: This work, mainly consisting of reading, can be fun.

A Collection is Your Best Investment

A fine *collection* is your best investment. I have always believed this. While a *miscellaneous accumulation* is far easier to acquire, a fine collection offers many advantages. In my book, A *Buyer's Guide to the Rare Coin Market*, I discuss this in depth.

1. First of all, in building a collection you acquire the common with the rare, the inexpensive with the expensive, giving you a "balanced portfolio."

2. Second, your investment is spread over a wide variety of issues.

3. Third, by forming a collection you develop a goal, and in trying to reach this goal you acquire knowledge. All of this will be beneficial to your investment success.

I suspect that if Louis Eliasberg in the 1940s had simply contacted coin dealers and said, "Send me whatever you want, I am interested in coins as an investment," and if he had spent $350,000 on a miscellaneous accumulation, instead of a breathtakingly beautiful collection, his investment, while it may have done well, would have in no way matched the brilliant performance it eventually demonstrated.

Similarly, Harold Bareford, who used to be "picky" when he acquired coins for his collection, would have missed out on much had he simply bought a group of coins for $20,000. As it was, he not only enjoyed the formation of a truly fantastic collection, but along the way he gained many friends and had countless enjoyable experiences.

1974 Revisited

The first edition of this book appeared in 1974. As was the case when I bought the 1894-S dime in 1957, or when I issued my previously-mentioned catalogue in 1958, the market in 1974 was "fully priced." There were those back then who remembered "the good old days" and thought prices could go no higher, just as you, today, when looking at *The Wall Street Journal* undoubtedly think all stocks are fully priced down to the last penny, or when you contemplate parcels of land near where you live, you feel these are as expensive as they are ever going to be. Thus it was with coins.

However, in 1974 I suggested that there were many opportunities for coin investment. As it turned out, if you had formed a collection of just about any series of your choice, and had done it carefully with an eye for quality, you would have seen a fantastic return on your investment. Back in 1974, an Uncirculated 1796 quarter dollar would have cost you $10,000; compare this to four or five times that price today for an average Uncirculated coin and well over $100,000 for a gem in MS-65 grade.

Liberty Seated quarter dollars dated in the 1840s were available for $300 each or so in MS-65 grade in 1974, about 1/10th of today's price. An 1849-O quarter dollar catalogued for $950 in Uncirculated grade. It was a rarity then, and I would be remiss if I didn't tell you that a lot of searching may not have yielded the opportunity to buy one. But, if you had located an example, the same coin, at auction today, would surely fetch well over $10,000!

An Uncirculated MCMVII High Relief double eagle was listed at $3,000 in the *Guide Book* back then. Recently, I sold one for $28,000—or about nine times more than the 1974 price! Indeed, in looking through the *Guide Book* of that year, and comparing it with the latest edition, I am hard pressed to find *any* pre-1940 coin among the thousands listed that did not increase in value! This is a truly remarkable situation. Contrast that to the stock market. A listing of, say, 4,000 stocks would be peppered with companies that lost money for their investors, or worse, went bankrupt and became valueless.

Since 1974 the market has had its ups and downs, and there are coins, including rarities, that sold for more during a peak in the market in 1979-1980 than they sell for today. There are also coins which went up in value sharply in the next peak, 1989 and 1990, but which now sell for half or less of their 1990 highs. This pattern of ups and downs, of cyclical effects, has characterized the coin market ever since day one—and is discussed in a separate chapter in this book. However, taken as a *long-term* investment, coins have done well—spectacularly well—since 1974.

Are There Any Good Values Today?

Now, in 1991 as these words are being written, we come again to the same question: Are coins fully priced? Are there any good investment values left?

These are the same questions I heard in 1974 when the first edition of this book was written, these are the same questions I heard in 1964 and are the same questions I heard in 1954. Undoubtedly, before my time in numismatics, collectors asked the same questions in 1944, 1934, and 1924. In fact, I know they did, for all one has to do is read old issues of *The Numismatist* (the official journal of the American Numismatic Association) or the *American Journal of Numismatics* (journal of the American Numismatic Society) to learn that collectors in 1900, or 1890, or just about any other year you mention, were amazed at auction price records and felt the peak had truly been achieved for all time!

I believe that today is a great time to invest in *certain* coins. Now, in the summer of 1991, there are values in the marketplace which have not been seen for five to ten years. Some coins are incredibly cheap. (Others, in my opinion, remain overpriced.)

I am an optimist. I believe in the future of America. I believe in the future of coin collecting and the coin market. I have devoted my professional life to rare coins, and with each passing year, my enthusiasm increases, as does my appreciation of the rich tradition of numismatics. I fully expect when the year 2000 rolls around, and we are on the threshold of a new century, anyone possessing a copy of this present book will look back and say, "Wouldn't it have been wonderful to have formed a collection back in 1991?"—just as today you might say, "Wouldn't it have been wonderful to have begun a collection back in 1974?"

History of the Coin Investment Market

The Lessons of History

 There is a lot to be learned from history. "Those who have not learned the lessons of history are condemned to repeat its mistakes," Santayana observed. Conversely, those who *have* learned the lessons of history can profit from them.

"The more things change, the more they stay the same," it has been said. Very little is new under the numismatic sun. The chances are excellent that some fad, some price movement, or some perceived popularity you may observe in the present market is not new; similar things have happened before.

If you are typical, you might brush this comment off with the thought that what is going on *today* is what is of importance, and that history is stuff for scholars, Harvard professors, and the like—not for live-wire coin investors. Not so. Lessons from those who have gone before us can provide valuable insights. How do you learn the lessons of history? The answer is simple: by reading.

I have read through issues of *The Numismatist* (published since 1888) on three different occasions, the latest being in the late 1980s when I was writing the two-volume work, *The American Numismatic Association Centennial History*. Each time I have learned something new. A set of this magazine from 1900 to date (the earlier years are more expensive) is apt to cost about $2,000 to $3,000 today. If there were only one such set in existence, it would be a bargain for 100 times the price! I am not suggesting that you rush out and buy a set of *The Numismatist*, for much of the information has been distilled in other publications, including *The American Numismatic Association Centennial History*. I am suggesting, however, that you build a decent library. Once you have a shelf or two of books, then adding a set of *The Numismatist* would be a fine idea.

In the spring of 1990 I had a conversation with a wealthy industrialist who had achieved worldwide success in his line of endeavor. Attending one of our auction sales for the first time, he informed me that he had already spent over $5 million on commemorative gold dollars and quarter eagles of the 1903-1926 period. These were a great investment and were very underpriced, he told me. Tiring of acquiring coins in such a limited field, he was now investigating regular-issue gold coins of the 1796-1834 years and Liberty Seated silver coins of the 1838-1891 era.

I asked him how he had determined that commemorative gold coins were such a good buy, and he stated that his own business judgment plus advice from a numismatic investment counselor enabled him to spot bargains that others could not.

"Do you have a numismatic library?" I asked. No, he did not, but he intended to start building one "soon." I happened to have an extra set of *The Numismatist* in stock, and I suggested that he buy it. We talked about the situation for a few minutes, after which he decided the magazine was primarily devoted to collecting, not to investment, and as such would not be worth buying. I said no more.

A few weeks ago I had another conversation with the same industrialist. "I am going to sell most of my commemorative gold coins," he said, "and I plan to consign some to your next auction. They were not a good investment at all. I don't know what I should do next."

I again suggested that building a library might be a good idea, but he still wasn't responsive, despite the fact that during the past year he had sustained a loss of over $2.5 million on his $5 million investment in commemorative gold coins. Perhaps another coin investment advisor will put him on to some more "good deals."

Another man, a refined gentleman and highly successful businessman in another field, decided that getting into the coin market was a great opportunity, and beginning in 1988 jumped into coins in a big way, spending, it was said, $15 million, mostly on common-date gold coins, common silver dollars, and other common coins in MS-65 grade. According to a dealer acquaintance of mine, at last reckoning this person had lost $11 million. He, too, had no numismatic library.

A numismatic library will not, of itself, make you a successful coin buyer. However, if you build a library, read it, and apply your knowledge when you buy, it is a virtual certainty that you'll be in the top 5% of successful coin investors and will sharply outperform just about anyone else you know.

I acquired all of the following information about the coin market of years ago by reading, and I enjoyed every minute of it. What I synopsize here is just the tip of the iceberg. An entire book could be written about the coin market of the late 19th century alone.

The Early Years

The beginning of the coin business in the United States dates from the mid-1850s, during which time several persons became full-time or part-time coin dealers. Edward Cogan claimed to have been the very first, his interest having been whetted by the discontinuation of the United States large cent and half cent and the coming of the new, smaller copper-nickel Flying Eagle cent in 1857. Prior to this time, the hobby of coin collecting was limited to just a few dozen numismatists in the United States. American coins were worth very little over face value. The main sources for such pieces were bankers and bullion dealers who, when alerted to watch for scarce dates, would pick them out and sell them to collectors for a modest premium.

The United States Mint in Philadelphia instituted the Mint Cabinet in 1838. During the 1840s and 1850s, the Mint Cabinet grew as officers of that institution actively bought, sold, and traded coins. Several trays of earlier-dated pieces—particularly large cents of the previous decades—were kept on hand for trading and public relations purposes. Collectors desiring specific dates could often obtain them for face value or for just a slight premium.

The few collectors who were interested in coins during this period—collectors such as Joseph J. Mickley and Matthew Stickney—were able to assemble extensive holdings for a moderate cost. For instance, in the year 1827, Mickley is reported to have obtained four Proofs of the 1827 quarter dollar from the Philadelphia Mint for face value! In 1962 a single 1827 quarter from the original Mickley four sold for nearly $15,000, a record at that time, but a price soon to be eclipsed. In 1980 an 1827 quarter from the Garrett Collection, which my firm offered at auction on behalf of The Johns Hopkins University, soared to a record $190,000, with the event taking place during a peak in the market cycle.

It is probably correct to say that the Philadelphia Mint was the leading "coin dealer" during the 1850s and early 1860s. In his book, *United States Mint and Coinage,* Don Taxay characterized the Mint as a workshop for the private gain of its officers and key employees. The attention of Mint officials was directed toward the acquisition of needed specimens, a process often enabled by the sale of restrikes of prized earlier issues. The Mint Cabinet was the focal point of the hobby. Today, portions of the collection, augmented by many additions over the years, are on view as part of the National Coin Collection in the National Museum of American History at the Smithsonian Institution in Washington, D.C.

The American Numismatic Society was founded in 1858. By the early 1860s there were several other societies, a handful of coin dealers, and several hundred coin collectors in the United States.

Edward Cogan's Sale of Cents

In 1863, Edward Cogan, in a mood of reminiscence, issued a small booklet describing a sale of cents which happened a few years earlier. The introduction tells of the cradle days of the coin business in our country. In Cogan's words:

"Having been repeatedly solicited by several of my numismatic friends to print a priced catalogue of the sale of my private collection of United States cents, which took place on the first of November 1858, and finding the desire to collect catalogues of coin sales considerably on the increase, I have determined to yield to their request. I shall briefly relate the circumstances connected with this sale.

"A friend had commissioned me to make a collection for him of every cent from the year 1793 [onward]. I commenced doing so, and had succeeded in obtaining some few unusually fine specimens—when nearing the completion of the collection, he very generously said that if I could make anything beyond what it would cost him, I should sell it on my own account, and insisted that I should do so. At this time there were comparatively few persons who paid any attention to collecting coins, but those who did were very anxious to obtain certain pieces out of this set. As, however, I determined not to sell any single piece out of it, one of my friends wrote me a letter, offering such prices for some of the pieces which at that time were considered extravagantly high, and suggested that every collector should be allowed to send in bids by letter for such pieces as he required, and the highest bidder to be declared the buyer. This arrangement was entered into, and as the letters were received they were numbered from one to 19, this being the total number of applicants.

"On the first of November 1858, the day named for the opening of the letters, some six or seven of the collectors who were interested in the results, and all having been invited, attended in my private room, and in their presence the letters were opened exactly in the order in which they had been received, and the prices put against such pieces as the writer wished to obtain, showing in this manner each bidding for every single piece throughout the whole collection, for which there had been any offer. Three pieces for which there was no written offer were disposed of after all the letters had been opened. These pieces were the 1830, 1833, and the 1857 nickel cents....

"In regard to the condition of the pieces, I cannot at this lapse of time say more, other than that some of them are remarkably fine specimens, and in the main, were much better than were ordinarily met up with at the time.

"At the time of publication of this sale in our Philadelphia papers I had but a very limited correspondence outside of this state, but within a few days after this appeared, I had scarcely time to answer the numerous inquiries respecting the prices of the coins, or to execute the orders that I received daily from all parts of the northern states. Believing, therefore, that a published result of this sale has been the chief cause of the unprecedented demand that has risen for obtaining coins, I have thought the publication of this catalogue would possess a peculiar interest with the collectors, and trust that I shall not be disappointed in my expectations."

Cogan went on to note that a 1793 Chain cent brought $12.67, a 1793 Wreath cent fetched $5.13, a 1793 Liberty Cap brought $7.25, while a 1799 cent (considered to be a great rarity) realized $7.00, and an 1804 (also very rare) brought $5.50, among others. The total amount realized for the collection of cents from 1793 through 1858 was $128.68, which at the time was a very satisfactory price.

The Market in the 1860s

The years from approximately 1860 to 1866 saw the first boom in the coin market. The most active area and the series in greatest demand by nearly everyone (including the Philadelphia Mint—which, as noted, was one of the most active "dealers" at the time) comprised—would you believe?—medals of George Washington. In a period when a choice 1793 large cent (now in the 1990s worth $5,000 to $10,000 or so) could be purchased for $5 to $10, certain scarce Washington medals would be bid in furious competition from $100 to $500 or even more! Also in vogue were medallic portraits of Admiral Vernon, Lafayette, and Benjamin Franklin, to mention just a few of the more popular figures. Today in the early 1990s few numismatists recognize the name of Admiral Vernon, and relatively few collect Washington medals. Here is a lesson from history: Popularity trends and fads change from time to time.

The 1870s and 1880s: Years of Expansion

The next few decades were expansive years in American numismatics. "Pure investors" were unknown. However, it was not uncommon for a collector to indulge in some speculation. At one time, a corner was set up in 1858 Proof sets, and from time to time various patterns and other scarce issues were held for high prices.

Beginning in 1879, speculation arose in gold dollars (and to a limited degree, $3 gold pieces), and many individuals, believing the pieces would rise sharply in value, placed orders for coins through their banks. The decade of the 1880s saw increased interest in this denomination, with the result that by the time the gold dollar was discontinued in 1889, the Proof mintage in the terminal year amounted to 1,779 pieces—an astounding figure for the era, and in sharp contrast to just 20 Proof gold dollars minted in 1878! Relatively large numbers of business strike gold dollars were set aside also.

In the 1950s I had the pleasure of distributing a hoard of several hundred gold dollars, all in Uncirculated preservation, dated 1879, 1880, and 1881, all from a Baltimore hoard. On another occasion, I acquired a small packet of Uncirculated 1889 gold dollars that had been kept intact since the time of issue and had been stored in a bank in Maine. Although the 19th-century investors who set these pieces aside were long since deceased by the time I handled them, I cannot help but think that today, when a single gem example of one of these gold dollars would bring a price in the $5,000 range, what a fine investment they were!

In the 1880s most coin owners were *numismatists*. Indeed, they had to be as a degree of numismatic knowledge was certainly necessary to intelligently buy the favorite series of the day, such as medals, United States colonial coins, tokens and store cards, and early American half cents and large cents. Coins increased in value gradually. A 1793 cent which sold for $7 in 1856 might sell for $15 in 1875, $25 in 1885, and $30 by 1890. Many collectors considered their holdings to be good investments, but investment in its own right was not the main consideration. Instead, investment was an auxiliary benefit, taken for granted, which came to anyone who carefully formed a cabinet of coins over a long period of time.

Collecting during those formative years had its problems, just as it does today. Forgeries lay in wait for the unwary, and the grading habits of collectors and dealers often sparked heated controversy in the pages of the *American Journal of Numismatics* and elsewhere.

Unlike today, there was virtually no interest in collecting coins from the various United States branch mints. Nearly all numismatists concentrated on Philadelphia Mint coins. Among regular issues, attention was focused primarily on copper and silver coins. Gold pieces, due to their high face value, attracted only the elite who could afford them. While certain advanced collectors desired rarities among $1, $2.50, $3, $4, and $5 issues, the large denominations, $10 and $20, were virtually, if not completely, ignored except for Proofs.

In the 1880s, the most complete collection of United States coins by dates was possessed by Lorin G. Parmelee, a Boston bean baker, who had in his cabinet such rarities as the 1804 silver dollar and 1822 half eagle, although it turned out that the latter coin was but a clever forgery. The Parmelee Collection was offered at public auction sale in 1890. Parmelee held out for the final dollar, and many coins were bid on by the consignor, only to be reoffered during the next several years.

Runner-up among collectors in the 1880s was T. Harrison Garrett, whose family was associated with the Baltimore & Ohio Railroad. Garrett, who met an untimely death in a boating accident in 1888, was a true connoisseur. From about 1865 until his death, he built his collection through purchases from the Chapman brothers, Ed. Frossard, W. Elliot Woodward, and many others. The story of his collection, and extensive excerpts from his correspondence, can be found in my book, *The History of United States Coinage*, which also contains additional information concerning the collecting scene at the time.

The 1890s: Collecting Comes of Age

By 1890 there were dealers in most cities in the Eastern part of the United States. Boston, New York City, and Philadelphia became the central points of activity. J.W. Scott, W. Elliot Woodward, the Chapman brothers, John Haseltine, Lyman H. Low, Ed. Frossard, and Charles Steigerwalt were among the leading dealers of the day.

Early in the 1890s a number of important things happened. The American Numismatic Association was formed in 1891, thus providing a common meeting place for the exchange of ideas and values among collectors from all parts of the United States and elsewhere. *The Numismatist*, which began publication under the private auspices of Dr. George F. Heath, a Monroe, Michigan physician and coin collector, in 1888, was eventually adopted as the official American Numismatic Association journal. Today, the ANA, as it is popularly called, ranks as the world's largest and most important non-profit organization devoted to the furtherance of numismatics.[1]

In 1893 Augustus G. Heaton, a professional artist by trade and a numismatist by avocation, published a treatise on coins from the United States branch mints, titled *Mint Marks* (two words; today, we use a single word: mintmarks).[2] At the time the presence of a "CC" (for Carson City, Nevada—a mint operated from 1873 to 1893) or an "S" on a coin (for the San Francisco Mint which was established in 1854) attracted little interest. In fact, there was no catalogue or guide listing which mintmarks were available! This seems incredible in view of today's values attached to certain rarities bearing tiny mintmarks, the previously mentioned 1894-S dime being but one of many examples. Heaton's *Mint Marks* booklet became popular, and hundreds of copies were distributed throughout the numismatic fraternity. Still, it took a number of years until collecting by mintmarks became popular. It was not until the end of the first decade of the 20th century that it caught on in a big way. Today, mintmark collecting is an inseparable part of numismatics.

Also important at the time was the publication by J.W. Scott in 1893 of the *Standard Catalogue*, the first generally used guide to coin values in America. Earlier, anyone seeking prices had to

---

[1] Address: American Numismatic Association, 818 North Cascade Blvd., Colorado Springs, CO 80903. Membership information will be sent gratis on request.

[2] Among his artistic commissions, Heaton designed the motif of a commemorative stamp issued in connection with the 1893 World's Columbian Exposition.

query a dealer or extract auction prices from sale catalogues or reports published in *The American Journal of Numismatics*. Such reports often had little meaning, for grading was apt to vary widely, and what one dealer called Uncirculated another might consider to be just Extremely Fine.

In 1893 the main topic of conversation in the United States was the World's Columbian Exposition held in Chicago. Numismatically, the fair was very active, with the firm of J.W. Scott & Co. having two separate coin sale displays, and with numerous other collectors, dealers, and museums participating. The event also saw the distribution of the first commemorative silver coins issued by the United States: the 1892 and 1893 Columbian half dollars and the 1893 Isabella quarter, all of which heightened the public's interest in coins.

There was considerable initial demand for the new Columbian halves. Many thousands were sold at the Exposition, but quantities remained unsold after the event ended. Following the fair closing, one syndicate offered to buy 100,000 Columbian half dollars from the U.S. Treasury, provided that any additional unsold pieces be melted by the government. This proposal was rejected, and large quantities of undistributed half dollars, mostly dated 1893, were released into circulation at face value.

1893 Isabella quarters fared a bit better as an investment medium. These pieces originally sold for $1 each, but due to the fact that for the same price a Columbian half dollar could be purchased (and human nature dictated that a 50-cent piece would be a better value than a 25-cent piece at the same cost), and also because the Isabella quarters were quietly distributed (the half dollars, in contrast were promoted with large displays), the quarters were poorly received at the time of issue. The unsold pieces were then wholesaled to coin dealers for a nominal premium above face value. These quarters were called a "good investment" by many, and words to this effect appeared editorially in *The Numismatist*. The price rose to $1.50, but the supply was too great for the demand at the time, and the value subsided to a lower level. Those who had the foresight to weather the price drop were able to sell large quantities for $2.50 to $5 per coin in the 1920s and 1930s, and this is precisely what several dealers and investors did. Today, of course, these prices in retrospect seem to be incredible bargains, and a superb Uncirculated Isabella quarter is worth several thousand dollars!

The Early 20th Century: Investment Interest Begins

By the early part of the 20th century there was a great interest in all American coins from colonial issues to $3 gold pieces. The higher denomination gold coins, the $5, $10 and $20 pieces, were not included in this popularity. Collectors belatedly learned that many Liberty Seated and earlier silver coins were really rare in top condition, as no one had the foresight to save them in quantity when they were available for face value.

Rarities emerged on the scene, with values of $1,000 to $5,000 being attached to such items as the 1804 silver dollar, the 1822 $5 gold piece, the 1787 Brasher doubloon, and a few others. The 1804 silver dollar in particular was the focus of much interest, and countless columns of print were devoted to it, more than to any other single United States coin issue.

It was announced in 1909 that a price of $10,000 each had been paid by a private collector, William H. Woodin, for two $50 pattern gold coins of 1877. A controversy arose; it was stated that these pieces had not been officially released by the government, and Woodin returned them. Today, these coins are in the National Coin Collection at the Smithsonian Institution. Theoretically, they would probably bring well over $1 million each if sold today—but, of course, they are not for sale.

The term "investment" came into use in the coin market and was mentioned in print many times. Coins were indeed a good investment, and while not all items increased in value, the collector or investor having diverse holdings almost always realized an attractive profit over cost when his collection was sold.

Numismatic knowledge was being translated into print, and articles in the *American Journal of Numismatics*, *The Numismatist*, and other periodicals, and in separate monographs, described die varieties of such diverse issues as Hard Times tokens (issued circa 1833-1844), large cents (1793-1857), silver dollars of the 1794-1803 years, and other specialties.

There was excitement in the air, and collectors were enthusiastic about the hobby. Coin club meetings were attended with enjoyment, and reports of the gatherings made interesting reading. B. Max Mehl, who started buying and selling coins in 1903 and ran his first advertisement in *The Numismatist* in 1904, by the teens was firmly established as one of America's leading dealers. *Mehl's Numismatic Monthly* gave *The Numismatist* and the *American Journal of Numismatics* a run for their money in terms of human interest and editorial content. Mehl was to go on to become the most colorful and most financially successful American coin dealer during the first half of the present century. He introduced thousands of people to the hobby of coin collecting, primarily through newspaper and magazine advertisements, later even a radio program, extolling the virtue of his *Star Rare Coin Encyclopedia*, which promised a small fortune to anyone lucky enough to find a 1913 Liberty Head nickel or some other rarity in his pocket change. Few found rarities, but many became acquainted with numismatics. The fortunate find of an 1894-S dime was all that was needed to send Junior to college. In the 1930s the American Numismatic Association gave Mehl an award for promoting the hobby.

Another prominent figure under the collecting sun was Farran Zerbe, a showman who set up booths and concessions at various expositions and fairs, most notably at the 1915 Panama-Pacific International Exposition in San Francisco, where he supervised the selling of commemorative coins ranging from the half dollar to the $50 issues.[1] In Chicago, Virgil M. Brand was in his glory years and spent most of his waking hours buying coins, including rarities in duplicate and triplicate. By the time of his death in 1926, he had amassed over 350,000 examples, including six of the 10 known 1884 trade dollars, quantities of 1793 large cents, and other treasures. The Brand Collection was subsequently disposed of over a period of more than a half century. In connection with the Morgan Guaranty Trust Company and the estate of Jane Brand Allen, my firm, Auctions by Bowers and Merena, Inc. had the pleasure of auctioning a number of Brand Collection rarities in 1983 and 1984.

The 1920s and Early 1930s: Years of Stability

The 1920s, years which saw dramatic changes in the American scene, with the great Florida real estate boom of 1925 and the stock market crash of 1929 being particularly notable, were fairly serene years in the numismatic hobby. To be sure, there were a few exciting events. The John Story Jenks Collection, auctioned over a period of 10 days in 1921, was a landmark, as was B. Max Mehl's James Ten Eyck Collection sold through mail bids the following year. The Judge Slack Collection, notable for its top-grade territo-

[1] Farran Zerbe also was the prime force in the issuance of the 1903-dated Louisiana Purchase Exposition gold dollars and the 1904 and 1905 Lewis and Clark Centennial Exposition gold dollars. Today, the American Numismatic Association's highest honor, the Farran Zerbe Award, is named after him.

The Bebee Collection Sale

1794 large cent
MS-63, $19,800

1861 Confederate States
of America cent, MS-60, $17,600

1879 $4 Stella
Proof-65, $50,600

1794 silver dollar
VF-30, $17,050

1877 pattern $50 gold in copper
Proof-67, $33,000

A sampling of United States coinage from the Aubrey and Adeline Bebee Collection sold by Auctions by Bowers and Merena, Inc. in 1987.

rial gold coins, was sold by Mehl in 1925 and delighted specialists in the series, among whom was John Work Garrett, son of T. Harrison Garrett, who was busy adding to the family collection.

By present-day standards, the coin business was in its infancy in the years before 1934. Most allied fields of endeavors such as rare books, Currier & Ives prints, and art shared in the stock market boom of the 1920s. Not so with coins. Collecting and investing in coins was limited to a select group of a few thousand persons. Coin values in this period increased steadily but not spectacularly or unnaturally.

Coin prices did not follow the stock market price rise in the 1920s, thus when the day of reckoning came to the stock market, coins held their values fairly well. There were some exceptions. Some of the higher-priced issues (such as territorial gold pieces) softened in price somewhat, and in general, it was a buyers' market for more expensive coins, but the pricing structure as a whole remained firm. B. Max Mehl, who sold on a consignment basis the Waldo C. Newcomer Collection, valued at several hundred thousand dollars during the early 1930s, found that sales were brisk for most low and medium priced issues. Rarities sold fairly well, but often price concessions had to be made.

Similarly, when Philadelphia dealer Henry Chapman and St. Louis dealer Burdette G. Johnson began breaking up the Virgil Brand Collection in the early 1930s, they had no trouble selling various pieces, including rarities. Among the buyers was Col. E.H.R. Green, a hoarder in the style of Virgil Brand. Green is best remembered for having owned all five of the five known 1913 Liberty Head nickels and, in a related field, buying the only known sheet of 1918 24¢ airmail invert "Jenny" stamps. The son of Hetty Green (who was popularly known as "the Witch of Wall Street"[1]), Col. Green collected everything from trains (he owned an entire railroad) to whaling ships. Following his death, his collection was dispersed in the 1940s.

The Mid and Late 1930s: Years of Change

Beginning in 1934 and 1935, the coin market entered a tremendous growth period. This was in the depth of the Depression in America, but an observer of the coin scene would have hardly known it! The early commemorative half dollars of this

---

[1] Her life was detailed in a biography, *The Day They Shook the Plum Tree.*

year—issues such as the 1934 Maryland and the 1935 Hudson, Old Spanish Trail, and Connecticut—all sold out and gave impetus to the growing market.

Activity was strong on all numismatic fronts, in contrast to the American economy, which was having tremendous problems. Prosperity did not return to the national scene until the 1940s, when production for World War II ensued. It is interesting to note that time and time again coin market cycles (about which I write more later) and periods of activity in numismatics have not correlated with trends in the economy, interest rates, or the stock market. A casual observer might think that when the economy is in a "recession" mode, the coin market would slump. However, history shows that there is no consistency in this regard. In the vast majority of instances, the coin market has moved independently. However, there has been a correlation in a number of instances with the inflation index, in that a rise in consumer goods prices is often paralleled by a rise in rare coin prices.

Spurred on by dealers' advertisements and news releases and by the reluctance of collectors and investors to part with what they owned during a rising market, the 1935 Old Spanish Trail half dollars rose in value to $4 within a few months of their issue, and then to $6 each. A boom was on in commemoratives.

What started it in earnest was the rare 1935-D and -S Boone Bicentennial half dollar set with small "1934" in the field. Only 2,000 of these sets were minted for distribution. Although these were advertised for sale in The Numismatist and were promoted by news releases, it is evident that the distributor, C. Frank Dunn of Lexington, Kentucky, sold only a few to buyers at the time, preferring to secretly hold the majority for private sale at higher prices later. Phony "sold out" notices were posted by Dunn, the sets were recognized as rarities, and the price jumped immediately to $50 per set and continued to the $80 to $90 level. The rush was on!

In 1936, commemorative half dollars were the main topic of conversation everywhere. Most of the new issues released early in the year were quickly oversubscribed, often with the supply being rationed at the time of distribution. The Rhode Island Tercentenary issue (totaling 50,000 coins) was ostensibly sold out in a matter of hours after the coins were first placed on sale. The 1936 Cincinnati half dollars (consisting of a set of three coins; one each from Philadelphia, Denver, and San Francisco) jumped immedi-

Gems From An Old-Time Collection

1652 Massachusetts Oak Tree shilling
Very Fine
$2,420

1877 cent
Proof-60/63
$1,430

1866 Shield nickel
Choice Proof-65
$3,080

1795 half dime
AU-50
$4,400

1796 half dime
EF-45
$3,740

1916-D dime
Choice Uncirculated MS-65
$6,050

1876-CC 20-cent piece
Choice Uncirculated MS-65
$66,000

1901-S quarter
Gem Uncirculated MS-67
$27,500

1859 Pattern half dollar
Select Proof-63 $880

1929 half eagle
Brilliant Uncirculated MS-60
$6,820

The Emery and Nichols collections came to light after spending many years in a bank vault. The quality of the pieces was superb, and the sale of them by Auctions by Bowers and Merena, Inc. in 1984 drew many record prices for the time.

ately from the issue price of $7.75 per set to $25 per set, then to $50! Great profits were made by collectors, investors, and dealers—and by certain favored insiders and distributors who, like C. Frank Dunn, posted fictitious "sold out" notices so as to artificially boost prices, enabling them to sell their holdings later at prices far over the "official" issue price. My book, *Commemorative Coins of the United States: A Complete Encyclopedia*, provides an interesting insight into the commemorative era.

The Numismatic Scrapbook, a magazine published by Lee F. Hewitt, came on the scene, and like *The Numismatist*, its pages soon contained many advertisements for commemorative half dollars. A new crop of professionals appeared: dealers specializing in commemoratives. Some, such as Rev. Elias Rasmussen and the Tatham Stamp & Coin Company, ran advertisements listing bid and ask prices for each commemorative issue. The first large speculative market in coins was on its way!

The commemorative market of the 1935 to 1939 years is one of the most interesting chapters in numismatic history. The activities set the scene for a number of other speculations and market peaks which were to occur in later years.

By late summer 1936 the bloom was gone from the rose. Interest waned. Large quantities of commemorative half dollars remained unsold, and many were returned to the Mint for melting. Others were sold to dealers and investors at large discounts from the original issue premium prices. Prices trended downward and continued to do so for the next several years. By 1939, the Cincinnati set had dropped in price from a high of $50 to just $15 per set, and no one was in a hurry to buy them.

The Case of the Cincinnati Halves

The price structure of the 1936-PDS Cincinnati set of three coins is typical of many of these issues. In 1936 the official issue price for the set of three pieces ($1.50 face value) was $7.75. By late 1936 and early 1937 the price had risen to $50 per set, amidst tremendous buying activity spurred by false "sold out" notices given by the distributor, Thomas G. Melish, a Cincinnati manufacturer of wire goods, who had persuaded Congress to create for him this special issue to be distributed and priced in whatever manner he saw fit.[1] Although no records survive, it is believed by many that

---

[1] Melish was also the official distributor for 1936-dated Cleveland Centennial half dollars released after the Cincinnati issue.

Melish sold many if not most of his sets for close to $40 each, instead of at his $7.75 official issue figure.

In 1939 the price of Cincinnati half dollars dropped to just $15 per set as the speculative fever subsided to a low point. Interest in commemoratives remained lacklustre through about 1941, after which the market turned around. By 1944 the price had inched upward to about $17 per set. By 1949 the price was $25. By 1954 the value doubled to $55. By 1959 the figure was $95. By 1963 a set had climbed to $350. In 1974, the price was over $750. During the market peak of 1979-1980 it crossed the $2,000 level. At the end of 1982, a nice set commanded about $1,500. By early 1987, a Cincinnati set in MS-63 preservation was worth about $1,300, with a hand-picked MS-65 set being worth close to $7,000. (The comparison of early market figures for any series with the figures used today must be tempered with the situation, discussed in my chapter on grading, that years ago a coin was described as either Uncirculated or in some other grade; today, in commemoratives and other series, there are such distinctions as MS-60, MS-63, MS-64, MS-65, and so on—classifications not used earlier.)

The price went slightly higher, after which it began to decline. In spring 1990 a Cincinnati set in MS-63 grade was worth about $1,000, while an MS-65 set fetched in the $5,250 range. By the summer of 1991 the prices had fallen further, to about $900 and $3,100 respectively.

The price analysis of Cincinnati half dollars demonstrates, in essence, that an investor buying at the peak of the market in 1936-1937 had to wait 15 years or more to break even, but as a *long-term* investment an attractive profit was shown. An investor buying at the slump period of the market (in this instance, 1939 to 1944) could have shown a profit in any of the successive years. An investor buying in 1974, when the first edition of this book was published, about doubled his money by 1987 if he bought a set which today would be described as MS-63, or multiplied his money by eight to 10 times if the set graded MS-65.

The Cincinnati set is representative of other commemoratives as well. Other issues did about the same. Anyone interested in the long-term price behavior of commemorative half dollars can find ample research material by looking through catalogues, price lists, and publications of the last half century, especially old copies of *The Numismatist*.

The illustration just given of the 1936 Cincinnati set represents a basically scarce and desirable numismatic item. Only 5,000 sets were issued—a very low mintage for a popular United States coin. The price slumped in 1939 because of several reasons. The price rose sharply at the beginning, too sharply. Non-numismatists (i.e., pure speculators) who had sets kept a watchful eye on the price structure. As soon as it leveled off and the "WE WANT TO BUY COMMEMORATIVES" type of advertisement became rare, the get-rich-quick boys sold their sets and took a quick profit.

The Importance of Collectors

Another factor was the minimal number of *collectors* interested in Cincinnati sets at the $50 level. All coin investment is predicated on the assumption that there will be a future demand for a particular coin or set on the part of the *collector*, who represents the ultimate "consumer" from an economic viewpoint. This is a very important precept to remember—one of the most important in this book, in fact—and yet it is one that many investors tend to overlook.

Further on this subject, I recall a conversation I once had with a gentleman who styled himself as a "numismatic investment consultant." He told me this: "The collector is not at all important, for coins are an investment in themselves, as long as new investors keep coming into the market, coins will be a good investment, simply because investors will buy them from each other."

While this theory might work well for the short term (so long as there is a continuing supply of freshman investors), in the long run it will collapse—when new investors fail to appear. The only—repeat, the only—solid basis for the valuation of a rare coin (apart from its intrinsic or face value) is the eventual demand on the part of a *numismatist*. In fact, the failure of a sufficient number of new investors to appear is what caused prices of investment-oriented MS-65 and finer coins in certain series to fall in value in the summer of 1990.

I stated the same sentiments in a feature article, "The Collector is King" which appeared in the *Monthly Summary*, published by *The Coin Dealer Newsletter*:[1]

"Over the years I have always recommended that investment be pursued in conjunction with collecting. The collector is the

[1] Issue of December 1986.

ultimate 'consumer' of a coin. Remove the collector from the scene, and there is no reason at all a Proof 1895 silver dollar should sell for $25,000 or so. Instead, it would be worth the meltdown value. The same goes for an 1858 $10 piece, an MCMVII High Relief double eagle, or for that matter, a 1916-D dime. The concept of a collectorless numismatic fraternity—many now like to call it an 'industry'—composed of investors selling only to investors, is simply 'the greater fool theory.'"

In the same article I went on to say this:

"The collector has a much easier time in coins than the pure investor. Without the knowledge of a collector, the investor has little or no information of value concerning how to make intelligent buys. The investor may rely on charts, taking a lead from the stock market, but if you think about it closely, what does past performance have to do with future performance in the rare coin field? In stocks, the past performance of a security, usually predicated on earnings and dividends (something coins don't have), can be a clue to the abilities of management and the possibility of future earnings and dividends. However, this concept cannot be logically applied to coins."

Among the many dealers and collectors responding to the article was David W. Akers, a professional who is especially well known for his studies of American gold coins. His words are worth repeating here:

"I have just finished reading and rereading your article, 'The Collector is King,' in the *Coin Dealer Newsletter*. Let me congratulate you on the superbly written and, in my view, completely accurate assessment of the collecting/investing/grading situation. More articles like yours in view of the investment hype variety are surely welcome and needed in our hobby. (I hate referring to it as an 'industry'—Ugh!).

"I also have been associated with numismatics for over 30 years, both as an advanced collector and as a professional and, almost without exception, the people I have known who made the most money when they sold their coins were collectors rather than investors. In fact, I shall even go so far as to say that the number of 'pure investors' I know who have done even marginally well is decidedly small."

Innovations

From time to time someone endeavors to invent an entirely new concept of coin investment. In 1980 a coin investment advisor wrote an article for *Coin World* stating that what should be considered is "the sizzle, not the steak," and that investment performance is more important than the coins themselves.

In the same vein, another firm proposed a novel scheme of keeping coins in its possession and offering to its customers paper certificates representing the coins. Storage and shipping problems would be minimized, and the investor would save money, so it was said. I could only smile when I read about a firm which had filed for bankruptcy, was not answering its telephone calls, and which apparently had several thousand investors clamoring to obtain coins that had been paid for but were being stored by the seller.[1]

Likewise interesting was an article I read about a creative enterprise which offered private vaults to people who wanted to store coins and other precious items without using the facilities of a bank. The only trouble was that during one weekend some burglars broke in, emptied the vaults, and fled undetected. "So sorry," said the president of the vault company. "The police are looking into it." Here is another piece of advice: *Always take physical possession of any rare coins you purchase.*

Still another method of rare coin investment was invented in the 1980s by an advisor who offered "bid" prices for coins purchased from him earlier, and so identified by certificates in special holders. Thus, for a given coin, an MS-65 silver dollar for example, he might pay $300, *if the coin was purchased from him earlier.* For an identical coin in the same grade he might not make any offer at all—if it was purchased elsewhere! Even this idea came to a screeching halt in 1985, when this person announced he no longer was bidding on his own merchandise but, instead, he would consider the asking prices submitted by his customers—and then would decide whether or not to buy them.

Another business with the same buy-back philosophy ran large and impressive advertisements in *The Numismatist* and other publications until 1990 when it was put out of business by the Federal Trade Commission. Investors were lucky to recoup even a few cents on the dollar.

---

[1] News of this appeared in the media in October 1982.

Still another innovator offered a certificate representing a fractional interest in an important rarity—with the rarity itself being stored out of sight from the owners.

In 1985 and 1986, the concept of encapsulated or "slabbed" coins—coins in hermetically sealed holders—became popular. I shall have more to say on this subject later.

So long as human beings are involved in the field of coin investment, new innovations will constantly come to the fore. My advice, however, is that while some new ideas may indeed have merit, it is often best to stick with the tried and true. If something looks too good to be real, it probably is false.

Back to Cincinnati

Return with me to the Cincinnati half dollars minted in 1936: Although 5,000 sets comprised a low mintage, there were not 5,000 *collectors* in 1939 interested enough in Cincinnati sets to support the earlier market price of $50 or more. Thus, the true value of the Cincinnati set was more nearly $15, the "bottoming out" price.

From this low figure the price rose steadily, based upon the increasing number of *collectors* who desired sets. Thus, when the Cincinnati sets broke the $50 mark again in 1953 to 1954 the $50 figure at this time was a solid and stable valuation, not a speculative one. There were enough collectors in 1953, thus the demand and supply curves equated themselves with the $50 price.

In the years since 1953 the number of collectors has increased many times over. Today's figure would seem to be more solidly based, although there is no doubt that certain buyers of Cincinnati coins today are investors, instead of collectors. There may be fluctuations in the future, for the commemorative market has always been characterized by ups and downs, but the chance that the price of the 1936 Cincinnati set will ever return to *substantially* lower levels is nil.

Diversification

The formative market of the late 1930s, although it may have hurt a few unwise investors in commemorative half dollars who purchased their holdings at the top of the market, had a tremendously favorable effect on numismatics. It introduced thousands of people to coin collecting. Some left coins in a hurry when the market fell, but thousands stayed on and benefited greatly.

Other things were happening in the coin market during the 1930s. In the early part of the decade you could have purchased an Uncirculated 1909-S V.D.B. cent (a rare issue, an example of which sells for over $1,000 in brilliant MS-65 grade today in 1991) for just 25 cents. By the end of the decade these coins sold for $2 to $3 each.

1885 Proof Liberty nickels, which were worth about $1,250 in Proof 65 grade in 1991 (against a high of about $2,500 in the late 1980s), were 25-cent items early in the 1930s and $1 to $2 items later in the decade. Similar price increases took place in other series—Indian cents, Washington quarters, half dollars, gold coins (except for large denominations), and so on. While many investors bemoaned their commemorative market losses, the irrefutable fact remains that if they had diversified their holdings and had purchased some Lincoln cents, Standing Liberty quarters, and other coins as well, their investment taken as a whole would have shown a spectacular profit! This brings me to another piece of advice, quoting the old saying: "Don't put all your eggs in one basket"—*diversify*.

Perhaps in response to the related axiom, "It is OK to put all your eggs in one basket, but be sure to watch the basket carefully!" an Iowa client, a physician, telephoned me a few years ago and stated he wanted to sell his collection of coins and invest the proceeds in a single rarity, an 1838-O half dollar. As the price involved was close to $100,000, I suggested his needs would be better served by reviewing his present collection and only selling pieces which he felt were undesirable. These pieces could be replaced by a number of other pieces which more closely filled his objectives. For his budget of $100,000 I recommended that, instead of a single coin being purchased, no individual coin should be worth more than about $10,000, and it would be better if most coins in his collection were worth substantially less than that. As it turned out, this advice was worth many thousands of dollars to my client, for during the period in question the 1838-O half dollar did not increase in value, but the coins he purchased instead did increase sharply. I have always felt that diversification is desirable.

Other Events of the 1930s

Of great importance to the coin market were several other events during the 1930s. Wayte Raymond, a prominent New York City dealer, published the *Standard Catalogue* beginning in 1934. Prior to the Raymond effort, the only price reference books in wide use were the J.W. Scott catalogue (which was last revised in 1913) and the Guttag Brothers' catalogue of the mid-1920s. The *Standard Catalogue* was issued on a regular basis with frequent new editions. Containing up-to-date prices, interesting information, and excellent illustrations, the various editions were distributed far and wide. Until the advent in 1946 of *A Guide Book of United States Coins*, the *Standard Catalogue* had the popular price guide field to itself.[1]

The *Standard Catalogue* educated collectors and investors alike. Prior to its appearance, even information concerning recent United States coins was sketchy at best. Several years before, a collector wrote to the editor of *The Numismatist* and asked whether any Lincoln cents had been struck at the Philadelphia Mint in 1922. The editor didn't know and asked help from readers. This lack of knowledge was not unusual, and few other people knew the answer either.

It was Wayte Raymond, by the way, who published one of the first advertisements specifically featuring the investment field of rare coins. In 1912 his firm, The United States Coin Company, advertised in *The Numismatist* (I quote from the first part of the advertisement):

"COINS AS AN INVESTMENT: Many harsh words are said about collectors who interest themselves in an actual speculation as to whether or not the coins they are buying today will have appreciated in value 10 years from now. Numismatists of the old school said the true collector is not interested in any such appreciation in the value of his collection but derives his entire profit and pleasure from the coins while in his hands. We feel, however, that the average American collector, while he greatly enjoys his coins, also feels very pleased if on disposing of his collection he realizes profits...."

There were many other influences during the 1930s. The activities of B. Max Mehl reached new heights, as impoverished American citizens hoped to turn grandma's souvenir coins into ready cash, and the best way to do this seemed to be to part with

[1] This book passed from the scene in the late 1950s, by which time the editor was John J. Ford, Jr., and the volume incorporated much research done by Walter H. Breen.

$1 to buy a copy of the *Star Rare Coin Encyclopedia*. At one time during this period, over half the mail handled by the Fort Worth, Texas Post Office went to Mehl's company! At the same time, Mehl was active in the serious side of numismatics, and each issue of *The Numismatist* carried his observations and selling offers for commemoratives, his auction service, or some other aspect of his business.

Perhaps to dispel the feeling that Fort Worth, Texas was out of the mainstream of numismatic activity, Mehl hastened to remind collectors that while many well-known dealers could be found in leading metropolitan centers, important collections had a way of traveling all the way to Fort Worth, where Mehl would include them in auctions (actually mail bid sales, for no public participation was ever involved). Mehl took particular delight in publishing announcements whenever large collections from New York City, Los Angeles, or other commercial numismatic centers were shipped by their owners to him in Texas.

M.L. Beistle, Wayte Raymond, and others marketed albums with celluloid slides which provided convenient coin storage for advanced collectors. (Plastic holders and polyethylene coin envelopes, popular for storing coins today, did not come into general use until the 1950s.) The number of coin collectors increased during the 1930s, and by 1940 nearly every large city in the United States had one or more full-time dealers.

The Coin Market
1940-1959

The Early 1940s

 During the period from 1940 to 1950 the modern structure of coin prices began to take form. Whereas all Proof Liberty nickels, for example, had been priced about the same during the 1930s, a different price structure emerged during the following decade. Figures taken from the 1934 and 1949 editions of the *Standard Catalogue* show this dramatically. In Proof condition, certain dates of Liberty nickels had the following values in 1949: 1884 $10, 1885 $25, 1886 $10, 1887 $4.40, and 1888 $4.50. Fifteen years earlier in 1934 these coins catalogued precisely 50 cents each!

The "key" dates such as 1885 and 1886 became more valuable than the others. In other series 1877 Indian cents, 1909-S V.D.B. Lincoln cents, 1916-D dimes, 1932-D and -S quarters, and other scarcities became the varieties most in demand. Collectors started looking through millions of coins in circulation. A new price structure emerged; the prices of coins in a given series increased in direct proportion to their scarcity in circulation. All of this was helped along by the marketing of so-called "penny boards" by Whitman and others; cardboard coin holders with spaces for date and mintmark varieties of Lincoln cents, Liberty nickels, Mercury dimes, and other series which could be extracted from pocket change.

As prices rose, coins in "Good" and "Very Good" condition— well worn examples—became valuable if they were scarce varieties. Previously, a 20th-century coin in any grade less than Extremely Fine or Uncirculated was fit only for spending. Early editions of the *Standard Catalogue* priced coins only in Uncirculated and Proof grades! At one time the editor of *The Numismatist* said it was a foolish thing to want to own a well worn 1901-S quarter dollar (a coin which in the early 1990s would be worth the best part of $1,000!). Only high-grade specimens were desirable, he told his readers.

It was soon learned, however, that there were not enough Uncirculated and Proof coins to go around as the number of collectors doubled and tripled, and then doubled and tripled again. Circulated coins of scarce dates were sought eagerly. Although I do not know of anyone who found a 1913 Liberty Head nickel in circulation, it was indeed possible to find "a treasure in your pocket," and many were the reports published in the *Numismatic Scrapbook Magazine* of "circulation finds." Lee F. Hewitt, founder of the publication, told me that this area was the most popular with his readers, probably because everyone could dream of someday being the lucky finder of a rare coin.

The Significance of the Higgy Sale

The years from 1942 to 1944 saw explosive growth in coins. The wartime economy and the attendant uncertainties caused many people to desire "hard" or tangible investments. All of a sudden coins were "discovered" by many people, including investors, who had paid them scant notice earlier. Abe Kosoff, who during the decade from 1944 to 1954 operated the Numismatic Gallery with Abner Kreisberg, reported that the Michael Higgy Collection Sale in 1943 saw many bidders send in "buy" or unlimited bids for the items offered. A bidding frenzy took place, and many coins sold for five to 10 times the estimates—an unheard of situation! Kosoff, a chronicler of the numismatic scene in his published articles in *Coin World* and elsewhere, credited the Higgy Sale as being the jumping-off point for an entirely new market, with wild prices not dreamed of earlier. Prices continued to rise dramatically, and by 1945 there were many pieces which sold for a couple dollars in 1940 but came to be worth $15, $20, or even more.[1]

Immediately following the war a new colossus appeared on the numismatic scene: the *Guide Book of United States Coins*, written by Richard S. Yeoman and printed by the Whitman Publishing Co. With the vast and varied distribution outlets of Whitman, the *Guide Book* was an instant success. Today in the 1990s it ranks as one of

[1] The high-water mark in the fortunes of the Numismatic Gallery was the sale of the F.C.C. Boyd cabinet of United States coins, billed as "The World's Finest Collection," in 1945 and 1946.

the most popular books ever published on any subject in America. Many millions of copies have been sold.

Prices continued to rise, although in 1949 the market suffered a temporary setback, due perhaps to doubts about the strength of the postwar economy and due to the rapid run-up in coin prices during the several previous years. However, a review of price levels at the end of the decade shows sharp increases across the board from half cents to double eagles. Territorial gold coins, patterns, tokens, and other items also came in for their share of attention.

It is worth noting that Wayte Raymond, a true professional numismatist as well as a rare coin dealer (yes, there is a difference), devoted substantial sections of the *Standard Catalogue* to tokens, medals, and other pieces separated from the regular coinage. In my opinion, present-day publishers of popular references would do well to take a leaf from Wayte Raymond's idea book!

During the decade of the 1940s the number of new collectors continued to increase, whereas the supply of coins remained constant, thus causing an inevitable price rise. The inflationary economy at the time contributed as well. Price increases were healthy and were based upon increasing demand from numismatists.

There were minor adjustments in certain series from time to time, but the long-term trend was upward. The Dunham, Higgy, "World's Greatest," Hall, "Bell" (Shapiro), Flanagan, Atwater, "Memorable" (Williams), Allenburger, Neil, and other collections came on the market. In most instances numerous price records were set, some of them fantastic for the time. If Rip Van Winkle had awakened in 1950 after a 20-year sleep he would not have believed the prices! Coins that were selling for $10 in 1930 were in some instances selling for $100 to $200 by 1950! But, as we shall see, the greatest increases were yet to come.

Growth in the Early 1950s

In 1950 the Philadelphia Mint announced it would resume the production of Proof sets. Earlier, Proof coins had been been sold to collectors from 1858[1] through 1916 inclusive and then from

---

[1] Prior to 1858, Proof coin distribution was primarily limited to Mint officials and their friends (some of whom were collectors), congressmen and other public figures, and foreign dignitaries.

1936 through 1942. Coinage was suspended after 1942 and was not resumed until 1950.

In 1950 the Philadelphia Mint produced 51,386 Proof sets. In 1951, 57,500 sets were made. As production climbed year by year there began to be considerable interest in Proof sets from an investment viewpoint, but the interest was limited. I remember that David Karp, of James, Inc., rare coin dealers of Louisville, Kentucky, showed me a nice "thank you" letter the firm received from the Mint in appreciation for its particularly large 1951 Proof set order! The years when millions of sets were to be produced and when ordering quantities would be restricted were yet to come.

In 1950 the Denver Mint produced only 2,630,030 nickels— the smallest nickel five-cent piece coinage since 1931. When the mintage figures were released, excitement prevailed! By May 1951, a $2 face value roll of 1950-D nickels was selling for three times face value, or $6. One dealer in the May 1951 issue of *The Numismatic Scrapbook Magazine* said: "1950-D Nickels. Hectic! Write for prices." Still there was no great widespread interest in modern coins. Sample retail prices of modern coins selected from that 1951 *Scrapbook* issue show offerings at tiny fractions of what the same coin sets would sell for today.

In 1951 a set of Lincoln cents in Uncirculated grade, and dated from 1934 to 1950 inclusive, cost only $2.50. A set of Jefferson nickels from 1938 to 1950 in like preservation cost $8.50, and a set of Washington quarters in the same grade from 1932 through 1950 cost $77.50. A bank-wrapped roll containing 40 1938-S quarters could be had for $35, and a roll of 1946-S quarters brought $11. A roll (20 pieces) of 1949 Philadelphia half dollars fetched $10.65, or just 65 cents over face value, and a roll of the previously mentioned low-mintage 1950-D nickels could be yours for as low as $5.10 if 50 or more rolls were bought.

In 1951 prices of individual rare coins were equally low in comparison to today's prices. A 1916 Uncirculated Standing Liberty quarter could be bought for $185. Today, this same coin would be worth $6,000 or more! A 1917 Type I Uncirculated quarter fetched $2.50, a 1909-S V.D.B. cent in the same condition brought $10.50, and a 1931-S cent brought $1.25—all of which are tiny, even *microscopic* fractions of today's valuations—as a check with current price lists will reveal. Many other examples could be cited.

In 1952 a new publication called *Numismatic News* was started in Iola, Wisconsin by Chester Krause. It proved to be very popular, and over a period of years it introduced thousands of new people to the field of coins.[1] Meanwhile, the American Numismatic Association was gaining thousands of new members, and *The Numismatic Scrapbook Magazine* acquired large numbers of new subscribers.

All of these new collectors wanted coins, and coin prices continued to escalate. The price rise was well founded and solidly based. Sometime around this point I became involved in numismatics, and by 1953 I was an avid reader of numismatic publications and was studying as intensely as I could, reading every book that came my way. My observations for the years 1953 onward are thus in the first person, for I was there when it happened. My observations of the 19th and early 20th century are from history books and are more theoretical in nature.

Not all collectors can have sets of Proof Liberty nickels (even if all Proof Liberty nickels ever coined were still in existence, there would be only 1,475 sets possible, for this was the number of pieces coined in the low-mintage year of 1907) or sets of Uncirculated Indian cents. There simply were not enough coins to go around. Accordingly, a strong demand for modern sets such as Jefferson nickels, Roosevelt dimes, and Franklin half dollars developed.

Prices Continue to Rise

By the end of 1955 the coin market was in the midst of a continuing strong price rise. Conventions, once scholarly gatherings of numismatists, were proudly chalking up record attendances as thousands of newcomers and beginning collectors visited these large affairs to see what coin collecting was all about. Purists and numismatic scholars were dismayed to see that the bourse or sales area became the focus of attention of such events, while the historical and educational aspects were often overlooked.

Attracted by the stories of price increases and profits, investors began to flock to the marketplace. The previously small trading activity in bank-wrapped Uncirculated rolls and modern (since 1936) Proof sets grew rapidly.

---

[1] *Numismatic News* was the seed that grew into an impressive business empire, Krause Publications, of Iola, Wisconsin, which went on to produce popular periodicals in many other fields, including sports cards, old cars, guns, and phonograph records.

A 1936 Proof set, a group of five coins which was issued for $1.89 in 1936 and which sold on the market for $100 by 1954, reached a new level of $300 in 1956. The prices of all Proof sets dated 1937 through 1956 rose also. Sol Kaplan, a Cincinnati dealer, started something when he took a large chalkboard to conventions and posted bid and ask prices for Proof sets—with the prices often changing within a matter of hours. Nothing like this had ever happened before!

Sol, whose background was in the securities market, also introduced the concept of "selling short." I recall that at one time he offered to sell me up to three 1915-S Panama-Pacific sets at whatever the going rate was at the time—say several thousand dollars per set, although he did not have them. "I'll make my profit by finding them somewhere and then selling them to you at what you are paying me now," he said.

Along with Abe Kosoff, who founded the organization, Sol Kaplan was one of the prime guiding lights in the Professional Numismatists Guild, which came on stream in a big way beginning around this time. Although Sol was a tough, no-nonsense businessman, and if something didn't go his way he was quick to speak out in no uncertain terms, including four-letter words, he had a soft side as well, and many were the schoolchildren he introduced to numismatics by giving talks to local classes, scouting organizations, and other groups.

In mid-1956 a current 1956 Proof set, although still available from the Mint for the issue price of $2.10 per set (note: issue prices have risen since then), commanded a price of $2.50 or so on the numismatic market.[1] A record 669,384 sets were struck in 1956, nearly doubling the preceding year's total and exceeding over a dozen times the number struck in 1950, six years earlier.

The market in Proof sets continued to trend upward during the second half of 1956 and the first part of 1957. The 1936 Proof set, which had previously advanced to $300, went on to $500 and then to $600. Other sets also found ready buyers at new levels. Every day more and more people desired them, thus it seemed.

A Setback in the Market

Late in 1957 the market for Proof sets fell. The 1936 set dropped back to $300, and other modern issues retreated to lower

---

[1] Although such sets could still be ordered for $2.10 each, those seeking to buy them had to wait several months for delivery, thus explaining the premium on the current market for sets already delivered.

Modern Series

Enlarged Illustrations.
Two popular modern series: Franklin half dollars and Jefferson nickels.

levels. Again, in 1957 those who were hurt by the drop of prices were those who had *all* of their holdings in Proof sets. Those who diversified fared well. During the same time that modern Proof sets fell, dealers were posting new high buying prices for 19th-century coins and scarcer 20th-century issues. The coin market taken in its entirety was stronger than ever!

Many of the collectors who were introduced to coins with the 1956-1957 bull market in Proof sets stayed with coins and went on to build collections or to invest in other numismatic series. The number of collectors continued to grow.

1958 and 1959 were good years for the collector, investor, and dealer alike. Anyone who purchased Proof sets at the reduced prices of those times would have no trouble in doubling or tripling his investment capital within the next five years. Likewise, anyone who bought Lincoln cents, half cents, large cents, colonial coins, late gold coins, $5,000 rarities, $5 Liberty nickels, or what have you, would show a very attractive long-term profit. It is probably accurate to say that $10,000 invested across-the-board in the market in 1957 or 1958 would have yielded $50,000 by the mid-1960s, and even this figure may be conservative.

Chapter 4

The Coin Market 1960-1980

The 1960s: A New Order

 The year 1960 marked the beginning of a new order in the numismatic market. Eventually, all that happened before 1960, including events of the 1950s, would be viewed as ancient history. After 1960, coin collecting and investing would not be the same.

1960 saw the inception of a new publication, *Coin World*. Beginning with its first issue, coin prices were available to collectors on a *weekly* basis. The market became more volatile and active. Within four years the circulation of *Coin World* climbed past the 150,000 mark, a level not considered possible earlier.[1] There were few secrets in the coin business now. Especially with actively traded modern coins, everyone was up-to-date on the latest prices.

In the same year the Philadelphia and Denver mints produced Lincoln cents with two sizes of dates, the Small Date and Large Date. 1960 Small Date Philadelphia cents were considered to be scarce, and soon after their release at face value, a $50 mint bag of such coins soared in value to over $12,000! *Time* magazine, newspapers, television programs, and other media reported the bonanza, and the search was on! Many people decided to investigate what rare coins were all about, and in the process tens of thousands of new collectors were created.

Beginning in autumn 1962, the U.S. Treasury Department released to the public hundreds of millions of dollars' worth of early silver dollars, mostly Morgan issues dated from 1878 through 1904, but with many Peace dollars in the 1921 to 1935 span as well.

---

[1] Circulation later drifted downward. By the summer of 1991 about 70,000 copies were distributed each week; it is the largest weekly periodical in the field. The first editor of *Coin World* was D. Wayne Johnson, followed by Margo Russell, then Beth Deisher (the incumbent). Also published are the reference books, *The Coin World Almanac* and *Comprehensive Catalog and Encyclopedia of United States Coins*, both of which have been highly acclaimed.

The appearance of scarce dates in this hoard caused great public interest and brought thousands of new collectors into the numismatic field. Leading the way in publicity was the 1903-O silver dollar, formerly a great rarity which in Uncirculated grade catalogued $1,500 in the *Guide Book*, which was released to the extent of over a million coins. Many obtained these erstwhile $1,500 rarities for just face value, while others had to pay from about $20 to $50 each. Harry Forman reported that Uncirculated bags of 1,000 coins each found a ready wholesale market at $17,000 to $25,000.

As a result of growing nationwide interest in rare coins in the 1960s, American Numismatic Association membership applications increased dramatically as did subscriptions to popular numismatic magazines. The story was the same: The increasing number of collectors matched with the static supply of available coins forced prices upward. Rising prices meant rising interest in rare coins. The more prices escalated, the more people were drawn to the field.

In 1960-1962 the collecting of coins by design type—the foundation of what are called type sets—took on new popularity. The introduction of the *Library of Coins* (published by the Coin and Currency Institute) and Whitman *Bookshelf* albums provided an attractive and convenient way to store and display coins by types. Important type set coins such as the 1796 quarter, 1796-1797 half dollars, 1917 Type I quarter dollars, and related pieces doubled and tripled in value. My firm was among the first to publish information concerning the desirability of design types. My recommendations appeared in 1963 in the *Empire Investors Report* and were widely heeded at the time.

Unbridled Speculation

By 1963 speculation in certain modern rolls and bags of coins reached what one dealer called "epidemic proportions." It seemed that anything bright and shiny and of circular shape was being called a "good investment" by some advisors. At one point a $2 face value roll of 40 1950-D nickels was worth over $1,200.[1]

Although experienced collectors were sitting on the sidelines for the most part, the general public was hoarding coins with a

---

[1] A.J. Mitula, a Texas dealer who liked to spend his leisure time in Colorado, was a primary trader in the hot market for 1950-D nickels. From his profits he built a vacation home in Cascade, Colorado, on the road from Colorado Springs to the western side of Pikes Peak.

frenzy. In fact, hoarding became so widespread that there developed a scarcity of new coins in circulation! The Treasury Department vowed to stop all the speculation, and rather drastic measures were taken. The numismatic community was called on the carpet and criticized, despite the protests of ANA officials and others that traditional numismatists were not the ones who were doing the hoarding. Much bad blood developed between Eva Adams (director of the Mint at the time) and the collecting fraternity.

Mintmarks were omitted on issues struck at branch mints from 1965 through 1967, an unprecedented step. The practice of dating coins according to the years in which they were produced, a philosophy which had been adhered to (more or less) for many decades, was suspended for a while. The result of this was to end speculation and to dampen prices, at least for a few years.

It is curious to note that the government itself then did a complete reversal and decided to go into the coin business in a big way in the late 1960s and 1970s. The government's manner of doing this caused considerable criticism. Much of this was voiced in various numismatic publications and involved unnecessarily high issue prices for Proof sets, thoughtless statements made by the government concerning the "investment" value of the coins it offered for sale, and so on.

The initial silver Eisenhower Proof dollars, released at $10 each, rather than $3 to $4 (prices which at the time would have shown a nice profit to the government), likewise met with negative editorial comments.

It is my personal opinion that the United States government should issue modern coins to buyers for nominal prices—and let any future price appreciation accrue to collectors and investors. Also, by doing this the government gives beginning collectors and those with limited budgets a chance to participate equally in new issues and to begin the numismatic hobby at low cost.

The 1950-D Nickel Story

During the 1960s the market for scarce and rare early coins of proven numismatic value remained strong. As an example, such early issues as colonials, 18th- and 19th-century silver coins, early gold coins, and related pieces never faltered (even a tiny bit!) in price when the 1965 to 1967 Treasury efforts against investors were in progress. The prices of certain speculative items fell, with the drop being led by the 1950-D nickel. During the beginning of the run-up of prices in the early 1960s, rolls of 40 1950-D nickels could be had for $100 to $200 each. During the height of the market, rolls sold for as much as $1,200 each, as noted. The drop was a long and a hard one, and before long the same rolls were selling for $300 to $400 each. The decline continued, with the result that by 1991 rolls could be purchased for about $225 or so each! I should point out that this example is not representative, and that the majority of other key issues among modern coins were selling for more—often much more—in 1991 than they were in 1967. However, for an objective discussion of coin investment, I consider it desirable to point out all aspects of the picture.

The 1970s: Coin Investment Comes of Age

After moving sideways for several years, the coin market in general picked up again in the late 1960s and very early 1970s. At the same time the stock market was at a low ebb. As I mentioned earlier, the price movements of stocks and coins do not appear to be related to each other. When stocks are strong then coins usually are also strong, for there is a general "good feeling" in the investment market, and this extends to all investment media. Also to be considered as a factor is the spending of stock market profits on coin collecting and coins for investment.

In the 1969-1970 years and again in 1973-1974 the stock market was weak—at a period when the coin market exhibited great strength. Time and time again I was told by disillusioned stock market investors that they were cashing in and turning their interest to coins. As the Salomon Brothers survey has shown, long-term investment in rare coins has sharply outpaced the Dow-Jones Industrial Averages, the most commonly quoted index of stock market value. However, to be objective I must mention that there are certainly selected individual stocks which have outper-formed coins, and vice-versa.

Just as no correlation between the stock market and the coin market can be found in history, there does not seem to be any connection between interest rates and the prices of numismatic investments. During 1972 to 1974, when commercial interest rates were at unprecedented high levels, over 12% at one point, and when record high rates were being paid on certificates of deposit and on savings account deposits, classical economists felt tre-

The Terrell Collection Sale

$16,000

$6,800

$16,000

17,000

$7,500

$4,600

On this page are shown some items from the Terrell Collection sale (May 1973) which now is "ancient history" so far as prices are concerned. In the nearly two decades since then, most items have multiplied in value over the 1973 record prices noted here! At the top of the page auctioneer George Bennett, who called sales for the author's firm until his death in 1981, says "Sold!" and a coin finds a new home.

mendous amounts of money would be channeled into banking areas and away from "hard" investments. As a student of economics myself, I realized that all past theory pointed toward this. However, the opposite was true. This time marked one of the greatest boom eras in modern numismatics! An explanation of this apparently contradictory phenomenon is that unusually high interest rates are symptomatic of rampant inflation, and, historically, investment in rare coins has been one of the best hedges possible against inflation.

The Great Gold Fizzle

The 1973-1974 years saw great growth in the rare coin field. During this time there was a tremendous interest in gold. It was announced by the government that for the first time since 1973 the American public could hoard gold bullion—beginning on December 31, 1974. Earlier, it was a criminal act to buy and sell gold bullion without special hard-to-get permits.

The popular press took a very bullish view of the changing situation and said that once gold bullion could be owned by the American people, prices would soar through the roof. One of America's most respected economic experts predicted that the price of gold, then in the range of $150 per ounce, would soon go to $400 per ounce! Numerous other "authorities" suggested bullion prices of $200 to $400, with $1,000 mentioned by one particularly aggressive forecaster.

As December 31, 1974 was too long to wait to acquire gold in bulk or bullion form, thousands of investors took a shortcut by purchasing common date gold coins of high intrinsic value. Others bought rare gold coins believing that when gold bullion jumped in price, as it was absolutely certain to do after December 31, 1974, rarities would also double and triple in value. Of course, this thinking was fallacious, for if one pays, for example, $5,000 for a rare gold coin with an intrinsic or melt-down value of $100, it doesn't make much difference whether the intrinsic value doubles or triples—for the collectors' value is so much higher. The anticipated gold boom spurred many artificial price increases.

During this frenzied activity I told interested investors and collectors to be cautious—to stick with tried, true, and traditional items and not to jump on a bandwagon which, to me, seemed to have very weak axles.

Richard Buffum, columnist for the *Los Angeles Times*, interviewed coin dealers and others to ask their reaction to the coming gold boom. I was a solitary voice in the wilderness, and instead of urging *Los Angeles Times* readers to spend their money as soon as possible on anything that was round and yellow, I urged caution. I even had the audacity to state that the gold boom would be a fizzle. I was the only one who said so!

December 31, 1974 came and went, and gold bullion which had nearly touched the $200 mark shortly before that magic date, didn't go to $400. In fact, it didn't even go to $300. In fact, it did something that no one else but me predicted: it dropped! With it dropped the value of quite a few gold coins and other items which were artificially inflated in price earlier. Later, in the autumn of 1976 the *Los Angeles Times* published a follow-up article on the subject, and I was given credit as being the only person who correctly predicted several years earlier what would happen.

In the meantime, selected choice type coins—Indian cents, Liberty nickels, Barber coins, Standing Liberty quarters, and the like—increased in value.

Investment Goes Wild

Beginning in 1977 and 1978, investing in coins became a popular public pursuit. Earlier, the knowledge of the success of coin investment was mainly limited to those who read coin publications or who were otherwise familiar with the hobby. An exception was provided by the 1973-1974 years, when there was widespread advertising concerning gold coins in particular, but by and large coin investment was a field known to relatively few.

In 1977 and 1978 things began to change. By 1979, coin investment was one of the hottest things going, and by early 1980 coin prices were riding a crest.

The situation was caused by several factors coming together all at once. First, under the presidential administration of Jimmy Carter the country had so-called double-digit inflation; inflation over 10% per year. At one time the annual inflation rate actually exceeded 13%. At the same time, money in savings accounts yielded less than 6% (and even this low amount was subject to high income tax rates). Certificates of deposit, a particularly popular way for wealthy people to invest, yielded higher amounts, but these, too, were subject to taxation at high rates. So, a quest began for fields of investment which were taxable at the low capital gains rates then in effect, and which at the same time performed sufficiently well to outpace inflation. As a result, many people with money in banks and elsewhere turned to coins.

The worldwide energy crisis received great publicity, and scarcely a day passed without newspaper headlines about the ever-increasing price of gasoline and oil and ever-escalating interest rates. Certain Arab oil interests publicly stated they did not want to be paid in paper American dollars but, instead, wanted payment in gold. Paper dollars were no good, it was implied. This in turn generated much unfavorable publicity about the future of the American dollar. The price of the dollar plummeted on overseas markets, causing more dollars to be dumped. Obviously, if Arabs wanted gold instead of paper money, they knew something we didn't know—or at least many people thought they did.

Numerous editors of newsletters, "hard money" advocates, and others proclaimed that anyone holding paper dollars was a fool, an idiot, or worse. Gold, and to a lesser extent, silver were the only way to go. Gold, which was selling for several dollars an ounce, was bound to go to $1,000 or, according to one of the most followed advisors of the time, to $2,000 or even $3,000. Investors scrambled to buy as much gold and silver as possible.

Investment for investment's sake increased in the coin market. Selected rare coins had been very good investments in the past, and anyone reading an earlier edition of the present book back in 1977 or 1978 would have been excited by future prospects. Similarly, others published accounts of coin investment success. The findings of Salomon Brothers received wide publicity, and the cachet provided by this respected New York financial advisory service drew more into the field. While investment news of this nature was hardly surprising to numismatists, information disseminated in financial markets drew still additional new investors to the field of coins.

New firms sprung up like mushrooms in the night. Airline magazines, financial publications, newspapers, investment guides, and other printed matter contained advertisements for firms proclaiming their knowledge and abilities in this regard. Companies which were virtually unknown to the established collector and dealer community were suddenly proclaiming themselves to be among the largest, best, and most reputable coin dealers in the

universe! Offered for sale were many types of investment programs. Employed to sell the programs were salesmen paid on a
commission basis. Indeed, I remember seeing a number of advertisements reading somewhat as follows: "WANTED: SALESMAN
FOR RARE COIN FIRM. Experience not necessary. Securities
knowledge helpful."

By means of beautiful brochures and advertising materials
many people were induced to spend their money on coins which,
in many instances, represented dubious values. Often such pieces
were either vastly overgraded, or correctly graded but vastly
overpriced.

Banks, savings institutions, pension funds, and others became interested in coins. Those who sought competent professional advice often did well. Others fared less well. Keogh Plans
and IRA accounts became a popular vehicle for coin investment
(until the government mandated several years later that rare coins
could not be used in this way). Many established numismatists
used these plans to augment their collections or holdings with
good success, but others simply purchased coins blindly, not
knowing what they were buying.

At the same time, auctions continued to set record prices.
Many of the price-smashing realizations were set by coin dealers
who were flush with profits from gold and silver trading. Silver in
particular became a popular passion during late 1979 and early
1980, when thousands of people sold tableware, vases, platters,
and other wrought articles to coin dealers and other similar
buyers who were paying ever increasing prices. The Hunt brothers,
Texas oilmen and investors, were particularly enamored of silver
and were responsible to a large degree for the price rising from
under $10 per ounce to $50 at one point.[1]

By early 1980 just about everyone was buying coins for
investment. There were, however, major exceptions called *numismatists*. True collectors were frightened by prices and were "staying
away in droves," as the popular saying went.

By the end of the decade of the 1970s, and until March 1980,
the coin market enjoyed a relatively continuous growth, with a big
spurt in prices at the end. The 1970s were excellent for the coin
investor. There were some exceptions, the up and down move-

---

[1] The price subsequently fell to about $6.75 per ounce by November 1987, and the Hunt
brothers subsequently sought court protection from their creditors. By the early 1990s the
metal dropped for a time below the $4 mark.

ment of gold from 1973 through 1974, for example, but by and large all went well. It is undoubtedly accurate to state that anyone building a fine collection and spending $100,000 on it in 1960 could have cashed in for several million dollars by 1980. However, most holders of coins were so excited about watching the rising prices that they came to believe that values would always continue to go up, and up, and up.

The Fall

Toward the end of March 1980 the market began to weaken. Although it is difficult to determine precisely when the turning point occurred, the Central States Numismatic Society convention in Lincoln, Nebraska represents the time that many consider to have been the end of the wild market. At the beginning of the show one of my clients, a Michigan doctor, told me that he received "an offer he couldn't refuse" for a group of Barber half dollars purchased from me a few years earlier. The offer? $15,000 per coin, about three times the then-going rate! The buyer was a dealer seeking to spend profits from silver trading. By the end of the show there seemed to be a change in attitude on the part of many, and enthusiasm disappeared.

During the next two to three years the market for many coins, especially those which had risen sharply in recent times, drifted lower. Investors who were not numismatists switched to other things. Money market funds, new high interest rates paid on certificates of deposit, the stock market, and other areas drew their attention. Coins were left behind. As numismatists went to the sidelines (beginning in 1978 and 1979) there were few people left in 1980 and 1981 to buy coins for the purpose of putting them in collections.

As dramatic as the crash of March 1980 was, it came as no surprise to anyone who had learned the lessons of history. Quite a few readers of the then-current edition of the present book told me that they had seen the crash coming and had sold out, taking nice profits. A Texas buyer of the book told me that, using ideas from this book, he turned a $125,000 investment in coins in 1975 into a cash-in value of $640,000 when he sold his holdings in late 1979. A Massachusetts entrepreneur told me that ideas in the book were responsible for his making a profit of nearly $2 million during the same period.

The Coin Market
of the 1980s

Strength Returns

 Prices continued to fall. Finally, toward the end of the summer of 1982, some strength returned. Investors were still largely absent from the scene, but collectors, realizing that prices had returned to sensible levels, became buyers. Auction '82, conducted by a consortium of dealers (Stack's, Rarcoa, Superior, and Paramount) before the American Numismatic Association convention in August, saw excellent activity, as did the ANA convention itself.

My firm offered at fixed prices the John W. Adams Collection of 1794 United States large cents. There were 75 pieces in the collection priced to total over $400,000. By the end of the ANA convention, fewer than 20 pieces remained! For some pieces, a half dozen to a dozen or more orders were received! The Eliasberg Collection of United States Gold Coins, catalogued by me and auctioned by my firm in October 1982, likewise created great attention, primarily on the part of numismatic connoisseurs. Containing one of each date and mintmark issue in the United States gold series, the auction realized $12.4 million, and in the process numerous world record prices were established. Clearly, the market had returned to the realm of the collector.

It is important to observe that the prices of certain tokens, medals, obsolete currency, and other pieces which did not share in the investment boom of the 1970s were not adversely affected by the subsequent market weakness. Indeed, prices in these series remained as firm as ever. Alan V. Weinberg, an astute observer of tokens and medals, wrote an enthusiastic article for the magazine of the Active Token Collectors Organization (ATCO) observing that the Clifford Collection auction, held by my firm in March 1982, saw many pieces far exceed previous price records.

New Commemoratives Issued

In 1982 the Treasury Department resumed the issuance of commemorative coins, the first since 1954. The Washington commemorative half dollar, designed by Elizabeth Jones, and with publicity and enthusiasm generated by Donna Pope, director of the Mint, was issued to observe the 250th anniversary of the birth of our first president. The pieces, made with Proof finish by the San Francisco Mint and with "Uncirculated" or business strike finish by the Denver Mint, were very well received, and within a year several million pieces were sold, with remainders being trickled out until 1985.

Commemorative 1983-1984 silver dollars and 1984 $10 gold commemoratives issued in conjunction with the 1984 Olympic Games, held in Los Angeles, were likewise popular, as were 1986 Statue of Liberty commemoratives of the denominations of 50¢, $1, and $5. Each of these helped publicize coin collecting to the general public.

In the autumn of 1986 the Treasury Department issued gold and silver bullion coins, called "eagles." The $50 gold issues in particular met with an enthusiastic reception, and many hundreds of thousands of examples were sold by year's end, so much so that *The Coin Dealer Newsletter* reported that the great expenditure on these bullion coins had sapped buying power from the rest of the market.

The years 1983, 1984, and 1985 saw an active market, with emphasis on numismatic considerations. Collectors continued to return to the fold, but not in such numbers that prices rose appreciably. Indeed, among rarities many prices set in 1979 and 1980 still stood. Still, there was a strong demand for quality material. My firm offered at public auction the Virgil M. Brand Collection, which saw numerous price records broken—especially for such esoteric items as territorial gold coins, Washington medals (a set of Washington Seasons medals fetched $55,000, for example), and other pieces. "The Collector Has Returned," pronounced a headline in one popular publication.

By and large, the investor was out to lunch, so to speak. Inflation had diminished, the oil and energy crises subsided, and things were relatively peaceful on the economic scene. Besides, coins as an investment were not a "fresh" subject. It is not that the problems had gone away. Although inflation was lower than in

The Harry Einstein Collection Sale

1895 silver dollar
Proof-67, $30,800

1918/7-S overdate quarter dollar
MS-60/63, $9,075

1825 quarter eagle
AU-55 $10,450

1802 restrike silver dollar
Proof-63 to 65, $39,600

1911 double eagle
Matte Proof-65, $28,600

1933 eagle
MS-63, $79,200

A sampling of United States coinage from the Harry Einstein Collection sold by Auctions by Bowers and Merena, Inc. in 1986.

previous years, the federal government was faced with a record peacetime deficit exceeding $200 *billion*—that's right, *billion*. There were more failures than "rescues" of banks and banking institutions than at any other time since the great Depression in the 1930s. On Friday, March 15, 1985 the governor of Ohio padlocked dozens of savings and loan institutions that were in trouble in his state, while officials tried to straighten out the mess. In the meantime, worried depositors spent a night-long vigil hoping they would be able to see a trace of their money. This situation was accelerated in 1986, which saw the dubious record of more bank failures than ever before in modern times. However, perhaps this record was not to remain for long, for early in 1987 it was announced that already a new record was on its way to being set! As most readers know, the worst was yet to come, and the years 1989, 1990, and 1991 saw many disasters in the banking industry.

In the meantime, the American dollar, strong overseas in 1984 and 1985, by 1987 became very weak, thus creating record trade imbalances. This was an important factor in causing the record 508-point drop in the Dow-Jones Industrial Averages on October 19th of that year.

Although investment was not in the mainstream of numismatic activity during the mid-1980s, the subject received new life through vast telemarketing organizations that were set up to promote the sale of coins by telephone solicitation. Common silver dollars, Proof sets, and the like were aggressively marketed, often at prices far above what knowledgeable collectors would pay.

An investigation conducted in 1986 by Phoebe Morse of the Federal Trade Commission revealed, for example, that one firm sold Liberty Walking half dollars to clients for several hundred dollars each, billing them as MS-65, when in reality they were worn pieces worth no more than $15 each! A typical group of coins sold for $10,000 was found to have a replacement value of about $2,000. Such abuses cast a shadow on all of numismatics, although reputable firms weren't involved. Over a period of time, fraudulent activities such as this caused the government to pay close attention to the entire coin field.

Long-established professional dealers of unquestioned reputation found themselves in the expensive and uncomfortable position of having to defend the field of rare coins to government agents, some of whom seemed to believe that all coin investment should be regulated and subject to controls, paperwork, etc. The Professional Numismatists Guild, long the leading American association of rare coin dealers, rallied to the defense of the field, but as of 1991 many problems remained. It was a case of a few telemarketers—certainly fewer than a couple dozen firms—causing untold aggravation and annoyance for several thousand thoroughly reputable professional individuals and companies.

Meanwhile, Back in the Collecting Fraternity

Among the collecting fraternity, quality was emphasized, and grading underwent a transition (as discussed in detail in my separate chapter on the subject). Market emphasis was put on pieces grading MS-65 and Proof-65 with the result that lesser grade pieces appeared to be bargains by comparison. This spawned a new wave of collecting interest in such issues as Liberty Seated coins, Barber dimes, quarters, and half dollars, and other issues which were and are basically scarce, but which had not participated in the great market boom of the late 1970s.

Interviewed at the close of 1984, Raymond N. Merena, president of Bowers and Merena Galleries, Inc., noted the previous 12 months had set a sales record. "If I could put the coin market on 'hold' and keep it this way forever, I would," he observed. He went on to say the market was primarily composed of experienced buyers paying reasonable prices for truly scarce and rare items. Clearly, it was a good time to engage in the formation of a meaningful collection.

In the last edition of this book, much of which was revised in 1987, I noted: "The numismatic market is strong. Certain areas which were popular with investors—MS-65 1881-S silver dollars being a popular example—are cheaper now than they were a year ago, but items with a more solid numismatic foundation; colonial coins, early silver, Liberty Seated issues, and the like, are higher in price—but hardly expensive in relation to their potential."

What Happened in 1989 and 1990

If coin investment was *wild* in 1979 and early 1980, it was *crazy* in 1989 and early 1990, a decade later. This time there was hoopla about many new things, including the invincibility of certified coins housed in plastic slabs, and the hundreds of millions or even *billions* of dollars that Wall Street investors were going to shower down upon every holder of rare coins, driving prices up to heights that would make the market boom of 1979-1980 look like kindergarten play.

Whereas years ago investment was a pleasant adjunct to collecting, in 1979 and 1980 investment became the tail that wagged the dog. Numismatics survived however, and while investors were investing, collectors were still collecting—especially in areas that weren't of so-called "investment quality," United States large cents for example.

Whenever the coin market has experienced excesses and has subsequently crashed, many people have been hurt. The bigger the crash, the greater the damage.

In the late 1980s investment in coins became a big business, and the word "industry" was used all over the place. (I share David Akers' view, quoted earlier, that the term is inappropriate; to quote David: "Ugh.") Slick brochures, fancy magazine advertisements, television spots, videotapes, and, especially, telemarketing were used in an effort to convince wealthy people such as investors, physicians, et al., that they were absolutely and positively stupid if they didn't have a large percentage of their net worth tied up in "investment quality" coins.

And what were these "investment quality" coins? Again, the lessons of history teach us something. They were, as in the last investment boom and bust, common coins in high grades. Leading the pack this time was the 1881-S silver dollar, a specimen of which in MS-65 grade was once said to be worth on a wholesale basis over $800, predicted to go to $1,000 or more. At auction some "clever" buyer actually paid close to $2,000 for one, a figure which just happens to be more than a dozen times what an MS-65 1881-S dollar is worth now in the summer of 1991.

A fool and his money are soon parted, P.T. Barnum said. Perhaps this is why noted numismatic researcher and sometimes cynical observer of the current scene Walter H. Breen called Barnum the patron saint of coin collectors, except that I think he meant to say coin *investors*.

Certified coins (more about these later) turned out to be idols with clay feet. Despite hopes and claims that all MS-65 coins of a given variety in slabs are worth the same amount of money, and can be bought and sold sight-unseen, reality turned out to be quite different. As Barry Cutler of the Federal Trade Commission pointed out, dealers who are eager to sell their customers coins sight-unseen are for the most part quite unwilling to buy coins sight-unseen themselves. Not making matters any better is the assertion by the *Certified Coin Dealer Newsletter* that the sight-unseen bids listed for coins are for "the worst possible examples" of the grades indicated!

As might be expected, it was a classic case of coin investors coming in last. Thousands of buyers were left holding common coins in high grades, purchased for far higher prices than *collectors* (remember them?) would ever pay.

At the same time, the anticipated deluge of Wall Street money failed to materialize, and by early 1991 it was likely that Wall Street funds had invested considerably less than $50 million in rare coins, a far cry from the hundreds of millions or billions of dollars once viewed as a virtual certainty.

The general economic recession of 1990-1991 didn't help either. While the national economy and the rare coin market usually have moved in opposite directions in the past, this time the peak of the coin investment market, which occurred in late spring 1990, coincided with a decline in the economy, a situation which exacerbated the decline of coin prices. After all, if someone is out of a job or expects to be, he is not going to be a candidate to buy coins.

What I Might Have Done But Didn't

With the rapid pace of business at Bowers and Merena Galleries, Inc., the related firm of Auctions by Bowers and Merena, Inc., and the newly-formed mail-bid sale subsidiary, Kingswood Galleries, not to overlook my spending several years writing the 1,768-page, two-volume *American Numismatic Association Centennial History*, I did not have time to put out another edition of the present book until now. As I like to speak of my actions, not what I was thinking of doing but didn't, I won't suggest that any edition of the present book issued in 1989 or early 1990 would have predicted the market break—but my feelings on the overpriced nature of certain aspects of the 1989-1990 market were adequately chronicled elsewhere, including in my monthly column, "Coins and Collectors," in *The Numismatist*, in articles for *Coin World*, in contributions to the *Coin Dealer Newsletter*, and elsewhere. My book, *A Buyer's Guide to the Rare Coin Market*, the manuscript of which was

A few of the many catalogues producted by Auctions by Bowers and Merena, Inc. over a long period of years.

mostly prepared in the early part of 1990, contains many warnings, especially on the subject of overpriced MS-65 and better coins. I refer anyone interested to these and other writings.

Why Isn't Everyone a Collector?

Collector demand tends to be stronger than investment demand, thus the market for collectors' coins tends to be steadier. In fact, since the market break in the late spring of 1990, the market for lower-grade Liberty Seated coins, for colonials, for scarce tokens and medals, for large cents, and for many other series not caught up in the investment boom has been very strong.

In May 1991, Liz Arlin, who manages the Want List Department at Bowers and Merena Galleries, reported the greatest sales volume in recent years to her clients (who consist almost entirely of experienced and knowledgeable collectors and dealers). Clearly, the market for *certain* rare coins was strong. At the same time, anyone with a collection of colonial coins, of half cents 1793-1857, of large cents 1793-1857, of Liberty Seated coins by date and mintmark, or of many other selected series saw no diminution of value. Indeed, during our auction of the George N. Polis, M.D. Collection in June 1991, many pattern coins sold for all time high prices, some of which returned to the estate of the owner 50 to 100 times the price he paid us for these same coins 30 years earlier in 1961!

It is logical to ask why investors don't copy collectors and desire to buy early issues and other series with a proven base of collector interest. There are several answers to this. The main one is that *knowledge* is necessary to collect and invest in earlier issues. The buyer possessing such knowledge traditionally has done well. However, the buyer who does not want to learn and who cannot or will not invest time in studying the field is apt to buy from someone who is primarily concerned with selling common items. A buyer consulting such a source would not be exposed to the advantages of investing in coins of proven numismatic desirability. Such sellers often buy up the things that are easiest to accumulate in quantity, and recklessly sell them as "good investments." Coins of true scarcity and rarity are never available in quantity, therefore these are not often recommended. In an article in *The Coin Dealer Newsletter* I discussed this very situation:

"The problem confronting the investor is that he is bombarded by numerous sales messages, many of which have little to do with the hobby of numismatics. Those with the most intense messages and the largest advertisements—the mass marketers of coins—seek for their clients pieces which are available in quantity. They are the people who sell Morgan silver dollars in quantity, who offer modern rolls and Proof sets, and the like, simply because these are coins that are common and can be acquired in large numbers. If an investment-oriented mass marketer sends out tens of thousands of brochures suggesting that clients buy Extremely Fine 1908-S Barber half dollars, AU 1846-O and 1859-S Liberty Seated silver dollars, and large cents of the 1820s in VF to AU grade, after the firm receives its first order its inventory would be wiped out—for such things simply do not exist in quantities. Instead, such sellers need to fill their hoppers with bags of common date Morgan dollars and other such things which can be obtained by the thousands. In that way, they can be assured that their inventory will remain good throughout the life of the sales presentation.

"Actually, the concept of RARE coins is at odds with the concept of mass merchandising. Rare coins are not available in quantity. Thus, the investor buying through a mass merchandising firm is apt to wind up with a portfolio of common issues. Indeed, this has happened and, paradoxically, has caused many common issues to rise in value sharply, especially in comparison to rare issues. This is a classical self-fulfilling prophecy. But will it last?"

In an editorial in *Numismatic News*, Cliff Mishler mused that it was indeed a strange world—this was in the height of the mass merchandising of the mid-1980s—in which common coins were often in greater demand than rare ones, and that common coins were, in some instances, just as expensive as their rarer counterparts!

In the late 1980s and early 1990s when the Federal Trade Commission, led by the efforts of Phoebe Morse and, later, by Barry J. Cutler, closed down a number of unethical firms engaged in the telemarketing of coins to unsuspecting investors, nearly all such firms were found to be doing one of two things: (1) Selling common coins at very high prices, or (2) selling rare coins at prices much more than reputable professionals would charge for the same coins. Investment writer and consumer advocate Scott Travers has furnished many details of telemarketing abuses in the books he has written on the subject of coin investment.

My own personal opinion, as stated before, is that the most successful investor is the one who takes the time to learn about coins and the coin market—and who along the way builds a meaningful *collection*. I have always recommended that our clients become acquainted with coins, buy reference books, subscribe to numismatic publications, join the American Numismatic Association, and so on. I have done this in full confidence that the coins my firm, Bowers and Merena Galleries, sells can stand up to close scrutiny in comparison to the offerings of other sellers. Unfortunately (for both the individual investor and for the good of numismatics as a whole) some types of coin sellers prefer that their clients read only their own literature and not become familiar with what is going on in the general numismatic marketplace. The disadvantages of this to the investor are obvious.

Chapter 6

The Market of
the Future

Short Term Outlook

 What about the future? From my vantage point in the summer of 1991, in the short term the market offers many buying opportunities. By short term I mean the next several years. On the other hand there are certain issues whose prices are still too high—a reflection of fast run-ups during the past few years. Subsequent chapters outline my picks of good buys in all series from half cents through gold, commemoratives, and other coins.

As a rule of thumb (please do not use this commentary alone; see my later, expanded commentaries), there are many coins in MS-63 and MS-64 grades in popular series such as commemoratives, semi-scarce varieties of Morgan dollars, late 19th- and early 20th-century "type" coins, etc. which are excellent values in comparison to MS-65 levels for the same pieces.

There has been a reorientation of philosophy in this regard, and over a period of time a number of investment advisors who earlier recommended only MS-65 coins have now come to recommend MS-60, MS-63, and other grades below MS-65. In an issue of the *Rosen Investment Advisory*, Maurice Rosen noted he was recommending MS-60 coins in certain series, but the only other firms he could find who were recommending MS-60 coins were Bowers and Merena Galleries and Stack's. It's not that our firm or Stack's are in the "recommending business," for both of our firms are primarily involved with the buying and selling of coins to established collectors, with investment being strictly a secondary consideration. However, both Stack's and ourselves feel that in the current market MS-60 coins offer many interesting opportunities.

Good Advice (In My Opinion)

I feel that the market in some areas still has to undergo a downward adjustment in MS-65 and Proof-65 grades and, especially, in MS-66, MS-67, and MS-68 Mint State levels and Proof-66, Proof-67, and Proof-68 categories. As money can be made by *not buying* coins as well as by buying them, I urge that you consider very carefully any coins certified above the MS-65 and Proof-65 levels. As more and more coins become certified by the leading grading services, the number of certified coins in such high grades will become more plentiful, and I predict that prices will fall. This will be especially true in instances of relatively common Morgan dollars, commemorative gold and silver coins, U.S. gold coins (especially issues minted after 1880), and certain "type" coins.

When making investment decisions in the coin market, ask yourself this question: For a given coin in a given grade, are *collectors* demanding it? If the answer is "No," and if the demand is primarily from investors, keep your checkbook in your pocket.

Long Term Outlook—United States Coins

Few will question that investment in United States coins has been spectacularly successful for those who have bought carefully and from responsible sources. Probably even those who bought at the peak of the market in the late 1970s through early 1980 will do well sometime in the future, just as those who bought Cincinnati commemorative half dollars in 1936 eventually did well later (but had to wait a long time to show a really attractive profit). In fact, many coins sell already for more now in 1991 than they did back at the 1979-1980 market peak.

A problem arises with grading in that what the American Numismatic Association, the arbiter of the field, certified as MS-65 in the late 1970s and early 1980s is what the ANA later stated was only MS-60 to MS-63 in many instances.

Later in this book I devote a chapter to grading. Also, I recommend that you read the introduction I wrote for the latest (4th) edition of ANA *Grading Standards For United States Coins* (available from most numismatic booksellers). This is an important and highly complex field.

Those who entered the investment market in 1989 and early 1990, and who bought so-called "investment quality" coins in MS-65

and Proof-65 grades in certain series, will probably find themselves in a loss position now. The future market *may* make you
whole, but I believe it will be a long time before MS-65 1881-S
silver dollars again sell for over $800 on a wholesale basis, or
common-date gold coins (such as 1901-S $10 and $20 pieces
dated 1904, 1904-S, 1908 no motto, and Philadelphia Mint coins
1924-1928) equal their highs of the recent boom market, etc. You
might want to cash in, swallow your loss, and buy some coins of
true rarity and scarcity.

The past is a known entity. But, what lies ahead? Are there
still some good investment opportunities in the long run (say, 10
to 20 years ahead) in the field of United States coins, or is
everything either fully priced or, in view of the flood of investment
newsletters available, "analyzed to death"?

Perhaps this is best answered by quoting some comments I
made 20 years ago in 1971 in an article in *The Forecaster*, an
investment newsletter (and a respected one, edited by John
Kamin, who considers himself to be a contrarian). I was discussing
the 1902 Proof Barber half dollar (although the comments would
have been relevant for any other Proof Barber-design half dollar of
1892 through 1912[1]), a coin which sold for $80 in 1963 and which
sold for $180 in 1971. I wrote the following:

"Will the 1902 Proof half dollar, a coin which might cost $180
today, be a good investment for the future? After all, quite a bit of
profit has already been made by others on the coins—by people
who bought them when they were cheaper 10 years ago.

"This is a logical and reasonable question to ask. Perhaps the
quickest way to answer would be to say that 10 years ago isn't now,
and we must concern ourselves with the present, not the past.
Valuable objects in any field—Rembrandt paintings, antiques,
etc.—have a history of price appreciation over the years. Waiting
to buy them for the prices of 10 or 20 years ago is not realistic. So
long as the trend of our economy is inflationary, prices seem to be
headed for an ever-upward spiral. Coins have shared in this spiral
and will continue to do so. Today [remember, this is written in
1971] the number of available 1902 Proof half dollars combined
with the number of people desiring them, have set the price at
approximately $180. Again we remind our readers that we have

[1] 1892-1912 only, for Proof Barber half dollars dated 1913 and, especially, 1914 and 1915 have
historically sold for above-average prices, due to the low related business strike mintages of
these particular dates.

picked the 1902 Proof half dollar merely as an example. The reasoning applies to many coins in the United States series."

As it turned out, the buyer of a 1902 Proof Barber half dollar for $180 in 1971 could have made a $100 profit by holding the coin for just one year and selling it in 1972! By 1978 the coin was worth over $850 and an even greater profit could be made. By early 1980 the same piece was trading at the $5,000 level, with one spectacular deal reported, as noted earlier, at $15,000 per coin! When the price adjustment came after 1980, the value of a Proof Barber half dollar drifted lower. By the end of 1982, a typical coin was trading in the price range of $2,750 to $3,250. By 1987, the price for a quality Proof-65 example had risen to the $5,000 level. By the summer of 1991 it had eased back to about $4,500.

There are always exceptions to market trends, and I should mention that in our sale of the Emery and Nichols collections in December 1984, a Gem Proof 1911 Barber *quarter* dollar (an issue theoretically worth *less* than a Barber half dollar of the era) soared to $6,600—far and away a fantastic record, and a price which would have made people blink even back in the peak years of 1979 and 1980![1]

In my opinion rare coins have an excellent future. The coin market is recognized as an important investment medium by many. As knowledge of the past success of the coin investment field spreads, more and more people will be attracted to this area. While unbounded enthusiasm for rare coin investment without a commensurate degree of knowledge can result in a boom and bust situation such as happened with commemoratives in 1936, or with many issues in 1979 and 1980, the spread of knowledge coupled with intelligent foresight and investigation should result in an orderly market. The supply of older coins remains static, so an upward price movement is a logical result as more and more people become interested.

Collectors, dealers, and others concerned with the hobby must remember that the ultimate "consumer" is the individual *collector*, as I have stated several times earlier. This is very important. For this reason, it is incumbent upon all of us to develop investors who are also collectors. It is my experience that a person

---

[1] The Emery Collection, begun in the 19th century and continued later (until 1941) by family member Walter P. Nichols, emphasized Uncirculated and Proof coins of remarkable quality. The collection remained in a bank vault for nearly a half century before being consigned to Auctions by Bowers and Merena, Inc.

who buys for investment alone will be a fickle purchaser. As soon as the market turns down in one of its periodic fluctuations he or she will lose interest, sell out, and never return to coins.

On the other hand, the collector, particularly one who has learned the lessons of history and who has studied coin prices and cycles (more about cycles in a special chapter later in the book), will stay with us and will continue to form a meaningful collection. Over the long term I expect this will produce positive results.

It is important not to be swayed by passions of the moment. There will always be high spots and low spots in the market. If coins are out of fashion as a popular investment, this is a good time to buy, although it requires quite a bit of fortitude to swim against the tide.

I suspect that right now, in the summer of 1991, coins are a bad word in Wall Street, especially in view of the diminished interest of investors in coin funds, in view of Federal Trade Commission prosecutions of certain unethical telemarketers, in view of the recent delisting of coins in the Salomon Brothers investment index, and in view of negative articles about coin investment which have appeared in the past year in money and investment publications such as *Consumer Reports* and *The Wall Street Journal*.[1]

However, looking at the big picture, just remember that two years ago the same Wall Streeters were looking at coins and believing them to be one of the best investments ever—and this was when many of their darlings (MS-65 and Proof-65 type coins, common silver dollars, etc.) were selling for double or more their prices now! The coins haven't changed. Popular investment psychology has.

I am not suggesting that common MS-65 and Proof-65 coins will go back to their 1989 and 1990 highs any time in the next 10 years, for I don't think most of them will. I am suggesting, however, that you ignore what Wall Street writers have to say about coins. They have a hard enough time writing about stocks (it is a sad commentary that most mutual funds, which are supposed to be

[1] As a general observation, I mention that articles about rare coin investment which are published in financial (i.e., non-numismatic) publications are usually somewhat superficial in nature, either stating that seemingly coins are the best investment ever (such articles usually appear when the market is rising), or the worst investment since Ponze coupons (such articles usually appear when the market is falling). Wanted are insightful articles written from the viewpoint of serious numismatic market knowledge. To profit readers of financial publications the most, such articles should be enthusiastic while the market is down and the opposite when the market has peaked!

managed by the best brains in the securities business, traditionally have not done better than stock averages), and what do they know about numismatics? Instead, think for yourself. Be a contrarian.

Writing about the stock market, Bernard Baruch, who earned millions of dollars by thinking for himself and bucking trends, observed that when other people were in a hurry to buy stocks at unreasonable prices, he would sell them his. On the other hand, when people were eager to unload stocks, he would be a buyer. In other words, Baruch encouraged investors to think for themselves. Thus it is with coins.

As these words are being written in 1991, many astute investors in contact with the writer believe the market to be one of great opportunity, as it has been in recent months. Compared to the levels of 1989 and 1990, many bargains are in evidence. Popular psychology is absent, and at this point few people recommend such esoteric areas as colonial and early American coins, early half cents and large cents, 19th-century "type" coins, circulated Liberty Seated and Barber coins, and so on (check my earlier recommendations).

However, to the informed investor this is an advantage. The performance of certain of these series in auction sales in early 1991 shows what many perceive as the start of an upward trend. In the past it has been dramatically proven that those who have made the greatest profits are those who have bought during inactive periods. Go back to my earlier illustration of Cincinnati commemorative sets. By 1939, these sets could be picked up for as little as $15 each (a third of their value three years earlier), but no one was in a hurry to buy them! *Then was the time to buy them.*

Coins will continue to be very much in the news in coming years. The 1776-1976 bicentennial coins created immense additional collector interest when they were released, in 1979 the Susan B. Anthony dollar, of a distinctive new size and format, stirred much interest among numismatists, although the general public was apathetic. The 1982 Washington commemorative half dollar, followed by the Olympics, Statue of Liberty, Constitution, and other commemorative issues all helped to create new collectors.

The commemorative program at the moment needs some fresh thinking and straightening out, for certain recent issues of

1989, 1990, and 1991 have been widely criticized for their designs. Sales have been below expectations. Recently, Donna Pope, the outgoing Mint director (under whose aegis many successful programs were launched in the early and mid-1980s), proposed that a committee study new designs and proposals, and that a representative of the numismatic community be included on such a committee. If this works well, we can look forward to many interesting new designs commemorating significant events, such as the many 50th anniversaries of World War II happenings.

Both the United States Mint and the Bureau of Engraving and Printing have in recent years mounted exhibits at the annual summer convention of the American Numismatic Association. This has served to acquaint collectors and others with the process of minting money and printing currency. The directors of these institutions during much of the 1980s, Donna Pope and Robert Leuver, have done much to interest the public in their products.[1]

Scholars and writers have been busy. There are more really excellent numismatic books available now than there ever have been at any other time in numismatic history, and the vast majority of these publications are available for low prices, mainly in the $10 to $50 range, with a few titles selling for up to $100. In the front rank, although expensive (list price: $100) is *Walter Breen's Complete Encyclopedia of United States and Colonial Coins*, a text which is fully equal on its own to a basic numismatic library! This and other books accrue to the benefit of all, to us now and to collectors in the future. Knowledge begets interest.

On a worldwide scale, increasing inflation combined with more money in the hands of the average citizen should increase interest in coins as a hobby and as an investment. On the American scene, the unprecedented and continuing federal deficits are sure to spark another inflationary spiral, at which time coins should participate in the upward movement of "hard" assets. It seems that energy and fuel costs, a major part of the American Consumer Price Index, are bound to increase over the long term as worldwide demand marches forward while at the same time sellers of fuel realize that supplies eventually will run out. The future of nuclear energy, once heralded as the answer to the problems in this area, is clouded by political and environmental controversy. Housing prices, another vital barometer, will

[1] Donna Pope announced her retirement from the Mint to take place in late summer 1991. After serving in a brilliant capacity at the Bureau of Engraving and Printing, Robert Leuver was hired as executive director of the American Numismatic Association, a position he holds now.

Ye Olde Mint

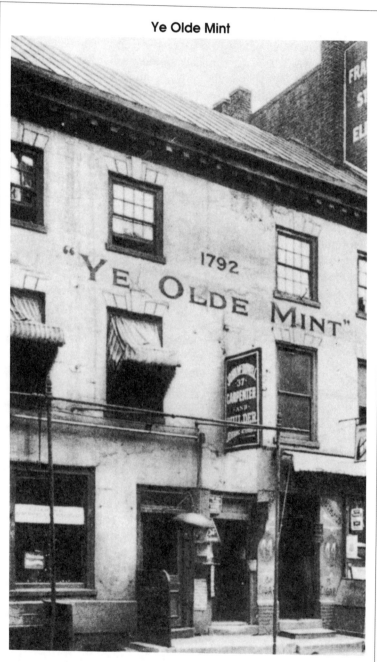

The 1792 Philadelphia Mint building as it appeared years later, circa 1905.

continue to increase as the cost of components such as labor, plywood, cement, glass, hardware, and so on escalate (although for the short term they are in remission, due to the national economy).

Early in 1980 President Jimmy Carter stated that "inflation is our number one enemy." By 1983, inflation had been brought in check by Ronald Reagan, and a new problem, unemployment (which was over 10%, a 40-year high), became a concern. Then, by early 1985, unemployment had been reduced to a new low for recent times. Prosperity and inflation marched forward in the late 1980s, fueled in part by reckless lending by banks and savings and loan institutions.

The piper had to be paid, and in 1989 there were signs of problems, followed by a full-scale recession in 1990. Now, in the summer of 1991, the recession isn't over (at least this is my opinion), although some economic indicators are beginning to show favorable trends. Unemployment is still high, many banks continue to be in disastrous condition, life insurers are developing financial difficulties, domestic automobile sales are low, real estate and housing starts are in a slump, Wall Street is having layoffs, and there are other problems.

On the other hand, there are many bright spots. Who would have dreamed two or three years ago that citizens of many communist countries would be able to have elections or that they would be able to experience the personal satisfaction and rewards of capitalism? This, truly, is one of the most exhilarating happenings of our generation! I envision a vast new market developing for consumer goods, collectors' items, and other things which we in America take for granted. I fully expect to see hundreds of thousands if not millions of new collectors created in countries with newfound freedom. This will bode well for coin investment.

In my own experience with numismatics, I have observed that the coin market has marched to its own drummer while the stock market has had its ups and downs, the unemployment rate has gone through different gyrations, the inflation rate has bounced around, and just about everything else has been unstable. Paraphrasing J.P. Morgan, the various economic indicators will probably continue to fluctuate. There are a number of chartists who keep their eyes on such indicators and try to predict the coin market from them, but I can see no consistent or long-term connection.

It seems to me that the years ahead will be good ones for numismatics. Relatively unaffected by external economic factors, the numismatic market should maintain its strength and growth. There will be ups and downs, for cycles are a natural part of the field (more about this later). And, there will always be promotions and speculations, some of which will do better than others. By and large, however, I expect great rewards will go to serious *collectors* who take the time to study coins and to invest carefully. With careful planning and with an awareness of the lessons of history, I expect you will do well!

Long Term Outlook—Coins of the World

As more and more countries gain the affluence that has characterized the United States in recent decades, more and more numismatists will come into being all around the world—and there will be a greater demand for *all* coins, including United States pieces. It is now quite common for numismatists in Germany, Japan, Italy, France, and other countries to desire type sets of United States gold or silver coins and other issues.

At the same time, numismatists will desire coins of their own countries. Foreign countries with large population bases, such as England, France, Germany, Spain, Italy, etc., plus all Eastern Bloc countries (especially these), will undoubtedly someday have large numbers of numismatists who will study minor coinages, die varieties, and other aspects which are not collected on a widespread basis now. At present, most emphasis is on crown-size (silver-dollar size) silver coins and on gold coins; minor issues are very inexpensive and are largely neglected. I strongly feel that there are some terrific opportunities in this area. However, before spending a cent, build a decent library on world coins, starting with the *Standard Catalog of World Coins* (Krause Publications) as your jumping-off spot. Spend a month or two reading and studying before you buy a single coin. Also, consult the later chapter on world coins.

Advantages of Coin Investment

Introductory Comments

As an investment medium, coins have many advantages. Earlier I discussed how coin investment has proven itself in the past. Now let me tell you some of the different aspects and advantages of investing in coins.

Easy Storage and Handling

Coins are small and are easy to store in a safe place. They require very little special attention. A beautiful collection can be kept easily in a bank safe deposit box or vault. Indeed, many of the finest collections ever formed—the Garrett Collection, the Norweb Collection, and the Eliasberg Collection come to mind—were stored in this manner.

In competition a number of years back my company made a bid for the Westwood Collection, one of the very finest collections of United States coins to come on the market. Our bid, a substantial one, was successful. The owner of the coins (who, incidentally, began collecting in 1953 and made a very substantial profit when he sold his holdings) kept his coins in a bank safe deposit box. His cost to store this magnificent group was a nominal sum, probably less than $50 per year. The compactness of this stellar group of coins is perhaps best illustrated by noting that after the purchase was made, the collection was brought to my office in a briefcase (after the proper security and insurance arrangements were made).

The Garrett Collection, the most valuable ever auctioned, which realized over $25 million, was shipped to my firm from a bank vault in Baltimore. The entire collection was stored in four metal containers weighing no more than 150 pounds for the lot! Obviously, with coins a large treasure can be housed in a small space!

For most collectors and investors a bank safe deposit box is the best way to store coins over a long period of time. Insurance rates are much lower for coins kept this way; much lower than for coins kept in a home or other location. In 35 years of dealing with numismatists I have yet to learn of even a single one of my clients who has ever had coins stolen from a bank safe deposit box. Certainly this is a remarkable record!

Except for coins used for study or appreciation (and with appropriate insurance coverage) coins should not be kept at home or in your office. Avoid private vaults of any kind, for I have heard of too many problems. The old tried and true bank safe deposit box, not very glamorous, quite inexpensive, and very secure, seems to me to be the best answer.

When storing your coins, be sure the humidity or moisture level is not excessive. Should the bank vault be damp, then a packet of silica gel (obtainable at a photographic supply store) put in the safe deposit box will absorb moisture. It makes good sense to put your coins in an airtight box or other container within the safe deposit box. For best results, if dampness is present, simply move to another bank—one with a drier vault. Also, be sure the vault is not subject to periodic flooding or in an area with harmful industrial fumes.

A policy can be purchased through your insurance agent to cover coins in transit and while they are at your home or office for enjoyment, evaluation, or study. Such a policy makes a great deal of sense.[1]

For the study of coins in your possession, or while storing them in a bank vault, I recommend the use of polyethylene envelopes, album pages with acetate slides, or small plastic holders.

The hermetically sealed plastic holders or "slabs" in which certain coins are purchased seem to be good in this regard as well. So far as I know, the slabs offered by the Numismatic Guaranty Corporation of America, the Professional Coin Grading Service, ANACS, and probably most coin grading services are fine for long-term storage, although I have seen some comments to the effect that there may be problems with high-grade copper coins. Only time will tell the full story.

---

[1] Coin insurance is available through the American Numismatic Association, among other places. If your local agent cannot help you, it may pay to check with the ANA.

Capital Plastics offers a large line of lucite holders at reasonable prices; holders which many collectors have found to be very satisfactory. The "Kingswood" holders sold by Bowers and Merena Galleries are manufactured by Capital Plastics (and are specially ordered by us with special arrangements and with gold stamping). Koin-Tains, a snap-together plastic product made in Sidney, Ohio, also has a good track record and has pleased many. So-called "flips" made of mylar plastic are also popular.

It is important to avoid certain types of flexible transparent coin envelopes which contain polyvinyl chloride (PVC) which can result in an unsightly deposit, often green, appearing on the surface of coins. If such flexible transparent envelopes are used to store coins which you purchase at auction (as of this writing, these envelopes are commonly used in this regard—so as to facilitate auction viewing over a short term, without harm to the coins), remove the coins from these holders once you get them. Such holders are definitely not recommended for long-term storage of any kind. However, if you do acquire coins that have been stored in PVC holders for a length of time, often the residue can be removed by use of acetone, a commercial solvent available in drug stores (the solution is highly flammable, should not be inhaled, and should be used with extreme caution).

In my opinion, the best way to go is to store your coins in polyethylene envelopes, small plastic or mylar holders, "slabs," or "flips" while your collection is being built. Once your collection is complete, or nearly so, transfer it to Capital holders (or other similar holders of your choice)—which are ideal for protection and display at the same time. It is not aesthetically pleasing to keep a meaningful collection in a series of small envelopes, slabs, or holders, and for maximum enjoyment of what you own, large display holders are strongly recommended.

Coins are easily portable and can be carried from one place or another or sent through the mail. This makes the market for coins a worldwide one instead of just a local situation. As an example of the convenience of mail shipment I mention our acquisition a number of years ago of the Robert Marks Collection. I was able to ship a substantial portion of the collection—a group which included a magnificent Proof 1884 trade dollar and many Proof gold coins—from Arkansas back to my office in several small, insured, registered mail packets.

Rick Bagg and Ray Merena, who do extensive buying for our firm and regularly visit collectors and attend coin shows, use registered mail as a quick and efficient method to safely send coins without security worries. It is likewise the policy of many other collectors and dealers to ship auction sale purchases and other particularly valuable acquisitions back home through the mail instead of carrying them personally. This is very convenient and represents a saving on insurance and handling.

When it was desired to ship the fabulous and priceless Hope Diamond from New York City to the Smithsonian Institution, various methods were considered. Finally selected was insured, registered mail. Needless to say, the precious jewel arrived safely.

You Can Buy or Sell Coins Easily

In the field of selected quality coins the typical dealer's main problem is buying coins, not selling them. Rare and desirable coins are easy to sell, provided they are priced in keeping with the market at any given time. It is buying coins that is difficult for the dealer. As a result, buying competition is intense among professionals, a situation which results in a higher price and a close-to-retail market value often obtained by the collector or investor who sells.

There is no "wholesale" market in the field of choice and rare coins. There is no opportunity for a dealer to say, "Please ship me 10 Uncirculated 1862 silver dollars, and while you are at it, send an Extremely Fine 1845-O dime," for example. A dealer must compete with collectors and other dealers for desirable pieces. At the same time it is important to remember that not all dealers want to buy all types of coins at any given time. The exact amount a dealer wishes to pay and what he wants is determined by such factors as his financial condition, the number of pieces of a given issue currently in his stock, whether or not he specializes in the field, and so on.

There is a wholesale market for common coins, and a few years ago it was envisioned that a great trading network for NGC, PCGS, and other coins would develop on a sight-unseen basis. This apparently was well and fine for the investors' market, for many investors, being basically uninformed, did not care if their coins were spotted, ugly, etc. as long as they were certified as MS-65 (or some other grade). However, this did not last for long, and as of this writing in the summer of 1991 there are very few people who will pay good money for a coin without having the opportunity to see it first.

At a recent convention I desired to buy several hundred thousand dollars' worth of certified commemorative coins in MS-60 to MS-64 grades (I avoided all but a few MS-65 issues, for I thought most were overpriced at this level). It took a lot of looking and a lot of effort to buy coins which I felt were not only graded correctly from a technical or numerical viewpoint, but which were also well struck, on quality planchets, and had a high degree of aesthetic appeal.

There are thousands of dealers who desire coins, therefore it is relatively easy to convert your holdings to cash if you have quality material of proven scarcity or rarity. (However, if you have coins which are neither rare nor attractive, you may have a problem.)

If you sell outright, there is no waiting for your money. It is a policy of Bowers and Merena Galleries, for instance, to pay instantly for all items purchased, and numerous others do the same.

Should you decide to auction your coins, typically you have the opportunity to receive a cash advance against the proceeds, or receive the proceeds after the sale. Competition in the auction field is intense, with the result that properties valued at large sums can often be sold for a very low commission rate. Not all items are appropriate for auction, however. Auction seems to be ideal for scarcities and rarities and pieces which are seldom seen, as well as higher grade examples in popular fields.

In over 35 years of numismatics I have never seen a situation in which there has not been extremely intense competition among dealers and auction houses when a choice *collection* has come up for sale. Any other leading professional dealer will verify this. This situation exists in boom markets as well as in slump periods.

At the same time, it is only fair to mention that when certain pieces have risen in value sharply, due to speculation or due to cyclical effects, demand on the part of dealers for these coins when the prices are beginning to drift downward is less than enthusiastic. Although prices vary from time to time, never has there been a softness in the market for first-quality coins of proven rarity and value.

Individual Rarities Have Done Well

In the coin market collectors and dealers all act independently. There is an orderly stream of *collections* being formed and later resold. Note that I am emphasizing collections. Investment groupings in a particular series, hoards, and groups of coins other than collections often are subject to different influences. Considering that there are hundreds of thousands of serious advanced collectors and millions of casual collectors (figures estimating as many as 8 to 10 million collectors have been published in recent years), the demand for true numismatic coins of proven rarity is stable and is usually not susceptible to sharp market fluctuations.

To illustrate this let me take as a random example a Proof 1870 Liberty Seated silver dollar. There were 1,000 of these pieces coined. If you take into consideration that various specimens have been lost or damaged over the years, then it is fairly safe to assume that probably only 500 to 600 pieces survive today. It is further a safe assumption that few if any dealers have more than one or two pieces in stock, and most dealers have not even a single specimen.

Collectors who own an 1870 Proof silver dollar have just a single coin. After all, why should they have two? Thus the available supply of 500 to 600 Proof pieces is spread out among as many owners, plus many are impounded in museums. Let us assume for purposes of illustration that this coin is in Proof-65 preservation and is worth around $13,000 at the moment (the actual market price may be different when you read this; I use this purely as an illustration of the market value in 1991). If you offer to pay $5,000 above the market or $18,000 totally, the chances are excellent you will not be able to buy more than a dozen pieces. In fact, even this estimate may be on the high side! Dealers who have 1870 Proof silver dollars will be happy to sell them to you, but why should the average collector spoil his set by picking out his prized 1870 and selling it separately?

On the other hand, should you have picked the 1870 Proof dollar as an investment item 10 or 20 years ago, and should you have, say, two or three dozen by now, you would have no trouble selling them for an attractive profit far above the price you paid. There is sufficient demand by many collectors who would like an 1870 Proof silver dollar for their type sets or date sets to readily absorb such a small quantity. Virtually any dealer would be happy to buy them all as a lot, knowing full well that they could be sold quickly and easily. Similarly, any auction firm would be proud to offer such pieces in catalogues. Thus, the market in 1870 Proof silver dollars is relatively stable. As the long-term trend of coin prices moves upward, the price of 1870 Proof silver dollars should move up with it. History has shown that in the past this piece has been a superb investment. It is appropriate to observe that the price of this coin in 1948 was only $45, which equates to 1/289th of its present value! The 1870 Proof silver dollar has been a relatively safe investment over the years, as supply and demand are both widespread. Coins of this calibre can rightly be called "blue chips."

I hasten to say that I feel that this coin was a better investment years ago at lower prices, and at $13,000 much if not most of its profit potential may have been used up. However, it does serve as a nice illustration.

The Market is International

The market for your coins is an international one. Compare this to real estate. If you purchase a piece of real estate on the wrong side of town and future growth doesn't happen to lie in that direction you are out of luck. In any event, your real estate will generally appeal only to a buyer interested in purchasing land in your specific geographic location. In February 1987, The Wall Street Journal told of apartments going begging in Houston for $6,000 each (as amazing as this might seem!) while, at the same time, in New England a boom was taking place, and builders couldn't erect structures fast enough. As the buildings located in Houston were not portable, there is no way they could be sold to a buyer in New England. Likewise, in October 1982 a 14-room stone "castle," replete with chandeliers, parquet floors, quartered oak paneling, art glass windows, 11 acres of land, a separate greenhouse, and other features, located in Vermont, was advertised in the real estate section of The New York Times for $285,000. At the same time a much smaller home on a lot only a fraction of the size, and apparently with few if any touches of artistry and craftsmanship was advertised for over $4 million in The Los Angeles Times. As you might suspect, the second home was located in Beverly Hills, California. Probably if the Vermont property could have been transplanted into Beverly Hills, with its quality workmanship and extensive acreage, it would have been advertised for $20 million!

In contrast, the market for coins is truly international. An 1870 Proof silver dollar (to cite the example used earlier) appeals not only to the collector or investor in Vermont, but also to the buyer in Beverly Hills—or, for that matter, in Tokyo, Copenhagen, London, or Rome.

Standardized grading nomenclature and terminology have played an important part in this. Hence the simple listing "1852 Original Proof half cent" was sufficient for Spink & Son, Ltd., prominent London dealers, to buy this coin from me—although they had not seen it previously and although I was located across the Atlantic Ocean from them.

When a Zurich (Switzerland) numismatist described a coin as "1926-D $20, Choice Uncirculated," I knew instantly whether the price was reasonable to pay. I did not have to hop aboard a Swissair jet, spend thousands of dollars in time, travel, and hotel bills, to "inspect the property." Instead, I knew the coin could be shipped to me quickly by mail and, if it proved unsatisfactory, could be returned just as quickly—all of this for a very nominal cost.

Seeking coins for our Want List Program, Liz Arlin constantly telephones and writes to collectors and dealers all over the world and, in fact, from time to time prepares printed lists of her customers' needs. A typical message is as follows:

"Dear Mr. Smith:

"I have clients for certain coins you purchased from us years ago. Please quote your best price on the following, or I would be pleased to make an offer: 1794 silver dollar, VF-20; 1921 Peace dollar, MS-64, sharply struck; 1878-CC trade dollar, EF-40; 1848 CAL. $2.50 EF-45. I look forward to the possibility of hearing from you soon.

"Sincerely,

"Liz Arlin"

In each instance, the coins were subject to the buyer's approval and inspection.

If still another example is needed to illustrate how standard descriptions are useful to buyer and seller alike, and to typify the ease with which transactions can be made, I mention that when Yale University selected my firm to purchase one of their coins— a Gem Proof example of the exceedingly rare MCMVII Extremely

High Relief $20 gold piece—I was able to give an instant purchase decision simply by hearing a brief description of it over the telephone. When my firm later sold the coin, a similar brief description was all that was needed to consummate a sale with a new purchaser who was located 2,500 miles away! And so it goes with countless numismatic transactions, large and small, day in and day out.

Coins Can be Privately Held

Your coin collection is your own personal business and no one else's. Whether you have $10 worth of coins in your safe deposit box, $10,000 worth, $100,000 worth, or $1 million worth is your business—and is not known by your neighbors or business associates. Assuming you do not choose to publicize your holdings, it is "mind your own business" so far as the value of your coins is concerned. Your investment is a private matter.

One of my clients, a doctor in a small midwestern town, was desirous of avoiding any appearance of "conspicuous consumption." He lived in a modest home, drove an inexpensive car, and few of his neighbors or associates knew that he owned one of the finest coin collections in the land.

There are many romantic stories of fortunes being carried across international borders by secreting a few selected rare coins on one's person while fleeing to escape tyranny or some other threat.[1] A selected group of rare coins can be a wonderful *private store of value.*

At any given time in American history there are doomsayers who state that our country is about to fall apart at the seams, that there will be blood in the streets, that the American dollar is going to become worthless, and that the end is near. From that extreme you can go to observers of the scene who feel that everything in the United States is perfect or nearly so. A number of people have recommended that it is good sense to have a portion of your investments in tangible or hard items, particularly those which are small, valuable, and easily transported. Although I do not advocate collecting coins as a defense measure against tyranny or international disaster, it is comforting to know that in times in which there have been problems, coins have held their values well

[1] The late I. Snyderman, proprietor of the Art Trading Co., New York City, related to me that during the 1940s he purchased several fine collections of European coins from refugees who were able to make fine starts in America using the proceeds from their numismatic holdings.

and have had a ready market. Indeed, history has shown that during periods of conflict (such as World War II) coin values have risen sharply. The same thing happened during the American Civil War nearly a century earlier.

In most places around the world there is no property tax levied on a coin collection (as opposed, for instance, to real estate—where taxes seem to reach new highs each year). When the time comes for you to sell your coins, any profit you make can be offset in your tax report by any expenses you have had during the course of acquiring your collection. Such items can include subscriptions to publications, memberships in numismatic associations, postage, interest, insurance, and even the cost of this book! I do not presume to practice either accounting or law, so for specifics you should contact professionals in these fields.

Coin Information is Readily Available

You do not have to be an expert to successfully invest in coins, although, as I have noted several times earlier, the more you learn about coins, the greater are your chances for investment success. Generally, coins are easy to identify and classify. Mintage figures, sales records, and price guides are available to help you with your investment decisions—aiding you in the same way that earnings records, dividend information, industry projections, and other information is of use in the stock market.

When analyzing coin investment advice it is important to consider the source. Is the writer or speaker really familiar with rare coins? Is he an established *professional numismatist* with an excellent reputation in the field? If you are subscribing to a newsletter, consider whether the writer of the newsletter is busy tooting his own horn (and offering you "bargains" which yield for him the highest profit margin) or whether he is truly familiar with numismatics and is acting in your best interest. He will profit, for your subscription guarantees this. The question is, will you profit?

Analyze information critically and objectively and then make your investment decision deliberately. *An established professional dealer is your best friend and advisor in this regard.* If you are uncertain of his or her reputation, ask around before committing money for purchases. Anyone can have fancy brochures printed, and anyone can call himself the "biggest," "best," "most reputable," etc. You should ask such questions as the following: How long has he been in business (and verify this by checking with *Coin World*, *Numismatic News*, *The Numismatist*, *Coins* magazine, COIN*age*, and other publications)? Is he a member of the Professional Numismatists Guild and/or the International Association of Professional Numismatists? How long has he been a member of the ANA? What important collections and rarities has he handled? While answers will vary, and not every fine dealer belongs to the Professional Numismatists Guild (for example), the more good answers you receive, the greater your chances will be for a good relationship. Of course, an occasional scoundrel slips into a fine organization or has been in business a long time. However, it does pay to investigate.

Today there are more excellent books available than at any other time in numismatic history. If you plan to spend several thousand dollars on rare coins, change your thinking and start by spending $500 to $1,000 for books and *read them*. Properly selected books are literally worth their weight in gold and, as I stated earlier, I would not sell my own reference library for its equivalent in gold if I could not replace it! If you are hesitant to buy books by their titles alone or by the reputations of their authors, consider borrowing interesting titles from the ANA Library, and then buy those you find to be of the greatest value. Alternatively, buy books from a seller who offers a money-back guarantee of satisfaction.

Coins Have a Steady and Strong Market

Coin prices are not as volatile as are prices in many other investment media. With the exception of certain speculative issues, coin prices do not change on a day-to-day basis. The historical trend of rare coin prices has been upward. There are hundreds of different coins which have averaged a 10% to 25% or more per year price increase over the past several decades.

Consider coins to be a *long-term* investment. While individual factors vary, I suggest a period of five to 10 years to be a good objective, and 10 to 20 years to be even better; the longer the time, the greater the returns have been on a historical basis. Of course, the exact period depends upon other considerations such as your own patience, your age, the position of your coins in the price cycle, and so on. If you buy at the top of the price cycle, it may take longer to show a profit. On the other hand, if you buy at the bottom of a price cycle, growth can occur within a relatively short time. In the past, my customers who have shown the greatest profits have held coins for five to 10 years or more, and those who have held coins for 20 or 30 years, or passed them from one generation to another, have made simply fantastic profits.

What the coin market lacks in day-to-day price fluctuations it more than makes up in long-term movement. One of the main sources of coins for my firm is buying and acquiring auction consignments from collectors who purchased pieces years earlier from us. Many of our customers have been very successful in the past. In the course of buying countless *collections* of United States coins over the years I am not aware of any seller who has experienced loss when he has formed a meaningful *collection* and when the coins were held as a long-term investment. It is not at all unusual to pay a client many multiples of the price he paid when the coins were acquired in the 1950s, 1960s, or early 1970s. Indeed, the rare coin market has done *fantastically well* for those who have approached coin collecting and investing from a serious and well-reasoned viewpoint.

Coins are Interesting to Own and Collect

Coins are interesting to own as well as being a potentially good investment. Coins provide infinite possibilities for historical appreciation. What stories coins could tell if they could only speak! But they remain silent—and therein lies a certain fascination. Perhaps your large cent of 1835 was owned by Abraham Lincoln when he was a struggling young lawyer. Was your 1883 Liberty Head nickel spent by a child for a souvenir at the World's Columbian Exposition in Chicago in 1893? Was your 1857-S gold double eagle once lost at sea? Not knowing the answers to these questions makes the ownership of such pieces intriguing. Coins keep their secrets well! As noted earlier in this book, in addition to whatever investment potential you may derive from coins, do not overlook the aspects of art, history, and romance, as well as psychological and social benefits.

Perhaps the story of Armand Champa, a fine gentleman and one of our firm's customers for many years, will illustrate the combined appeal of collecting and investment. Over a period of years Mr. Champa carefully built a choice collection. He subscribed to many different numismatic publications, ordered from a variety of dealers, attended coin conventions, and generally participated in the mainstream of numismatics. Whenever an important numismatic event took place, chances were that Armand Champa would be there!

A main function of a professional dealer is to furnish advice to his customers, advice in addition to selling coins. Thus it was with my firm's relationship with Armand Champa. Many times I would help him determine the rarity of a particular piece, to help him decide whether he should "reach" to buy that piece now or whether he should wait for another which possibly might be offered for a slightly lower price later.

Although Mr. Champa's collection covered many areas of American numismatics, he concentrated on United States pattern coins—a specialized field containing experimental, trial, and pattern pieces of various designs manufactured at the Philadelphia Mint from 1792 through the early 20th century. Mr. Champa subsequently decided to sell his fabulous collection. My company was chosen to sell the coins at a combined public auction and mail bid sale. A fine catalogue was prepared. The preface to this large, illustrated volume pointed out the quality of the coins offered:

"Welcome to our combined public auction and mail bid sale of the Armand Champa Collection and other important consignments. Whether you attend the sale in person or bid by mail you will receive some truly beautiful coins if your bids are successful.

"Armand Champa, the well-known Louisville, Kentucky numismatist, appreciated the finest. His collection, formed over a period of many years (and including many purchases from us), is replete with many scarcities and rarities. United States pattern coins were a special interest. Mr. Champa's collection, offered here in its entirety, contains many spectacular pieces—including 21 specimens of the famed pattern half dollars of 1877, the rare and beautiful Amazonian silver dollar of 1872, and many other prize coins, many of which trace their pedigrees to the collections of Dr. J. Hewitt Judd, King Farouk, Col. E.H.R. Green, and other prominent numismatists.

"The rare coins in this sale are many. We might mention the gem condition silver and other coins at the beginning of this catalogue, a consignment which includes some of the most beautiful Bust type quarters we have ever handled. Early Proof coins such as silver three-cent pieces of 1854 and 1857, an 1842 half dime, an 1848 dime, and half dollars of 1847, 1848, and 1857 will surely create interest among specialists. Silver dollars, always a popular series, are highlighted by examples of 1858, 1871-CC, 1873-CC, 1889-CC, 1892-S, 1893-S, and two examples of the famous 1895—not to mention many other beautiful coins.

"If spectacular rarities are your forte you'll have your choice of such pieces as a Gem Uncirculated 1876-CC 20-cent piece (the specimen once owned by noted composer Jerome Kern), an 1879 Flowing Hair $4 Stella, the ultra-rare (just 10 are believed to have been struck!) 1879 Coiled Hair Stella, a superb 1803 Proof restrike silver dollar, and many more celebrated coins—many of which have not appeared on the market in years.

"We have enjoyed cataloguing these coins for you. If you are a successful bidder in person or by mail—and we hope you will be—you'll experience the same enjoyment, but to an even greater degree as it will be combined with the *pleasure of ownership*. Good luck. We hope you can attend the sale in person. If this is not possible, then we'll represent your mail bids. A wonderful sale is now about to take place. Thank you for your participation."

The sale, which spanned two days, was one of the most exciting events of the 1970s. Hundreds of bidders participated. While the excitement, enthusiasm, and action of the Armand Champa Collection Sale would make an interesting story in itself, I shall mention one coin here: Lot 1086, a beautiful Amazonian pattern silver dollar which is considered to be one of the most beautiful of all American pattern issues, attracted quite a bit of pre-sale attention. Bids by mail and telephone in the amounts of $4,750, $5,000, and $5,300 had been received before the sale. It was my expectation that the piece would be awarded to the $5,300 bidder, a Wisconsin gentleman, at a nominal advance over the second highest bid—perhaps a realization of $5,100 or $5,200.

It didn't work out that way. The coin was sold on the floor for $5,500 to a prominent numismatist who flew from Iowa to California to bid on that piece plus a number of others he needed for his collection. Thus a new price record was set!

The sale of this particular coin points out several interesting things; it is a small object lesson in itself:

First, Mr. Champa realized a profit of *several thousand dollars* over what he had paid for it a few years earlier.

Second, the coin is part of the United States pattern series— a field not considered to be in the mainstream of "hot" issues by many people, thus pointing out that the careful buyer can make tremendous profits by purchasing coins in specialized areas.

Third, rarity never goes out of style—and when scarce and rare coins come up for sale during an upward time in the market cycle, new price records are almost always set. I imagine that the same coin, if sold in 1991 in one of our auctions, would have brought $30,000 to $50,000 or more!

The story of the 1872 pattern Amazonian silver dollar doesn't end there. The underbidder, the Wisconsin gentleman previously mentioned, telephoned me after the sale to see if he had purchased the coin. Naturally he was disappointed to learn that he hadn't. He then asked if I could find another specimen for him. This was a challenge, and I responded by searching my memory and writing a number of letters to collectors and dealers who might be a possible source. Within a month or two luck was with me, and I obtained not only an 1872 Amazonian silver dollar, but the other two Amazonian coins of the same year that were issued with the dollar: the Amazonian quarter and the Amazonian half dollar! This splendid set, an American numismatic classic, is now a prized possession of my Wisconsin numismatist friend.

How well did Mr. Champa do with his investment? This, of course, is Mr. Champa's business and not ours. However, we know he did well for Mr. Champa then did something unprecedented in the annals of American numismatics: He was so pleased with the results of the sale of his collection that he placed advertisements thanking us in leading numismatic publications! The advertisement which appeared in The Numismatist, official journal of the American Numismatic Association, is typical:

"Thank you Dave Bowers and Jim Ruddy [my business partner in the years from 1958 to 1977] for the excellent handling of my coins through your auction. I was well pleased with your wonderful description of my coins, especially the patterns. The prices realized for my coins nearly doubled the offers I received from other dealers. [signed] Armand Champa."

A few months after the sale took place I saw Armand Champa again when he attended the American Numismatic Association Convention in New Orleans. "Since I have been at the convention here several people have asked me whether these advertisements were your idea—and I was happy to tell them they were completely unsolicited by you," he said with a merry twinkle in his eye! And the statement was absolutely true.

The pleasure of helping a discriminating numismatist over the years and then later helping him to sell is one I have experienced many times. It is a satisfying experience which is difficult to describe in words. Helping others to achieve success is very, very gratifying—and I do not mean gratifying from just a monetary viewpoint.

What did Armand Champa do after he sold his coin collection through my firm? He did what many other numismatists have done before and since: he found another numismatic interest and busily set about building still another fine collection! Now, he is the proud owner of one of the finest collections of numismatic reference books and auction catalogues ever put together. Undoubtedly, when and if this vast treasure is sold, Armand Champa will again make numismatic history![1]

[3] The Numismatic Bibliomania Society (NBS), publisher of the quarterly Asylum journal, is comprised of collectors of numismatic literature. Armand Champa has endowed the organization with money to finance an annual award.

Rarity vs. Value

Determinants of Value

 What determines a coin's value? Stated briefly, important factors include rarity, popularity (demand), grade, and face or intrinsic value. For any given coin, the weight given these factors varies. Moreover, for any given coin the importance of any one of these aspects can change from time to time.

Analyzing the relative importance of these factors for a given coin is useful in understanding the current market value and, relevant to the present text, determining its potential for future price appreciation. Little has been done in the way of such studies elsewhere. Most collectors, dealers, and investors study the current market price and perhaps consider what the price was in the past, but do little thinking as to what determines the current value. Rarity, popularity (demand), grade, face or intrinsic value— I discuss each of these now in turn. For a typical scarce or rare coin of proven numismatic value, none of these factors acts alone. They are intertwined, as you will see.

What is a "Rare" Coin?

In popular terms, numismatists collect *rare* coins. Signs such as "Rare Coins Bought and Sold" and "Dealer in Rare Coins" are common in the profession. When an 1804 silver dollar crosses the auction block, or a record price is paid for an 1879 $4 gold piece, accompanying news articles proclaim each such coin to be a *rarity*.

What exactly does "rare" mean? In general, a rare coin is one which in its series is seen less frequently than the majority of others. For example, among Washington quarter dollars from 1932 to date, the issues which are seen with less frequency than the others are the 1932-D and 1932-S. Many cataloguers would call these rare. In absolute terms they may not be rare. Tens of thousands of examples of each survive from an original mintage of 436,800 for the 1932-D and 408,000 for the 1932-S. Nor are such coins necessarily expensive. In Fine-12 grade the *Guide Book* posts the value of a 1932-D at $55 and a 1932-S at $40. Still, within the Washington series the 1932-D and 1932-S can be considered rare.

Similarly, among Indian cents the 1877 is considered rare, as is the 1909-S. Among Lincoln cents, the 1909-S V.D.B. and 1914-D are considered rare, and because of its low mintage many would consider the 1931-S to be rare as well. In the field of nickel five-cent pieces, the 1885 Liberty Head is rare, as are the 1912-S, the 1918/7-D overdate, and several others, not to overlook that rarity of rarities, the 1913 Liberty Head (of which only five are known to exist).

The dime series is sprinkled with numerous rarities, including not only the previously mentioned 1894-S Barber dime, of which only about a dozen are known, but also such issues in the same design series as 1901-S and 1913-S, followed by rare Mercury dimes including 1916-D, 1921, 1921-D, and the 1942/1 overdate. Most of the pieces I've enumerated among cents, nickel five-cent pieces, and dimes exist by the thousands, but still in a *relative* sense they can be considered rare.

A writer in the field of antiques once said that for an antique to be considered rare, it should be an example of an issue which appears on the market only once every two or three years. By this criterion, most of the coins I have just mentioned would not be considered rare. Instead, rare coins would be limited to select issues which appear on the market only when great collections are dispersed—among them such memorable coins as the 1802 half dime; the 1894-S dime; 1876-CC 20-cent piece; 1873-CC quarter dollar without arrows at the date; 1838-O half dollar; 1804 silver dollar; quarter eagles of 1841, 1854-S, and 1863; $3 pieces of 1875 and 1876 (not to overlook the unique 1870-S); certain half eagles dated from 1815 to 1834 plus the 1854-S; and so on—in other words, the great classics of numismatics.

Dr. Sheldon's Rarity System

It is increasingly evident that the question "how rare is rare?" is the numismatic equivalent of the classic query "how many angels can dance on the head of a pin?" There is no set answer. Different people have different ideas.

In 1949 Dr. William H. Sheldon, a psychiatrist with the Presbyterian Hospital at Columbia University, New York City, wrote *Early American Cents*, later retitled *Penny Whimsy*, a study of copper cents of the years 1793 to 1814. Being of an analytical turn of mind (Sheldon earlier compiled a reference text dividing human body types into specific categories), the doctor set about evaluating large cents in a scientific procedure.

Price, according to Dr. Sheldon, was based upon a combination of three factors: (1) the condition or grade of a coin, (2) its rarity, and (3) "the history of the numismatic market with reference to the variety, in comparable condition."

He further observed that "a professional numismatist devotes his life mainly to becoming an expert at these three matters—recognition of condition, knowledge of rarity, knowledge of what prices particular coins have brought and will bring in various quarters."

In the field of rarity, Sheldon proposed a quantitative scale ranging from Rarity-1, or "common" (not otherwise defined), to Rarity-8, a category reserved for unique or nearly unique—a piece of which one, two, or three are known. Sheldon's complete scale is as follows: Rarity-1 Common; Rarity-2 Not so Common; Rarity-3 Scarce; Rarity-4 Very scarce (population estimated at 76-200); Rarity-5 Rare (31-75); Rarity-6 Very rare (13-30); Rarity-7 Extremely rare (4-12); Rarity-8 Unique or nearly unique (1, 2, or 3).

While useful on a quantitative basis, such terms as "not so common" still were not satisfactory to many, and among the higher condition ranges such as Rarity-6, Rarity-7, and Rarity-8, it was felt by some that there should be a further breakdown. Not all Rarity-7 coins are created alike, and one of which four are known is much more desirable than one of which 12 are known, or three times as many, although both are Rarity-7 on the Sheldon scale. Accordingly, several proposals were made to refine the Sheldon scale. Representative is the expansion suggested by Don Taxay in *Scott's Catalogue & Encyclopedia of U.S. Coins* 1971 edition (with another edition published in 1976):

Rarity-1 Over 1,250 known to exist

Rarity-2 501-1,250

Rarity-3 201-500

1794 Large Cent

This example of a 1794 large cent. Sheldon No. 59, was in the fabulous specialized collection of cents formed by John W. Adams and sold by the author in a fixed price catalogue in the 1980s.

Rarity-4 76-200

Rarity-5 31-75

Rarity-6 13-30

Low Rarity-7 10-12

Rarity-7 7-9

High Rarity-7 4-6

Rarity-8 2-3

Unique (called Rarity-9 by some) 1

Other Scales for Rarity

Dr. Sheldon was not the first to suggest a quantitative scale for rarity, nor was he the last. At the turn of the century Lyman H. Low in his book, *Hard Times Tokens*, proposed a scale with the following categories: V.C. (very common), C (common), N.C. (not common), S (scarce), followed by Rarity 1, 2, 3, 4, 5, 6, 7, and 8.

A decade or so later, in *United States Experimental, Pattern, and Trial Pieces*, Edgar H. Adams and William H. Woodin set forth a scale ranging from Rarity-1, the most common, to Rarity-15, the rarest.

In 1919, Henry C. Miller and Hillyer C. Ryder, in *The State Coinages of New England*, used a scale ranging from Rarity-1 to Rarity-6, although no specific quantities were associated with each.

In 1929, M.L. Beistle, in A *Register of Half Dollar Die Varieties and Sub-Varieties*, described varieties of this denomination adjectivally, such as rare, very rare, and exceedingly rare.

With relatively few exceptions, rarity ratings can only be approximate. Witness the description of an 1894-S dime I cited earlier, for which catalogues of the 1957 to 1961 period stated that seven examples were known to exist, but today research has shown that about a dozen can be traced. A better case in point is the 1817/4 overdate half dollar. When the first specimen came to light, in the 1930s, it was believed to be unique. Later, others were found, and three were known. Today, specialists can trace five examples. Perhaps a few more will be unearthed as decades go by.

Dr. Sheldon states the situation succinctly:

"No student of cents ever says that such-and-such a number of a variety 'are known.' He states simply that such-and-such a number have been reported or are known *to him*. The reader should realize, of course, that most errors arise from overrating, not from underrating a rarity. If a coin is rare, it may be common, but if it is called common, it almost certainly is not rare. If Jones was seen, he probably was there. If he wasn't seen, he still may have been there."

In the numismatic world, adjectival descriptions of rarity are still the most common. Thus, typical catalogue headlines are as follows:

"The Rare 1877 Cent"

"The Extremely Rare 1871-CC Liberty Seated Quarter Dollar"

"The Very Rare 1836 Reeded Edge Half Dollar"

"The Classic 1868 Large Cent"

"One of 12 Known 1927-D Double Eagles"

"The Key 1889-CC Morgan Dollar"

and so on....

European catalogues sometimes use a succession of Rs, with R meaning rare, RR designating rarer yet, RRR denoting very rare, and the highest degree, RRRR, representing extremely rare, without quantitative definition. In the 1950s and 1960s this terminology was used by the New Netherlands Coin Company, when that famous firm was under the management of Charles Wormser and John J. Ford, Jr. A typical "R" rarity description is as follows: "1854-S $2.50 gold. EF-40. RRRR."

A Tale of Three Coins

Among privately issued tokens produced during the Civil War, especially in the year 1863, are thousands of varieties. Just one variety was produced for a merchant in the state of New Hampshire, a token issued by a certain A.W. Gale, who operated a concession at the Railroad Depot in Concord. Several hundred specimens of this particular token are known, probably somewhere between 300 and 500, many of which are Uncirculated. In terms of Civil War tokens, no specialist in the series would designate the Gale piece as being rare, for it isn't in a *relative* sense. However, in an *absolute* sense, the coin is probably at least 20 to 50 times rarer than an 1877 Indian cent. This illustrates that rarity, as expressed in adjectival terms, is a matter of *context*. Stated numerically, the problem of nomenclature would disappear. The 1877

Indian cent, using Don Taxay's expansion of the Sheldon scale, would be designated as Rarity-1, because over 1,250 are known. The 1863 Civil War token issued by A.W. Gale can be designated as Rarity-3, a coin of which 201 to 500 are known. Thus, anyone reading catalogue descriptions of either piece can determine more or less where these coins stand.

So far so good, but, really, this does not tell us much about the 1877 Indian cent. We find that it is Rarity-1, or more than 1,250 pieces known, but the same can be said for every other date in the Indian cent series! Thus, a 1907 Indian cent, a coin of which 108,138,618 were minted (a mintage over 100 times greater than the 1877), a coin of which probably hundreds of thousands of coins exist today, would also be called Rarity-1. So, for purposes of disseminating useful information, a catalogue description such as "1877 Indian cent, rare" and "1907 Indian cent, common" are far more useful than "1877 Indian cent, Rarity-1" and "1907 Indian cent, Rarity-1."

In 1991, approximate values in MS-60 grade for the coins just discussed are as follows:

A.W. Gale Civil War token (Rarity-3): $75

1877 Indian cent (R-1): $1,250

1907 Indian cent (R-1): $25

Limits of Rarity Ratings

Rarity ratings, adjectival or numerical, can be useful, but they are only part of the story. They must be employed in context within a given series, and in conjunction with other information.

Regarding value, in general, and *within a given series*, rare coins sell for more than common coins.

For example, within the Indian cent series, an Extremely Fine-40 grade Indian cent of 1877 catalogues in the current *Guide Book* for $900, while the relatively common 1907 is listed for $8. The rarer issue sells for more. However, in other series a coin can be rare, very rare, or whatever and still not sell for a great deal of money if other factors such as high grade and strong popularity are not present.

While the 1877 Indian cent is rare in all grades, there are numerous coins in the United States series which are common in one grade and rare in another.

For example, among Washington quarter dollars, the 1936-D is quite common in worn grades, as its mintage of 5,374,000 would suggest. However, in MS-65 condition it is worth the best part of $1,500, simply because in MS-65 preservation the 1936-D is quite rare. The reason for this? In 1936, collectors were preoccupied with the commemorative boom and other things, and the bulk of 1936-D Washington quarters simply slipped into circulation un-noticed. A few years later, it was realized that few Uncirculated 1936-D quarters were to be had, by which time it was too late.

Similarly, in the Washington quarter series the 1936 Philadel-phia Mint issue is quite common in grades from well worn to Uncirculated (MS-63 catalogues $30, MS-65 $100 in the *Guide Book*), but in Proof finish just 3,837 were minted—a low figure for modern times—so a Proof-65 example sells for well over $1,000.

Going back earlier in history, an 1803 half dollar is not rare. Given an appropriate checkbook balance, you would have no trouble acquiring dozens of specimens within a year's time. However, in Uncirculated preservation, particularly MS-65, the picture changes dramatically. An MS-65 1803 half dollar is a great rarity, and it might be the case that you would have to wait five to 10 years or more before a purchase opportunity occurred! The "bid" price (there is no "ask" given) in *The Coin Dealer Newsletter* (7/5/91) is $45,000! By contrast, a well-worn Good-4 coin has an "ask" price of only $130.

Thus, certain coins are rare in an absolute sense (the 1894-S dime, 1913 Liberty Head nickel, and so on—of which very few specimens are known to exist). Other pieces are rare in a relative sense (the 1877 Indian cent, of which thousands exist, is rare within the Indian cent series). Still other coins are rare only in certain grades of finishes (such as the 1936-D quarter which is rare only in Mint State, the 1936 quarter which is rare only with Proof finish, and the 1803 half dollar which is common in worn grades but extremely rare in Mint State).

If you have followed my commentary to this point, you probably know as much about the "technical" aspects of rarity as does anyone in the numismatic fraternity!

Popularity
vs. Value

Popularity or Demand

 For a coin to sell for a premium price, someone has to desire it. In other words, there has to be a demand for it; it has to be popular. Coins are popular for many reasons, thus the category of demand and popularity is a catch-all which admits many different considerations. And, what one collector may find desirable or popular may not be desirable or popular to another. Here are some of the observable factors in this regard:

Type Coins

Ever since the early 1960s, collecting coins by design types has been an important part of the numismatic spectrum. (Forming a type set will be discussed in a subsequent chapter.) The collector of coins by design types desires not scarce date and mintmark varieties but, instead, simply a single representative of the design in question. Thus, to illustrate the Barber dime minted from 1892 to 1916, any date is satisfactory. Often a type collector will opt to acquire one of the commoner issues, perhaps a Philadelphia Mint coin of the early 1900s. A rare variety such as the 1894-S, of which only a dozen or so are known, would not be chosen in this regard.

For most United States design types, abundant examples are available. Certain early design types may be rare in higher grades, but in lesser preservation there will be no trouble in acquiring a piece. An example is provided by the Draped Bust half dollar with Heraldic Eagle reverse, the general type minted from 1801 to 1807. In grades from Good through Extremely Fine, examples appear on the market with some frequency. As noted in my earlier illustration of an 1803 half dollar, in higher grades, such as MS-65, a half dollar of the 1801 to 1807 span is a rarity, but in lesser grades there is no problem.

However, there are some issues in American numismatics which are essential to a type set, and which at the same time are scarce or rare in all grades. While such pieces are desired by date and variety collectors, the main demand comes from those putting together type sets. Thus, a generous portion of today's market price can be attributed to the demand for inclusion in a type set collection. Examples abound. The 1793 half cent is the only year of the Liberty Cap type, head facing left. Thus, not only is it needed by collectors of half cents but, more important, anyone aspiring to own a complete set of United States coins by design types must acquire a half cent dated 1793; no other date will do. Thus, there is a strong demand for this issue for type set purposes. Among large cents, the 1793 Chain and Wreath types were produced only in that year and are needed for type sets.

In the small cent series, the 1859 Indian Head with laurel wreath reverse represents the only year in which the laurel wreath was used. On the other hand, the copper-nickel Indian cent with oak wreath and shield reverse was minted over a span of years from 1860 to 1864, thus the type set collector has a choice of several issues. The effect the demand for type sets has on the price of a coin is illustrated by this issue. The 1859 Indian cent posted a mintage of 36,400,000. The current *Guide Book* lists an example in EF-40 grade for $70. On the other hand, the 1862 Indian cent, with a mintage of 28,075,000 is slightly scarcer today, but yet it catalogues in the same reference for less than a third of the price: just $20. The reason is that the 1859 Indian cent is needed for type set purposes, whereas the 1862 is not.

Among half dimes, the 1796 and 1797 style with Draped Bust obverse and Small Eagle reverse is the scarcest of all major design types, and much of the market strength of coins of this motif can be attributed to demand for type set purposes.

In the quarter dollar series, the 1796 is the only year with Draped Bust obverse and Small Eagle reverse. Today, an MS-65 coin is worth the best part of $100,000, not because there is a tremendous demand on the part of those collecting quarters by date and variety sequence, but because thousands of people desire the issue for inclusion in type sets. The same analogy can be drawn to the 1796-1797 half dollar of similar design.

Washington Quarters

In 1932 the first Washington quarters, the design of which was modelled by John Flanagan after a portrait bust by Houdon, appeared. Originally they were intended to be a commemorative issue, but the motif proved so popular that it was continued for decades afterward. Today, Washington quarters are collectors' favorites. Scarce issues include 1932-D and 1932-S (elusive in all grades), 1936-D (common in worn grades but scarce in Uncirculated preservation), and several others.

Liberty Walking Half Dollars

Designed by Adolph A. Weinman, Liberty Walking half dollars were made from 1916 through 1947. All are of the same design type. Generally, issues dated prior to the 1930s are very elusive in Uncirculated grade, with certain issues being particularly elusive, 1921-S for example. A favorite pursuit with numismatists is the assembling of a "short set" of Liberty Walking half dollars of the 1940s, a collection which contains many beautiful pieces but no major rarities.

Among gold coins, the 1808 quarter eagle is the only year of the denomination which has the Capped Bust to the Left obverse on a large diameter planchet. Thus, the piece is in fantastic demand for this reason. Numerous other examples can be cited. In general, if a coin is of a restricted mintage or a limited series and is needed for a type set, a strong demand and consequent higher price will result.

First Year of Issue Coins

While the majority of type set collectors are satisfied with any issue of a given design, some desire the first year of production. Thus, to illustrate the Barber dime minted from 1892 to 1916, only the first year, 1892, will do. Similarly, to illustrate the Mercury dime, a 1916 is wanted, for the Washington quarter, a 1932, for the Liberty Walking half dollar, a 1916, for the Morgan silver dollar, an 1878, and so on. The first year of issue situation does not represent a strong element of demand, but still it is a factor, thus I mention it here.

Artistic Coins

Beauty is in the eye of the beholder, and many beholders have pinpointed certain United States coin designs as being quite beautiful and have therefore decided to collect them. Among popular series, prime in this regard is the Liberty Walking half dollar. The work of artist-sculptor Adolph A. Weinman, the Liberty Walking design made its debut in 1916. Miss Liberty is shown in the form of a goddess, striding toward the sun, with a star-spangled cape in the background—a motif borrowed from Saint-Gaudens, and somewhat resembling other world coin issues, specifically certain pieces of France. This classic design has always been admired, and more than just a few collectors have aspired to complete sets of these half dollars from 1916 through 1947 because of the artistic value of the motif. A tribute was paid to the design in 1986, when the Treasury Department, seeking ideas for a silver bullion coinage, found nothing more artistic than the old Weinman Liberty Walking design, and it was resurrected for further use! Similarly, for the new issue of American gold bullion coins in 1986, the old design by Augustus Saint-Gaudens, first used on $20 pieces of 1907, was brought back.

The Mercury dime, the Standing Liberty quarter, the Indian cent, the Indian $10 piece, and certain other issues have scored high marks in popularity polls, and part of their demand and price today is attributable to their perceived degree of artistry. In the field of United States pattern coins, the great popularity and consequent high price given to such issues as the 1872 Amazonian silver coins, the 1879 Schoolgirl dollar, and the 1882 Shield Earring coins is because of their great beauty of design; certainly these are among the finest motifs ever used on products of the U.S. Mint.

Interesting Varieties

Throughout American numismatics there are numerous die varieties and other issues with characteristics which can best be described as interesting. Such pieces often have a higher value because of this. An example is provided by the 1794 Starred Reverse large cent. An early diesinker placed around the reverse of the die used to strike this coin a circle of 94 five-pointed stars, so minute that they can be seen clearly only under magnification. Thus was created one of the most fascinating and enigmatic varieties among coins of this denomination, a variety which Dr. Sheldon said collectors viewed "with religious awe." For this reason, a 1794 Starred Reverse will sell for many multiples of the price that a 1794 cent of another variety, of equal rarity, will fetch.

The 1828 half cent with 12 stars on the obverse instead of the normal 13 and the 1817 large cent with 15 obverse stars instead of 13 have always been in strong demand, not because they are very rare but because their varieties are interesting. In 1987 my firm sent a mailing to our clients, offering examples of the 1828 12-stars half cent from a hoard of several hundred pieces bought from an old-time collector. In the first two days the listing was distributed, over 150 coins were sold, for a total of $23,000!

Numerous overdates in the United States series, caused by punching one digit over another in the die, have attracted numismatists, and in many instances premiums are paid for them. Among state coins of Vermont, the 1788 issue with the C in the inscription VERMON AUCTORI punched in the die backward, a die variety attributed as Ryder-30, has always been in great demand and has brought high prices from specialists because of the curious backward C feature. The 1787 Massachusetts cent with the arrows on the left side of the coin instead of the right is a classic issue for the same reason; every other variety in the series is different from it, thus this particular 1787 is particularly interesting and desirable—and high priced. Many coins have interesting stories to go with them, and if the story is well publicized, an additional demand will be created.

Availability

The availability of coins in a given series contributes to the demand and popularity of them. In the years prior to the Treasury release of Morgan dollars in 1962, coins of this series were not particularly popular. Indeed, a survey conducted several years earlier by Abe Kosoff did not show them even in the top 10 favorites of American collectors! The same survey, if it had been taken in 1991, would probably have shown Morgan silver dollars to be at or near the top of the list! Since 1962, hundreds of millions of silver dollars, previously hidden away in Treasury vaults, have come to light. The result is that today almost anyone can afford to collect Morgan silver dollars. True, some rarities are hard to find, but issues such as 1879-S, 1880, 1880-S, 1881-S, 1884-O, 1885-O, 1886, 1887, and numerous others are quite common. As they are available, people collect them. This availability has caused an increased popularity, and in the Morgan silver dollar series even common dates are apt to sell for medium to high prices because of this added factor.

Similarly, series such as Lincoln cents, Jefferson nickels, Mercury and Roosevelt dimes, Washington quarters, Franklin half dollars, and Kennedy half dollars are in demand because they are available; these are coins from our own time. The Littleton Coin Company scored a success and added many names to its mailing list by running nationwide advertisements offering a set of modern Susan B. Anthony dollars for sale in a display case for a reasonable price; clearly, the public likes familiar, modern coins. Similarly, in the early 1990s the Philip Wing Company placed many advertisements in widely-distributed publications such as USA Today, offering modern Proof sets for sale.

If a coin is part of a popular series, it will bring a higher price than if it belongs to an obscure area. Going back to my earlier example, the 1877 Indian cent in Uncirculated grade will sell for much more than an 1863 Civil War token issued by A.W. Gale, for tens of thousands of collectors desire the 1877 Indian cent, whereas perhaps a few thousand at most desire the Civil War token. The Civil War token is many times rarer, but it does not sell for an equivalent price. Similarly, an MS-65 1796 quarter dollar of which several dozen or more pieces are known is worth the best part of $100,000 as noted earlier.

If you were to show me an MS-65 streetcar token from Emporia, Kansas and we were to both agree that fewer than a dozen specimens are known to exist, I doubt if the coin would bring more than $50—or one-thousandth of the price of the 1796 quarter—simply because the 1796 quarter is in tremendous demand, but few people collect streetcar tokens of this particular Kansas community. Availability equates to popularity, and popularity affects price.

Fame and Publicity

Hand in hand with the concept of interesting varieties is the aspect of fame and publicity. In the American series, certain classic rarities have engendered much public notice. Perhaps no two coins are more famous in this regard than the 1913 Liberty Head nickel, used as the centerpoint of B. Max Mehl's advertising campaign involving sales of his *Star Rare Coin Encyclopedia*, and the 1804 silver dollar. Around the turn of the present century, more columns of print were devoted to the 1804 silver dollar than to the next two or three most famous coin varieties combined! Describing an 1804 silver dollar in an auction catalogue, B. Max Mehl called it "The King of American Coins," an appellation which caught on and which has been used by other cataloguers since.

Both the 1913 Liberty Head nickel, of which five specimens are known to exist, and the 1804 silver dollar, of which slightly over a dozen are known, have been desired for their fame and publicity value. In 1972, the World-Wide Coin Company acquired examples of these coins, and the fame which resulted probably was worth many hundreds of thousands of dollars—more than the coins themselves were valued at the time!

J.V. McDermott, a prominent coin dealer of the 1940s and 1950s, carried as a pocket piece (as unbelievable as this may seem to the present reader!) a 1913 Liberty Head nickel which he eventually encased in a small green plastic holder. In his monthly advertisement in *The Numismatic Scrapbook Magazine* McDermott

The Famous 1802 Half Dime

Of all coins in the series of silver half dimes minted from 1794 to 1873, the most famous issue is the 1802, a coin of which only a few dozen are known to exist. The one illustrated here (enlarged as well as regular size) sold for $45,000 in our sale of the Garrett Collection. It was described as follows: "Choice Extremely Fine. Obverse very well struck with excellent definition in all areas except certain of the lower curls. The reverse is slightly impressed above the eagle's head, as is characteristic for this design. Full borders and smooth, even surfaces grace this piece."

The coin, purchased by T. Harrison Garrett from the Newlin Collection in the 1880s has an interesting pedigree. In 1883 Newlin described the same piece as follows:

> No. 7 [in his enumeration of the 16 known to him]. This piece was picked up in Europe and was bought by Mr. Betts, for $125. It was sold in Cogan's sale, September 16-20, 1878 and was described as follows: "This is one of the best specimens of this half dime I have ever known to be offered at auction, and certainly the best, if I except the one sold in the Redlick sale by Mr. Scott, which had been too highly polished to cause me to value it very highly. This is unusually fine, and the rarest half dime known. The piece was purchased at the sale by Mr. Haines for $130." It was again sold in W. Elliot Woodward's sale of the Haines Collection, October 13-16, 1880, and was thus described: "1802. Barely circulated, having only the slightest marks of friction; polish surface believed to be as fine as a half dime of the date exists." This piece was bought by Mr. E. Burton for $240, and was purchased indirectly by Mr. Garrett, of Baltimore, in whose possession it remains. It is undoubtedly the finest known if we except the Uncirculated specimen in the collection of Mr. L.G. Parmelee. As I have never seen this piece, I cannot give my opinion. One gentleman, who has seen both pieces, informs me that Mr. Parmelee's is the better. Another gentleman, who likewise examined them both, declares this to be much the finer. So I think that the honors should be divided.

The $45,000 sale price in 1979 represented more than a hundred-fold increase over the $400 purchase price of nearly a century earlier. Today, in the 1990s, this coin would bring even more.

would often mention the coin, and would describe how he had "teased" numismatists who desired to buy it. In particular, P.B. Trotter, Jr., a Memphis banker, desired to own the coin—but after many thrusts and parries, the coin remained with McDermott. After he died, his widow, Beth, consigned it to Paramount International Coin Corporation for sale at public auction. In 1967 it crossed the block for $46,500, with the buyers being Aubrey and Adeline Bebee, well-known Omaha dealers. In the 1980s the Bebee's presented the coin to the American Numismatic Association Museum in Colorado Springs, the most valuable single specimen that institution had received up to that date. Later, the same couple presented an 1804 silver dollar to the ANA.

In 1975 I owned a 1913 Liberty Head nickel, which I exhibited all by itself in a case at the American Numismatic Association convention. A long line of people formed to see this fabulous coin, and it was one of the major attractions of the show. Later, it went into the Jerry Buss Collection, to be subsequently sold at auction in 1985 by Superior Galleries for $385,000. At present it is in the collection of Reed Hawn, a Texas connoisseur (who also has the good fortune to own an 1804 silver dollar!).

In 1980 I catalogued the Garrett Collection example of the 1804 silver dollar and presented it in an auction catalogue. Pre-sale estimates were all over the map, with $150,000 to $200,000 being the most favored guesses. Shortly before the auction took place, a Wisconsin coin dealer came up to me and said he wanted to buy the coin and was prepared to pay $250,000 for it. I asked him if he had a customer for it, and his answer was interesting:

"No, I am just buying it for publicity for my business. I would like to show it in my store window, with appropriate security, during business hours—as it will create a sensation in my town."

As it turned out, the piece sold for $400,000—still a record for the coin—to the team of Larry Hanks and Bill Pullen, who subsequently resold it at a profit to Sam Colavita. (Several years later, when the market was at a quieter level, the piece resold for $187,500, then shortly thereafter was sold for a reputed $225,000). In 1985 Superior Galleries sold the Jerry Buss example for $308,000—a coin which I had owned a decade earlier—with the buyers being Aubrey and Adeline Bebee, who already owned a 1913 Liberty Head nickel. The Bebees were not endeavoring to collect Liberty Head nickels by date and mintmark varieties, nor were they collecting early silver dollars by date. Instead, they recognized the fame of these two classic rarities, and desired to own them for this reason. As noted, the Bebees later gave both to the ANA Museum.

In 1985 John Abbott, a Michigan dealer, consigned to Auctions by Bowers and Merena, Inc. the only known specimen of the 1870-S half dime, a coin which had been discovered a few years earlier. Previously,the issue was unknown to numismatists. In furious bidding competition the coin went to $176,000, with the buyer being Martin Paul, a leading dealer. I asked Martin why he bought it, and he said he wanted to own it for its rarity value. Subsequently he put it on the market for resale. In the meantime, he had the satisfaction and pride of having a classic go through his hands.

Not everyone desires publicity when they buy rarities, and when my firm sold the only known Uncirculated 1787 Brasher doubloon for $725,000 as part of the Garrett Collection Sale, the buyer acquired it through an agent and wished to remain anonymous.

While some numismatists desire publicity and others do not, the fact remains that rarities which are surrounded by great fame and public notice have traditionally sold for more than their less publicized counterparts.

Grade vs. Value

Art or Science?

 Of all subjects under the numismatic sun, none has evoked more intense feelings, more controversy, and more discussion in print than grading.

Is grading an art or is it a science?

Do dealers (and collectors) buy a coin in one grade, then when they want to sell it, suggest that the grade is higher?

How does one define a coin as EF-40? Or AU-55? Or MS-65? Even if several people agreed that three coins are each MS-65, do all three coins necessarily have the same value?

Are certificates, "slabs," and "guaranteed grades" of any value, or are they just so much publicity?

The questions could go on and on, but you get the idea!

Grading as a Determinant of Values

Grading is an important determinant of coin values, and in general, the higher a grade is, the higher the price is also. The concept is basic.

In the *Guide Book* the 1907 Liberty Head nickel is listed for 60¢ in G-4 grade, $1 VG-8, $3 F-12, $6 VF-20, $18 EF-40, and $75 MS-60. Although the *Guide Book* does not list the category of MS-65, other sources in 1991 pegged the value in that grade at about $750. From 60 cents in G-4 to $750 in MS-65—what a difference!

A broader spectrum of prices as related to certain grades is provided for some series by *The Coin Dealer Newsletter*. The issue of July 5, 1991 posts the following valuations for an 1886-O Morgan silver dollar:

VG-8	$8.50
F-12	$10
VF-20	$13
EF-40	$18
AU-50	$40
MS-60	$235
MS-63	$1,350
MS-64	$5,000

MS-65 $20,000 (approximately; no "ask" price is given, but a "bid" of $17,500 is listed).

In MS-65 with a prooflike surface, the same issue is listed at over $60,000!

In this illustration, the value of an 1886-O dollar can be just $8.50 if well-worn, or over $60,000 if in MS-65 preservation with a prooflike surface!

Continuing the 1886-O example, if an issue is MS-63 it is worth $1,350 according to this source. For an MS-64 grade, just slightly better than MS-63, the value nearly quadruples—to $5,000! If you are offered a coin described as MS-64 at $4,000, it may be a good buy if it *is* MS-64, but what if it is just MS-63? In the latter instance, you may be paying three times more than you should. Of such stuff controversy is made, and you can readily see that heated debates can ensue.

While it would be nice to think that the MS-64 grade of Dealer A is precisely the same as the MS-64 of Dealer B and Dealer C, in practice this is not the case. While it would also be nice to think that among various commercial grading services, the MS-64 of Grading Service A is the same as the MS-64 of Grading Services B and C, such is not necessarily the case.

Accuracy (or Lack Thereof)

In a well-known study, Kevin Foley, editor of *The Centinel*, official journal of the Central States Numismatic Society, sent 10 different coins to four different professional grading services. You have probably guessed what I am going to say! In not a single instance did all of the four grading services agree. In one instance—that of a 1919 Standing Liberty quarter—the professional opinions ranged all the way from AU-55 to MS-65.

At the 1990 convention of the ANA, Barry J. Cutler, head of the Consumer Protection Division of the Federal Trade Commission, told how he subjected several professional graders to a blind test. Beforehand, each person said that he was sufficiently expert that not only could he determine whether a coin was MS-63 (for example), but he could further tell if it was a "low end," "regular," or "high end" MS-63. In the blind test the participants were each shown the same 1908 $20 gold piece. Their professional opinions ranged all the way from AU-58 to MS-64!

As if this situation were not perplexing enough, let me cite a brochure issued by the American Numismatic Association, *Basic Facts About Grading and Authentication*, which specifically notes:

"No two coins are ever exactly alike in every respect and thus values vary. In some instances AU-55 graded coins could be valued nearly equal to MS-63 pieces because of superior eye appeal; conversely,some MS-65 coins are valued lower than MS-63 for reasons of poor strike, lustre, or flaws."

Before you throw in the towel and say, "I give up!" let me suggest that you learn more about grading. Do so, and the entire concept will fall into place. Grading controversies or no, the coin market has gone merrily along its way for well over a century. Grading controversies are nothing new. In the pages of the *American Journal of Numismatics* in the last century, grading sparked lots of controversy. Probably, grading will be controversial a century from now. However, in 1991 grading is more consistent than ever before. It may not be precise, as Kevin Foley's previously cited survey shows, but at least grades are not "all over the map" like they used to be. However, there are exceptions.

What is grading? Grading is the art (some say it is a science) of examining a coin and determining its classification, depending upon the experience—the amount of contact with other coins or wear—the piece has had since it left the dies at the moment of striking.

Dr. Sheldon's Numerical Grading System

Today, many use the numerical scale of grading formulated by Dr. William H. Sheldon. Making its debut in 1949 in *Early American Cents*, later reiterated in *Penny Whimsy*, Sheldon's numerical grading system ranges from 1 to 70, with 1 representing a coin worn smooth to the point of barely being identifiable, whereas 70

How Important is Condition?

Among later United States coins condition is an exceedingly important factor. However, among colonial and state coins, such as the 1787 New York copper shown above, one does not always have a wide choice. The *Guide Book of United States Coins* notes that just three examples are known to exist of this particular variety, and all are very weakly struck with part of the design missing. The piece was sold by us for $20,000 at auction in 1979.

This piece is believed to have been made in the late 1780s by Capt. Thomas Machin, who operated a private mint on the shores of Orange Pond near present-day Newburgh, New York. Operations there were conducted in secret and were viewed with suspicion by local residents. It is said that a guard wearing a hideous mask was employed to frighten curiosity seekers! More information concerning Machin's enterprise can be found in Sylvester S. Crosby's *Early Coins of America* book.

stands for a piece which is flawless. In between are many different categories. Why a scale from 1 to 70 instead of from 1 to 100 or some other range? The answer is that the Sheldon Scale was part of a market formula for United States large cents of the dates 1793-1814 and was specifically created to produce the desired result within that series. First, let me give the Sheldon Scale, slightly abbreviated:

Basal State: Identifiable and unmutilated, but so badly worn that only a portion of the inscription is legible.

Fair-2: The date and more than half of the inscription and detail can be made out, although perhaps faintly.

Very Fair-3: The date will be clear and practically all of the detail of the coin can be made out, although faint areas are to be expected, and the coin as a whole may be worn nearly smooth.

Good-4 (with slightly better coins designated as **Good-5** and **Good-6**): The date together with all the detail must be very clear. The general relief of the coin may be well worn down.

Very Good-7 (also 8 and 10): Everything is boldly clear, but the sharpness of the coin may be largely gone. Signs of wear are seen uniformly over the whole coin.

Fine-12 (and 15): All of the design and all of the inscriptions are sharp. Wear is appreciable only on the high surfaces. If the coin is examined with a glass, the microscopic detail is gone.

Very Fine-20 (and 30): All of the details are in sharp relief, and only the highest surfaces show wear, even when a glass is applied.

Extremely Fine-40: Only the slightest trace of wear, or of rubbing, is to be seen on the high points.

About Uncirculated-50: Close attention or the use of a glass should be necessary to make out that the coin is not in perfect Mint State. Typically, the AU-50 coin retains its full sharpness but is darkened or a little off-color.

Mint State-60 (also 65 and 70): Free from any trace of wear, and the color should be that of a copper coin which has been kept with great care. The color will vary from mint red to light brown or olive. For condition 60 a minor blemish, perhaps some microscopic injury, or light trace of discoloration may be tolerated. For condition 70 the coin must be exactly as it left the dies, except for a slight mellowing of the color.

The Sheldon Pricing Formula

In 1949, when the Sheldon Scale was proposed, there was not a great deal of market emphasis on Uncirculated (also known as Mint State) condition, and a coin described as VF-30 was apt to have a market value of half that of an MS-60 coin.

Dr. Sheldon's formula stated that all one had to do to determine the value of a coin was to multiply the Basal Value of a coin (determined by a figure such as $1, $5, or whatever, based upon the rarity of the coin and its popularity as a die variety) with the numerical grade. Thus, a coin with a Basal Value of $5, if in VF-30 condition, would have a market value of 5 X 30, or $150, while an MS-60 example of the same piece would have a market value of 5 X 60, or $300.

This formula was fine and dandy for the time, and subsequent studies showed that the ratios held true until about 1953, after which they became completely obsolete as the market placed increased emphasis on higher grades. Today, the formula is meaningless. If we assume that a typical 1802 large cent with a Basal Value of $10 in VF-30 grade is worth $300, according to the Sheldon formula an MS-60 piece would be worth twice the price, or $600. However, an MS-60 piece is apt to be worth several thousand dollars instead!

The Evolution of Grading

One cannot blame Dr. Sheldon, with his scientific turn of mind, for trying to make order out of relative chaos. Earlier, there had been little consistency in grading. Nineteenth-century auction cataloguers, and certain early 20th-century numismatists as well, often gave preference to a coin based upon the rarity of the piece. Thus, a 1799 large cent, a particularly rare date, might be graded as "Fine *for the coin*," because it was rare, but an 1800 large cent, a common date, in the same preservation might be graded only as Good!

There were no published guides on grading, and in one interesting instance, what a well-known professional numismatist called Proof, one of his colleagues irreverently suggested might be only Fine! Grading did not make a great deal of difference then, for if you were to go back to the year 1880 to be a numismatist on the scene at that time, there would have been little market price difference among coins in higher grade levels. Although one high-grade piece might a century later be called AU-50, and another might be called MS-63, back then both were apt to sell for the same price. If a coin was well-worn or unsightly, it might be rejected, but if it had a "nice" appearance, many numismatists were satisfied with it. This situation persisted for a long time. Market values were low, and grading was not important.

When my firm acquired the Norweb Collection and moved it into our vaults in 1986, I noted that the grading system used by Emery May Holden Norweb and others of her family, in a collection that was formed beginning around the turn of the century, was simple: The number 1 meant Proof, 2 stood for Uncirculated, and 3 represented worn. I earlier observed that in 1934, when Wayte Raymond's *Standard Catalogue* made its first appearance, Proof Liberty nickels catalogued precisely 50 cents each, no matter whether they were dated 1885 (a key date recognized by a later generation) or 1887 (a more plentiful date). With such low values, who cared whether a coin was EF-40, EF-45, AU-50, and so on? Indeed, the first edition of the *Standard Catalogue* priced most later coins in just two categories: Uncirculated and Proof!

As the 20th century progressed, efforts were made to standardize grading. The American Numismatic Association named Henry Chapman, Virgil M. Brand, and several others to a grading committee in 1908. Similarly, several coin clubs took up the idea and studied the situation. Nothing came of it.

Several decades later in *The Numismatist* Loyd Gettys and Frank Catich prepared a series of articles titled "AU or BU" which discussed grading for certain issues. Numerous other ideas appeared in the numismatic press, including the novel suggestion that coins could be graded by weight, for this would determine the amount of metal that had been worn away. This might have been fine for well-worn pieces, but for top grade pieces in which distinctions were small, it would not serve—especially since freshly minted coins were apt to vary slightly in weight anyway.

James F. Ruddy on Grading

In the introduction to *Photograde*, first published in 1970 and which has since become the best-selling guide on grading ever produced, James F. Ruddy had the following to say:

"People have been collecting coins for over 2,000 years—making numismatics one of the oldest hobbies in the world.

Before the 20th century most collectors graded their coins as being either 'new' or 'used.' Rarely did the price of a coin dictate that a finer distinction in grading be made. Most often, coins could be purchased for a small premium over their face value.

"The story today is much different. Since the numismatic boom began in the 1950s there has been an ever-increasing demand for rare coins. The supply remains constant as the mintage of a given issue cannot be changed. The natural result is a rise in values. This happened in the 1950s. And when it did, it became increasingly more important to grade coins carefully. The difference between Good and Fine might have meant $1 to $2 in the price of a particular coin in 1950. By the 1970s this same grading difference might have meant $50 to $100.

"The numismatic hobby of the 1950s fully realized the need to provide information that would keep the collector well informed. The *Guide Book*, the standard pricing reference, was expanded and improved. A weekly newspaper, *Coin World*, appeared in 1960 and offered a regular section which featured coin values. *Numismatic News*, another weekly paper, offered its 'Tele-Quotes' guide to values.

"However, in the field of coin grading much less progress has been made, In 1958 Messrs. Brown and Dunn pioneered the standardization of grading with a book which used line drawings to illustrate wear on a coin. Attempts were made by others to create grading reference books by using photographs of actual coins. Unfortunately, the photographic reproduction and, in a few cases, the grading information was inadequate to warrant the acceptance of these works as a standard.

"Today we are faced with the paradox of excellent progress in pricing information, but we have little that is new in grading guidelines since 1958. Pricing and grading are equally important as the value of a coin depends not only on its date and mintmark but on its grade as well. For example, if a coin catalogues $100 Fine, $200 Very Fine, and $300 Extremely Fine, not knowing whether a coin is Very Fine can be expensive. If you are offered a purported Very Fine for $200, and it is really only Fine, you've lost $100! Check the prices in Fine, Very Fine, and Extremely Fine grades of a cent of 1793 or 1877, a 1916-D dime, or any one of hundreds of other examples, and you will see well the need for all collectors and dealers to have an accurate modern pictorial grading guide!

"In 1968, after carefully considering the problems involved, I decided to write a book that would fill this need. I knew that four important factors were necessary to produce a successful photographic grading guide:

"First was the access to hundreds of thousands of dollars' worth of coins needed for photography. For two years I systematically took pictures of every coin that came through my hands which best represented the average grade for its type....

"Next came research. Fortunately I have had nearly two decades of professional coin dealing experience to draw from. In this time I have graded tens of millions of dollars' worth of coins. My schooling and professional training was originally in scientific research. This background taught me to be precise and methodical on very minute details—important factors when formalizing a universal grading system.

"Next came photography—by far the most formidable feature to master. The main problem was the extremes involved; the wide range in detail from About Good to About Uncirculated; the size differential from silver three-cent pieces to silver dollars; the variations from a dark, porous copper surface to a brilliant silver or gold one...."

Photograde did enjoy an excellent reception with collectors, with the American Numismatic Association naming it as an official grading guide in 1972. However, the photographs in that reference were limited to pieces from AG-3 preservation to AU-50. It was not possible to clearly illustrate the difference between various gradations of Mint State issues from MS-60 to MS-70 by photographic means, nor is it possible to do so today.

The ANA Gets into the Grading Business

In 1973, the American Numismatic Association decided to step into the grading situation and see what it could do. Abe Kosoff was named by President Virginia Culver to head a committee to investigate the field. Stanley Apfelbaum also formed a study group to gather information. In 1977 a new book, *Official ANA Grading Standards for United States Coins*, with an introduction by me and with the grading standards defined by Kenneth Bressett and Abe Kosoff, appeared. Subsequently, the book was updated to include additional numerical categories. The second edition listed the following grades for a typical issue: AG-3, G-4, VG-8, F-12, VF-20,

VF-30, EF-40, EF-45, AU-50, AU-55, MS-60, MS-63, MS-65, MS-67, and MS-70.

As a result of action by the American Numismatic Association Board of Governors in the summer of 1986, in which *all* grades from MS-60 through MS-70 were adopted as "official," the third edition, released in April 1987, included MS-60, MS-61, MS-62, MS-63, MS-64, MS-65, MS-66, MS-67, MS-68, MS-69, and MS-70. Another "new" grade also made its appearance, AU-58. In 1991 the fourth edition was released, but no new grades (grades other than those in the third edition) were added.

As Donn Pearlman pointed out in an interesting address given to the Numismatic Literary Guild shortly after the ANA Board of Governors adopted 11 grades in the Mint State category, now with 11 obverse grades and 11 reverse grades, this makes possible 121 different grading possibilities in the Uncirculated category alone! As Alexander Woolcott said, "Backwards reels the mind!"

In practice, the printed definitions for MS-60, MS-61, MS-62, MS-63, MS-64, MS-65, MS-66, MS-67, MS-68, MS-69, and MS-70 are hardly scientific. In my opinion, in the third edition, the first one with 11 degrees of Uncirculated grades, the situation became such that few could understand it. Where will it all end?

What is MS-65?

The American Numismatic Association states that to be MS-65 a Morgan silver dollar must have:

"no trace of wear; nearly as perfect as MS-70 except for a few minute bag marks or surface mars. Has full lustre but may be unevenly toned. Any unusual striking traits must be described."

For a tiny silver three-cent piece, an MS-65 coin, according to the American Numismatic Association, must have:

"no trace of wear; nearly as perfect as MS-70 except for some small blemish. Has full Mint lustre but may be unevenly toned or lightly fingermarked. A few barely noticeable nicks or marks may be present."

For a Morgan silver dollar, what are "a few minute bagmarks or surface mars"? For some buyers, "a few" might mean five, for someone else 50 marks might be acceptable, and still someone else might feel that 117 would be okay.

Let's suppose for purposes of argument, you and I agree that 50 marks fit the requirement for a silver dollar. Now we go to the tiny silver three-cent piece. What are "a few barely noticeable nicks or marks" on this tiny coin? Fifty marks, which we agreed might be satisfactory on a Morgan dollar, would probably severely disfigure a tiny silver three-cent piece, thus for a silver three-cent piece "a few barely noticeable nicks or marks" has to have some other standard—but that standard isn't given.

Also overlooked is the placement of the marks. For my money, I would rather have a Morgan silver dollar with 50 nicks on the reverse, scattered in relatively unnoticeable positions on the eagle's feathers, than have five prominent marks on the obverse on the cheek of Miss Liberty, right out where all the world can see them. And, likewise to be considered is that if a mark or disfigurement appears on the date or mintmark it may severely damage a coin's worth, but the same mark if in a hidden area would impair the value little if at all.

Commercial Grading Services

In an attempt to standardize the situation, and also to turn a profit, a number of commercial grading services appeared on the market in the late 1980s. By 1986, *Coin World* was able to run a survey of over a dozen different companies. In an article the same year in the *Rare Coin Review*, Dr. Joel Orosz said the situation was becoming such that "one can hardly heave an egg without hitting a new grading service!" As noted earlier, the findings of the services were apt to vary widely, as evidenced by "official" grades from AU-55 to MS-65 being given by four different grading services who examined the same 1919 Standing Liberty quarter and by professional graders evaluating the same 1908 $20 piece as grading all the way from AU-58 to MS-64.

The American Numismatic Association set up the ANA Grading Service, usually abbreviated as "ANACS" (with a C instead of a G), from the concurrently existing ANA Certification Service.[1] Even the same coin graded by the same service at different dates was apt to vary. In a discussion on grading held at a meeting of the ANA Board of Governors, Harvey Stack pointed out that a gold dollar was submitted to the ANA Grading Service and was re-

[1] In 1990, ANACS was sold by the American Numismatic Association to Amos Press, Inc., of Ohio, and the ANACS staff and facilities were moved from Colorado Springs, Colorado to Columbus, Ohio. After the sale, ANACS had no official connection with the ANA.

turned with a grade of AU-50. Then it was resubmitted, without mention being made that it was the same coin. When it came back it had jumped to MS-60—an About Uncirculated coin had become fully Uncirculated!

Conversely, in 1986 a client sent me an example of another gold dollar which was sent to the ANA Grading Service and was certified as MS-60. He sent it back again, and it was called AU-50.

In my office is a Morgan silver dollar which was sent to the ANACS four times, and each time it was returned with a certificate giving a different grade.

Changes in Grading Interpretation

As if this were not enough, grading interpretations changed during the 1980s. What the hobby designated as MS-65 in the early 1980s, and what the ANA Grading Service itself certified as MS-65 then, by January 1986 was apt to be MS-60 or MS-63, according to an official statement made by the ANA Board of Governors at that time.

The tightening of grading interpretations admits of no easy explanation. My feeling is that it was brought about by dealers posting successively higher "bid" prices for MS-65 coins, but then saying that most coins submitted were not "up to our expectations." In order to qualify for such "bid" figures, coins had to be "super" MS-65 pieces.

Bit by bit, interpretations changed, and what was MS-65 in 1980 or 1981 became the new MS-60 or MS-63. The corollary of this is beneficial for you: today, when you buy certain MS-60 or MS-63 coins, you are buying coins which in many instances are fully equal to the MS-65 coins of a few years ago!

Certified Coins

Certain numismatic firms, particularly those in the investment sector of the business, developed an active trading market for certified coins. In 1986 a new factor, the Professional Coin Grading Service (PCGS) appeared on the scene. Its coins, firmly encapsulated in hermetically sealed holders, were the subject of many bid and ask quotations, as were those of the American Numismatic Association Grading Service and the Numismatic Guaranty Corporation of America. Overlooked was the admonition given by the ANA itself, as quoted earlier: "No two coins are ever exactly alike in every respect and thus values vary. In some instances AU-55 graded coins could be valued nearly equal to MS-63 pieces because of superior eye appeal; conversely, some MS-65 coins are valued lower than MS-63 for reasons of poor strike, lustre, or flaws."

In response to collector demand for certified coins, my firm, Bowers and Merena Galleries, Inc., developed a policy of offering *selected* certified coins which not only met PCGS, NGC, or ANA requirements for the technical or numerical grade, but, in addition, met our own strict requirements and, further, were outstanding examples of their issue—with aesthetically pleasing surfaces, a nice planchet, a sharp strike, and so on.

Single or Unit Grades

Prior to the advent of PCGS in 1986, many collectors and dealers used split grades, as did many grading services. Due to peculiarities of striking, due to protective high rims, and due to the intricacies of design, certain coins commonly exist with one side in a lower or higher grade than the other. Common examples include these:

◆Barber dimes, quarters, and half dollars have on the obverse the portrait of Miss Liberty with her prominent, plain cheek being one of the highest design features. The reverse design of the dime (wreath and denomination) and quarter and half dollar (Heraldic Eagle) have no single points which are higher than the others and are intricate. The cheek of Miss Liberty, when it received even slight contact with other coins, was apt to show nicks, scuff marks, or friction. By contrast, the reverse with its intricate design could sustain a moderate amount of handling without prominently showing marks, nicks, etc. Before 1986 a typical 1900 Barber half dollar, for example, might be graded MS-60/63, meaning that the obverse graded MS-60 while the reverse on its own merited the grade of MS-63.

◆Morgan silver dollars have the large, plain, unprotected cheek of Miss Liberty as the most prominent area of the obverse design and one of the highest points. The reverse of the Morgan dollar displays an intricate eagle (with many feather details), a wreath with many leaves, etc. A typical Morgan dollar can show extensive handling marks on the obverse and virtually no marks at all on the reverse. Before 1986 a typical 1893-CC Morgan dollar, for example, might be graded MS-60/63 or even MS-60/64.

Today in the early 1990s, in an effort to make grading and pricing more scientific and to eliminate variables, all of the main commercial grading services (ANACS, NGC, and PCGS) use just a single grade. While there may be exceptions, the coins just given in the above examples would be called by PCGS as follows: 1900 Barber half dollar, MS-60, and 1893-CC Morgan dollar, MS-60.

As grading scholar F. Michael ("Skip") Fazzari has pointed out, this situation is illogical so far as imparting information is concerned. An 1893-CC dollar certified as MS-60 might truly be in any one (or more) of these grades: MS-60/60 (obverse and reverse both MS-60), MS-60/61, MS-60/62, MS-60/63, MS-60/64, MS-60/65, etc. Obviously, you or any other buyer would rather have a PCGS 1893-CC "MS-60" dollar that has an MS-65 reverse than one that has an MS-60 reverse, but unless you examine the coin in person there is no way to tell the overall *complete and true grade.*

Widely Differing Values

After slabbed coins became a reality, the publishers of the *Coin Dealer Newsletter* (which was founded in 1963) came on stream with the *Certified Coin Dealer Newsletter,* giving values for coins issued by certain grading services (again without consideration of differing characteristics between various coins).

The July 5, 1991 issue of that publication noted, for example, that a 1922 Grant With Star commemorative half dollar (a rarity in the commemorative series) in MS-65 grade had the following values, depending upon which grading service certified it:

ANACS: $7,500

Numismatic Certification Institute: $1,850

Numismatic Guaranty Corporation of America: $9,800

Professional Coin Grading Service: $10,500

Obviously, the values of "certified" coins can vary widely! Further, the *Certified Coin Dealer Newsletter* notes: "Client or sight-seen sales may command a substantial premium above CCDN dealer-to-dealer bids. Certification does not guarantee protection against the normal risks associated with potentially volatile markets."

Advice On Grading

Concerning grading, my general advice is summarized in this paragraph:

Acquire copies of *Photograde* and the *Official ANA Grading Standards for United States Coins*. Read them. Also buy or borrow a copy of a reference book I edited, *The Coin Dealer Newsletter: A Study in Rare Coin Price Performance* 1963-1988, which gives the why and wherefore of many grading and market subjects, including changing grading interpretations and changing popularity trends.

Then couple your reading with some practical knowledge, by examining coins from different certification services. You will probably have little difficulty with worn grades, from coins graded from Fair through AU-55. However, for Mint State coins some hands-on experience is necessary. Even the experts disagree, and you will find that some vendors are more conservative than others.

Do not be a slave to certificates or holders, or you might end up owning a bunch of "technically correct" coins which are not worth as much as you expect. Going back to the admonition given by the ANA that certain MS-65 coins are worth less than MS-63 coins, you do not want to have the false security of owning a bunch of MS-65 certified coins only to find that upon selling them they will sell for less than MS-63 prices. Although the subject of grading is complex—and the preceding paragraphs exemplify this—it *can* be understood, and experienced professionals can usually agree within a point or two, what constitutes an MS-63 coin or an MS-65 example. There will be some differences, as noted, but it is unlikely that I as a professional will grade a coin as MS-65, and then another professional at the same point in time will grade the same coin as AU-50! I might consider a coin to be MS-65, and someone else might think it is MS-64. Or, I might think a coin is MS-63, and someone else might think it is MS-64 or MS-65— but such differences are within a relatively narrow range.

In instances in which a very, very tiny difference in grading means a very, very big difference in price—such as the 1886-O silver dollar earlier discussed—my recommendation is if you acquire an 1886-O dollar, study it carefully, and be sure that it is nicely struck, has an excellent surface, and is an outstanding example of its variety and grade.

Also, determine how much *value* you are receiving for the price paid. Recall the price structure of the 1886-O dollar: MS-60 $235,

MS-63 $1,350, MS-64 $5,000, and MS-65 approximately $20,000. Unless you have more money than you know what to do with and don't care about value, a nice MS-63 coin for $1,350 seems to me to be a better item to own than an MS-65 for $20,000. Remember, even the grading services aren't all that accurate when it comes to minute differences.

In 1990 I sent an 1893-S Morgan silver dollar to PCGS, which graded it MS-63, and then sent it to NGC, which graded it MS-65. For the 1893-S dollar, this amounted to a difference in market value of about $100,000.

It certainly wouldn't hurt to show your newly-purchased 1886-O Morgan dollar (or any other coin for which a tiny difference in grade causes a tremendous difference in price) to a few knowledgeable friends. However, at the same time, be aware that all reactions might not be complimentary. By way of analogy, if you purchase a new Ford automobile and take it to a Chevrolet showroom, the Chevrolet dealer will probably not congratulate you on making a good buy!

Similarly, if you buy a coin as MS-65 from Dealer A, and if you take it to Dealer B, Dealer B might view it as business lost to him, and may criticize it. Indeed, in an article in the *Coin Dealer Newsletter*, dealer Barry Stuppler pointed out that one of the great problems in professional numismatics was that many dealers spent a good amount of their energy criticizing the activities and coins of other dealers, instead of doing positive things to help the hobby. In an article in *Coin World*, Donald Kagin stated the same thing. So, if you "consider the source" you may get some valuable insight by showing your coin around, but you may also receive some unfair criticism. In any event, be aware of any return period which may come with the sale of a coin (such as a three-day, seven-day, or 30-day money back guarantee), and make your observations within the required time.

It takes a degree of self confidence to be certain about grading and to be pleased with what you own. Unfortunately, it is easier to criticize something than to praise it. Just be aware of this quirk of human nature, and you can understand a lot of what you hear and see in print.

It may be comforting for you to remember that grading today is much more conservative and much more consistent than at any other time in the history of the hobby. And, you might likewise be comforted by the realization that most other areas of collecting activity have grading standards which are defined much more loosely than are those of coins. For example, how do you grade an antique sofa, a 1953 wooden Chris Craft boat, or an old master painting by Vermeer?

Don't be afraid to ask about a coin. If you buy a coin from any dealer—me included—and if it doesn't seem "right" to you, or you have a question about it—state your feelings. Dealers are used to such questions and are, for the most part, happy to answer them. For my money, a knowledgeable buyer is the best buyer—for a knowledgeable buyer knows what he or she wants and appreciates it when it is acquired.

I'm sorry I cannot give you the final answer to the grading situation, but no one else can either. At least you are aware of the state of the art, and at this point, after reading this, you know more than most coin buyers do.

More Grading Advice

In recent times it seems that the certification services are grading more coins than ever before in grades above MS-65. Whereas these were once few and far between, now they are becoming increasingly common. Part of this is due to repeated resubmissions of the same coin to a given grading service. As has been said in print many times before (for example, in letters to the editor and the "Striking the Issues" section of *Coin World*), certain valuable coins will be resubmitted until they have exhausted their grading potential.

For example, a particularly "nice" MS-65 silver dollar in a slab may be resubmitted several times, until it becomes an MS-66. If this happens enough times, there won't be many "nice" MS-65 coins in MS-65 slabs; they will all be in MS-66 or MS-67 slabs.

The July 5, 1991 issue of the *Certified Coin Dealer Newsletter* lists MS-66 and MS-67 prices for many PCGS- and NGC-certified coins. Here are some examples (I have included the lower grades as well) of PCGS coins, but the illustrations could just as easily apply to those of other services:

◆1936 Rhode Island commemorative half dollar:

MS-61	$71
MS-62	$72
MS-63	$73
MS-64	$87
MS-65	$314
MS-66	$1,700
MS-67	$4,000

◆ 1923-S Monroe Doctrine commemorative half dollar:

MS-61	$30
MS-62	$45
MS-63	$130
MS-64	$420
MS-65	$3,300
MS-66	$6,300
MS-67	$13,000

◆1884-O Morgan silver dollar

MS-61	$17
MS-62	$19
MS-63	$25
MS-64	$39
MS-65	$110
MS-66	$555
MS-67	$7,000

◆1898-O Morgan silver dollar

MS-61	$18
MS-62	$19
MS-63	$26
MS-64	$39
MS-65	$110
MS-66	$520
MS-67	$5,000

◆1922 Peace silver dollar

MS-61	$14
MS-62	$15
MS-63	$17
MS-64	$34
MS-65	$168
MS-66	$2,100
MS-67	$8,000

◆Liberty Head $5 gold type of 1866-1908

MS-61	$170
MS-62	$275
MS-63	$760
MS-64	$1,775
MS-65	$5,700
MS-66	$10,400
MS-67	$16,500

What do you think my advice is about the above (and other similar) coins in such grades as MS-66 and MS-67. Using the knowledge you've acquired from this book thus far, contemplate how much *value* you are getting (or not getting) for an MS-67 coin in comparison to an MS-64 or MS-65 example.

By educating you to *not buy* such coins, this book may *make* tens of thousands of dollars for you! I might be wrong, and perhaps MS-66 and MS-67 coins will go up and up, but for the future as far as I can envision it, I see a downward trend. On the other hand, some of the MS-63 and MS-64 prices are very cheap now, especially when you stop to think that MS-63 in 1991 is often better than what the American Numismatic Association Grading Service officially certified as MS-65 a few years ago!

Still More Advice

When contemplating the grade of a coin, think carefully about how much *value* you are getting for the money. If you have to pay three, five, or 10 times more to get a coin which is only *slightly* nicer in numerical grade, and if even the experts cannot be sure about grading precision, then please, please think very carefully. It's your money you are spending not mine, but I am concerned for your best interests.

Other Determinants of Value

Quality of Strike

 Somewhat related to grading are several other considerations affecting the value of a coin, namely quality of strike, quality of the planchet, centering, and aesthetic appeal (such as lustre, toning, and other artistic considerations).

A Morgan silver dollar can be theoretically worth $1,000 in MS-65 grade, and you may see bid and ask prices at this figure, but if it is poorly struck, with areas of obvious flatness and lack of definition, it may have a true market value of half that, or less.

There is no hard and fast rule concerning striking. In general, issues that you expect to be sharply struck—the 1881-S silver dollar is an example—carry no particular premium if they are, and are worth quite a bit less if they are not.

Issues that are usually weakly struck—the 1926-D Buffalo nickel is an outstanding example—may be worth several times the price if they are sharply struck. Continuing in this example, of a given 100 1926-D Buffalo nickels, only two or three will show needle-sharp definition of design detail.

Knowing which coins are apt to be found lightly struck and which are sharply defined is a matter of experience and study. A numismatic library will help in this regard, for many series have been explored in detail—early half cents (by Walter H. Breen and Roger S. Cohen, Jr.), early large cents 1793 to 1814 (by Dr. William H. Sheldon), and so on. In the Morgan silver dollar series, such authors as Wayne Miller, Leroy Van Allen, and A. George Mallis have had much valuable information to impart.

Another piece of advice: If you are about to spend a large amount of money on a specific coin or in a specific series, by all means buy whatever standard reference books you can on the subject!

Do not be a slave to sharp striking. There are numerous issues in American numismatics which simply do not exist in sharply struck condition, for they were not minted that way to begin with! Perhaps no area is more relevant to mention than 1785 to 1788 state copper coinage. Many issues were produced with exceedingly weak detail and, as they left the dies appeared to have the definition of a well-worn coin! For example, the reverse of a certain 1787 Vermont copper coin with BRITANNIA in the legend normally is found as flat as the proverbial pancake. There is no such thing as a sharply struck, well-defined 1787 Vermont BRITANNIA copper, and if you lived to be as old as Methuselah you will not find one.

On the other hand, if a coin is available sharply struck—the previously mentioned 1881-S dollar comes to mind—by all means demand a sharp strike when you write out your check. Again, experience with a given series and study of books on the subject are important considerations.

Planchet Quality

Planchet quality is important also. While modern coins are usually struck on excellent planchets, among early issues there are numerous mint-caused adjustment marks (series of parallel striations caused by filing away unwanted metal to reduce an overweight planchet prior to striking), laminations, fissures, porosity, and so on. For certain of these issues, acquiring a piece on an excellent planchet may necessitate paying a premium.

For example, among Flowing Hair silver dollars of the 1794-1795 years, adjustment marks are the rule, not the exception—and pieces struck on superb planchets are apt to sell for more. On the other hand, virtually all 1776-1976-dated bicentennial coins were produced on good planchets, so such is to be expected if you acquire a coin; it is not necessary to pay a premium.

In the field of early Proof coins—pieces struck on special planchets using a slow-speed press and employing polished dies—lint marks are often seen; these are impressions of hairs or threads left on the die, and transferred to the surface of a coin in the form of little lines and curlicues. A piece can be in perfect condition at the time of minting—Proof-70—and yet have a surface with lint marks. If the lint marks are particularly severe, the piece is not worth as much as a coin free from such marks.

Centering

Centering is another determinant of value. Among modern coins, nearly all are well centered, but among early pieces, perfectly centered issues may be difficult to locate. For such series, well-centered coins are worth a premium.

Surface Coloration

For the connoisseur there are certain aesthetic values that contribute to a coin's worth, often significantly. If a piece possesses attractive light natural toning, as acquired over a long period of years, it may exhibit a rare beauty which merits an extra value.

Conversely, a coin with dull, spotted, dirty, or otherwise unpleasing surfaces usually sells at a discount, often a significant one. Among early copper coins, pieces with glossy surfaces are worth more than those with porous or granular surfaces.

Aesthetic Appeal

The aesthetic appeal of a coin is a quintessential consideration, but it cannot be defined easily. It is a combination of grade, quality of strike, quality of the planchet, and (especially) the quality of the lustre or toning.

Moreover, aesthetic appeal admits to differences of opinion. What I might think is a truly beautiful example may be considered less so by you, or vice versa. Aesthetic considerations are the reason a group of coins can all be graded in a specific numerical category and yet have vastly differing market values.

In a letter to the editor of *Coin World*, a West Coast numismatist told how he appraised a group of silver dollars, and of several pieces with precisely the same technical or numerical grade, his idea of market value ranged from $400 to $1,200!

Similarly, if I were to get together a group of specialists in early American large cents and were by some stroke of extraordinary luck able to acquire 20 cents of the year 1803, all of the same die variety, and all which we agree are, say, MS-60, I'm sure that the aesthetic considerations would vary from coin to coin and from observer to observer sufficiently that the most desirable coin in the lot from an aesthetic viewpoint would be valued at two or three times the figure of the least desirable.

Face or Intrinsic Value

The face or intrinsic value of a coin is another determinant of worth. The prices given to worn common-date $20 pieces, say those dated 1904, 1926, 1927, and 1928 (to pick several of the more plentiful dates) are apt to fluctuate with the rise and fall of the value of the gold bullion they contain. If gold bullion is worth, say, $360, then an EF-40 example of a 1904 double eagle might be worth $25 or so more than that (for purposes of illustration; actual values might vary).

If the value of gold bullion jumps to $700 per ounce, the value of the double eagle might jump to, say, $750 or $800. Stated differently, the coin is worth its bullion value, plus a *slight* numismatic premium. The same goes for various silver coins of the 20th century, worn pieces which are not rare. Liberty Walking half dollars in the 1940s and Franklin half dollars of common dates in Fine to Extremely Fine grades have values determined primarily by their silver content.

A separate niche of the coin investment market has been built up around coins with significant bullion values, and the worth of these fluctuates depending upon the metal market. Bid and ask prices are available for such things as bags of circulated silver half dollars, worn silver dollars, silver-content Jefferson nickels of the 1942 to 1945 years, and so on.

Certain other coins are apt to be worth just face value, current pocket change for example. The market value of a worn 1982 Jefferson nickel, 1959-D Lincoln cent, or 1986 quarter dollar is face value and nothing more. Years ago, when coins could be easily collected from circulation, a common saying was, "If I ever tire of coin collecting, I can always spend my collection!"

The Value of a Coin: Putting it All Together

We have seen that the value of a coin depends upon a number of factors acting in concert: rarity, popularity or demand, and grade, plus other ancillary factors such as quality of strike, planchet quality, centering, surface coloration, and aesthetic appeal. For certain other pieces the bullion value or face value may be a consideration as well.

None of these factors can stand alone. Here are some examples:

The rarest of coins, if in a miserable grade, is apt to be worth little. A rare 1793 Chain AMERI. large cent, worth thousands of dollars in Fine grade, is apt to be worth less than a couple hundred dollars if holed, gouged, or worn to the point of virtual smoothness.

A very rare coin in a very high grade can also be worth very little, if there is not much demand for it (witness the hypothetical streetcar token from Emporia, Kansas mentioned earlier).

A coin in a popular series and in very high grade can be worth very little if it is not rare—for example, a 1986 Roosevelt dime in MS-65 condition is worth face value and no more.

Put high rarity, great popularity, and high grade together, and you have a terrific formula. When all three come together in a high degree, a record price is apt to result! Thus, a famous rarity in a popular series, and in a high grade is apt to be the focus of attention for the entire numismatic community.

Take, for example, an MS-65 1808 quarter eagle. Here is a coin which is basically rare, which is in great demand due to its necessity for inclusion in type sets, and which is in extremely high grade. I suspect that if I were to offer one in an auction sale it would bring $200,000 or more!

Will Grading Interpretations Change Again?

While the interpretation of grading has changed in the past, I believe that from this point forward interpretations will change very little. The market has been through a transition, and it is a reasonable expectation that a coin certified as MS-65 by NGC, by PCGS, by ANACS, or by another qualified grading service will stand a good chance of being MS-65 a number of years down the line. Values may vary, depending on striking, planchet, and aesthetic considerations earlier noted, but the "technical grade" should remain fairly constant. At least I hope so.

At the same time, the rarity, or, more accurately, the *perceived* rarity, may change. It is often the case that study brings additional

Early United States Issues

The U.S. Mint in 1792

1792 half disme

1793 half cent

Three different types of 1793 one-cent pieces

pieces to light, and coins earlier believed to be Rarity-4 (on the Sheldon Scale) may now be Rarity-3, or a Rarity-8 coin may descend slightly to Rarity-7. In a relative sense, however, rarities tend to remain in the same order.

Coins can also increase in perceived rarity, as strange as this may seem. Such coins are called "sleepers." Often the rarity of a coin is overlooked, then when it is studied, the rarity becomes evident. In a series of articles in the *Rare Coin Review*, Andrew W. Pollock III pointed out sleepers in the field of half dimes, Barber coins, and other series—pieces which have nominal catalogue values but which appear on the market much less frequently in certain grades than catalogue values suggest.

A dramatic instance of increased rarity happened in the 1940s, when the Numismatic Gallery (Abe Kosoff and Abner Kreisberg) put up for sale an 1873-CC Liberty Seated dime without arrows at the date. Prior to handling the piece, numismatists believed the coin was rare, but they did not know how rare it was. After due research, it was determined that there was only one coin in existence! A scramble ensued at the auction, Dayton (Ohio) dealer Jim Kelly purchased it, and it later went into the Eliasberg Collection. Today, the issue remains unique.

The Case of an 1876-S Half Eagle

There is much yet to be discovered in numismatics concerning rarity. Many issues, particularly in higher grades of preservation, are much scarcer than catalogue values or printed information suggest. This is nowhere more evident than among early coins, especially those from about 1790 to 1890. In his studies on American gold coin auction records and appearances, David Akers uncovered much fascinating information which pointed out that certain coins listing for nominal catalogue values were extreme rarities in Uncirculated grade. Nowhere is this better pointed out than by a situation which happened in 1979 when I catalogued the Garrett Collection for The Johns Hopkins University. Lot 487, a half eagle, was described by me as follows:

"1876-S prooflike Brilliant Uncirculated, MS-65. 4,000 examples of the half eagle were minted at San Francisco this year, which makes it scarce in its own right. In this instance it happened that all specimens were released into circulation and received extensive use. This specimen is the single exception.

"Walter Breen comments that this piece is 'apparently unknown above Very Fine' grade and reinforces his opinion with the fact that even the F.C.C. Boyd specimen, as part of one of the finest collections ever formed, was well-worn. David Akers, who included the Garrett Collection in his survey (it is apparent Walter Breen examined only a portion of the Garrett Collection but not all of it by far; certainly not the 1876-S), uses the present Garrett coin as an illustration on page 236 of his *United States Gold Coins, An Analysis of Auction Records, Volume IV*, and notes, 'There is one gem Uncirculated example in The Johns Hopkins University Collection...and I have seen one other at the AU level.... Most known specimens are well worn, grading Very Fine or less, and I consider this to be one of the rarest and most underrated half eagles in any condition.'

"Whatever price this example brings will be a tribute to the scholarship of Walter Breen, David Akers, and the others who have studied the relative rarity of coins in recent years. A decade ago, the rarity of the 1876-S half eagle was largely unappreciated. A glance at the *Guide Book of United States Coins*, 1979 edition, shows an Uncirculated 1876-S valued at $275, making it by comparison *one of the least expensive issues of its era!*"

The coin brought $34,000!

Determining sleepers among early issues is a fertile field for research, and I assure you that time spent acquiring a numismatic library and studying various series will repay you with great dividends in this area. I have often "cherry-picked" the offerings of other sellers, buying $5,000 coins for $1,000 or less, simply by knowing which varieties were rare and which issues were scarcer in certain grades than the sellers realized. There's no reason you can't do the same. Others have.

Population Reports

In recent years, "population reports" issued by PCGS and NGC have provided useful information concerning the *relative* rarity of certain coins, especially in higher Mint State grades.

However, these ratings must be taken with a grain of salt. Recently, a leading dealer told me of an instance in which he owned an rare 1916-D Mercury dime and desired to have it certified as MS-65. Again and again he submitted it to a grading service, and again and again it came back as MS-63 or MS-64.

Finally, on the 26*th* submission, it was graded MS-65. He did not mention whether he told the grading service that he was repeatedly submitting the same coin, but if he did not, then the population report of that firm indicates 25 more specimens of Mint State 1916-D dimes than exist!

Further, as time goes on, more and more coins are certified or re-certified. A coin that is "rare" today in some such high grade, say MS-67, might not be rare, per the population reports, a year or two from now. Certainly, the number in existence of any given coin as listed in the population reports cannot diminish; it can only become larger—a fact overlooked by many investors in 1989, 1990, and 1991 who paid royal sums for coins in MS-66, MS-67, MS-68, and other lofty grades.

Popularity May Fluctuate

Popularity of a given series is apt to fluctuate. As noted earlier, Morgan silver dollars, now at the top of the list were not represented at all on Abe Kosoff's nationwide survey of favorite American series a few decades ago.

At one time in American numismatic history, medals of George Washington topped the popularity list. At another time the leader was the Buffalo nickel series.

Turn the calendar back to 1959 or 1960, and the most popular series was that of small cents; Lincoln cents and Indian cents. Today these are popular, but they are far from the position they held a quarter century ago.

Never in the history of numismatics has one series remained consistently popular and at the top of the list of collectors' favorites year after year. Popularity fluctuates, and because of this there are some great advantages. Later in the present book I shall discuss market cycles. A lot of money can be made by buying series which are out of favor at a given time, for prices are cheaper and there are apt to be many really great buys. Popular psychology is such that it is difficult to be a contrarian—but if you can swim against the current, you will reap many rewards!

Be aware of the influences of rarity, popularity, and other considerations, and study the given price of a coin at any particular time, and you can better evaluate its potential.

Pedigree

Before departing the subject of coin values and treading on new ground, let me mention one other consideration: pedigree. Form a nice collection over a period of years, and when the collection is sold, the collection as a whole may well attract great attention—thus imparting an extra "pedigree value" to your pieces. In instances of landmark collections, this value can be considerable.

There is no question that many collectors, dealers, and others bid liberally to acquire coins from the Garrett, Eliasberg, Brand, Norweb, and other famous collections which have crossed the auction block in recent decades. The Rothert, Champa, Getty, Fairfield, River Oaks, Einstein, Kosoff, Levine, Taylor, Bebee, Dreyfuss, Boyd, Brand, Ryder, Schenkel, and other notable cabinets sold by my firm have each attracted bidders who were desirous of acquiring a piece pictured in a specific auction catalogue or with an established prior record of ownership.

Undoubtedly, many collections now being formed today will become famous in the future and will have their own pedigree values. Often, the whole is worth more than the sum of its parts. When my firm sold coins from the Virgil Brand Collection in 1983 and 1984, they undoubtedly brought more money in many instances than the same pieces would have brought if simply scattered hither and yon over a series of miscellaneous offerings.

As I conclude the present chapter I cannot resist stating that the contents of this chapter formed a good part of the curriculum of my "All About Coins" course which I gave for the American Numismatic Association Summer Seminar for a number of years, a course which hundreds of students paid several hundred dollars each to attend!

Coin Market Cycles

A Pioneering Study

 In February 1964 in the *Empire Investors Report* I wrote the first article ever published on the subject of cycles in the rare coin market. Since then I have observed many cyclical performances of individual coin issues and series. Significantly, the entire coin market as a whole has never been in step so far as cycles are concerned. Each series marches to the beat of a different drummer, so to speak. When commemorative half dollars are active, perhaps Indian cents may be sluggish, Civil War tokens may be just beginning an intense interest, gold coins may be setting new records, and silver dollars may soften in price. Never has there been a market in which all series were "hot" at the same time, and never has there been a market in which all series slumped simultaneously.

The Anatomy of a Coin Cycle

The anatomy of a coin cycle can be traced. The following stages are typical of certain numismatic issues and serve to illustrate price movement. Coin "X" may be a commemorative, it may be a roll of coins, it may be a type coin, it may be a foreign Proof set, it may be one of many different coins, groups, or sets which have commanded the attention of collectors and investors during the past few decades. In general, *the more a series is dominated by investor (rather than collector) buying, the more susceptible it is to wide cyclical fluctuations.* To elaborate on this, I mention that 1794 large cents have never been subject to fluctuations, because the market consists nearly entirely, or perhaps absolutely, of dedicated collectors. By contrast, modern Proof sets and bank-wrapped rolls have fluctuated widely, for a large part of the market has consisted of investors.

I have divided a typical cycle into several stages. In actual practice the time span of each stage varies. Broad cycles encompassing many different series (but not all of numismatics, as noted) may encompass periods of five to 10 years. Cycles within individual coins are apt to be much shorter, with some cycles occurring in a matter of months or even weeks. Such factors as dealer promotions, the breadth of the market, availability of pieces, the quality of demand (whether from collectors primarily, from investors, or from a combination of both), and other considerations must be evaluated.

Stage I

The market for coin X is not particularly active. Some dealers price X for $120 each; some for $110. One dealer offers a group of 10 X for $990. At a convention, a sharp buyer (who knows that a dealer has had trouble selling his large holding of X) succeeds in buying 375 pieces of X for only $80 each. In various numismatic publications there are few, if any, dealers stating realistic buying prices for X. In other words, there just isn't much life to X at all!

Popular psychology being what it is, there isn't much support for X from anyone. A dealer is apt to say: "X is dead, so I'm not even interested in discussing buying any for stock." A collector might say: "Why should I bother collecting items like X? There doesn't seem to be much interest in them, and apparently they would be a poor investment—I don't see any buying ads, and the last dealer I talked to said that he could care less about X."

Stage II

Some alert persons note that X is selling for $100 to $120 and has been selling at that price for quite some time without any extensive market activity and without any increase in price. In fact, as time wears on, the price weakens as dealers give discounts and special deals to move unwanted quantities of X out of stock.

In the meantime item "Y," which is not as scarce as X, but which is in a currently popular field, sells for $250. Dealers are publishing many advertisements offering to buy Y; many of these are offering to pay close to the $250 retail price. Item Y is hard to buy in quantities, as most people owning Y are busy watching the price go up! Other investors who have been watching X stagnate price-wise decide that X is underpriced and start buying. Dealers are contacted by telephone, letter, and by personal visits in shops and at conventions, and by any other feasible means. The formerly unwanted supply of X is now dried up!

Stage III

Having bought all of the available X at $100 and $120, collectors and investors are now willing to pay $140 and $150, and say so in print and in voice. Dealers run "wanted to buy" advertisements for X offering $130 for all specimens submitted, knowing that a few dollars of profit awaits them for each X acquired. These "buy" advertisements prompt thousands of collectors, dealers, and other investors to start thinking about X. After all, why is X selling for a super-bargain $150 when Y, which is not as scarce, finds a ready market and a new high price of $300?

Stage IV

X becomes a hot item! Everyone is talking about X! Everyone wants to buy X! There are not enough Xs to go around! X is exciting! The price of X rises to $200, then to $250, then to $300. Meanwhile, many sell their supply of Y to raise money to buy X. Y drops in value to $180.

Stage V

Those who bought X at prices from $80 to $120 each find the $300 price very attractive. Some sell. Others hold out for still higher prices. The great activity in X has lessened somewhat as investors turn to other things. X advances to $305, then $310. Noting that the market is not rising as sharply as before, thousands of X are now sold by many different investors and speculators. The first ones to sell realize $300 to $310 each. Some of the later ones have to be satisfied with $270, and a few are able to get only $250. At the $250 point the supply and demand appear equal, and the price stabilizes—for a short time.

Stage VI

At the new $250 price very few people want to invest in X. It takes fortitude to buy in a falling market, and they have just seen the price of X fall from $310 down to $250. Other investors, who missed the opportunity to sell at a greater profit, are now willing to sell additional X for less than $250. The market is sluggish. X is available in quantity for just $220 each! If you are in the market for a large quantity you may be able to drive a hard bargain and buy some X for $190. The story is told of a large metropolitan convention at which an investor helped a dealer unload 243 pieces of X by offering him $180 each, an unheard of low price in the recent market. In other words, Stage VI brings us back to Stage I. The cycle is complete!

Be Aware of Cycles

The preceding illustration is typical of many past coin price movements, particularly those of recent decades. Each cycle seems to take place at a higher plateau. In the next cycle X may start out at $190 and may rise to a new high of $500 before settling back to, say, $350.

If you are aware of cycles you have an advantage which will permit you to buy "dead" coins and series at favorable prices and which will caution you to pass by "hot" coins until they settle in price somewhat. Right now in 1991 there are many coins, particularly those in higher Mint State and Proof grades, which are selling at half or less of what they were during the high point of their cycle a year or two ago.

The Coin World Almanac

A number of years ago the editors of the Coin World Almanac commissioned me to write an essay on coin investment for that publication. In subsequent issues—the fifth issue appeared in the summer of 1987—I have updated my earlier thoughts, and along the way I have discussed cycles in the United States coin market.

The Market in 1976

In the 1976 issue I said: "Right now gold coins are 'hot' and sell very well. At the same time, Indian cents are 'quiet' and there's no rush to buy them."

The Market in 1977

In the 1977 issue of the same publication, I reported: "Gold coins are now 'quiet' and Indian cents are more active! Perhaps in 1980 this situation will reverse itself again."

The Market in 1978

In 1978 I wrote the following: "Gold coins have indeed picked up in activity, particularly scarcer issues. Indian cents remain active as well. Perhaps a few years from now gold coins will become intensely active and Indian cents will become quiet once more."

The Market in 1984

After that, there was a lapse of several years before the next edition of the *Coin World Almanac* appeared. For the following issue, in 1984 I wrote this:

"I find that gold coins are 'quiet,' with very little activity among common or bullion-type issues, particularly in comparison with the activity of the recent past. Indian cents are neither active nor dormant but, instead, are somewhere in-between. Moving to other series, I note that colonial coins are very quiet. Large cents and half cents, never the scene of frenzied activity, are moderately active in keeping with interest by collectors. The same goes for Indian and Lincoln cents. United States 'type' coins are fairly quiet but seem to be stirring. These were the heroes of the 1979-1980 boom market. Commemoratives are fairly active at levels less than they were several years ago. Silver dollars are very active, down from 'extremely active' a few years ago, but still a lot of buying and selling is going on."

The Market in 1987

In an earlier edition of the present book (*High Profits From Rare Coin Investment*) I wrote the following in autumn 1987:

"The market for colonial and early American (pre-1792) coins is fairly active, much more than it was two or three years ago. A definite awakening has occurred in the field, and I suspect that strength will increase. The Frederick B. Taylor Collection, sold by Auctions by Bowers and Merena, Inc. in March 1987, saw many pieces sell for double or triple the pre-sale expectations. The Norweb Collection Part I, sold in October 1987, saw many record prices established for colonial and state issues.

"Half cents in the Norweb Collection 'went through the roof' and virtually every price record established earlier in the series was shattered, as specialists, dealers, investors, and others competed to buy specimens from this great American cabinet. Large cents are also active and several recent collections and other offerings have drawn strong bidding, again often far above pre-sale estimates.

"Although such series as colonials, half cents, and large cents are not popular with investment newsletter writers, they are indeed popular with collectors, and it is probably safe to say that a fine collection of early copper coins, if auctioned today, would do as well as any other series you can name—and probably better than many series. This is quite a reversal from the situation a few years ago.

"Lincoln and Indian cents are fairly quiet, but when quality pieces come on the market they receive good bids. The Norweb Collection Sale in October 1987 saw a world's record price established for a Proof 1864-L cent, which crossed the block at $47,300. This was more than double the price realization for a comparable specimen earlier!

"Two-cent and three-cent pieces are sluggish. Nickel five-cent pieces, sluggish until recent times, seem to be picking up in interest, with a lot of new attention being paid to them. Liz Arlin, who takes care of the Want List Department at Bowers and Merena Galleries, reported numerous want lists for Shield, Liberty, and Buffalo nickels, particularly for scarcer varieties, with more requests than there were coins to fill them—an indication of market strength to come.

"Type coins are active all across the board, from the 1790s onward. Activity seems to be most intense in grades from VF-20 through MS-63. MS-65 coins of very early dates, say pre 1860, are in strong demand, but relatively few pieces appear on the market. Certain MS-65 and Proof-65 pieces of later issues are considered to be high priced by many buyers, especially in view of the strong demand for these on the part of investors (which demand has pushed the price up). Modern series such as Mercury dimes, Standing Liberty quarters, Washington quarters, and Liberty Walking half dollars are all active.

"The market for silver dollars is mixed. A number of 'investment quality' coins, as popularized in certain newsletters, have dropped in value, and an MS-65 1881-S silver dollar, to cite one of the most actively traded issues, can now be purchased for less than half of its value at the height of its market activity in 1986. Many other common date Morgan dollars have likewise slackened in value. On the other hand, demand for key issues such as 1879-CC, 1881-CC, 1885-CC, New Orleans and San Francisco issues of the mid-1890s, the 1895 Proof, 1903-S, 1904-S, and other issues variously described as scarce or rare is very strong. Indeed, I believe that there are many Morgan dollar issues that are severely undervalued in comparison to the prices commanded by common pieces.

"Peace silver dollars for some reason have never caught the fancy of collectors and investors, even when Morgan dollars have been extremely active all across the board. The Peace dollar market is quiet, although for higher-grade coins such as MS-64 and MS-65, which for most issues dated from 1921 through 1928 are particularly elusive (less so for certain issues dated 1934-1935), there is a good market, but not broadly based. Grading is a particular consideration among Peace silver dollars. Although a coin can have a grade of MS-60, MS-65, or some other number, one piece in a given grade may have an aesthetic appeal far greater than another piece of an identical technical grade. So, some degree of discernment is necessary when purchasing these.

"Gold coins are very active, especially for popular 'type' issues as well as scarce dates. An exception is provided by bullion-type pieces such as AU half eagles, eagles, and double eagles of the late 19th and early 20th centuries. The interest in these has been transferred to a degree to the new (first marketed in 1986) $50 and fractional denomination bullion coins issued by the United States government.

"Among gold coins there are many outstanding sleepers, with the most fertile fields for these being scarce date and mintmark varieties pre 1880, especially in such series as $5, $10, and $20, and in grades from AU-50 upward. There are numerous pieces listed in A *Guide Book of United States Coins* at "type" prices, which are so rare that many months, or even many years may elapse between offerings! Similarly, among later issues, particularly $2.50 issues 1908-1929, $5 issues of the same span, $10 pieces 1907-1920, and $20 pieces of the With Motto style 1908-1916, there are many sleepers in higher grades such as MS-63 and MS-65. The tightening of grading interpretations, in effect in the market in recent times, has yet to be analyzed in detail, and I firmly believe that many issues now considered to be 'common' will emerge as being quite rare, once the actual number of available MS-65 coins (for example) is studied.

"Commemorative silver and gold coins are active, not quite as active as they were last year, but still sufficiently so that a strong market exists. Particularly in demand are MS-63 and MS-64 coins, although there is a market for MS-65 coins on the part of those who can afford them—primarily investors.

"Paper money is in the doldrums, as it has been for several years. Despite optimistic reports in *The Currency Dealer Newsletter* and other places, I have yet to see anything which vaguely resembles the activity currency enjoyed a decade ago. Clearly in the field of currency the buyer can acquire many excellent values.

"As these words are being written in November 1987, the world financial market has sustained a sharp drop, with the 508-point loss in the Dow-Jones Industrial Averages on October 19, 1987, being far and away the stiffest loss ever registered by this index. The long-term effects of this shakeout have yet to be assessed, and the numismatic market, as well as the American financial market in general, will await happenings in 1988. The president of the New York Stock Exchange, interviewed on television in late October, stated that he had no idea at the time whether stocks would be rising or falling, but that he was praying they would rise. Obviously, if the president of the New York Stock Exchange can't make a prediction, it would be foolish for someone such as myself, a professional numismatist, to make any guesses as to what will happen in the securities field. However, in the past when the stock market has taken its lumps, this has often had an opposite effect on the coin market.

"Each day, each week, each month, untold millions of dollars come onto the market from earnings, dividends, retirement funds, and the like, and this money has to be spent. I feel that it will be at least a year or two, possibly longer, until the so-called 'man in the street' regains confidence in the stock market. In the meantime, alternative investments will be explored. Among such alternative investments are money in savings accounts, real estate, and 'tangibles.' In the latter category, coins have been attractive for years, and I expect that their attractiveness will increase. I am not an advocate of large numbers of unknowledgeable buyers coming into the coin market to buy anything that is round and shiny, but this will probably occur whether or not I like it, and when it does, it will infuse a certain amount of strength to the coin market.

"This strength will result from two factors. First, the specific issues which appeal to investors, such as certified silver dollars, gold coins, and the like, will undoubtedly experience a market resurgence. Second, this market resurgence will bring an element of prosperity to rare coin dealers. Time and time again, when dealers are doing well, they seek to spend their own funds not on 'investment-type' common coins, but, instead, on scarce and rare pieces. I remember vividly that during the height of an earlier investment market in 1979-1980, a number of major buyers at the Garrett Collection Sale bought rarities with profits earned on coin investment sales. So, the market continues, as do prices cycles of individual series."

The Market in Spring 1990

My investment predictions of autumn 1987 came true more quickly and more vividly than I could have ever imagined! During 1989, interest in rare coins as an investment increased dramatically. "Large numbers of unknowledgeable buyers" indeed came into the market and bought anything that was round and shiny. Telemarketing was the name of the game, and boiler-shop operations had a field day selling coins for prices that informed collectors would have found to have been ridiculous. Many of these operations sold perfectly nice certified coins, but often they were of very common issues. The Salomon Brothers index (which, as I mentioned earlier, consists of *rare* coins) was used as a selling tool, and numerous other misrepresentations occurred.

This great and unprecedented demand for common coins in high grades drove many issues to new high levels. Collectors sat on the sidelines as they saw common and semi-scarce Morgan and Peace dollars, gold and silver commemoratives, 19th- and 20th-century "type" coins, and other issues ascend to heights which seemed to be very unreasonable. Predictions became self-fulfilling, and common coins rose even higher in price. Wall Street money was said to be interested, and this caused still more increases.

As interest in coins approached the epidemic stage, just about every dealer in existence was approached by eager buyers, no matter whether he or she was an investment specialist. Dealers who were deep in the investment market turned to old-time dealers and auction sales as a source of material, and in an era of good feeling nearly all prices of MS-65 and Proof-65 coins rose. Coins in higher grades such as MS-66, MS-67, and MS-68 defied logic even further. Professionals who had been in business for a decade or two scratched their heads in amazement.

Then the music stopped. Coins were no longer the darling of investors or of Wall Street. At the new high prices few collectors were interested in buying. Few new investors appeared, thus there was no market at inflated levels for common-date MS-65 Morgan dollars and other such "investment quality" goods. Prices plummeted. (Few if any readers of earlier editions of the present book were surprised, however.)

The Market in 1991

In the summer of 1991 the numismatic fort is back in the control of numismatists, and Wall Street investors have been vanquished, leaving behind them a trail of tears, laments that coin investment wasn't what it was cracked up to be, etc. Amid all of this I have seen no introspection, no self-analysis, no realization on the part of outside investors that what they were buying were common coins in high grades.

Readers of the very first edition of this book in 1974 saw this comment: "To buy common coins with the hope they will magically become rare is an exercise in futility." This philosophy hasn't changed, and in the meantime I have seen many people sustain great losses because they ignored it. At least when disillusioned Wall Streeters sell their coins (probably for losses) they won't have to wonder what to do with the books in their numismatic libraries, for they probably don't have any.

In the meantime the market for collector-oriented coins such as colonial coins, half cents, large cents, etc., in lower Mint State grades and in circulated grades has fared quite well, all things considered. I view the present market as one laden with many opportunities, although there may still be some adjustments to be made in the prices of MS-65 and better coins and Proof-65 and better coins. Especially do I feel that certain MS-66, MS-67, and

MS-68 coins are overpriced, for there is little *collector* demand for coins in these grades at high prices.

I was one of the first to suggest in print that all MS-65 coins (for example) are not created equal, no matter what service certified them. I pointed out, and continue to emphasize, that numerical grading is *only one* aspect determining a coin's value (refer to my earlier chapters on the subject). Now that sight-unseen trading has just about collapsed, I feel vindicated, for I bore quite a bit of criticism a few years ago when I dared suggest that slabs were not equal to the Second Coming.

Today in 1991 there are many fine opportunities to build a fine collection of coins, and at prices which in most instances are no higher than you would have paid a year or two or three ago, and which, in some instances, are a lot less. Elsewhere in this book I give some specific recommendations.

The Coin World Market Index

Over a period of years, Keith Zaner, of *Coin World*, has built a broad-based index of 16,576 coins distributed over certain Mint State categories, known as the Coin World Market Index, using the benchmarks of MS-60, MS-63, and MS-65.

In each instance December 1983 equalled 100.[1]

Selected excerpts from the index are quoted herewith:

◆MS-60 Index:

December 1983: 100.00

December 1984: 99.76

December 1985: 108.32

December 1986: 102.75

December 1987: 99.51

December 1988: 101.83

December 1989: 110.38

December 1990: 110.59

June 1991 (latest data, also historic high): 115.60

---

[1] Figures are from *Coin World*, July 17, 1991, page 1 and continuations.

◆MS-63 Index:

December 1983: 100.00

December 1984: 96.46

December 1985: 114.43

December 1986: 114.63

December 1987: 110.34

December 1988: 116.19

May 1989 (historic high) 165.30

December 1989: 141.19

December 1990: 106.38

June 1991 (latest data): 117.00

◆MS-65 Index:

December 1983: 100.00

December 1984: 106.13

December 1985: 140.42

December 1986: 133.61

December 1987: 151.31

December 1988: 191.79

December 1989: 287.12

March 1990 (historic high) 324.95

December 1990: 228.83

June 1991 (latest data): 253.16

Analysis (by Q.D.B.): During the past eight years, MS-60 and MS-63 coins have remained at about the same price levels. MS-65 coins increased sharply in value, peaking in March 1990, and since subsiding to 78% of the high price.

As noted, this is a broad-based index, perhaps comparable to the Standard & Poor 500-Stock Composite Index in the securities market. Although I haven't analyzed the individual entries in the Coin World Market Index, I suspect that common-date Morgan dollars, commemoratives, and other popular series in MS-65 grade went up more than the general index for MS-65 and have fallen farther since. For example, the common 1881-S Morgan dollar, which was quoted in the $700 to $800 range in 1986 (the top of its particular market) now can be bought for less than 25% of that range.

I have never advocated buying everything across the board in the coin market, any more than a conscientious securities advisor would recommend that you buy one each of the stocks listed on the New York Stock Exchange or in the NASDAQ quotes. However, like the S&P stock index, the broad-based Coin World Market Index is quite interesting and is an indicator of the market in general.

The *Numismatic News* Coin Market Index

Beginning with the issue of July 18, 1981, Bob Wilhite of the *Numismatic News* staff has tracked a group of coins, not specified, but including a "broad base" with "heavily traded issues."[1] Key points in the index are as follows:

Opening figure, July 18, 1981: 5040

Historic low, September 11, 1982: 3540

Historic high, June 20, 1989: 10,190

Closing figure, July 23, 1991: 5832

Editorial comments in *Numismatic News* included the following: "In the long rum the market is up from 10 years ago. The [figures show] that prior to 1988 the Coin Market Index rested below the 5000 mark for most of the previous seven years. Even with the large market downturn in 1990, the index still stands as of July 23, 1991, at 5832, some 792 points above its resting point on July 18, 1981.

"When and if the Coin Market Index will ever again break the 10,000 mark is a question of time. Market cycles are a well-known phenomenon within the world of rare and not-so-rare coins."

The Long-Term Outlook

For the coin investor with a long-term outlook, cycles provide the opportunity to buy low and sell high, a classic advantage. If you are contemplating building a specialized series, I recommend

[1] Information is from *Numismatic News*, July 23, 1991, pp. 1 and 8.

picking a specific area which is slow, not one which is at or near its peak. A collector of coins by design types will find that the importance of cycles is minimized, for by acquiring pieces over a broad spectrum of American numismatics, the market activity differences among individual series cancel themselves. Instead, the value of a type set tends to move with the coin market as a whole—historically upward.

The reader wanting to study coin cycles has but to review past literature and price lists to determine numerous trends. Commemorative half dollars have gone through a number of well-defined cycles over the years. United States gold coins have likewise felt the effect of cycles, with a great increase in interest and value taking place during the years 1973 to 1974, followed by a slump in 1975 to 1976, a gathering of interest in 1977 and 1978, new high price levels in 1979-1980, followed by a slump, then a boom which peaked in early 1990, after which prices dropped. Now, the current commemorative market of 1991 shows great strength for scarce and rare pieces as well as issues in grades such as MS-63 and MS-64.

During the 1940s, 1950s, and 1960s rolls and Proof sets underwent many cycles. Numerous other examples can be cited.

Answers to
Coin Investment Questions

 In the course of advising many collectors and collector-investors over the years my staff and I have answered just about every type of question imaginable. Throughout this book I have endeavored to answer in a direct way the most significant of these. The present chapter is a catchall and includes some topics not specifically treated elsewhere.

Investment Objectives

QUESTION: What are typical coin investment objectives? Does one's age or career position matter?

ANSWER: Coins are a mid- to long-term investment and do not produce income. Thus, coins should be considered from the aspect of capital appreciation, not as a source to pay living or everyday expenses.

At any given time the percentage of assets you may wish to put in coins depends upon your comfort level. Many conservative investors have placed 10% to 25% of their discretionary investment funds into building a coin collection. This minimizes the risk. On the other hand, I have seen many people invest all or nearly all of their discretionary funds into numismatics; this is particularly true of people who have studied this situation carefully and who are sure of themselves.

Historically, selected *rare* coins have done superbly well as a long-term investment, as the now-discontinued Salomon Brothers study indicated. However, my recommendation is that even if you are an ardent numismatist, I would set some funds aside elsewhere for instant use if needed. Although I know some other professionals will take issue with me, I have never been an advocate of buying coins on "margin" or making leveraged purchases. If an important opportunity comes up to acquire a rarity, borrowing to pay for it may be a good idea, for the next time it comes around it may cost you significantly more, or perhaps a purchase opportunity will not recur for a long time. However, for everyday purchases of coins for your collection, I recommend that these be made from discretionary income, not from borrowing. However, in the case of the Salomon Brothers survey period, the price appreciation of coins cited there has been far above the interest rates on money, thus anyone borrowing from a bank and investing in coins during the period indicated, would have done well (without consideration of the liquidation or selling cost).

I recommend that at any given age level the prospective coin buyer have certain liquid assets (for example, money in a savings account or money market fund) to defend against an emergency. As cash investments are hardly the way to accumulate wealth, my own feeling is that other funds should be invested in areas with capital appreciation potential, a fine coin collection being a possibility. Such well-known economists as Howard Ruff, Eliot Janeway, James Blanchard, and John Kamin have recommended coins as an investment.

Here are my thoughts concerning age levels:

10 TO 20 YEARS OF AGE: While it may seem facetious to include youngsters in a discussion of coin investment, time and time again I have seen many high school students collect coins and invest in them. If anything, people in this age bracket have a fresh-faced enthusiasm for numismatics unequalled by their elders. Perhaps their minds are not cluttered with as many things! From a legal viewpoint, any coin investment should be made through a parent or guardian. However, it has been my experience that most "investment" at this level consists of building collections of series of interest—Jefferson nickels, Kennedy halves, modern commemoratives, and the like. My recommendation is to concentrate on learning about coins and collecting what you enjoy.

20 TO 30 YEARS OF AGE: These are career-building years; a time perhaps for marriage, building a family, and buying a home. I recommend intense concentration on numismatic education (which is quite inexpensive) while, at the same time, building a collection of interest. By starting one or more collecting areas, and by studying the areas in advance to determine what issues are available and for what prices, you should be able to purchase

wisely. Time is on your side, and you have an ample opportunity to build a numismatic treasure.

30 TO 40 YEARS OF AGE: For many, these are the years of career success. Income often outpaces living expenses, and amounts of extra money become available for discretionary investment. Again I recommend that you build a fine collection—perhaps in some of the more difficult and expensive series such as early United States coins by design types, scarce gold, and the like. There is no limit to the possibilities.

40 TO 50 YEARS OF AGE: These, too, are years of success. Perhaps more so than any other time, you will have the enthusiasm of youth and growth combined—I hope—with a feeling of career achievement, success, and security. And yet, retirement is still sufficiently distant that it is almost an abstract concept. These are excellent years for building definitive collections in areas which interest you. It is probably correct to say that the majority of important numismatic collections I have seen formed in recent decades have been started by people in this age bracket.

50 TO 60 YEARS OF AGE: Success in life is yours, I hope, and you may be able to afford the best. Continue building a fine collection. In the past, many truly great numismatic holdings have been gathered by buyers in this age range. A survey of American Numismatic Association members shows that many are aged in or about their 50s and 60s.[1]

60 TO 70 YEARS: If you have been collecting for decades, these may be the "harvest years," the time to cash in. On the other hand, if you are involved in numismatics, there is no reason not to continue adding to your collection. One key to longevity is to continue to participate in a hobby or something of great personal interest. "Retirement has killed more people than hard work ever did," is a saying which has some merit. Too often in retirement, oldsters have little to stimulate them. Coins can be an intellectually stimulating pursuit, and for this reason alone they are desirable. Some estate planning is in order as you build your collection, to insure that your heirs will handle the collection properly. I recommend that you give specific directions in your will that your coins be handled by a specific firm of your choice, preferably at auction. If a large and reputable firm is selected, your coins will be presented to a wide spectrum of bidders.

---

[1] This is not viewed as a desirable situation by the ANA, and in recent times effort has been expended to increase the appeal of coin collecting to younger citizens through the Young Numismatists group within the ANA.

70 OR OLDER: Once I received a letter from an 81-year-old man who inquired about coins as a *long-term* investment. Perhaps his optimism has carried him to the 100-year mark by now! Enjoy your collection, add to it as you see fit. Again, if you don't plan to sell your collection during your lifetime, make specific estate plans, selecting in advance the procedure by which your coins will be sold and by whom. (Actually, it is never too early to make such plans.)

Sources for Advice

QUESTION: What are the best sources for coin advice?

ANSWER: First of all, avoid anyone except a *professional numismatist*. Anyone giving you advice should have years of experience in buying and selling rare coins and also should have a basic grounding in economic theory. I suggest that you discuss your objectives in correspondence or conversations with several respected rare coin dealers, and then pick one or two who seem to please you the most (by giving you the most logical advice, not necessarily the most rosy forecasts).

Your best single source for advice is a numismatic library. By building one and consulting it you can sample the writings and opinions of many different people.

Especially important advice: Join the American Numismatic Association and invest in subscriptions to *Coin World*, *Numismatic News*, *Coins* magazine, and *COINage* magazine, for a wealth of general information. For information specific to the coin market and investment, add *The Coin Dealer Newsletter* and the *Certified Coin Dealer Newsletter* to your subscription list.

Quantity as a Factor

QUESTION: What factor does quantity play in coin investment? Is it better to have a single $50,000 coin, or 10 $5,000 coins, 100 $50 coins, or a vast quantity of $5 coins?

ANSWER: There is no definite right answer to this. A charting of values over a period of years reveals that great rarities which cost thousands of dollars in the 1950s have soared in value since then—as have pieces which cost just a few dollars at that time. My answer to this question is that it depends upon the amount of money you have to spend. If you want to invest $100 per month in

Raymond N. Merena, president of Bowers and Merena Galleries, Inc.

your collection, then it would be foolish to save up your money for two years to own just a single coin, a rarity costing $2,400. Recall my earlier commentary about the gentleman who wanted to have just one coin in his collection, an 1838-O half dollar worth the best part of $100,000!

Instead, you would undoubtedly experience much more satisfaction of ownership if you were to have a nice collection of coins valued from $25 to several hundred dollars per item. If, after several years of collecting, you wanted to buy a $1,000 rarity, then would be the time to save up for it or purchase it in installments.

If you have $1,000 per month to spend on your coin investment, then a $2,400 coin would be a logical thing to own—assuming, of course, that it meets your other requirements as well.

Coin Price and Marketability

QUESTION: Does the price of a coin affect its marketability?

ANSWER: This is a question I am often asked. Some buyers are worried that expensive coins might not find a ready sale when they are put on the market. This fear is unfounded, and here is the reason:

The price of a coin is usually based upon its rarity and the demand for it. As the coin market is an active one, prices have equated themselves with supply and demand. Thus, an 1838-O half dollar (to cite a previous example) is an extremely salable item, for only a dozen or so specimens are known of this rarity. In fact, only 20 were originally coined!

Of course, the number of people desiring 1838-O half dollars is also small—but the number of collectors desiring one, even taking the price into consideration, has always been more than the available supply. So, despite the ups and downs of certain segments of the coin market, the 1838-O has always been a "blue chip." A single specimen, among several that I have owned, illustrates the price movement of this famous rarity. In April 27, 1962, I purchased for $9,500 the example offered by Stack's in the sale of the R.E. Cox, Jr. Collection. I subsequently resold the coin to a prominent eastern numismatist. Today the coin would be worth approximately 10 times the price. The 1838-O half dollar has always been a famous American coin. *There has never been a period in American numismatic history in which it was not in demand*—in good economic conditions and in bad. However, prices have tended to vary. Over the long term the trend has been upward. An 1838-O half dollar was worth more in 1960 than it was in 1950. It was worth more in 1970, than it was in 1960, and so on. Probably 10 and 20 years from now it will be worth far more than it is now.

Prime American rarities can perhaps be likened to Rembrandt paintings in the art field. They are expensive to be sure, but when a choice one comes on the market it creates a lot of excitement, and often a new price record is set! Apart from the desirability a rarity may have on its own, it is important to remember that when great collections are marketed, all eyes are riveted on the classics. Thus, a collection of large cents, but without specimens of 1793, 1799, and 1804 (the three rarest dates), would not be particularly exciting, even if the remaining coins were in high condition. My auction sales of the Fairfield, Garrett, Eliasberg, Brand, Norweb, and numerous other collections attracted a lot of attention because of the stellar rarities they contained. Often the attention given to a rarity will catch other coins in the same net, elevating the realization for these as well—obviously a beneficial situation for the seller.

Returning to the general subject of coin price and marketability, the higher in price the coin becomes, the fewer in number are the collectors who can afford it. Obviously, there are more buyers for a $100 coin than for a $1,000 coin. Likewise, there are more buyers for a $10,000 coin than for a $100,000 coin. Offsetting this is the often-quoted observation that "you only need two buyers." In an auction sale you need a successful bidder and an underbidder. When I sold the Uncirculated 1787 Brasher doubloon for $725,000 for The Johns Hopkins University in our auction of the Garrett Collection, all I needed was an underbidder who bid the piece up to $700,000, and the successful bidder, who carried it away for $725,000. In fact, there were a dozen or more hands in the air during the early stages of the bidding—but, really, only two bidders were needed!

My advice concerning rarities is that they are beautiful and thrilling to own. As noted, I would not recommend that you own a $100,000 rarity and no other coins. However, if your finances can accommodate this and there is a space for it in a collection you are forming, it is great to have a $100,000 rarity as part of a series comprising many other coins. Indeed, the rarity might well be the centerpiece, the coin you enjoy most—and the one which creates the most attention when your collection is sold.

How High Can Prices Go?

QUESTION: How high is high? How far can coin prices go?

ANSWER: The future is unknown, of course, no one can predict it with accuracy. However, on a comparative basis it can be said with certainty that the prices of many coin issues have a long way to go in relation to prices of rarities in other fields. Among the highest prices United States coins have ever been sold for at auction, with seven of the top eight world record prices being held by my firm, are the previously noted 1787 Brasher doubloon for $725,000, the 1822 $5 for $687,500, the 1870-S $3 for $687,500, a 1861 Paquet $20 for $660,000, an 1851 Augustus Humbert octagonal $50 Proof at $500,000, and a pattern 1907 $20 gold piece for $475,000.

As spectacular as these prices are in the numismatic field, they pale in significance to other collecting fields. In January 1985, Sotheby's sold an antique American chair for $2.75 million. A rare stamp was sold by another firm for $935,000. In 1987, one painting by Van Gogh sold for $39 million and, later, another brought $54 million at auction! In 1990 *Au Moulin de la Galette*, by Renoir, crossed the block at $78.1 million, and *Portrait of Dr. Gachet*, by Van Gogh, realized a staggering $82.5 million.

In our sister field of philatelics, the 1918 24-cent air mail stamp with an inverted airplane, a stamp of which 100 specimens were specifically distributed to collectors, has fetched in the $200,000 range at auction, although the current value is more like $75,000 to $100,000. At current market prices it is possible to buy Proof quarter eagles and eagles from the 1860s and 1870s, coins of which fewer than two dozen specimens exist, for in the range of $10,000 to $25,000.

If a 1918 24-cent invert air mail stamp is worth $100,000, and 100 are in the hands of collectors, then perhaps the 1838-O half dollar, of which about a dozen are known to exist, should by comparison be worth in the range of $1 million!

The $82.5 *Portrait of Dr. Gachet* painting sold for more than the theoretical total combined market value of all known specimens of such major coin rarities as the 1804 $1 (15 known), 1787 Brasher doubloon (seven known), 1894-S 10¢ (c. 12 known), 1822 $5 (one in private hands), 1870-S (one known), plus the values of dozens of other rarities added! Are coin rarities overpriced? You be the judge!

Of course, the majority of coins you will confront will not be major rarities. What about the typical coins needed to build a type set of United States designs, or scarce mintmark varieties among Liberty Walking half dollars, or key issue Morgan dollars, or scarce gold coins? As noted earlier, at any given time in the market these seem to the observer to be "fully priced." Back in the 1950s, collectors considered them to be "fully priced," but history shows they multiplied in value many times since then. I'm reminded of a sign I once saw in front of a Downey, California real estate agency. It showed a bearded old man hobbling along with a cane, with a caption that went something like this: "The *young* man who is still waiting for real estate prices to come down."

With an inflationary worldwide economy, with increasing demand for coins on the part of collectors, and with a heightened appreciation of collectibles in general, plus numerous other factors, the outlook for the hobby seems bright indeed. I fully expect anyone reading this present volume a decade or two from now will marvel at the many rarities that could have been purchased in the present market!

Rare Coins vs. Common Coins

QUESTION: The average investor will not have an opportunity to own great rarities such as the 1894-S dime, 1838-O half dollar, 1804 silver dollar, 1913 Liberty Head nickel, and other classics. If one cannot own great rarities, then should a collector concentrate on just owning common coins of low value? Or is there a happy medium?

ANSWER: I repeat one of my favorite sayings, an aphorism which I conceived in the 1950s and included in the first edition of this book in 1974, a philosophy which has never been challenged: *The coin that is common today will be common in the foreseeable future.* A common coin by very definition is common and is not rare! To buy common coins with the hope they will magically become rare is an exercise in futility. This simple observation is overlooked by many people who buy coins as an investment. This is so important that I suggest you underline it in your copy of this book!

Untold millions of dollars have been expended by people who prefer quantity to quality. This situation is not unique to coins; it exists in stamps as well. In the field of philatelics countless misguided souls religiously "invest" in sheets of new postage stamps as they are issued. The sad truth of the matter is that one can purchase from any stamp dealer sheets of stamps that are 10 to 30 years old, and pay only face value for them! Often such sheets are sold for less than face value, for the post office doesn't want them back, and few people have use for quantities of denominations that are currently obsolete. The investment potential, or lack of it, needs no further explanation. Thus it goes with the hoarding of modern coins issued by the untold millions.

Let me recite two experiences. The first concerns a gentleman who lived in the western part of Pennsylvania. For many years he purchased coins, always looking for bargains, and preferring quantity to quality. Deciding to liquidate his holdings, he telephoned our offices and told us about what he had—coins which he felt might be worth the best part of $500,000. Our representative visited him, and upon inspection found he had hundreds of pounds of circulated Mercury dimes, Franklin half dollars, Liberty Walking half dollars, and the like, of common dates, primarily worth bullion or meltdown value. We weren't interested in the group and referred him elsewhere. Eventually, the coins were sold for a tiny fraction of the sum he had hoped for.

The second story involves a gentleman who lived near Philadelphia. For a period of many years he acquired Proof coins dated from 1858 through 1916, carefully selecting each for quality. His total investment was something on the order of $75,000. Upon resale about 20 years later, he cashed in for $600,000. Instead of having hundreds of pounds of coins, his complete collection fit neatly in an attaché case. Today, the same collection would be worth several million dollars.

In my opinion, the best path is to purchase coins which have a *present* scarcity and value—either realized or unrealized by the marketplace.

To be desirable for investment purposes (as part of a collection) a coin does not have to be rare or even extremely scarce. It can be moderately scarce and still do quite well. Scarceness and rarity are relative. Consider the 1917 Type I Standing Liberty quarter issued by the Philadelphia Mint. This particular piece is in great demand for type sets—to illustrate a design which was made in only two years; 1916 and 1917. The mintage for the 1917 Type I was fairly large; 8,792,000 pieces. However, 1917 Type I quarters were issued during an era when coin collecting was in its infancy. Few people bothered to save these quarters. Although no figures are known, probably all but a few thousand went into circulation and became worn as they passed from hand to hand. If we assume that just a few thousand Mint State coins are known today, then the pieces are fairly scarce when you consider that there are perhaps several hundred thousand collectors desiring to assemble type sets of 20th-century United States coins—and that each will need a Standing Liberty quarter of the 1916-1917 design. Even when one considers that many collectors will be satisfied with a coin in worn grade, the investment possibilities of an Uncirculated 1917 Type I quarter remain obvious. In 1963 I wrote "the 1917 issue sells well for $22.50 to $25 [in Uncirculated grade]. I believe this price is a strongly based one and that it will continue to advance." Today, the same coin could be sold for over $1,000!

By building a collection, you will necessarily accumulate some common pieces along with scarce and rare ones. However, the common pieces will cost less, thus by the mathematical arrangement known in the stock market as "dollar averaging," most of your investment will be concentrated in the scarce and rare pieces—which is as it should be. However, if you collect Washington quarters, for example, you will want to own *all* of the issues—including low-value pieces of current times. However, these later pieces will cost virtually nothing, so you don't have to think twice about them.

Let me repeat: when you buy coins, concentrate on those of proven scarcity or rarity. To buy common coins and hope they will magically become rare is a fool's errand. And yet, common coins provide the basis for many careless "investment recommendations," simply because common coins are very easy for telemarketers to buy and promote. Investors are often a "dumping ground" for common silver dollars, rolls of later coins, and other plentiful coins. Be careful, and think for yourself!

Expansion of the Coin Market

QUESTION: What will make the price of coins rise above today's levels?

ANSWER: Of course, this is basic economics, but if the number of collectors increases, then the demand for rare coins will also increase. Now the question becomes: will the number of collectors increase?

This seems quite likely. The average citizen is working an ever-shorter week. More and more time is being directed toward leisure activities. Coin collecting is an ideal leisure activity. It can be conducted in privacy, does not require a large amount of space (a fine collection can be assembled by an apartment dweller, for instance), does not require any undue consumption of gas or electricity, can be conveniently and cheaply stored, often is immune from property taxes, and so on. As leisure time activities increase, coin collecting will surely increase also. An increase in the number of collectors will bring an even greater demand.

Then there is the international expansion of the market to consider. Other countries are developing large numbers of collectors. As the "affluent society" spreads throughout the world there will be more and more attention paid to pursuits such as coin collecting. This is presently taking place in a number of overseas countries. Japanese collectors and dealers are an important factor in the American market and have been for several years. England, which had only four major dealers and just a few thousand collectors in the early 1960s (when I used to spend a lot of time there), now has dozens of dealers and tens of thousands of collectors. Germany has many enthusiastic collectors who are important factors in the market. Italy, France, Switzerland, Denmark, Norway, Sweden, and other countries have been bidding ever-increasing prices for their own coins as well as for coins of other countries. Max Humbert, chief executive officer of Paramount International Coin Corporation, told me that certain limited-edition modern coins marketed by his firm sold better in West Germany than in any other country on earth.

It makes sense for other buyers around the world to desire American coins—just as American collectors for years have avidly assembled sets of crowns, gold coins, patterns, and other desirable issues of foreign states. Coin collecting, long an international hobby from the viewpoint of the variety of coins collected, is now becoming an international hobby from the viewpoint of collectors collecting them.

Then there is the important consideration of monetary inflation. In 1986, John Jay Ford, Jr. sent me a study of inflation in America, and by using these figures I was able to correlate price jumps in the coin market with increases in the inflation rate. In recent years, the purchasing power of the American dollar has depreciated severely, not only in our own country but even more so in terms of international commerce. If this continues, then the thought of paying $1,000 or $5,000 won't seem to be very important.

It wasn't long ago that $200, for instance, would have been a "big" price for an Uncirculated 1796 quarter. I mention this particular coin for I remember that dealer Aubrey Bebee showed me a 1796 quarter with a prooflike surface at the American Numismatic Association convention held in Omaha in 1955. He stated he had paid $200 for it, a "staggering price" at the time. Today, it seems absurdly cheap. In 1974 I sold a comparable piece for $18,500 at auction, and today the same coin would undoubtedly bring in the $100,000 range. I don't mean to suggest that the average coin purchased for $200 today will be worth $100,000 35 years or so from now, for I don't think it will be. On the other hand, it certainly is reasonable to expect many of today's $200 coins to multiply in value several times. Come to think of it, if Aubrey Bebee had asked me in 1955 if I thought the 1796 quarter would be worth $100,000 by 1991, I would have stated that under no condition would this ever happen! Coin investment returns in recent decades have been simply amazing. Sometimes I think I am far too conservative in my outlook!

What Grades of Coins Should I Buy?

QUESTION: What grades should I buy? Is it better to buy, for instance, 100 coins in Good-4 condition or 100 in MS-65 grade for the same price?

ANSWER: From an investment viewpoint all grades of coins have done well. Scarcer coins in lower grades such as Good-4 and Very Good-8 have been excellent investments over the years, as have been Mint State and Proof pieces. However, Mint State and Proof coins and other high-grade issues (such as Fine to Very Fine or better for certain 19th-century and earlier examples) have been in stronger demand and are scarcer than lower-grade pieces, thus the dealer's margin of profit is less, representing more solid value for you.

Take as a random example an Mint State coin which sells for $500. A dealer might well pay $400 to buy the coin for stock, giving him a profit of 25%. It is often the higher-grade pieces that turn over the fastest in a dealer's stock, so he's willing to take a smaller margin of profit for them. On some high-grade items the profit margin may be as low as 5% to 10%.

On the other hand, if a dealer were to have 10 coins in stock, all of the same variety, that were priced at $5 each, he may want to pay only $2 or $3 per coin to buy such pieces for stock, as more handling per item is involved. I'm assuming that the latter are in worn grade. From an investment viewpoint, I would rather have one Uncirculated $500 coin than 100 well-worn $5 coins. There is no right or wrong answer to this—it is more a matter of personal preference. It has been said by many others that collectors should "buy the best grade they can afford." Generally I agree with this advice.

When the first edition of this book appeared in 1974 I recommended that Uncirculated (Mint State) and Proof pieces represented the best value for one's money. Since that time the market has become quite heavily investment-oriented, and thousands of people have heeded my advice (and the suggestions of others) and have purchased pieces in higher grades. Now, Uncirculated and Proof coins are further divided into numerous grading categories unlike the situation in 1974, thus a buyer of Morgan dollars is confronted with new choices. Is MS-60 better than MS-63? What about MS-65? Tell me about MS-64, won't you? And so on. Then there is MS-70, the "Perfect Uncirculated" grade—largely a theoretical situation, for in practice such coins do not seem to exist—except for modern Proofs and pieces minted in recent times.

In reality there are few if any perfect regular issue United States coins made prior to the 1930s, simply because business strikes of these issues were produced on high-speed presses, were dumped into hoppers, were sorted, and then put into bags for shipment and were, from that point on, roughly handled. There are inevitably some imperfections, even if minute. This is evidenced by analyzing Mint bags of Morgan silver dollars kept sealed since the 1880s. A typical Mint bag consists primarily of MS-60 to MS-63 coins, with relatively few MS-65 samples. The nicks, marks, etc, were acquired during the handling process in the Mint after striking, and the subsequent years of storage and moving around.

In 1974, when the first edition of this book appeared in print, it was a typical situation that if a given issue fetched $100 in Extremely Fine grade, an Uncirculated piece might sell for $250. Today, with increased attention to the Uncirculated category, particularly MS-65 pieces, the price structure has become severely skewed. For example, the same coin that sold in Extremely

Fine grade for $100 back in 1974 might sell for $200 today, but an Uncirculated example, instead of selling for $250, might today sell for $1,000 in MS-60 grade and $5,000 in MS-65 preservation. Now, I recommend that potential buyers examine the true rarity and market demand and determine whether an MS-65 piece at $5,000 is truly worth 25 times the price of an Extremely Fine coin at $200. In a recent edition of this book I warned that "a number of choice Uncirculated [MS-65] and Choice Proof [Proof-65] pieces have become overpriced." This comment came home to roost in 1990 when prices of certain MS-65 and Proof-65 coins tumbled, while Extremely Fine coins held their values well.

There are many coins in Extremely Fine-40 to MS-64 grade which represent better values than MS-65 coins, in my opinion. Among worn coins, such grades as EF-40, EF-45, AU-50, and AU-55 still have all of the main design details, lettering, and other features sharp and visible and are available at reasonable prices. From a collecting viewpoint, it might be better to have several dozen nice EF-45 coins than just a single MS-65. One investor I know told me early in 1980 that he was assembling a set of Liberty Seated quarters in Extremely Fine grade, simply because he felt they were absurdly cheap in relation to their Uncirculated counterparts. Since then, Extremely Fine Liberty Seated quarters, to continue this example, have advanced in value—but for my money there is much potential yet to come.

Among Uncirculated coins, I currently feel MS-63 and MS-64 represent ideal grades for such popular series as Standing Liberty quarters, Liberty Walking half dollars, commemorative half dollars, and Morgan silver dollars. Such pieces are apt to be quite attractive, lustrous, and have characteristics which closely approximate MS-65 coins. And yet, in many instances, prices are but a fraction of MS-65 levels. It may be that in the future MS-63 and MS-64 coins will increase in value to a point at which I might recommend AU-55 or MS-60 for these series, but right now MS-63 and MS-64 seem to be a nice way to go. There are exceptions, of course, and for certain rarities one's budget might not permit buying MS-63 or MS-64 coins. For such pieces, lesser grades can be used to fill out a collection.

Accurate Grading is Important

QUESTION: I read a lot about coin grading. Do all dealers grade the same? What about certified coins?

ANSWER: Grading is very important, and my earlier discussion of the subject points this out. When you purchase coins as part of your collection you are faced with the uncertainty of what they will do in the future. Will they go up in value or won't they? Of course, we both hope they will. Why add to this the uncertainty of whether your coins are in the correct grade? Instead, learn about grading, shop around, and satisfy yourself that the grade you received is the grade you are paying for. Be aware that grading practices do vary among dealers and among grading services, and that certified or "guaranteed" coins may have a "technical grade" of a given number, but the market value may vary widely. Educate yourself—which is, of course, one of the reasons you are reading this book.

In recent years many coins have been "treated" and "processed." Lower-grade coins have been given the false appearance of "Uncirculated" or of "Proof." There is a lot of money to be made by selling processed and treated pieces, often called "whizzed" coins. Such operations prey on the bargain seeker. In the 1970s, Virgil Hancock, then president of the American Numismatic Association, led a movement to combat this situation head on, with the result that several operators were put out of business, and the situation today is far less serious. However, stray "whizzed" coins still appear on the market, and one should buy from an experienced professional in order to avoid them. One decided advantage of certified coins is that, with few exceptions, the pieces encapsulated in slabs have not been whizzed or processed. Most certification services have a guarantee under which the owner of a coin can be reimbursed if it is later found that the service by mistake encapsulated a coin treated in this manner (however, it is best to check with the grading services to ascertain the guarantees in effect at any given time).

When selecting a dealer source for coins, bear in mind that a large advertising budget has little to do with the seller's experience or the quality of the coins he sells. Indeed, some of the most successful dealers enjoy a fantastically large business by modestly circulating price lists and auction catalogues to a selected number of proven clients who have been with them over the years. They do not need a continuing stream of new faces!

In the market there are many investment-oriented firms who sell overgraded coins at full retail prices, or even more, to potential investors—hoping these collectors will never gain access to other established collectors who might tell them the true condition of their coins. Knowledge of the American Numismatic Association and other organizations is "hidden" from their clients. They want stupid buyers, not smart ones! My reaction to this you can easily guess.

Learn as much as you can about grading. Buy different references on the subject, including *Photograde* and *Official* ANA *Grading Standards for U.S. Coins.* Read the introduction, written by me, to the latter reference—for it gives many ideas.

When buying coins, remember the statement made years ago by Lee Hewitt, founder of *The Numismatic Scrapbook Magazine:* "There is no Santa Claus in numismatics." If somebody offers you a coin worth $500 for just $300, watch out! Of course, if someone offers you a coin worth $500 for $500, this does not mean it is a good buy, for it may be overgraded or may have other problems. However, there is no way you can buy a properly graded $500 coin for $300 or some other low figure unless the coin has planchet problems, looks unattractive, or is deficient in some other way.

Take with a large grain of salt much of what you read in print. In "The Hunting of the Snark," Lewis Carroll wrote, "Whatever I tell you three times is true." Many investment-oriented sales organizations spend lots of time in print telling you how wonderful they are, and how fast your coins will increase in value. The question is: are their coins as wonderful as their advertising? I strongly urge you to do some checking on your own. Ignore fancy advertisements, ignore color brochures, ignore promises of fantastic gains, and, plain and simple, study carefully any group you purchase to be sure what you are getting is graded properly and is priced correctly. *The time to be careful is when you buy; when the time comes to sell, it will be too late.* So get your education now, not later!

Again and again I have stressed the concept of *education.* I realize this is not as romantic as giving you the recommendation to drop everything, whip out your checkbook, make a mad dash to the nearest person with coins for sale to load up on Morgan dollars, Lincoln cents, commemoratives, or something else. A lot of people demand instant action and go where they can find it. I urge you to take a more measured pace. It takes time to learn, and poring over books and studying the coin market isn't everyone's cup of tea. I do not promise you that you can become an expert without effort. I do promise you, however, that if you are willing to spend a reasonable amount of effort to learn about coins before making major purchases, you will be ahead of about 95% of your competition and will have a much, much better chance of doing better than most others!

Slabbed Coins Can Be Beneficial

QUESTION: Inasmuch as slabbed coins give only the grade of a coin, and you have said that the grade is only one of several factors affecting the value of a coin, is it beneficial to buy slabbed coins?

ANSWER: Yes, in many instances. While there are many fine coins available outside of slabs—"raw" coins as they are sometimes known—for the beginning buyer in the rare coin field, coins in slabs are apt to be graded (from a numerical or technical viewpoint) better than raw coins offered by many sellers.

Use the number on a slabbed coin as the *starting point*. Ask yourself, or consult an advisor, and determine beyond that point if a coin is well struck and of attractive appearance. As a general rule, if a coin is spotted, darkly or irregularly toned, or stained (and *many* such coins exist in slabs), and if it is not attractive to you, don't buy it—no matter what anyone tells you. If you don't find it to be pleasing, chances are good that when you sell it, a potential buyer won't find it to be pleasing either.

The Importance of Authenticity

QUESTION: How concerned should I be with the genuineness of coins offered to me?

ANSWER: Authenticity is important. If you do not know the technical aspects of coin authenticity (and few amateur collectors or investors are expected to know this), then by all means do business with one of the many dealers who guarantee the authenticity of what they sell. Members of the Professional Numismatists Guild (to mention the most prominent American organization of rare coin dealers) guarantee the authenticity of pieces sold. A refund in full awaits the purchaser of any coin which is later proven false. This is a tremendously important protection, for a fake coin is absolutely worthless and is, in fact, illegal to own. In addition, there are many other fine dealers who are not members of the PNG (for reasons including insufficient time spent in the business, or lack of capital, or in some instances, because they have not applied for membership) who offer guaranteed authenticity.

Further, most of the larger commercial grading services offer a guarantee of authenticity (although, again, I remind you to check what guarantees may be in effect at a given time), a valuable protection.

Is fakery something which the average person is likely to encounter? Yes. For example, Joe Flynn, the well-known Kansas dealer, told me he once purchased a collection which contained what ostensibly was a complete set of Indian Head half eagles beginning with the first date, 1908, and continuing to the last, 1929. Beautifully displayed in a plastic holder and comprising 24 different dates and mintmarks—at first glance it appeared to be a collection of great beauty and great value. There was one problem: 22 of the 24 coins were forgeries! And, when Joe returned the set to the owner he learned it had been purchased from one of the largest advertisers in the rare coin field. What eventually happened to the set when it went back to its source, I don't know. Perhaps now it has been resold to someone else, with the seller hoping it won't find its way into the hands of Joe Flynn or someone else knowledgeable again. Ignorance is bliss, so they say!

In the same vein, John Kamin, who publishes *The Forecaster*, told me about one of his clients who had purchased for a bargain price a beautiful type set of United States gold coins. I heard the description of the coins and the price and knew immediately that the collector must have made a real steal—for his purchase price was considerably below what our firm would have sold the set for. However, there was a fly in the ointment. You probably have guessed it already: John Kamin informed me that the two most important coins in the set, the Type II gold dollar and the $3 piece, were worthless forgeries! John Kamin then did his best to help the collector get his money back, but I do not know if he was successful.

Never buy a coin "as is." Buy from an established professional dealer who will guarantee his or her merchandise.

There are many fake coins for sale in the marketplace. The number of forgeries in the numismatic field is less than those in certain other collecting fields. However, unlike the situation in other fields (modern art being an outstanding example), publications in the field of coin collecting give great publicity to counterfeiting and the problems it causes. Should this aspect be publicized or shouldn't it be? There are two sides to this question, and I'm not sure which side I am on. My stand on the subject of fakes is well known: I am against them. My staff and I have spent countless hours working with the American Numismatic Association Certification Service (now known as the ANA Authentication Bureau), the Treasury Department, the Secret Service, numismatic publications, and others to combat these. I am happy to say that many arrests and convictions have been made as a result of my efforts in this direction.

Concerning publicity, however, one camp advocates that fakes should be widely publicized and played up so that everyone takes notice. However, this undoubtedly scares off many would-be collectors who are afraid to enter the hobby. This emphasis on fakery is not a featured part of publications on art, antiques, and so on—although, as noted, the problem exists there to an equal or greater extent than it does in coins. (I should mention that among antique publications, *The Maine Antique Digest*, edited by Samuel Pennington, "tells it like it is" and discusses forgeries and other problems—and for this reason, the periodical enjoys a circulation far beyond its home base in Maine.) The other camp advocates that fakes be handled privately without fanfare. The second idea would be feasible if all coin dealers would guarantee their merchandise and collectors could be persuaded to buy only from those dealers. But, no license or even experience is needed to hang up a "Rare Coins For Sale" or "Coin Investment Center" or "Professional Numismatist" sign. Perhaps it is best that fakes be nipped in the bud by publicizing them. This is a controversial point.

Aspects of Investment Timing

QUESTION: How long should I hold my coins?

ANSWER: The answer depends upon your investment objectives. Generally speaking, my staff and I recommend coins as a long-term investment. In an up-part of the cycle for a given series, I have seen attractive profits made in three to five years, but the most spectacular profits I have observed have been by clients who have held their coins for 10 to 20 years or even longer. It is probably correct to say that anyone who spent $50,000 with me 35 years ago would have coins worth far over $1 million today—assuming the coins were purchased as part of a meaningful collection.

I have seen many fabulous profits made by collectors and investors who assembled fine groups of coins over a period of years and then sold them upon their retirement. It is not at all unusual for my firm to pay hundreds of thousands of dollars for coins which cost the owner a tiny fraction of that. This is a very gratifying aspect of my business. Whenever I look through catalogues I wrote decades ago, I know that people who bid in my firm's auctions or who ordered from catalogues can be nothing less than delighted if they still have the coins now. Undoubtedly, many millionaires have been created in the process. The coin market has done wonderfully for our clients in the past. This in turn has contributed greatly to my firm's success, for there is no better client than one for whom you have made a lot of money!

I have nothing against your buying and selling coins on a shorter term basis, but often this results in simply making money for the dealer, not for you. It's a virtual certainty that if you buy a coin for, say, $1,000 today and decide to sell it a few months or even a year or two from now, you will lose on the transaction. I recommend long-term investment as being best.

A few years ago the late Herb Melnick ran a clever advertisement titled "Where are the Customers' Yachts?" The text of the advertisement related to the securities business. Many stockbrokers prospered greatly and could afford yachts and other pleasures. Who paid for these? The customers, of course. How well were these customers doing? That was another question entirely. Herb Melnick's point was that the customers should do well also. And, I agree. For a customer to do well, long-term involvement is needed. By holding coins for a long period of time, the most consistent profits have been realized in the past. I speak from much experience in this regard.

Learning About Coins

QUESTION: How can I learn about coins?

ANSWER: At the risk of being overly repetitious, here is my advice: When building your coin collection, it will pay you to learn as much as possible. If you plan to spend several thousand dollars or more on rare coins, by all means you should begin by spending several hundred dollars or more right away on coin books, by subscribing to *Coin World*, *Numismatic News*, the *Coin Dealer Newsletter*, and other periodicals, and by joining the American Numismatic Association. Once you start a numismatic library, add to it.

There is no substitute for knowledge. None. Any success I have personally had in the rare coin field I can attribute directly to studying and learning about the coins I have sold. The coin investors who have done the best over the years have been the ones with the most knowledge, the ones who took the time to learn about what they were buying, and incorporated their knowledge into the formation of a fine collection. This point is not even debatable. In my opinion it is basic.

Besides, the more you learn about coins, the better position you are in to spot excellent buys. Walter Breen once found in a dealer's junk box a well-worn cent of 1794 worth at the time just a few dollars. He looked at it, but something didn't seem quite right. It was a new die variety! Purchasing the coin at the price asked, Walter became the owner of a piece worth several thousand dollars! In an auction held by a leading dealer I once purchased for $200 a pattern coin worth $7,000, simply because the seller was not a student of patterns and overlooked one of the coin's most significant features. Luck was with me, and apparently no one else attending the sale had taken the trouble to look at what seemed to be an ordinary piece.

How much should you spend on a reference library? $250 to $500 will get you a good bookshelf of basic volumes. Beyond that, you can add specialized references of interest. If you join the American Numismatic Association, you can borrow books free of charge (except for mailing expense) from the ANA Library—a nice way to try out a book before you buy a copy for yourself. Also, through the ANA Library you can borrow books which are out of print.

Buying coins is a learning process. When you make purchases, compare the prices and qualities of several different dealers. Don't compare price alone, for such a comparison is absolutely meaningless. Compare grading, aesthetic considerations, and other aspects, and you can see why one certified MS-65 coin can be a good buy for $1,000, and another MS-65 with the same technical grade can be a poor buy at $600. Don't be a slave to price, and don't go bargain hunting (although there is nothing wrong with making good buys—but bargains—coins at substantially less than their true worth, are apt to be bargains only until you try to sell them).

I vividly recall an instance in which my firm advertised a certain Peace silver dollar in one of the leading weekly numismatic periodicals. If memory serves, the price at the time was around $400. We had two or three pieces in stock but received a dozen or more orders. We sold out immediately. At the same time in the same publication another company, a heavy advertiser, was listing the same piece for $150! As obviously the market value was significantly higher than this, and as we had received many orders at $400 and would have been pleased to have paid, say, $350 to buy additional coins to supply our unfilled requests, there was "something rotten in the state of Denmark." I had a friend order one of the $150 coins from the other advertiser. You guessed it: what arrived in the mail was a piece over-graded by several grade categories. It not only wasn't worth $150, I wouldn't have paid $100 for it. In actuality, the piece was really worth about $75.

Feeling such competition was unfair to me, I contacted the periodical in question. The reply received was something like this: "We are a publication and concentrate on news. We simply cannot police all of the advertisements that are sent in, nor can we check if the prices are correct." I still wonder how many people have these coins for which they paid $150, thinking they were worth much more, when in reality they were worth only $75. The moment of reckoning will come when the pieces are offered for sale!

Rick Sundman, then associated with Littleton Coin Company, related an incident a few years ago when his firm shopped around and purchased for a good wholesale value an original mint bag of 1,000 1884-O silver dollars in Uncirculated grade. Seeking to add names to their mailing list, Littleton offered the coins for sale in a leading numismatic publication, charging the wholesale price they had paid. Obviously, they expected to be deluged with orders, for even dealers would find the asking price to be a bargain. But, when the advertisement appeared, lo and behold, someone else was advertising 1884-O dollars described as "Uncirculated" for substantially less! How could this be? Rick Sundman wondered, and ordered an example. Through the mail came a polished Extremely Fine dollar, not at all comparable to an Uncirculated piece. He voiced a complaint with the publication in question but was given a polite brush-off.

Investigate before buying coins. Once you have determined where your best values are, then take advantage of the knowledge by concentrating your purchases with those dealers who give you the best quality and value for your money. By doing so you will greatly enhance the chances for your investment success.

Now that I have given you some basic information about building a coin collection, I shall discuss in the following chapters the coins themselves—and different ways to acquire them as a potential treasure for the future. I preface this with a brief history of United States coins.

The History of United States Coins

The Beginnings of American Coinage

It was not until 1792 that the United States government established its own mint. The need for coins in commerce before then was filled by many different issues from many different sources. Prime in importance were coins issued by major European countries, most prominently England and Spain. It was the usual practice in America to calculate transactions in terms of English pounds, shillings, and pence or in Spanish dollars and fractional parts thereof.[1]

In addition to the official issues of England, Spain, France, and other countries there were many foreign-made speculative coins which circulated in the early American colonies. William Wood, an English entrepreneur, obtained a royal patent from King George I of England whereby Wood was authorized to privately strike coins for circulation in America (which was an English possession at the time). These coins, bearing the legend ROSA AMERICANA ("the American rose"), were issued in the denominations of halfpenny, penny, and twopence. In the 1722 to 1724 years William Wood also issued a series of coins with a HIBERNIA inscription. These pieces, issued in the values of farthing (one-quarter of a penny) and halfpenny, were not popular with the Irish people for whom they were originally intended, so quantities of them were said to have been shipped to America.

Later, mainly in the 1780s and 1790s, a large number of English-made tokens, some of which bore patriotic legends or inscriptions honoring President George Washington, were widely circulated in America. Other tokens and coins with American

---

[1] Certain currency issues printed under the authority of the Continental Congress were denominated in Spanish milled dollars. In was not unusual for legal instruments, invoices, and contracts to be given in English or Spanish currency units as late as the early 19th century.

inscriptions or made with use in the colonies in mind were struck in France, Holland, Spain, and elsewhere.

Among the most interesting of early American pieces are those struck by the colonies and states themselves, either by state mints or on a contract basis.

Massachusetts produced a distinguished series of silver coins beginning in 1652 and continuing for several decades thereafter. Prominent among these issues are the Pine Tree shillings; coins which have been mentioned in many romantic tales. In 1787 and 1788, Massachusetts produced copper cents and half cents at a state-run mint. The venture was soon abandoned, however, when the state learned that each coin cost twice its face value to produce!

In 1785 the first copper coins of Vermont appeared. Coined by a group of individuals who obtained a contract from the Green Mountain State, the first pieces bore a design of the early morning sun peeking over a forested ridge—just the type of scenery one might expect to actually find in Vermont. Later Vermont issues (which were continued with dates through 1788) were changed in appearance to conform more or less to the appearance of British halfpennies of the same era in an effort to make the coins more acceptable in the channels of commerce by giving them a familiar design.

Of all states which issued their own coins Connecticut was by far the most prolific. Coinage was performed by private individuals under a contract. Over 300 die varieties of Connecticut cents, which were minted with dates from 1785 to 1788 inclusive, are known today. Most bear the legend AUCTORI: CONNEC: ("by the authority of Connecticut"), but interesting blunders and errors can be found. One variety reads CONNECT instead of CONNEC, and others read AUCIORI, AUCTOPI, and AUCTOBI instead of the standard AUCTORI.

New Jersey issued coins at several different mints. Generally, New Jersey copper coins (dated 1786 to 1788) are of the same basic motif: a representation of the state insignia with a horse head and plow on the obverse and with a shield on the reverse. New York copper coins were made in many varieties, some of which are major rarities today. Some bear variations of the inscription NOVA EBORAC, a Latinization of NEW YORK.

The Frederick B. Taylor Collection

1776 Continental Currency Issue
AU-50, $13,200

1786 Immune Columbia Standing
Eagle copper, VF-30, $33,000

1786 New Jersey copper
MS-63, $17,600

1785 Vermont Landscape type
AU-50, $5,720

1788 Massachusetts cent
MS-60, $2,860

A sampling of United States coinage from the Frederick B. Taylor Collection
sold by Auctions by Bowers and Merena, Inc. in 1987.

There were many privately issued coins circulated in the colonies during the 17th and 18th centuries. Perhaps the most famous of these is the 1787 gold Brasher doubloon, a coin which many numismatists consider to be the most valuable and desirable American issue. The finest known example, an Uncirculated coin, was sold by my company for $725,000 as part of the Garrett Collection. Ephraim Brasher, a New York City goldsmith and jeweler, produced this heavy gold coin in 1787, possibly as a pattern for a proposal seeking a coinage contract from the state. The coin, equal in value (about $16 at the time) to a Spanish doubloon of the era, bears certain New York-related inscriptions such as EXCELSIOR (the state motto) and NOVA EBORACA.

Near Granby, Connecticut, John Higley owned a small, private copper mine. From his own metal he and family members produced halfpenny-size copper coins dated 1737 and 1739. The first pieces bore the inscription THE VALUE OF THREEPENCE. The self-assigned high value of threepence caused the pieces to be rejected. Higley, undaunted, changed the inscriptions to read VALUE ME AS YOU PLEASE.

Standish Barry, a goldsmith and silversmith of Baltimore, Maryland, issued tiny silver threepence pieces dated July 4, 1790—perhaps indicating that this was a commemorative issue in observation of Independence Day.

Prior to establishing its own mint in 1792 the United States government explored several avenues for producing coinage. The 1776 Continental coin, usually seen in pewter metal (but struck in silver as well), bears a design similar to that found on a variety of Continental currency (paper money) and may have been made under the auspices of the Continental Congress. No official documentation in this regard is known, however. Small halfpenny-size copper coins dated 1783 and 1785 bear the legend NOVA CONSTELLATIO ("the new constellation") and were struck privately to the order of Gouverneur Morris, who was assistant financier of the Confederation at one time.

The first coins specifically documented as having been issued under the authority of the United States government are the Fugio cents of 1787. These pieces portray a sundial on the obverse and have the inscription FUGIO ("I fly"—pertaining to the rapid passing of time) and MIND YOUR BUSINESS. These were struck on a contract basis by James Jarvis of New Haven, Connecticut and by others.

Tokens and medals honoring President George Washington are eagerly sought by numismatists. Most were produced in the 1790s. The study of Washington pieces is a fascinating field in itself. W.S. Baker's *Medallic Portraits of Washington*, originally issued in 1885 and vastly updated and revised in 1985 by Russell Rulau and Dr. George J. Fuld, serves as a basic guide to the field. My book, *The History of United States Coinage as Illustrated by the Garrett Collection*, contains a chapter concerning Washington numismatic items. During the writing of the book I found this segment to be one of the most enjoyable from research and interest standpoints.

Washington medals? Many dealers and collectors would scratch their heads in puzzlement if you asked about them. And yet, at one time in the late 19th century these were the hottest things in American numismatics. As an intellectual exercise you just might enjoy reading about them today. Such things are what numismatics is all about.

The Various United States Mints

In 1792 the United States established its own mint in Phila-delphia. During the first year of operation several different pattern and experimental issues were produced. The decimal system was adopted. The dollar became the standard unit, and the 100 units which made up a dollar were called *cents*. The United States, a relatively new country at the time, emphasized the intrinsic value concept. Legislators decreed a copper one-cent piece should contain a full cent's worth of copper metal, a silver dollar a full dollar's worth of silver, a gold $5 piece a full measure of gold metal, and so on.

In 1792 it was realized that to be worth full intrinsic value a cent would have to be of very large size—about the size of a present-day half dollar! An interesting solution was proposed by the so-called silver center cent. A tiny plug of silver was inserted in the center of the copper disc or planchet prior to striking it with the dies. This combination of silver (a more valuable metal than copper) and copper sufficed to maintain the metallic value at the desired one-cent figure and permitted the diameter to be smaller. Soon the intrinsic value concept for copper coins was abandoned. Much later in American coinage history the intrinsic value con-cept for silver and gold coins was abandoned also. Today we have a fiat currency; coins and paper money are based not upon

Coins, Tokens, and Medals Honoring George Washington

Only a few specimens are known to exist of the 1792 Washington "Roman Head" cent. The father of our country is depicted as a Roman emperor.

The 1793 Washington and Independence token was made in England, but intended for sale and use in America—as were many early Washington coins and medals.

1791 Washington cent with small eagle reverse.

"HE IS IN GLORY, THE WORLD IN TEARS" reads the inscription on this sentimental token issued shortly after President Washington's death.

Following George Washington's death at Mount Vernon on December 14, 1799, America was plunged into mourning. Within a matter of a few weeks Jacob Perkins, of Newburyport, Massachusetts, had produced a medal depicting Washington on the obverse, a funeral urn on the reverse, and with the sentimental inscription: HE IS IN GLORY, THE WORLD IN TEARS. Thus was set the stage for hundreds of different Washington tokens, medals, and coins which would be issued during the next two centuries.

Added to these are many issues produced during Washington's lifetime, particularly coins and tokens made in England during the 1790s.

intrinsic value of their composition but on the good faith and credit of the United States government.

One of the most interesting issues of 1792 is the half disme. *Disme*, the early spelling of *dime*, was later simplified by dropping the middle letter. Silver bullion for the production of about 1,500 pieces is said to have been personally supplied by President Washington. The first public notice of the first coinage for circulation, the 1792 half disme, was mentioned in Washington's fourth annual address on November 6, 1792: "There has been a small beginning in the coinage of half dimes, the want of small coins in circulation calling the first attention to them."

The Philadelphia Mint, which has expanded over the years and which has been in a number of different buildings and locations, remains the largest and most important United States mint today. With the exception of certain nickel five-cent pieces minted from 1942 to 1945 (and which have a "P" on the reverse), and certain issues made in recent times which also have "P" mintmarks, Philadelphia-issued coins do not bear a distinctive letter.

In 1838 three branch mints began the production of coins. The New Orleans Mint issued coins with the mintmark "O"—the previously mentioned 1838-O half dollar (of which only 20 were coined) being the most famous rarity from this mint. Coinage was conducted at New Orleans from 1838 to 1861 and again from 1879 to 1909. In 1861 the New Orleans Mint was seized by the Confederate States of America. Using earlier United States-made dies, the Confederacy produced a modest quantity of silver and gold coins during that year. Also produced were four specimens of the 1861 Confederate States of America half dollar with a distinctive reverse design.

Also in 1838 mints were opened in Dahlonega, Georgia and in Charlotte, North Carolina. Coins issued at these mints bear distinctive "D" and "C" mintmarks. Both of these mints were operated from 1838 to 1861 inclusive, and each produced gold coins only.

The Carson City Mint opened for business in Nevada in 1870 and struck pieces from metal primarily obtained from the Comstock Lode. Many varieties of silver coins from the 10-cent through trade dollar denominations, and gold coins from $5 to $20, were produced from 1870 through 1885, and again in certain series from

1889 through 1893. In general, mintages of Carson City issues were considerably restricted, with the result that today some of the most prized rarities in numismatics bear the coveted "CC" mintmark. The Carson City Mint building is still in existence and serves as the Nevada State Museum, although no coins have been struck there for nearly a century.

The Denver Mint, in operation today, commenced producing coins in 1906. Denver-issued coins have a "D" mintmark, similar to that used earlier in Dahlonega.

The San Francisco Mint produced its first coins in 1854.[1] Bearing "S" mintmarks, coins were made there until 1955. In that latter year it was announced that the San Francisco Mint was to close its doors—evidently forever. Collectors were delighted when the San Francisco Mint again began producing S-mintmarked coins in 1968. Today Proof coins are made there (in earlier years Proof coins were made at Philadelphia) as are issues for general circulation. A tiny "S" mintmark on the back of an 1870 dime caused it to sell for $176,000 in an Auctions by Bowers and Merena, Inc. sale in 1985. Without the "S," the same piece would have been worth just a few hundred dollars!

In recent years a special minting facility has been operating at West Point, on the grounds of the United States Military Academy. With the exception of certain modern commemoratives which bear a "W" mintmark, the pieces struck at West Point have no distinguishing mint letter and in this regard resemble typical Philadelphia issues.

A synopsis of the various United States mints follows:

◆Philadelphia Mint: 1792 to date; no mintmark until the 1942-P through 1945-P nickels, then in recent years the P mintmark has been used on most denominations.

◆New Orleans Mint: 1838 to 1909; O mintmark.

◆Charlotte Mint: 1838 to 1861; C mintmark; gold coins only.

◆Dahlonega Mint: 1838 to 1861; D mintmark; gold coins only.

◆San Francisco Mint: 1854 to date; S mintmark.

◆Carson City Mint: 1870 to 1893; CC mintmark.

---

[1] The San Francisco Mint was housed in facilities formerly owned by Curtis, Perry & Ward, private pioneer gold coiners. In 1870 the cornerstone was laid for a new San Francisco Mint building, which was employed until the present facility was utilized beginning in 1937.

The 1838-O Half Dollar

One of America's classic rarities is the 1838-O half dollar. The specimen illustrated above, from the R.E. Cox, Jr. and the Century Sale auctions, has been purchased and resold by us several times. In many instances famous rarities have become "old friends." When a fine collection is formed—the "Century Collection" being an ideal example—the owner often commissions us to acquire important pieces. Then when the collection is sold years later we often have the chance to handle the coins again. Over the years my firm has handled nearly every important United States and world coin rarity.

Only 20 1838-O half dollars were coined. Of that number, only about a dozen are known today. Several different specimens have passed through our hands over the years.

◆Denver Mint: 1906 to date; D mintmark.[1]

◆West Point Mint: 1965 to date; W mintmark used since 1984 on commemoratives.

Coinage Metals

Several different types of metals have been used over the years to make United States coins. Usually the basic metal has been alloyed with other metals in order to impart extra strength or other desirable characteristics. Thus most American silver coins are .900 fine, which means they are 900 parts silver and 100 parts alloy (mostly copper). Likewise, the gold in American gold coins is alloyed with copper to give the otherwise soft metal extra strength.

Copper, nickel, silver, and gold have been the main metals used, in alloy form. However, pattern coins have been produced in other metals; platinum[2] and aluminum, for example. The zinc-coated steel Lincoln cents of 1943, an issue produced during World War II when the usual bronze alloy was needed more for war material, represents an unusual use of steel metal.

The previous intrinsic value concept whereby a silver or copper coin contained full value or nearly full value in metallic content is no longer used for regular United States coinage. Whenever the prices of metals rose so the metallic content of a coin was greater than its face value the coins would be melted in wholesale quantities. This explains why $5 gold pieces of the 1820s and 1830s—coins produced by the tens of thousands—are extreme rarities today. Most went to the melting pot. During the late 1960s history repeated itself and all United States silver coins dated prior to 1965 became worth more than their face value, a situation which led to the melting of an untold number of pieces.

Denominations

Today there are five denominations of coins produced for circulation: the cent, nickel, dime, quarter, and half dollar. In practice the half dollar does not circulate actively. The Treasury Department has on hand hundreds of millions of undistributed Susan B. Anthony dollars minted during the 1979 to 1981 years.

[1] Although the Dahlonega and Denver mints each used a D mintmark, the years of operation did not overlap; thus there is no confusion on the part of numismatists today.

[2] Three 1814-dated Capped Bust half dollars struck in platinum are known to exist, the only platinum coins produced at a U.S. government mint. Aluminum was widely used to make pattern coins in the late 19th century.

Although sporadic attempts were made several years ago to encourage circulation of these pieces, including giving them out in military pay envelopes, they are seldom seen today.[1]

From the early 1980s to date, such denominations as the silver dollar, gold $5, and gold $10 have been used on occasion for commemorative coins. From 1986 to date, gold bullion coins denominated $5, $10, $25, and $50 have been made for sale to investors. However, none of these denominations has been produced for circulation in modern times.

Since 1792 many different denominations of United States coins have been issued for use in commerce. They are as follows: half cent (1793 to 1857), cent (1793 to date), two-cent piece (1864 to 1873), three-cent piece in nickel metal (1865 to 1889), silver three-cent piece (1851 to 1873), half dime or silver five-cent piece (1792 to 1873), nickel five-cent piece (1866 to date), dime (1796 to date), 20-cent piece (1875 to 1878), quarter dollar (1796 to date), half dollar (1794 to date), silver dollar (1794 to 1981, the later issues being clad composition without silver content), trade dollar (1873 to 1885), gold dollar (1849 to 1889), $2.50 gold piece (1796 to 1929), $3 gold piece (1854 to 1889), $4 gold piece (1879 to 1880 pattern issues), $5 gold piece (1795 to 1929), $10 gold piece (1795 to 1933), $20 gold piece (1849 to 1933), and $50 gold piece (1877 pattern issue and 1915 commemorative issue).

Coinage has not been continuous in most instances. As an example, silver dollars (later made of clad non-silver alloy) were struck bearing the following dates—with large gaps between coinages: 1794 to 1804, 1836, 1838 to 1873, 1878 to 1904, 1921 to 1928, 1934, 1935, and 1971 to 1981. One-cent pieces have the best record for continuity; they have been struck every year since 1793 with the solitary exception of 1815, when a fire closed the Philadelphia Mint.

Minting Procedures

With just a few exceptions coins are meant to be used to fill the need for a circulating medium to aid commerce. Coins struck for circulation are referred to as *business strikes*, which differentiates them from the fewer pieces struck as Proofs or presentation

[1] Around 1980, the toll bridges leading from Manhattan in New York City were emblazoned with signs noting that Susan B. Anthony dollars could be used in the automatic machines. A frequent visitor to the city, I thought many times that a picture of one of these signs would make an interesting page in some future book, an ephemeral reminder of a great government idea that was viewed as less than great by the general public.

pieces. Business strikes are produced at the highest speed possible. After striking the coins fall into a hopper or bin. After being subjected to various sorting and handling, they are put in a bag and shipped into the channels of banking and commerce.

An Uncirculated or Mint State coin is one which has never passed hand-to-hand in circulation. It is typical, however, for Uncirculated pieces to show bagmarks due to the coinage method just described. Sometimes an Uncirculated or Proof coin will show one or more tiny lintmarks. Believe it or not, a strand of human hair or a piece of cloth lint (from a wiping rag used to clean a die) is stronger than the coin metal—and such particles are often impressed into a coin's surface.

A coin which possesses only a few bagmarks and is in above average Uncirculated condition may be designated as MS-63, MS-64, MS-65, or another of the intermediate Mint State classifications. Especially nice pieces merit the MS-65 category, with a very occasional piece being graded as MS-66, MS-67, or finer.

In practice, for early United States coins, MS-65 is generally the finest condition available, and many are the varieties for which no MS-65 coins exist. An absolutely perfect coin would be designated MS-70, but in reality there are few if any such coins among business strikes—simply because these were struck for utilitarian purposes at high speed, as noted in the preceding paragraph. In European catalogues the term FDC (for *fleur-de-coin*) is used for a superb condition piece which in America would be designated as MS-65 or finer.

There are always sellers trying to find a way to make an extra profit without working. An obvious way is to overgrade or to confuse the buyer. For example, a coin might be described as MS-65, however when the MS-65 coin is seen, it in no way resembles what I or a respected grading service would call MS-65! Spotting a two-page advertisement containing what I considered to be impossible bargains in a coin newspaper, I read the fine print, only to learn that "Uncirculated coins are graded by our own system," whatever that means!

Be Realistic in Your Expectations

When collecting coins it is important to be realistic in your expectations concerning which coins are available in which grades. An MS-63 example of a common Washington quarter in the 1940s may readily available, but the finding of an MS-63 $20 gold piece dated in the early 1850s is a virtual impossibility. In fact, studies by David Akers have demonstrated that there are numerous gold issues of the 1850s and the 1860s of which not even a solitary example of an MS-60 coin exists! Large and heavy gold coins were struck for use in commerce, were stored and shipped together in bags, and no thought whatsoever was given to handling them carefully for future collectors. Seeking to complete a collection of MS-60 or MS-65 eagles or double eagles in the 1850s and 1860s would only lead to frustration! A more reasonable expectation for these two decades, in the $10 and $20 series, would be Very Fine to Extremely Fine, with the hope that an occasional AU or MS-60 could be obtained to spice the collection.

On the other hand, the numismatist seeking to put together a date run of Philadelphia Mint double eagles from the early 1920s would have no trouble finding MS-60 coins, for these coins circulated very little and, today, Uncirculated examples are the rule, not the exception.

In the same vein, most commemorative half dollars, especially those dated 1934 and later, went primarily to numismatists who preserved them. The 1938 New Rochelle commemorative half dollar, for example, is usually seen in Uncirculated grade. A worn specimen would be a great rarity! So, when compiling a "want list" it is important to know what can be obtained reasonably and what cannot. A competent professional numismatist can share his or her experience with you in this regard and give you ideas and suggestions.

Mint Procedures Not Always Uniform

The production of coins was not always as efficient or uniform as it is now. Dies were used until they were well worn or until they literally broke apart. In the early days the pressures used in striking and the planchets (metal discs or blanks) were often irregular and inconsistent. As James F. Ruddy has written in the *Photograde* book:

"Variations in variety or striking must be taken into consideration [when grading a coin and comparing it to the *Photograde* photograph], especially for coins minted before 1836 and for certain Denver and San Francisco issues in the teens and 1920s, for example. The reader must average the plus and minus factors when comparing a coin to the average picture. If an early large cent, for example, shows weak letters on the right, it must be assumed that the coin could not have been worn only on one portion of its surface. Examples such as this result from an improper strike, an uneven planchet, or an improper die alignment. When grading a coin, take into consideration all of the features on each side—not just an isolated weak spot which is not a result of wear."

There is no formula to determine which coin issues are commonly found in sharply struck condition and which are rarely (or not at all) found that way. Experience is your best guide—your own experience or that of a professional dealer. The 1926-D quarter is an interesting case in point. Nearly all known specimens are flatly struck on the head. In late 1972 an Uncirculated 1926-D quarter catalogued $35 in the *Guide Book*, and a choice specimen (relatively free of bagmarks; what we would call MS-63 in the 1990s) sold in the $40 range. At the same time Lot No. 1128 of my firm's sale of the Robert Marks Collection was catalogued thus:

"1926-D quarter. Brilliant Uncirculated. Full Head, and of *extreme rarity* as such. The importance of 1926-D, a coin which nearly always is weakly struck, in this sharply struck condition cannot be overemphasized. It would not surprise us at all to see the coin sell for several hundred dollars, and it would be worth it. The final bid is up to you, however." The coin sold for $240 to a specialist who recognized its rarity. Today, of course, the coin would be worth far more.

When a coin leaves its shipping bag or roll and is placed into circulation it acquires signs of use. Coins in worn grades are classified as About Good (the lowest collectible grade), Good, Very Good, Fine, Very Fine, Extremely Fine, and About Uncirculated, with appropriate numerical equivalents in each case. I refer you to *The Official ANA Grading Standards for U.S. Coins* and to the *Photograde* book for advice.

Proof Coins

Proof coins have a mirrorlike finish and are especially struck for collectors. Due to the extra care involved in striking them, they are sold by the Mint for a premium price. Proof dies are carefully made to insure that all details (such as star points, lines in Liberty's hair, etc.) are sharp and distinct. The die surfaces, both obverse and reverse, are polished to a high degree. The coin blanks or planchets are carefully selected to be free of flaws, are cleaned, and then fed by hand into the coinage press. Sometimes several blows or impressions from the dies are used to bring up the coin design to its full sharpness. The Proof-making process is done at slow speed on special presses using dies carefully spaced so as to bring up all of the design details during striking. When a Proof coin is struck it is removed by hand from the press and carefully set aside to prevent contact with other coins.

Although the Philadelphia Mint produced Proofs in limited numbers from 1817 (the date when suitable equipment for this purpose was first installed) through the 1850s, early Proofs were not generally offered for sale to the public at the time. Instead, they were reserved for dignitaries, visiting foreign officials, and for other presentation purposes.

In 1858 Proof sets were first offered for public sale. In that year an estimated 80 silver Proof sets were sold. Contrast that to the 3 million plus sets produced on the average each year a century or more later during the 1960s and 1970s.

1858 to 1916 Proof Coins

From 1858 to 1916 Proof coins were generally available from the Mint on this basis:

◆1. "Minor Proof set" containing copper and nickel denominations from one cent to five cents could be purchased.

◆2. "Silver Proof set" containing denominations in that metal from the three-cent silver piece through the silver dollar and/or trade dollar could be bought.

◆3. Proof gold coins could be purchased individually.

Only rarely would a purchaser buy a full run of Proof coins from the cent through the $20 gold piece. The Proof mintages for 1888 illustrate this: (1) 4,582 minor Proof sets containing the Indian cent, nickel three-cent piece, and Liberty nickel were sold. (2) 832 silver Proof sets containing the dime, quarter, half dollar, and silver dollar were distributed. (3) Individual Proof gold coins were sold as follows: gold dollar 1,079 pieces, $2.50 gold 97 pieces, $3 gold 290 pieces, $5 gold 95 pieces, $10 gold 75 pieces, and $20 gold 105 pieces.

The number of pieces in a Proof set of a given year depended on which denominations were currently being struck for circulation. Contrast the number of pieces in an 1888 set (as just noted) with those in the largest set of all, the 1873.

In an 1873 Proof set you will find the following: Indian cent, two-cent piece, nickel three-cent piece, silver three-cent piece, Shield-type nickel, half dime, dime without arrows at the date, dime with arrows at the date (the arrows signified a change in the weight of the coin), quarter without arrows, quarter with arrows, half dollar without arrows, half dollar with arrows, silver dollar, trade dollar, and gold coins of the denominations of $1, $2.50, $3, $5, $10, and $20!

Certain Proof coins of the early 20th century are known as Matte Proofs or Sandblast Proofs. These have specially prepared surfaces with a grainy or matte finish and are entirely unlike the so-called "brilliant" Proofs in appearance. Matte Proofs were coined in the Lincoln cent series from 1909 to 1916 and in the Buffalo nickel series from 1913 to 1916. Sandblast, Roman Finish, and Satin Finish Proofs were coined in the $2.50 and $5 gold series from 1908 to 1915, and in the $10 and $20 Saint-Gaudens series from 1907 to 1915. Today Proofs are of the "brilliant" finish.

Proof Sets 1936 to Date

From 1936 through 1942 inclusive the Philadelphia Mint again issued Proofs for collectors. Sets could be ordered (cost $1.89 each at the time), or individual coins could be bought separately. Proof coinage was suspended after 1942 and was not resumed until sets were offered again in 1950 (at the issue price of $2.10 per set). Proofs were sold by the set only (individual coins could not be ordered) until 1964. In the latter year the critical shortage of coins in circulation resulted in a suspension of such "extra" activities as making Proof sets. A few years later in 1968 production was again resumed—this time at the San Francisco Mint. For the first time in history Proof sets were issued with mintmarks on all of the coins.

Building a Collection (With Investment in Mind)

Different Ways to Collect and Invest

 There are a number of ways to invest in United States coins. Which is "just right" for you depends upon several factors: your objectives, the amount of money you wish to spend, whether you are interested in forming a collection or whether you want to be a "pure investor," how involved you wish to become in die varieties and numismatic sidelights, and so on. There are many opportunities among United States coins. A coin collection has the potential for being an investment you can thoroughly *enjoy* if you want to—with all the aspects of art, history, and romance along with the possibility of price appreciation.

Over the years I have encountered many "pure investors" who have done well, although by and large it is the collector who has done the best of all. Those who have approached coins for the sake of investment only have done well if they learned at least something about coins, and had the wisdom to buy from established professional numismatists (instead of from promotional outfits).

I recall a Pennsylvania client who felt Proof nickel three-cent pieces of the specific years 1879, 1880, and 1882 through 1887 would be good investments. The related business strike mintages were low, and each issue was a key date, and yet the prices at the time were not high. Through my firm he bought dozens and dozens of these, cashing in a few years later at a profit many times over his cost.

Similarly, a friend and client decided to hoard Proof trade dollars of the dates 1879 through 1883, accumulated dozens of them, and realized a great profit upon their sale.

Still another acquaintance felt worn 20-cent pieces would be a good investment, set about buying as many Fine, Very Fine, and

Extremely Fine coins as he could, eventually acquired several hundred of them, and likewise made a generous profit upon their resale. Numerous other experiences could be related.

In the following chapters I shall discuss different ways to form a collection, giving tips and insights which I feel will help you make better buys—and at the same time will increase your chances of making a profitable investment. But first let's review how well United States coins as an investment have done during the past several decades.

A Study of Coin Prices

How have coins fared in comparison with other investment media? At the beginning of this book I discussed the Salomon Brothers survey of various investment fields, and noted that as a long-term investment coins have placed at the very top of the list in recent years prior to its discontinuation in 1991.

Years ago, long before the Salomon Brothers survey became publicized in the coin field, my staff did a survey of rare coin prices from the 1940s to the present time. The results were first published in the 1974 edition of this book. I selected at random 10 coins representative of the types I have sold to investment-oriented clients over the years. I made no attempt to select pieces by hindsight so as to show super-exceptional performance. Instead, I picked pieces which, in my opinion, are truly representative—not "special situations."

I charted the price totals at approximate five-year intervals, updating the intervals in the years since the values were first compiled:[1] 1946, 1950, 1955, 1960, 1965, 1970, 1975, 1980, 1985, and 1990, plus the recent addition of 1991, using the *Guide Book of United States Coins* as a pricing reference. Bearing in mind that the cover date of the *Guide Book* is one year ahead of the publication date, I used the 1981 edition to obtain the 1980 prices, the 1986-dated edition to obtain the 1985 prices, and so on. I express appreciation to the Western Publishing Company for permission to use figures from this popular reference.

---

[1] In editions one through 12 of this book, the intervals used were 1948, 1953, 1958, 1963, 1973, etc., at five-year intervals. I did this so that 1953, my first full year in numismatics, could be included. Beginning with the 13th edition, I revised the years to begin with 1946 (the first year *A Guide Book of* U.S. *Coins* was issued), but continuing in more standard five-year intervals, as 1950, 1955, 1960, 1965, etc., plus the addition of the most recent single year.

The coins used in the study were:[1]

1786	Vermont copper Baby Head variety, Fine
1910	Liberty nickel, Proof
1852	silver three-cent piece, Uncirculated
1842	half dime, Uncirculated
1807	dime, Uncirculated
1875-S	20-cent piece, Uncirculated
1815	half dollar, Uncirculated
1847	silver dollar, Uncirculated
1878-S	trade dollar, Uncirculated
1893	Isabella commemorative quarter dollar, Uncirculated

The group of 10 coins used in the study catalogued at $116.75 in 1946. By 1991 the value had risen to $15,125, an increase of 12,855%.

By five year intervals, plus the years 1946 and 1991, the values rose as follows:

1946	$116.75
1950	153.75
1955	259.00
1960	504.00
1965	1,642.50
1970	2,430.00
1975	7,077.50
1980	13,325.00
1985	14,895.00
1990	15,375.00
1991	15,125.00

Stated another way, every $1,000 invested in such a group of coins in 1946 would have increased to $129,550 by 45 years later!

---

[1] The figures listed here and also in the appendix to the book were researched and compiled by Richard A. Bagg, Ph.D. and Andrew W. Pollock III of the Bowers and Merena staff.

Selecting the Index

When selecting the 10 coins for the study back in 1974, I endeavored to pick representative coins of good *numismatic* quality of the type I have been recommending for many years. I could have used hindsight to come up with some really dramatic figures (although the figures used are dramatic enough!).

For example, it is not unusual in the present day to have some investment-oriented writer look through old price lists, ignore the coins that have not done particularly well, and to pinpoint issues which have had particularly immense gains, even though he or she did not buy, sell, or recommend such issues years ago. Such "performance" figures can then be presented to show increases of multiples above what I give here. However, I do not consider them to be particularly representative, for they are selected after the fact.

There are many people who have studied the market carefully and who have endeavored to come up with meaningful indexes. Among popular periodicals in the hobby, *Coin World* and *Numismatic News* each have compiled indexes of coin market performance, although these do not date back far in history, having been started in 1983 and 1981 respectively.

Walter Perschke, who achieved a measure of fame in 1979 by paying $430,000 for the Virgil Brand specimen of the 1787 Brasher doubloon and subsequently refusing an attractive offer for it, noted around the same time that his studies showed that typical coin investment gains were in the 30% per year range. Other studies have shown figures from 15% to 40% (not including data for the market decline of 1990).

A common feature of virtually every study I have seen is that all indicate that coins as an investment have dramatically outperformed nearly all other media. I haven't tried this, but I imagine if you were to set up a 35-year-old copy of the *Guide Book* on an easel, spread out the pages, and throw darts at it, the coins selected would have increased in value more than stocks, bonds, real estate, or anything else you can come up with. Of course, this does not mean that all coins are good investments and, importantly, it does not mean that people buying coins 35 years ago automatically made good buys. Thirty-five years ago, as today, numerous well-intentioned coin buyers were trapped by overpaying for coins at the time, or acquiring pieces which were vastly overgraded.

**Coin Investment
Comparison Graph***
1946-1991

Rare Coin Prices $129,550

Standard & Poor's Stock Index $25,914

Return on a 5% Savings Account $8,985

130,000
125,000
120,000
115,000
110,000
105,000
100,000
95,000
90,000
85,000
80,000
75,000
70,000
65,000
60,000
55,000
50,000
45,000
40,000
35,000
30,000
25,000
20,000
15,000
10,000
5,000
0

1946 1950 1955 1960 1965 1970 1975 1980 1985 1990 1991

In conjunction with a study prepared years ago for my firm, I selected at random 10 United States coins typical of the types my firm has been recommending over the years. I made no attempt to select pieces for exceptional performance (which would have been easy to do by hindsight). Rather, I picked coins of the type which you as an investor would have bought on our recommendation 10 or 20 years ago. A list of these coins appears on page 229. As you can see, the comparisons are startling!

* Computations reflect price data from the 1990-dated edition of A *Guide Book of United States Coins* reflecting 1989 prices in comparison with the Standard & Poors 500 Stock Index and the return on a 5% savings account as of July 18, 1991.

If 35 years ago you bought a coin for $500, but if it was worth only $100 at the time, your investment would have performed much less attractively. Again, the answer is knowledge—and doing business with established professional numismatic firms.

Investments in Other Fields

During the same approximate period covered by my study, the Standard & Poor's 500 Composite Index of Stocks[1] went from 15.30 in 1946 (last date of trading figures used) to 381.18 in July 1991 (when the present text was being written). Actual five-year figures, plus 1946 and 1991, are:

1946 15.30; 1950 20.41; 1955 45.48; 1960 58.11; 1965 92.43; 1970 92.15; 1975 90.19; 1980 135.76; 1985 211.18; 1990 330.22; July 1991 381.18.

Stated another way, a $1,000 investment in the S&P stock average, not including purchase and sale commissions or reinvestment of dividends, would have stood at about $25,914 by July 1991.

At the same time an investment in a savings account at 5% (although such interest was not readily available in the United States in the late 1940s and 1950s), compounded annually would have risen from $1,000 in 1946 to $8,985 by July 1991.

During the same period inflation caused the purchasing power of the dollar to decline very sharply. According to the United States government statistics, $1,000 would have declined in purchasing power to less than $200! Today, many elderly people who placed their faith in savings accounts and who anticipated a golden retirement are faced with living at the poverty level simply because the return on money in savings accounts or their pension benefits did not come even close to keeping pace with inflation. Do you remember the advertisements from years ago, promoting retirement policies, which had a headline something like, "We retired on $300 a month!"? On the other hand, *modest* amounts carefully set aside each year for building a coin collection during the 1940s, 1950s, and 1960s have made many people *wealthy* upon retirement.

---

[1] In editions 1 through 12 we used the Dow-Jones Industrial Index. Beginning with the 13th edition we substituted the Standard & Poor's Composite Index of stocks, as we felt it was more representative of the stock market in general and covered a much wider base.

In summary, here are the approximate amounts that $1,000 would have yielded in these different ways. Values in 1946 are compared to values at the end of the year 1990:

$1,000 cash in 1946 equaled just $181 by 1990

$1,000 5% savings account yielded $8,985 by 1990

$1,000 S&P 500-Stock Composite Index yielded $25,914

$1,000 RARE COIN INVESTMENT yielded $129,550

The preceding figures are rather dramatic, aren't they! Data at the end of this book show a number of United States coins and how well they have done from 1946 to date. Keep in mind that past performance is not necessarily an indication of what will happen in the future, for the future is unknown.

The coins used in the survey are the general type that my firm has been supplying for many years to our clients. In the process, many buyers have made tremendous amounts of money. I and my staff members could not be happier, for by making many clients successful, we have been successful also. Our business has grown steadily over the years to the point at which it is one of the largest and most respected in the world. What greater reward could be asked for?

Our Collection Portfolio Program

The following paragraphs are not written objectively, in that they describe the Collection Portfolio Program offered by Bowers and Merena Galleries, Inc., and managed by personal account representatives who work closely with individual clients.

The object of the program is to enable clients to build meaningful *collections* over a period of time. It could be that the idea of approaching coin collecting through a program may not be your cup of tea—you may wish to scout around and get pieces individually on your own—but for what it is worth, I tell you about what we have done here. The Collection Portfolio Program has appealed especially to busy professionals who wanted to acquire quality coins with a minimum of searching. The Program is not a substitute for knowledge or enjoyment of coins, and all along I have encouraged participants to build a library and to learn as much as possible about the field.

In the mid 1950s, I believe the year was 1957 or 1958, a number of clients approached me with the idea of acquiring coins automatically on a monthly basis. These were knowledgeable people—numismatists who knew about coins—but they were busy professionals who did not want the fuss and bother of ordering coins only to find out that certain items were sold out from catalogues, nor did they want the frustration of submitting want lists to many different locations and getting leftovers. Today, the concept is known as the Bowers and Merena Galleries Collection Portfolio Program, an opportunity for the collector who desires quality pieces but who wants us to assist with selections. The Collection Portfolio Program enables collectors to acquire scarce and rare pieces—items of proven numismatic value. One of our brochures notes the following, among other things:

"We invite you to join our Collection Portfolio Program. As a member you will receive first choice of coins you need from old-time collections, estates, and our inventory. Whether you need a $500,000 rarity (and we have handled just about every rarity in the book) or a $10 item, you've come to the right place. From our location deep in the heart of New England we have access to some of the finest and most sought after coins in all of numismatics. Our credentials are second to none.... While the outstanding collections and rarities we have handled make headlines, we hasten to say that the majority of our business is with clients who purchase from us regularly over a period of years, perhaps a $500 coin last year, a $200 coin last month, and a $100 item this month.

"If you are a busy person, you will find that the Collection Portfolio Program simplifies the building of a meaningful coin collection. By means of monthly (or other interval) payments, you can build over a period of time an exhibit of choice, rare, and desirable coins which you will be proud to own and display. Let us help you assemble a beautiful collection of Morgan dollars, commemoratives, gold coins, 'type' coins, or any other area of interest.

"You will develop a close working relationship with our staff of professional numismatists, which we consider to be the finest in the world. Have a question about a coin? About pricing? About aesthetic or other considerations? We are just a telephone call or letter away. The Bowers and Merena Galleries team constantly keeps abreast of market conditions and monitors prices in America, Europe, and other trading centers. Our library of thousands of publications is constantly consulted. We are perhaps the only numismatic firm to have a Research Department, and the list of numismatic reference books we have published is unequalled by any other rare coin company in the United States.

"We specialize in selecting pieces which are the type which collectors and dealers are looking for. Each year our staff spends untold hours searching for coins which have the ideal combination of quality, appearance, and price. Sometimes 10, 20, or even more coins are examined before we find one that is just right!

"As a member of our Collection Portfolio Program you will be in the 'inner circle' of our favorite customers. Not only do you have first choice of desirable and interesting coins as we acquire them, you will also receive a special VIP identification number which will entitle you to unadvertised specials and discounts on numismatic books, supplies, and special coin offers.

"Each month we will send you coins for the program you choose. These coins will be individually packaged and will be accompanied by a description of the piece, the grade, and the price. While most of our clients prefer monthly shipments, the programs are flexible, and other time intervals can be arranged. Programs are available for $100 per month upward, depending on the program selected.

"Sometimes you may have additional money and may want to send us a lump sum. You can make extra payments at any time in order to acquire rarities, special groups or collections, or just to get a substantial head start on the Collection Portfolio Program you choose. Each program is *personally* supervised. We keep your needs in mind and will work with you in this regard. If you already have coins in a certain category, let us know what they are at the beginning, and we will avoid duplicates. From the outset, we will set up a 'want list' so we know what you need and what grades you prefer....

"Each and every coin you receive as part of our Collection Portfolio Program is guaranteed to be authentic forever—no ifs, ands, or buts.... No Collection Portfolio Program client has ever received a counterfeit coin, but we mention this anyway to assure you. What about grading? Each coin shipped is personally inspected by our professional numismatic staff, with a minimum of *several* qualified numismatists viewing each piece.... Year in and year out we have pleased thousands of customers. We feel that you, like many others, will like the grade, appearance, and surface quality of the coins you receive. Each and every piece comes with a 30-day money back guarantee, so if you are not pleased with any aspect of grade, appearance, or price, an instant refund awaits you within the return period....

"The Collection Portfolio Program is ideal for advanced numismatists as well as beginning collectors. If you are an old-timer, and if you are to the point at which you need hard to find scarcities and rarities, then you will appreciate all the work we do for you in tracking down pieces which are seldom seen. It's almost as if you have a desk right here in our office and you can look over each new collection as it arrives! If you are a beginning collector, then the depth and breadth of our quality inventory will give you an excellent start on building a numismatic treasure."

The balance of the brochure is devoted to details of the Collection Portfolio Program, letters from past clients, and an outline of different areas available, including type sets, gold coins, commemoratives, and other specialities, then follows a brief summary:

Advantages of the Program

"As a participant in the Bowers and Merena Galleries Collection Portfolio Program you will enjoy the prestige and satisfaction of doing business with one of the world's largest and most respected numismatic firms, a firm of unquestioned financial reputation and integrity. To our knowledge, we've handled more important collections than any other company.

"By means of our Collection Portfolio Program you can build an important and meaningful collection of coins by having our staff work closely with you. You receive truly personal service of a kind which is all too rare in today's world.

"Over the years many of our clients have found rare coins to be a wonderful hedge against inflation. While past performance is no guarantee of future success, and while the future is unknown, and no guarantee, warranty, or representation, expressed or implied, is made concerning the future price or performance of any coin (nor, in our opinion, can any *responsible professional* numismatist make such a guarantee), the record shows that over a long period of years the performance of coins has been equalled by few other areas.

"As a Collection Portfolio Program participant you pay just our regular competitive prices for coins—sometimes even less (in the instance in which we pass a special buy on to you), but *never* more! There are no advisory fees, service charges, or any other charges for the time we spend in making selections or supervising your account. You are under no obligation when you join one of our programs. You sign no contract. If you are not 100% delighted with the coins you receive, you can cancel your participation at any time by simply notifying us and discontinuing your payments—or if you are ordering on open account, simply by requesting us to discontinue shipments to you, and by taking care of any balance due to us.

"Over the years the Collection Portfolio Program has had many advantages for our firm. We are able to place directly many beautiful coins without the expense of 'sold out' letters, credit problems, advertising preparation and listing, and so on—resulting in a savings for us. In a high-volume, low-margin business this savings can be quite important.

"Over the years, our main problem has been buying coins or acquiring them on consignment for our auction sales; our problem has not been selling! By placing coins with Collection Portfolio Program clients, we may have the opportunity to buy them back someday."

I have never suggested or intimated to a client that he or she has any obligation in that way—for my recommendation is that when you have coins for sale, investigate all possibilities, and sell through the channel that seems to be most attractive, for the marketplace is free and competitive. However, it has been my happy experience that many clients who purchased coins from my firm years ago have kept us in mind, and we have handled their holdings when the time came to sell.

Pardon the preceding "commercial"—and in the interest of returning to objectivity, I suggest that if you desire to acquire coins on a monthly acquisition basis, you might also shop around to see what services are offered elsewhere. However, here at Bowers and Merena Galleries we are all proud of what we have done, and of our track record in the past.

Building a Portfolio of Rare Coins

Working with collectors and investors over the years I have formulated a number of guidelines which I now pass on to you.

The precepts will give what I believe to be the best possible chances for your coins to appreciate in value. At the outset I state that these guidelines are not the most profitable for rare coin firms, ours included, for the margins of profit on high-quality coins are not what they are on low-value, common pieces. Moreover, many of my recommendations involve coins which are really difficult to find. My recommendations are apt to be in direct contradiction with what you might find from a mass-marketing coin investment company. Here are some of my ideas:

Recommended Grades

In earlier editions of this book I recommended that nearly all coins dated within the past 100 years be in grades which now in the early 1990s are stated as MS-65 and Proof-65 (for this reason, I use them in the book; bear in mind that numerical grading was not in general use in earlier years, except for large cents). I stated at the time that there should be no particular preference between MS-65 and Proof-65.

I went on to express the opinion that there was no reason at the time why a group of coins should be limited to either all Uncirculated or all Proof pieces. Proof is a *different* grade from Uncirculated, not a superior grade. In many instances Uncirculated coins are far rarer than Proofs, for Proofs were specifically saved by collectors whereas Uncirculated pieces were not. Of course, Denver, New Orleans, pre-1968 San Francisco, and other mintmark varieties are normally not available in Proof state.

The market of the late 1970s, following my recommendations in part, placed *extreme* emphasis on MS-65 and Proof-65 pieces (to translate into today's terms), with the result that by the early 1980s these coins sold for far greater sums than their Extremely Fine, AU, or lesser-condition counterparts. When early editions of this book appeared in the 1970s, MS-65 and Proof-65 coins sold for more than Extremely Fine or AU pieces, as might be expected, but not usually for tremendous amounts more.

Earlier I gave the instance in which an Extremely Fine coin would have been worth $100, while an MS-65 could have been bought for $250. Now, we have the situation in which the Extremely Fine coin has advanced just a modest amount, say to $200, while an MS-65 is worth thousands of dollars.

In general, I like the grades MS-63 and MS-64 for popular series such as Morgan dollars, Peace dollars, commemoratives, and most "type" coins. For very early type coins, such as half cents and large cents of the 1790s and early 1800s, grades such as Fine, Very Fine, and Extremely Fine are quite acceptable. I believe that many Capped Bust and Liberty Seated coins have excellent potential in grades from EF-40 to MS-64. For very modern coins from the 1930s to date I like MS-65, cherrypicked for good strike and lustre. Some of these will become the expensive coins of tomorrow. The market of the early 1990s offers many opportunities.

I shall be more specific in the pages to follow.

Be "Fussy" About Quality

I recommend that you purchase *choice* examples of each grade desired. I'm using the word *choice* as an adjective here. If you are buying an Extremely Fine piece, pick one which is relatively "clean" and which does not have deep surface scratches, unsightly edge bumps, or other "problems." Uncirculated and Proof coins should be of good quality for the grade indicated.

If you are buying an MS-60 coin, a piece which is Uncirculated but at the lower end of the scale, you will, of course, expect a generous number of bagmarks and contact marks. But, don't buy one that has gouges, deep scratches, severe edge knocks, or anything else which renders it unsightly. When purchasing higher-grade pieces, such as the MS-63 and MS-64 grades I recommend, or if you are buying MS-65 coins, strive for specimens that are visually attractive and aesthetically pleasing. Remember the advice issued by the American Numismatic Association itself—which stated that a coin can be technically graded MS-65, for example, but be worth the market value of an MS-63 piece or less, if the aesthetic appeal is not there. This is a very important consideration, and I strongly urge you not to overlook it. The greatest temptation here will be to go bargain hunting. Remember, in coins, as in other walks of life, you usually get what you pay for—and if an MS-65 coin of a given variety is worth, say, $2,000, and you are offered one for $1,200, you can almost be assured that while it is *technically* MS-65, it has some aesthetic problems.

With regard to my strong recommendation for MS-63 or MS-64 coins in popular series, be "fussy" when you buy these. If you do, there will be many instances in which coins you buy as MS-63, for example, will be fully as nice as coins some others buy as MS-64 or MS-65. Select only bright or attractively and lightly toned coins. Avoid spotted, stained, and deeply toned coins. Leave these for others. At Bowers and Merena Galleries we often have to check a dozen or two certified or slabbed coins in order to find *just one* that has what we consider to be the ideal combination of technical grade, striking quality, aesthetic appeal, and price.

Avoid like the plague any coin which has been treated by buffing or "whizzing." Coins should have natural surfaces; either brilliant or attractively toned. Also, avoid coins which have been retooled, holed, plugged, repaired, or which show evidence of tampering. Such coins do have a numismatic value, and it may be the case, for example, that a gold dollar worth, say, $2,000 in AU grade might be worth $200 if holed and repaired—but for my money you should just pass it by and save your funds for a better piece.

Insist upon quality, no matter what the technical grade. A coin with poor aesthetic aspects, even if it is surrounded by all sorts of fancy words, guarantees, and is in a certified holder, still is a poor item—even if you have to pay a lot to buy it!

Diversify

If you are collecting coins with an eye for investment, I recommend diversification. If you are a "pure investor" and are not interested in collecting at all, diversification is still important.

Spread your investment over a number of different series. The reason for this is simple: No area of United States coins ever moves upward steadily. Instead, the movement is a series of spurts of activity, then a period of lessened activity, then another leap forward—as outlined in my chapter on coin price cycles. By averaging your investment among denominations and types of coins you spread your risk and lessen the speculative element. A type set is an ideal way to practice this.

Of course, if you wish to become a specialized collector, then concentrating on a certain limited area is fine. In fact, few things in numismatics are as thrilling as the discovery of a long-sought rarity needed to fill in a group of tokens, early half cents, or some similar set. However, it could be that you would pick an area which has relatively little price movement. For example, during the years from about 1980 through 1986, colonial and state coins remained dormant. In 1987 the field of colonials began to experience a sharp renewal in prices and interest. From about 1980 until the present time, the field of currency has been relatively inactive.

Each of these two examples represent wonderful areas for the dedicated numismatist, but the point is that an investor buying these a number of years ago would have to wait a long time for a price movement. Perhaps the price movement will come soon, and when it does these pieces may jump forward strongly in the price cycle, thus amply rewarding those who bought coins and notes in 1982, 1983, and other years. However, I believe that the typical collector would be more satisfied if such pieces were part of an overall collection with other series in it—so while currency was inactive, scarce Morgan dollars or some other collection would have appreciated in value.

Buy Scarce or Rare Coins

Unless you are a commodities expert or specialist (in which instance you might be interested in bulk bags and quantities of bullion coins), I recommend purchasing numismatic items of proven scarcity and rarity. As I mentioned before, coins which are common today will be common tomorrow. A common coin cannot magically become rare! Also to be remembered is the fact that a dealer's handling effort is usually the same on a $10 coin as on a $100 coin, thus if you buy 10 $10 coins rather than one $100 coin you pay 10 times more for the dealer's efforts.

As an example of this, in the current *Guide Book* modern Lincoln cents in Uncirculated grade list for 10 cents each, or 10 times face value—but they would be a poor investment at this price, at least for the foreseeable term, for they are common, and nine cents of the 10 cents represents the dealer's handling efforts. If you went out and bought 1,000 pieces for 10 cents each on an individual basis, for a total of $100, you would still have 1,000 Lincoln cents worth face value, or $10. At the same time, if you are building a set of Lincoln cents and want completion, then by all means you want to fill in the modern issues. However, using the dollar averaging mentioned earlier, your expense in the modern issues will be very little compared to the earlier ones, thus the added cost is not significant.

By building a fine collection of the best quality you can afford, you will automatically acquire a preponderance of scarce and rare coins, for once you go beyond recent decades, nearly all coins in higher grade levels have a degree of numismatic scarcity.

So far as great rarities are concerned, the prestige of owning the "rarest of the rare," and the fact that rarity has always added a dimension of desirability, distinction, and extra value to a group of coins when they are offered for sale, particularly at auction, make the ownership of such pieces a source of pleasure to those who can afford them.

The acquisition of a 1913 Liberty Head nickel, an 1804 silver dollar, an 1822 half eagle, or any one of various other classics, automatically projects the purchaser into the "numismatic hall of fame." The names of collectors who have gone before—Col. Mendes I. Cohen, Charles I. Bushnell, T. Harrison Garrett, Lorin G. Parmelee, Matthew A. Stickney, William Sumner Appleton, George H. Earle, H.P. Smith, John Story Jenks, James Ten Eyck, Waldo C. Newcomer, Virgil M. Brand, Col. E.H.R. Green, F.C.C. Boyd, William F. Dunham, Will W. Neil, Josiah K. Lilly, Louis Eliasberg, Amon Carter, the Norweb family, and others are remembered today for the *rarities* they once owned. Had these same people possessed mere accumulations of low-value coins, no one would have heard of them!

Keep In Touch with the Market

As mentioned earlier, I recommend that you keep in touch as closely as possible with the coin market. In addition to whichever dealers' publications you subscribe to (and I hope you will consider those of my firm in this regard), I recommend *Coin World, Numismatic News, Certified Coin Dealer Newsletter*, and *Coin Dealer Newsletter* for starters. Beyond this, there are two monthly magazines which are primarily oriented toward beginners, but over a period of time each contains many really dandy articles. They are *Coins* and COIN*age*. Further, I recommend that you join the American Numismatic Association. This will bring you a subscription to *The Numismatist*.

In addition, I recommend that you establish a close relationship with one or more rare coin firms. It is important to remember that there is no substitute for *professional* experience, and your friendship with a leading dealer can repay itself many times over. Compare quality, value, service, and expertise and do business with the ones who treat you the best.

Large-Scale Investing

For profit-sharing programs and funds with large amounts of investment capital, rare coins offer interesting potential. Over the years my firm has worked closely with many accountants, banks, financial institutions, and professional financial planners in this field. Often the initial inquiry has come about in this way:

"My clients keep reading about the coin market and its investment potential. Right now we are mainly invested in stocks, bonds, cash, and real estate. I think my people would find coins to be interesting also."

I recommend that any group, fund, or other non-personal entity investing in coins also go the *collection* route. Building a type set, a specialized collection, or some other specific numismatic program will result in forming a meaningful collection over a period of time. Then, when time comes to sell the holding, purchase interest will be greater than if just a miscellaneous accumulation is involved.

Selling Your Coins

What about liquidity? Are coins easy to sell? These are logical questions to ask. Coins are indeed easy to sell, perhaps more so than any other collectible. It would be difficult to think of any other type of collectors' item which has a more active market or has more dealers involved.

Rare coins in higher grades have always been in demand. In the many years I have been in the coin business I have never seen a lack of demand for pieces of proven quality—and this includes periods of international uncertainty, stock market plunges, recessions, political problems, and so on. If anything, such uncertainties *increase* the demand for "hard" items such as rare coins.

As a dealer I know the main problem of my firm has been buying coins, and not selling them. In eager competition dealers will vie to obtain your material for outright purchase or auction. In our advertising in numismatic publications we spend much more effort and expense seeking to buy coins or obtain them for consignment to our sales than we do seeking to sell coins, an indication of the appetite we have for quality collections.

There are several ways to sell your coins. Here are some of them:

◆**Outright Sale:** You can have one or several dealers submit offers for your coins—then take the highest offer. It is to be remembered that certain dealers specialize, and if you have a collection of United States paper money for sale, for example, then your best bet would be to contact specialists in this area. Likewise, a collection of early American half cents and large cents would be best offered to specialists in those fields. Not all dealers want to buy all coins at all times. Factors such as the dealer's financial position, the amount of money owed to banks, the number of pieces of a given issue in stock, the dealer's perception of how easy pieces will be to sell, the position of a given series in the market cycle, and other considerations enter into the equation. For example, if my own firm has just purchased a group of Proof $10 gold pieces, our desire for an additional group of coins of the same dates and series would be less than if we did not have any in stock. At the same time, we might be very eager to acquire a group of Proof $5 gold pieces or $20 pieces, if we had few or none of these on hand. Perhaps while we are "fully stocked" on Proof $10 pieces, one of our competitors may be without even a single piece and would be a very enthusiastic buyer. For this reason it is desirable to "shop around."

◆**Consignment to a Retail Dealer:** You can consign your coins to a dealer who can then sell them over a period of time to his customers, to other dealers linked with him via the inter-dealer Teletype system, and to other customers. Of course, you hope that he will sell not only your rare items and gems but your lesser coins as well.

◆**Sale at Auction:** You can consign them to be sold at public auction sale or mail bid sale. This is a popular way to go, for your coins will be offered in competition to thousands of potential buyers, and if you have particularly scarce or rare pieces, or coins that create special attention, you may well do better than by any other method.

How Soon Can I Get Paid?

"How soon can I get cash for my coins?" is a question often asked. Well, if you sell your coins directly to a dealer then you can get instant payment. You don't even have to wait seven days or so (as is the case with most security investments). My firm pays cash on the barrelhead for the coins it buys—"the fastest check in the

East"—simply because the market is so competitive that if we didn't want to pay for the coins right away, someone else would!

Auction also offers fast payment. If you consign your coins for sale, then you will be paid on the settlement date after the sale takes place. The total time from consigning your coins to the time you get your money is several months—usually less time, in fact, than it takes to put a piece of real estate on the market, sell it, and complete all of the "paperwork." If immediate cash is a necessity, then a cash advance can often be made against the final auction proceeds.

In practice, the situation of liquidity and ease of sale has never been a problem for any of our clients who have built meaningful collections of choice and rare coins.

Summary

For the investor, coins offer what I consider to be the ideal investment if the investment is pursued in combination with a collecting interest. Past performance has been spectacular, and with continuing worldwide inflation, world monetary problems, the recurring uncertainties of certain other investment fields, the energy crisis, absence of property taxation on coins in most areas, and so on, coins offer an attractive alternative. My firm has helped many people make fortunes by assisting them in the building of collections.

You need not be a numismatic scholar to invest successfully, but a general interest in the field and a basic knowledge certainly help. As noted earlier, the record shows dramatically that those who have pursued the investment route by building a meaningful collection have done much better than those who have simply accumulated coins. In any instance, it is necessary to follow some common-sense rules when you spend your money. Enlist the assistance of one or more professional numismatic firms—companies with established and unquestioned professional and financial reputations. Remember that what you see in print often has to be taken with a large grain of salt, and that some with the fanciest advertisements often have the least substance behind them—particularly if the advertisements are in non-numismatic publications.

Take time to investigate coins, build a basic numismatic library, and get involved in the hobby. Embark on building a meaningful collection. Do these things, and chances are excellent your investment will do very well for you. In addition, you will find your investment is *interesting* to you, your family, and your business associates (if you choose to share your hobby with them)—for coins and money are something they can relate to; something of interest to everyone.

When the time comes to sell your coins you have several methods to choose from. The coin market is very competitive, and there has always been a strong demand for fine collections.

In this chapter I've discussed some general guidelines for building a potentially profitable "portfolio" of rare coins through the medium of forming a collection, and I have given you some of the philosophies that have meant great success in the past. At this point, I am sure, you are interested in some *specific* ways to go about forming a holding of coins, particularly if you want to combine your investment with an interest in collecting as well. Various numismatic areas and specific ideas will be discussed in the following chapters.

U.S. Type Set Investment

A Recommended Way to Collect

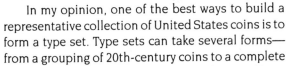 In my opinion, one of the best ways to build a representative collection of United States coins is to form a type set. Type sets can take several forms— from a grouping of 20th-century coins to a complete type set including one of each major design regularly issued from 1793 to date. Unlike a specialized set containing many date or mintmark varieties of the same design, a type set has but a single example of a given design.

Years ago it was possible to build a virtually complete collection of United States coins by date and mintmark sequence. Today it is nearly impossible to do this. First of all, the existing fixed supply of scarce and rare issues has been widely dispersed among hundreds of thousands, if not millions, of collectors. Second, the cost of a nearly complete collection of each and every variety of United States coins ever issued would be prohibitive. For example, when we sold the Eliasberg United States Gold Coin Collection in 1982, a holding consisting of one of each date and mintmark variety within the gold series from $1 to $20, it brought $12.4 million—and this for just the gold part of a collection of United States coins; had the collection contained copper, nickel, and silver issues it would have brought many millions of dollars more. Even if you have a bottomless checking account, certain issues are not readily available. It took Mr. Eliasberg over 20 years to form his collection, and this was in an era with little competition. A practical alternative today is the type set.

Advantages of a Type Set

A complete type set of United States coins is of immense historical interest. Each design has its own story to tell. Such a set provides an excellent opportunity to learn about the design, history, and romance of each coin. At the same time a type set can be an excellent investment. Years ago I always recommended a type set of United States coins as the ideal way to begin a collection. My many clients who followed my earlier advice have profited spectacularly in the intervening years. It seems assured that collecting by design types will be even more popular in the future. With increasing popularity, price increases are bound to come.

The price of a type set depends on the condition of the coins. This is illustrated by considering the price of a 1793 half cent, for example. The value of this coin as listed in the latest edition of the *Guide Book of United States Coins* is: Good-4 $1,700; Very Good-8 $2,400; Fine-12 $3,500; Very Fine-20 $5,500; and Extremely Fine-40 $9,000. Extremely Fine is the best grade listed, simply because specimens are rarely seen in higher grades of preservation. Indeed, Extremely Fine pieces are great rarities. An Uncirculated coin, if indeed one could be found, would probably fetch in the $20,000 to $35,000 range at auction.

Establish a Goal

It is therefore important to establish a goal as to the condition desired. Unless you have in mind spending many hundreds of thousands of dollars, it would be impractical to aspire to form a complete type set of Uncirculated and Proof grades (Proofs of many issues are available after 1858, but they are seldom seen among earlier issues). As a matter of practical consideration I recommend that the various copper and silver issues from 1793 through about 1850 be collected in Fine to Very Fine or Extremely Fine grades, perhaps with particular rarities in slightly lower grades. Designs from 1850 through the early 20th century can be collected in Extremely Fine or better grades, with Uncirculated or Proof examples for pieces which are readily available, depending upon your checkbook. For example, I suggest that your Morgan silver dollar be Uncirculated, for there is no supply problem.

Another possibility is to collect issues from 1793 to 1850 in Good to Fine condition, from 1850 to 1900 in Very Fine or better condition, and from 1900 onward in Uncirculated and Proof preservation. There is no rule about this, and historically all conditions have advanced in value. The selecting of grades desired is dependent upon your personal financial considerations. It would be folly to aspire to collect a complete Uncirculated or Proof type set of United States coins from 1850 to date on a budget of $100 per month. You might not live long enough to complete it! In general, I recommend buying the best grade you can afford.

In a complete set of copper, nickel, and silver United States coins by design types there are a number of rarities.

The 1793 half cent mentioned earlier is one of these. The 1793 half cent, to continue the same example, is desirable for several reasons:

1. It is essential for a type set, for 1793 was the only year in which the design with the Liberty head facing left and a cap on the pole was used. In the following year, 1794, the design was changed.

2. It is the first United States half cent (half cents were minted from 1793 to 1857).

3. It is one of just two denominations (the cent is the other) struck for circulation in the first full year of the Philadelphia Mint's operations.

4. The coin is rare in its own right. Only 35,334 were minted. Using the *Guide Book* as a reference, a 1793 half cent in Fine grade was valued at $45 in 1946.

Forty-five years later in the latest edition (1992 edition, released in 1991), the same coin catalogues for $3,500. You can see that a piece held for this span would have yielded a profit of 7,678%! Further, if the price movement of the 1793 half cent is charted by five-year intervals there was no period in which a profit was not shown from the earlier five-year time. The same is true, by the way, for nearly all United States type coins. In fact, the performance of 1793 half cents is exceedingly *conservative* in comparison to many other issues. As an appendix to the present work indicates, numerous coins advanced more than 10,000% during the same time period!

Another rarity is the 1796 quarter, a design issued only in that year. A Fine specimen catalogued $65 in 1946. By 1991 (1992 edition) the catalogue value had advanced to $7,000, and it was by no means an easy task to acquire one at that price.

Very rare also is the half dollar design of 1796-1797. In fact, this is the scarcest of all silver design type coins. A Fine specimen of the 1797 half dollar was valued at $200 in 1946. By 1991 the price had jumped to $17,000! Interestingly from 1980 to 1985 (a period in which many series were relatively quiet and in which some decline was noted because of the earlier boom times being followed by a normal adjustment) a Fine 1797 half dollar rose in value from $8,500 to $15,000! Since that time it has remained fairly constant in price.

Among United States gold coins, the scarcest major design type is the quarter eagle ($2.50 gold piece) of 1808. In Fine grade this coin was valued at $100 in 1946. By 1991, 45 years later, the piece had advanced to $9,000. In Uncirculated grade the progress of the 1808 was even more dramatic: from $250 in 1946 to $50,000 in MS-60 grade in 1991. If you had a $50,000 balance in your checkbook, this does not mean that you can buy an MS-60 example readily for few are known in that lofty state of preservation, and it may be the case that should one appear in an auction sale, $100,000 or more would be needed to capture the prize. In MS-65 grade, if one could be found at that level, an 1808 $2.50 piece would probably be worth over $200,000.

Additional Considerations

The *Guide Book* does not predict prices, it *reports* them, and often among rarities the situation is that pieces change hands infrequently, and prices listed reflect sales of several years earlier. When another sale occurs, often at a higher level, then subsequent editions will list a new figure. The present writer has seen only two Uncirculated 1808 quarter eagles, including a specimen formerly in the J. Hewitt Judd Collection, later going to the Jimmy Hayes Collection. If this coin were to come on the market today, I imagine that the current $50,000 catalogue valuation would be left far behind when the bidding finally stopped!

When building your type set, select one of the more common issues within the design range. For example, Liberty Walking half dollars were first minted in 1916 and last struck in 1947. Within this span there are dozens of different date and mintmark varieties. In MS-65 condition such issues as 1921, 1921-D, and 1921-S are major rarities, with the 1921-S being the rarest in the series. Other issues, particularly Denver and San Francisco mint pieces from 1918 through 1919, are usually indistinctly struck at the center of the obverse and portions of the reverse. Rather than select a rare issue for your type set, or an early issue which is not

Major Design Types of United States Coins

TYPES OF HALF CENTS

(1) 1793 Liberty Cap with head facing left.
(2) 1794-1797 Liberty Cap with head facing right.
(3) 1800-1808 Draped Bust.
(4) 1809-1836 Classic Head.
(5) 1840-1857 Braided Hair.

TYPES OF LARGE CENTS

(1) 1793 Chain.
(2) 1793 Wreath.
(3) 1793-1796 Liberty Cap.
(4) 1796-1807 Draped Bust.
(5) 1808-1814 Classic Head.
(6) 1816-1839 Coronet.
(7) 1839-1857 Braided Hair.

TYPES OF SMALL CENTS

(1) 1856-1858 Flying Eagle.
(2) 1859 Indian. Laurel Wreath reverse.
(3) 1860-1864 Copper-nickel. Oak Wreath reverse.
(4) 1864-1909 Indian. Bronze.
(5) 1909 V.D.B. Lincoln.
(6) 1909-1958 Lincoln with wheat ears reverse.
(7) 1943 Steel cent.
(8) 1944-1945 Shell case metal cent.
(9) 1959-1982 Lincoln Memorial reverse. Bronze.
(10) 1982 to date. Lincoln Memorial. Copper-coated zinc.

TWO-CENT PIECES

(1) 1864-1873 two-cent piece.

NICKEL THREE-CENT PIECES

(1) 1865-1889 three-cent piece.

SILVER THREE-CENT PIECES

(1) 1851-1853 No outlines to star.
(2) 1854-1858 Three outlines to star.
(3) 1859-1873 Two outlines to star.

NICKEL FIVE-CENT PIECES

(1) 1866-1867 Shield With Rays on reverse.
(2) 1867-1883 Shield Without Rays.
(3) 1883 Liberty Without CENTS.
(4) 1883-1913 Liberty With CENTS.
(5) 1913 Buffalo with raised ground.
(6) 1913-1938 Buffalo with level ground.
(7) 1938 to date, Jefferson.
(8) 1942-1945 Jefferson "wartime" metal.

Major Design Types of United States Coins

HALF DIMES

(1) 1794-1795 Flowing Hair.
(2) 1796-1797 Draped Bust; Small Eagle.
(3) 1800-1805 Draped Bust; Heraldic Eagle.
(4) 1829-1837 Capped Bust.
(5) 1837-1838 Liberty Seated; No Stars.
(6) 1838-1859 Liberty Seated; With Stars
(7) 1853-1855 Arrows at date.
(8) 1860-1873 Liberty Seated; Legend On Obverse.

DIMES

(1) 1796-1797 Draped Bust; Small Eagle.
(2) 1798-1807 Draped Bust; Heraldic Eagle.
(3) 1809-1828 Capped Bust; large size.
(4) 1828-1837 Capped Bust; small size.
(5) 1837-1838 Liberty Seated; No Stars.
(6) 1838-1860 Liberty Seated; With Stars.
(7) 1853-1855 Arrows at date.
(8) 1860-1891 Liberty Seated; Legend On Obverse.
(9) 1873-1874 Arrows at date.
(10) 1892-1916 Barber.
(11) 1916-1945 Mercury.
(12) 1946-1964 Roosevelt. Silver metal.
(13) 1965 to date. Roosevelt. Clad metal.

20-CENT PIECES

(1) 1875-1878 20-cent piece.

QUARTER DOLLARS

(1) 1796 Draped Bust; Small Eagle.
(2) 1804-1807 Draped Bust; Heraldic Eagle.
(3) 1815-1828 Capped Bust; large size.
(4) 1831-1838 Capped Bust; small size.
(5) 1838-1865 Liberty Seated, Without Motto.
(6) 1853 Arrows at date, Rays On Reverse.
(7) 1854-1855 Arrows at date.
(8) 1866-1891 Liberty Seated, With Motto.
(9) 1873-1874 Arrows at date.
(10) 1892-1916 Barber.
(11) 1916-1917 Liberty Standing Type I.
(12) 1917-1930 Liberty Standing Type II.
(13) 1932-1964 Washington. Silver metal.
(14) 1965 to date. Washington. Clad metal.
(15) 1776-1976 Bicentennial. Copper-nickel clad metal.
(16) 1776-1976 Bicentennial. Silver clad metal.

HALF DOLLARS

(1) 1794-1795 Flowing Hair.

Major Design Types of United States Coins

(2) 1796-1797 Draped Bust; Small Eagle.
(3) 1801-1807 Draped Bust; Heraldic Eagle.
(4) 1807-1836 Capped Bust; Lettered Edge.
(5) 1836-1837 Capped Bust; Reeded Edge; 50 CENTS reverse.
(6) 1838-1839 Capped bust; reeded edge; HALF DOL. reverse
(7) 1839-1866 Liberty seated, without motto.
(8) 1853 Arrows at date; rays on reverse.
(9) 1854-1855 Arrows at date.
(10) 1866-1891 Liberty seated, with motto.
(11) 1873-1874 Arrows at date.
(12) 1892-1915 Barber.
(13) 1916-1947 Liberty Walking.
(14) 1948-1963 Franklin.
(15) 1964 Kennedy. Silver metal.
(16) 1965 to date. Kennedy. Clad metal.
(17) 1776-1976 Bicentennial. Copper-nickel clad metal.
(18) 1776-1976 Bicentennial. Silver clad metal.

SILVER DOLLARS
(1) 1794-1795 Flowing Hair.
(2) 1795-1798 Draped Bust; Small Eagle.
(3) 1798-1804 Draped Bust; Heraldic Eagle.
(4) 1836-1839 Gobrecht issues.
(5) 1840-1865 Liberty Seated, No Motto.
(6) 1866-1873 Liberty Seated, With Motto.
(7) 1878-1921 Morgan.
(8) 1921-1935 Peace.
(9) 1971-1976 Eisenhower. Silver metal.
(10) 1971-1978 Eisenhower. Clad metal.
(11) 1776-1976 Eisenhower Bicentennial. Silver clad metal.
(12) 1776-1976 Eisenhower Bicentennial. Clad metal.
(13) 1979-1981 Susan B. Anthony. Clad metal.

TRADE DOLLARS
(1) 1873-1885 trade dollar.

GOLD DOLLARS
(1) 1849-1854 Liberty Head.
(2) 1854-1856 Indian Head; Small Head.
(3) 1856-1889 Indian Head; Large Head.

QUARTER EAGLES ($2½ GOLD)
(1) 1796 Capped Bust, No Stars.
(2) 1796-1807 Capped Bust Right; Stars.
(3) 1808 Capped Bust Left; large-size.
(4) 1821-1834 Capped Bust Left; smaller-size.
(5) 1834-1839 Classic Head.
(6) 1840-1907 Coronet.
(7) 1908-1929 Indian.

Major Design Types of United States Coins

$3 GOLD PIECES
(1) 1854-1889 $3 gold piece.

$4 GOLD PIECES
(1) 1879-1880 Flowing Hair. (patterns).
(2) 1879-1880 Coiled Hair. (patterns).

HALF EAGLES ($5 GOLD)
(1) 1795-1798 Capped Bust; Small Eagle.
(2) 1795-1807 Capped Bust Right; Heraldic Eagle.
(3) 1807-1812 Capped Bust Left.

(4) 1813-1829 Capped Head Left; large size.
(5) 1829-1834 Capped Head Left; smaller size.
(6) 1834-1838 Classic Head.
(7) 1839-1866 Coronet, Without Motto.
(8) 1866-1908 Coronet, With Motto.
(9) 1908-1929 Indian.

EAGLES ($10 GOLD)
(1) 1795-1797 Capped Bust Right; Small Eagle.
(2) 1797-1804 Capped Bust Right; Heraldic Eagle.
(3) 1838-1866 Coronet, Without Motto.
(4) 1866-1907 Coronet, With Motto.
(5) 1907-1908 Indian, Without Motto.
(6) 1908-1933 Indian, With Motto.

DOUBLE EAGLES ($20 GOLD)
(1) 1849-1866 Liberty Head, Without Motto.
(2) 1866-1876 Liberty Head, With Motto. TWENTY D. reverse.
(3) 1877-1907 Liberty Head, With Motto. TWENTY DOLLARS.
(4) 1907 MCMVII Saint-Gaudens Roman numerals issue.
(5) 1907-1908 Saint-Gaudens Arabic date, Without Motto.
(6) 1908-1933 Saint-Gaudens, With Motto.

readily available with a sharply struck appearance, pick one of the so-called "common" dates in the 1940s of which a sharply struck MS-65 specimen can be obtained for less than $200, about half the price of a couple years ago.

It may be interesting if you salt and pepper your type set with a few scarce or rare varieties, particularly if these do not cost much more than so-called common issues. For example, among Barber silver coins, it is often possible to acquire a rare San Francisco or New Orleans piece for just slightly more than a commoner Philadelphia issue.

Among Morgan dollars you might want to add a Carson City issue, for although these are hardly inexpensive, the prices are still within reason, and you will have the opportunity to contemplate the romantic background of this historic mint.

Interesting die varieties, low-mintage issues, and other situations may attract you. As long as the price is not tremendously greater than the cheapest piece available, such coins are recommended for inclusion and can lend additional appeal. You can customize or personalize a type set in any way you wish. For example, if you are forming a 20th-century type set, you may want to include coins of your birth year.

Like ice cream, cats, pizza, and automobiles, type sets come in many different varieties. Here are several ways to build type sets:

A 20th-Century Type Set

A type set of 20th-century silver coin designs makes a very beautiful display. In what we now call MS-63 to MS-64 grades a set was available in the late 1960s in the $1,000 range. In the early 1970s James F. Ruddy, my business associate for many years, hand-picked 100 different sets, encased them in Capital Plastic holders, and offered them for sale in the $1,500 range. By 1978 such a set had advanced in value over $2,500. Now, in the early 1990s, the value of the set is even higher, with the Barber dime, quarter, and half dollar by themselves costing more than the entire set cost in 1978. In my opinion, such a set, which has performed well in the past, will continue to be a great investment in the years to come. The set is a nice steppingstone to a larger type set if you later decide to expand your collection to include earlier issues.

Coin Designs of Our Own Century

Above is a montage of the obverses of most of the different coin designs (and different metal types) needed to form a complete set of 20th-century United States coins from the cent to the silver dollar.

Today I can recommend a collection in nicely matched MS-65 grades (for the prices now are much less for certain issues than they were in 1989 and early 1990) containing an example of each of the following major 20th-century coin designs:

1. Indian cent

2. 1909 V.D.B. Lincoln cent

3. 1909 to 1958 Wheat reverse Lincoln cent

4. 1943 steel Lincoln cent

5. 1944 to 1945 shell case alloy Lincoln cent

6. 1959-1982 bronze Lincoln Memorial cent

7. 1982 to date copper coated zinc Lincoln Memorial cent

8. 1883-1912 Liberty Head nickel*

9. Type I 1913 Buffalo or Indian nickel

10. Type II 1913 to 1938 Buffalo or Indian nickel

11. 1938 to date Jefferson nickel

12. 1942 to 1945 "wartime" Jefferson nickel

13. 1892-1916 Barber dime*

14. 1916 to 1945 Mercury dime

15. 1946 to 1964 Roosevelt dime

16. 1965 to date clad Roosevelt dime

17. 1892-1916 Barber quarter*

18. 1917 Liberty Type I Liberty Standing quarter*

19. 1917 to 1930 Type II Liberty Standing quarter*

20. 1932 to 1964 Washington quarter

21. 1965 to date clad Washington quarter

22. 1776-1976 bicentennial quarter in silver

23. 1776-1976 bicentennial quarter in clad metal

24. 1892-1915 Barber half dollar*

25. 1916-1947 Liberty Walking half dollar*

26. 1948-1963 Franklin half dollar

27. 1964 Kennedy silver half dollar

28. 1965 to 1971 Kennedy half dollar in silver-clad metal

29. 1972 to date Kennedy half dollar in nickel-clad metal

30. 1776-1976 bicentennial half dollar in silver

31. 1776-1976 bicentennial half dollar in clad metal

32. 1878-1921 Morgan silver dollar*

33. 1921-1935 Peace silver dollar*

34. 1971-1974 Eisenhower dollar in silver clad metal

35. 1971-1978 Eisenhower dollar in copper-nickel clad metal

36. 1776-1976 Eisenhower bicentennial dollar in silver clad metal

37. 1776-1976 Eisenhower bicentennial dollar in copper-nickel clad metal

38. 1979 to 1981 Susan B. Anthony dollar in clad metal.

What a beautiful set this would be to own and display. Each coin design has its own story to tell. With the exception of the items asterisked(*) each costs less than $100 in MS-65 grade, and some modern issues cost less than a dollar or two each!

A 20th-century type set can have fewer or more coins than I have just listed. For example, if you want more coins, then the piece I have described as No. 3, the 1909 to 1958 type cent could be further broken down to the style from 1909 to 1917 without the initials of the designer (Victor David Brenner), and the issues from 1918 onward with the designer's initials on Lincoln's shoulder.

On the other hand, if you want to abbreviate the set, then the 1776- 1976 bicentennial pieces can be collected in just one metal rather than both silver and clad varieties; the design is the same in both instances. A like situation exists for the Eisenhower dollar.

New Coin Designs Needed

The coinage panorama is constantly changing. Since the first edition of this book was published in 1974, a number of new varieties have appeared. The Lincoln cent obverse has been with us since 1909, a span of more than 70 years. In fact, the design is over three-quarters of a century old! Perhaps it is a candidate for change. The Jefferson nickel has been with us since 1938. The Washington quarter dates back to 1932.

In 1986 Kurt Krueger made a proposal, which was subsequently passed by the American Numismatic Association Board of Governors, endorsing the concept of design changes for our current coinage. *Numismatic News, Coin World,* and other periodicals had been discussing the situation in print for several months earlier. Diane Wolfe, an enthusiastic spokesperson for the numismatic community, took up the call in the late 1980s. However, the Treasury Department in 1990 declared that it was opposed to the modification of current coin designs.[1] In my opinion, the time has come for some changes.

By 1904 President Theodore Roosevelt had become interested in the subject of American coinage. He selected Augustus Saint-Gaudens to completely redesign the motifs of American denominations from the cent through the double eagle. Extensive correspondence and a heated controversy arose.[2] The result was the magnificent MCMVII High Relief double eagle, the 1907 Indian $10, and several interesting pattern designs.

With relatively few exceptions, and these being of a comparatively recent time, Treasury Department officials have not shown a close personal interest in new designs during the intervening decades. Now we have an era in which the Bureau of the Mint is taking an active part in numismatics. Mrs. Donna Pope, director of the Mint from 1981 to 1991, has been a familiar face at the yearly American Numismatic Association conventions.

During the last few years of his tenure as chief engraver of the Mint, Frank Gasparro had many meetings with coin collectors. When a new smaller-diameter dollar was proposed Gasparro came up with the beautiful Liberty Cap design reminiscent of the cent and half cent of 1793. Despite great interest and enthusiasm shown on his part and by collectors and journalists who viewed it, the idea was scrapped in favor of the Susan B. Anthony obverse, a style dictated by political interests.

Elizabeth Jones, the chief engraver from 1981 to 1991 and successor to Frank Gasparro, is likewise numismatically inclined. Her 1982 Washington commemorative half dollar has been widely praised. During her tenure she made many trips to give talks at numismatic events, much to the delight of those attending.

Mike Iacocca, an assistant engraver at the Mint until his retirement in 1991, was involved in numismatics and, in fact, participated in several educational seminars at American Numis-

[1] One reason for this is that the Mint was busy with designs for several current and proposed commemorative coin programs.
[2] Much of this correspondence is quoted in my *United States Gold Coins: An Illustrated History* book (specifically pages 277-291, 305-307, and 315-329).

matic Association conventions. During a visit to the Philadelphia Mint in 1980, Mike Iacocca showed me the technique by which he impressed S and D mintmarks into dies made at Philadelphia and shipped to the branch locations. John Mercanti, Mint engraver who has created several modern commemoratives, has attended a number of numismatic events. Robert Leuver, who headed the Bureau of Engraving and Printing until he resigned in the late 1980s to accept the position of executive director of the American Numismatic Association, offered many fine programs to collectors during his tenure in the B.E.P. office.

At the risk of being "political" myself, I urge *you* to make it known to your elected public officials that coins and coin designs are indeed important. For many decades stamp collectors have had a wide variety of new designs to maintain their interest each year. Why can't coin collectors have new designs as well? Just as I have suggested you do with coin investment, Treasury Department officials as well as senators and representatives on legislative banking committees would do well to observe "the lessons of history" with regard to coinage designs. Theodore Roosevelt furnishes an example of what can be done.

A glance through Dr. J. Hewitt Judd's *United States Patterns* book will show many designs which are extraordinarily beautiful but which were rejected for political or other reasons which seem unimportant now. For starters, the 1872 Amazonian coins, George T. Morgan's 1879 "Schoolgirl" dollar, and the 1882 Shield Earring designs would be worth reviewing. The half dollar patterns of 1877 would undoubtedly generate additional enthusiasm. Let's get behind the idea!

A Complete Type Set of U.S. Coins

A complete type set of United States coin designs from 1793 to date is a beautiful collection to behold. As mentioned earlier, such a set has been a wonderful investment in the past. As collecting coins by types is growing in popularity, it seems probable that these will be excellent investments in the future as well.

There are several ways to formulate what a complete type set of United States copper, nickel, and silver coins should contain. The number of pieces depends upon whether certain early issues are considered to be "types" or simply varieties of major types. You can leaf through the pages of the *Guide Book of United States*

Coins and come up with your own ideas. Or, you may wish to consult my book, *United States Coins by Design Types: An Action Guide for the Collector and Investor.* Separate pages are devoted to each of the major designs, with a discussion of the rarity and availability of each.

Generally, a type set should contain one specimen of each major design of each denomination from the half cent through the silver dollar, covering the span from 1793 to date. At the conclusion of this book I list what are considered to be the major varieties. There are several excellent album-type holders as well as display-type plastic holders on the market. There are several varieties of cardboard albums with plastic slides, some of which have interchangeable pages, which are convenient while your set is being formed. After your set is completed, or when it is nearly so, you may wish to investigate having custom plastic holders made. The "Kingswood" brand holders sold by Bowers and Merena Galleries have been highly acclaimed, but there are many other fine products on the market as well.

Your complete type set of coins will contain from one to over a dozen each of the following denominations: half cent (issued from 1793 to 1857), cent (1793 to date), two-cent piece (1864 to 1873), silver three-cent piece (1851 to 1873), nickel three-cent piece (1865 to 1889), nickel five-cent piece (1866 to date), half dime (1794 to 1873), dime (1796 to date), 20-cent piece (1875 to 1878), quarter dollar (1796 to date), half dollar (1794 to date), silver dollar (1794 to 1981), and trade dollar (1873 to 1885).

Some denominations will be represented by only a single coin in your type set. For example, all of the 20-cent pieces issued from 1875 through 1878 are of the same design, thus you will need only one piece. The same is true of the two-cent piece (1864 to 1873), nickel three-cent piece (1865 to 1889), and the trade dollar (1873 to 1885).

Other denominations offer a wide variety of types. In the half dollar series, for example, there are the following designs: (1) Flowing Hair type of 1794 and 1795; (2) Draped Bust, Small Eagle type of 1796 and 1797; (3) Heraldic Eagle reverse type of 1801 to 1807; (4) Capped Bust type with Lettered Edge, 1807 and 1837; (5) Small Bust type with Reeded Edge, "50 CENTS" on reverse, 1836 to 1837; (6) Small Bust type with Reeded Edge, "HALF DOL." on reverse, 1838 and 1839; (7) Liberty Seated type Without Motto, 1839 to 1865; (8) Liberty Seated type With Arrows At Date, Rays on

Reverse, issued only in 1853; (9) Liberty Seated type With Arrows At Date (but without rays on reverse), 1854 and 1855; (10) Liberty Seated type With Motto IN GOD WE TRUST, 1866 to 1891; (11) Liberty Seated type With Motto, With Arrows At Date, 1873 and 1874; (12) Barber type 1892 to 1915; (13) Liberty Walking type of 1916 to 1947; (14) Franklin type of 1948 to 1963; (15) Kennedy type in silver, 1964; (16) Kennedy type in silver-clad metal, 1965 to 1971, (17) Kennedy type in nickel-clad metal 1972 to date; (18) 1776-1976 bicentennial in clad metal; (19) 1776-1976 bicentennial in silver metal. Such a set will be very attractive!

A beautiful set containing carefully selected coins of quality will be an excellent investment over the years, in my opinion. This has been my often-expressed opinion in the past (in print years ago in the *Empire Investors Report, The Forecaster,* my *Coin World* column, and in our own coin company catalogues, for example). If you followed my advice then you've seen your investment multiply in value. However, "there's no future in the past," as the saying goes—and you are concerned about tomorrow, not yesterday. I think the outlook for collecting types is very bright and that these represent an excellent way to collect and invest at the same time. I am sure you'll do well!

If you want to build a first-class set, then a general guideline for grades is as follows:

1. Early issues, circa 1793-1807. VF-30 to AU-50

2. Issues circa 1807-1836. AU-50 to MS-63

3. Issues circa 1837-1891. MS-63 to MS-64

4. Issues after 1891. MS-65

Such a set will be beautiful in appearance and will be a treasure to own. There are a few exceptions to the guidelines, and these are dictated by price. For example, a Morgan dollar of the 1878-1921 design can be obtained in MS-65 grade inexpensively.

Type Sets of Gold Coins

United States gold coins were issued for circulation from 1795 through 1933. The series is replete with many rare date and mintmark varieties and many different design types. The following gold coin denominations were issued: $1, $2.50, $3, $4, $5, $10, $20, and $50. The $4 denomination was issued in pattern form only; no pieces were made for circulation. The $50 denomination was issued by several different California minters (the U.S. Assay Office of Gold being among them) in Gold Rush days, in pattern form by the United States government in 1877, and as a commemorative coin for the Panama-Pacific International Exposition in 1915. $4 and $50 coins cost thousands of dollars each and are not regular issues, thus many collectors and investors consider them to be in the realm of the advanced collector or buyer. More important for my present discussion are the issues which are readily available:

1. $1 gold pieces minted from 1849 to 1889

2. $2.50 from 1796 to 1929

3. $3 from 1854 to 1889

4. $5 from 1795 to 1929

5. $10 from 1795 to 1933

6. $20 from 1849 to 1933.

These six denominations are generally available to the collector and investor today. Gold $1 pieces are fairly scarce, and $3 pieces are all rare, for these denominations (with the exception of a few dates) were made only in limited numbers, and both denominations were discontinued in 1889. It is surprising to note that the massive $10 and $20 gold coins were often minted by the millions each year—not because they were in demand for circulation in hand-to-hand transactions, but because they formed a convenient monetary unit for bulk bank-to-bank and international transactions. More about this later.

There are several interesting ways a basic gold type set can be formed. Here are some of the most popular:

•**A Basic Denomination Gold Type Set:** Such a set consists of just six coins; one specimen each of the following denominations used from the mid-19th century through the early 20th century:

1. $1 1849 to 1889

2. $2.50 1840 to 1929

3. $3 1854 to 1889

4. $5 1839 to 1929

5. $10 1838 to 1933

6. $20 1850 to 1933

Mounted in a Capital or other plastic display holder, or kept in slabs, such a set is quite interesting to own. For grades I like MS-63 for each, except that for budget purposes some buyers may opt for a lesser grade $3, such as AU-50 to MS-60.

•**20th Century Denomination Gold Type Set:** This set consists of just four coins; one each of the denominations minted during the 20th century. Most collectors include these designs (instead of the earlier Liberty Head designs): Indian $2.50 (minted 1908-1929), Indian $5 (1908-1929), Indian $10 (1907-1933), and Saint-Gaudens $20 (1907-1933). For grades I like MS-63 or MS-64 for each.

•**Comprehensive Gold Type Set:** This set consists of one each of the major design variations of the mid to late 19th and early 20th centuries:

1. $1 small-diameter type 1849-1854
2. $1 small Indian Head or "Type II" type 1854-1856
3. $1 Indian Head type 1856-1889
4. $2.50 Liberty Head type minted 1840-1907
5. $2.50 Indian Head type minted 1908-1929
6. $3 1854-1889 type
7. $5 1839-1866 Liberty Head type without motto
8. $5 1866-1908 Liberty Head type with motto
9. $5 1908-1929 Indian Head type
10. $10 1838-1866 Liberty Head type without motto
11. $10 1866-1907 Liberty head type with motto
12. $10 1907-1908 Indian type without motto
13. $10 1908-1933 Indian Head type with motto
14. $20 1850-1866 Liberty Head type without motto
15. $20 1866-1876 Liberty Head type with motto and TWENTY D.
16. $20 1877-1907 Liberty Head type with TWENTY DOLLARS
17. $20 1907-1908 Saint-Gaudens type without motto
18. $20 1908-1933 Saint-Gaudens type with motto

This set displays a beautiful panorama of gold coinage.

Recommended Grades

Some advice: the spread between the prices of many of the gold coins in worn grades (Very Fine, Extremely Fine, etc.) and Uncirculated grade is much less than it is on copper and silver coins. I recommend acquiring 19th-century issues in MS-60 through MS-63 grades and 20th-century issues MS-63 or MS-64.

Leave lesser-graded coins, especially late 19th- and early 20th-century coins below MS-60, to the many buyers who don't know about grade distinctions and who are interested in buying the coins for their intrinsic or metallic value. Often the spread is so little that an Uncirculated piece can be obtained for just slightly over the price of a worn EF-45 or AU-50 20th-century $20 gold piece of a common date.

MS-65 coins are, of course, dandy to own, but in recent years the prices of these have gone up sharply, thus your budget may be a consideration here. However, in general, MS-65 United States gold coins, with just a few exceptions, are very elusive, especially if they are dated prior to about 1880.

Gold coins are very appealing. There is something indescribably romantic about owning a heavy (about one ounce of gold) $20 piece from many years ago.

Two Categories

In terms of investment, gold coins can be divided into two major categories: (1) those which are rare from a *numismatic* viewpoint, and (2) those which are scarce (for all United States gold coins are "scarce") but whose value is dependent more upon the price movement of gold bullion than upon numismatic considerations.

Thus a $3 gold piece, all examples of which are truly rare, is an ideal example of the first category. An Uncirculated specimen of the 1854 $3 gold piece has been valued at the following prices over the years in the *Guide Book of United States Coins*: 1946 $22.50, 1950 $27.50, 1955 $45, 1960 $140, 1965 $275, 1970 $350, 1975 $1,650, 1980 $3,500, 1985 $3,500, 1990 $3,200, 1991 $2,500. This amounts to an increase on the investment of about 11,000% over the years!

A 1928 $20 gold piece, one of the most common of all 20th-century $20 issues, has had a price movement characteristic of the second category. The price movement of such a coin is more dependent upon the price of gold metal as a commodity. The coin contains about one ounce of gold. As it is a collectors' item, it sells for a premium over the bullion price, but the two prices are closely related.

The *Guide Book* prices show the following price movements for an Uncirculated 1928 $20 over the years: 1946 $70, 1950 $60, 1955 $55, 1965 $80, 1970 $85, 1975 $340, 1980 $850, 1985 $775, 1990 $575, 1991 $500. This amounts to an increase over the years of 614%, a return more reflective of gold bullion prices than of any numismatic considerations.

My personal recommendation concerning gold coins has been this: if you want the best return on your investment, buy *numismatically rare* gold coins (of which the above is not one). If you are a commodity specialist or speculator, then the "common date" $10 and $20 issues are interesting, but this is an investment in *commodities*, not *numismatics*, and is hence out of the scope of this book.

A Complete Type Set of Gold Coins

United States gold coins were first minted in 1795. From then until 1933, the last year of regular coinage for circulation, many different design types were issued.

The year 1834 represents a turning point in gold coins. By that year the price of gold metal had risen to the point at which each coin was worth more than face value. Thus, for example, a group of $5 gold pieces could be melted down, and gold metal retrieved could be sold back to the Mint for several dollars' profit! This caused all 1795 to 1834 gold coins of the early weight standard to become quite scarce. Most were melted down, including nearly all of certain issues. Mintage figures reveal that 17,796 gold pieces of the $5 denomination were produced in 1822, and yet only three pieces are known today! It is thought that most of the 17,796 were never released, and sometime around 1834 they were melted down. In October 1982 my firm auctioned one of these for $687,500!

As a result of the 1834 situation, all early United States gold coins are very rare, and many are extremely rare. Completing a type set of all gold designs thus entails both a generous sum of money and a determined search, for some of the scarcer issues are seldom seen on the market. The *Guide Book of United States Coins* gives an indication of the amount needed to complete a type set

Early United States Gold Coins

1796 $2½ gold (quarter eagles). The variety at the left has no stars on the obverse. The specimen at the right has stars.

1795 and 1805 $5 gold pieces (half eagles). 1795, with the reverse eagle on a palm branch, is the first year of issue.

Later styles are typified by these $5 pieces of 1812 and 1818. Note that the head is smaller on the 1812 type.

Early $10 "eagles." 1795 is the first year of issue. The 1797 illustrates the heraldic eagle reverse.

of gold coins. However, as is also the case with rare early United States copper, nickel, and silver coins, the prices of certain rarities are on the low side in this reference. It has been my experience that auction records for top grade pieces and rarities are often far over catalogue values, sometimes many *multiples* of those values. Which coins are worth close to catalogue prices and which ones are worth much more? This is an excellent example of the need to seek the professional counsel of an experienced dealer.

A reasonable goal in forming a complete collection of the different design types of United States gold coins would be to have the 1795 to 1834 issues in grades of Extremely Fine or AU. Later issues can be Uncirculated. When complete, your type set will be a prize-winning display, a set with few equals anywhere in the world!

Comfort in Gold Ownership

Concerning type sets of gold coins, I mention that, like Silas Marner did, many investors and collectors feel a certain comfort in owning gold coins. These massive gleaming yellow coins have a certain solidity and "heft" about them, an aura of security. An Oklahoma client, who had made a fortune operating a chain of retail stores, and, later, building industrial properties in Colorado, once purchased from me a very substantial quantity of common-date gold coins. I tried to persuade him to become a numismatist, but my efforts were to no avail. I asked why he bought the coins, and he replied that they gave him a *comfortable feeling*. He had read numerous predictions of the collapse of the United States monetary system; he was familiar with reports of international problems, and the like. While he was a flag-waving American citizen of intense loyalty, he still thought "what if?" His cache of gold, ensconced in his safe deposit box, still provides him with a measure of satisfaction. In addition, he must have a smile on his face now, for when he bought the coins from me gold was selling for $135 per ounce!

Beware of Counterfeits

I cannot resist making a few additional comments here. First, if you are disregarding my advice and are buying so-called "common date" $10 and $20 issues, be sure you are getting *genuine* pieces. Perhaps more so than in the field of rare coins, common pieces are the ones usually counterfeited. The counterfeiters are very clever. Whereas genuine pieces contain 90% gold and 10% copper, counterfeits often contain 70% to 80% gold and a corresponding amount of other alloys. To the naked eye such pieces are difficult to detect.

I am dismayed to report that on a trip to Europe I visited a number of banks which maintained an active trade in selling United States and other gold coins. I hastened to examine the $10 and $20 pieces offered, with the anticipation that perhaps a scarce date or two could be acquired for the price of a common one. Alas, just about all the common date gold coins I saw on display in several banks in Holland, Belgium, Germany, and Greece were counterfeit! Even in Switzerland, where certain banks maintain numismatic departments and should know better, I have run into forgeries. For example, the rare coin department of a leading bank in Zurich offered me a $3 gold piece, unaware that I was a professional coin dealer and a member of the International Association of Professional Numismatists (among other qualifications). I was perceived as being an American tourist! I cautioned that the piece was a counterfeit, and not a good one at that. I was then told: "Well, I guess you won't want the piece then." Where did the coin go? Back into the display case!

Similarly, anyone caring to peruse back issues of *Numismatic News* or *Coin World* will notice instances of cleverly forged krugerrands and other bullion-type gold coins being sold to gullible buyers. When the perpetrators are caught, and reports appear in the numismatic publications, usually it is too late to do anything about it. Typically, the buyer for such things wants to deal only in cash, wants no records kept, and thinks he is pulling something over on the Internal Revenue Service. Often he is fooling just himself! How disappointing it must be to spend thousands of dollars for quantities of double eagles or krugerrands only to find out when selling them that they are forgeries.

There will always be sellers who turn a neat profit by offering misrepresented goods to people who believe they are gaining an advantage by acquiring a "bargain," by avoiding the Internal Revenue Service, by not keeping records, or by some other "clever" action. While some people may succeed in such endeavors, probably most are victimized. A few years ago a California industrialist visited with me. He was a casual collector, not a serious numismatist, and had seen one of our recent *Rare Coin Review* issues. We had offered a number of $3 gold pieces. These coins were of high quality and were priced not at super-bargain levels but, instead, to be good values. Indeed, we had sold out. Still, to my visitor the prices seemed high, for a number of them were priced in the range of several thousand dollars each.

A few months later the same gentleman visited me again. "Look at what I bought in Europe!" he said proudly as he showed me a red-covered plastic "wallet" with clear envelopes within displaying nearly a dozen different $3 gold pieces. "What will you pay me for them?" was his next question.

"I am sorry, but each and every one is a counterfeit," I replied. "Here, look at them with this magnifying glass. You will notice that the obverse die of each coin is precisely identical, although the first coin in your holder is dated 1854 and other coins in your holder are dated in the 1880s! The only value they have would be their gold content if melted down. In fact, they are illegal to hold."

My visitor departed, taking his "bargains" with him. While I suppose I might have thought "I told you so" as he walked out the door, in reality the situation was sad. Not only did he lose his original investment, he apparently became disillusioned with coin collecting. I have neither seen nor heard from him since, and this happened quite a few years ago.

A Treasure for the Future

When I think of type sets of United States coins I often think of Oscar G. Schilke, who formed one of the nicest type sets I have ever seen. Mr. Schilke, who is now deceased, was a close friend and advisor for many years.

I first met Oscar at one of the early Metropolitan New York Coin Conventions around 1955. He had read some of my advertisements in *The Numismatic Scrapbook Magazine* and had some coins to offer for sale. If memory serves, they were a few large cents and colonial coins—$200 or $300 worth in all. Oscar never put a price on anything, so I made an offer—which was accepted.

At the time I attended most of the major conventions in the eastern United States. Oscar was a habitual convention-attender, and at most shows he would have five or six or perhaps even a dozen coins for me to see first. He knew I liked unusual coins, so he would nonchalantly include a surprise in each selection. As I looked through the envelopes he would wait until I came across the "special coin" and commented on it. On one occasion it was a blazing mint red Uncirculated 1823 large cent, another time it was a large cent with a small counterstamp commemorating the return visit of Lafayette to the United States in 1824, and still another time it was an unlisted variety of 1795 Talbot, Allum & Lee cent.

In time Mr. and Mrs. Schilke and I became good personal friends in addition to our business acquaintance. Soon I considered a yearly visit to his tranquil lakeside home in Connecticut a "must" on my calendar. During these visits Oscar would tell stories of the "good old days" and the experiences he had with collectors and dealers in the 1930s and 1940s.

Many of Oscar's stories remain in my mind. One that is particularly vivid concerns his purchases from one of New York City's dealers. This dealer, the late Wayte Raymond, would ask Oscar a certain price for a desired coin and then grant a discount if Oscar could tell him, before buying it, of the coin's background and history!

As did many collectors of the past, Oscar really enjoyed his coins. To aid in appreciating what he purchased and also to learn about coins in general, he built up a large numismatic library— much of which simply "grew" as he saved periodicals, auction catalogues, and other references.

Over a period of time, I purchased many of his coins and sets. Oscar would delight in telling me that "I paid $5 for that one in 1938" as he accepted my offer of $50 for a coin!

Numismatics made Oscar Schilke's life richer in many ways. From a pleasure viewpoint he really enjoyed the company of other collectors and dealers, many of whom can recall today his warm hospitality and his love for the coins he owned. From a financial viewpoint his coin collection made a nice nest egg—an investment whose performance would have been hard to duplicate in any other financial medium. Oscar was a businessman himself, and over a period of years he tried many investment areas. Finally he decided—and this was in an era when few people had ever heard of coin investment—that the best investment of all was to spend money on his coin collection. His interests knew no limits, and he formed a fine collection containing United States one-cent pieces, colonial coins, quarter eagles, colonial and United States paper money, California gold, and other series.

Coins were very good to Oscar. His life story is an interesting case in point: coins can be a *wonderful investment* in combination with a *fascinating hobby*. Literally, you get the best of two worlds!

To paraphrase Ben Franklin: "Mind your collection carefully, and the investment will take care of itself." By carefully collecting choice coins you'll build a financial treasure for the future. In the meantime you'll have lots of enjoyment in the search for the pieces you need!

Investing in U.S. Copper Coins

Collecting By Varieties

 In this chapter I tell of ways to invest in and collect specialized United States copper coins (including bronze and other various alloys after 1863). In numismatic parlance this is called collecting by dates and mintmarks or collecting by varieties.

Collecting by dates and mintmarks has been popular since the early years of the present century. Indeed, many collectors and investors begin their interest today by endeavoring to assemble one of each variety of modern coinage: Lincoln cents, Jefferson nickels, Roosevelt dimes, Washington quarters, and Kennedy half dollars. Unlike a type collection (which includes but a single specimen of each major design) a specialized collection contains one of each and every major variety.

Examples of Specialized Collections

Each series has its specialists. Some numismatists have combined their collecting interest with the close study of coins and have published research articles and books. Often an auction sale catalogue featuring an outstanding specialized collection will be an important reference work in itself. Over the years my firm has handled many superb specialized collections. The Armand Champa, River Oaks, Rudy Sieck, and Major Lenox R. Lohr collections of United States pattern coins were milestones in that field. In fact, the Lohr Collection was the largest and most comprehensive (over 1,500 different pieces) collection of United States patterns ever priced and offered for sale.

The celebrated collection of United States currency formed by Matt Rothert, distinguished past president of the American Numismatic Association, will long be remembered, as will the Terrell

Collection of United States coins by design types, the Gilroy and Fuller collections of United States large cents, the state copper coins, Hard Times tokens, and other specialized series within the Garrett Collection, the Frederick Taylor Collection of state copper coinage 1785-1788, the fantastic and complete Louis Eliasberg Collection of United States Gold Coins (sold by my firm for $12.4 million in October 1982), and many others.

The most valuable group of United States coins ever auctioned was the Garrett Collection sold by my firm for over $25 million for The Johns Hopkins University from 1979 to 1981. T. Harrison Garrett, who was described as "the ultimate connoisseur" by one observer, endeavored from 1865 until his death in 1888 to form a collection as complete as possible in superb condition. Our handling of the sale involved the preparation of a major reference book, *The History of United States Coinage as Illustrated by the Garrett Collection*, as well as four specialized catalogues. The result was a series of sales the likes of which the coin market has never seen before or since. Interesting from today's viewpoint is that Garrett did not collect mintmark varieties, for this was not a popular discipline during his lifetime.

Often the completeness and quality of a choice specialized collection will result in the coins bringing well over current values when sold at auction. This compounds the desirability of the investment—the pieces, when sold, may bring not only the current value but even more! What could be more ideal from an investment viewpoint? This extra reward is an additional compensation for hours of study and patience.

The Adams Collection of 1794 Cents

An example of a specialized collection within the copper series is provided by the remarkable collection of 1794 United States large cents formed over a long period of years by John W. Adams. In 1982 my firm catalogued this holding and offered it for sale at fixed prices. A 132-page volume featuring the cents, one coin per page plus extensive introductory, historical, and editorial material, was offered for $10 per copy. Borrowing an idea used by Sylvester S. Crosby when he issued his *Early Coins of America* in 1875, a deluxe hardbound edition was offered at $100 by advance subscription. This special version contained tipped-in photographic color plates, and autographed inscriptions by me, Richard

A. Bagg, Ph.D. (who assisted with the research), and John Adams. At the end of the book there was a printed listing of each and every one of the subscribers, nearly 300 names in all. Collecting numismatic *books* has been a popular pursuit, and some good investment stories could be told about this field as well. Suffice it to say, no sooner had the limited edition been distributed than a collector who missed out on the earlier ordering opportunity saw a copy and offered $250 to our firm if we could persuade someone among the subscribers to part with one! Since that time, several copies have sold in the $300 to $450 range at auction.

John W. Adams was and still is a *numismatist* first and a numismatic investor second, if at all. Indeed, as the head of a securities firm he noted that since he was in the investment business he preferred to invest in stocks and bonds and that coins were for pleasure only. However, when his coins were sold, the profits obtained would have made any securities analyst envious! The following story of John Adams and his 1794 cents is excerpted from our catalogue of his collection. I urge you to read the text carefully, not because it will tell you how to turn $1,000 into $10,000 in your spare time without effort, but because the words illustrate one of my favorite philosophies: The greatest investment successes have gone to knowledgeable numismatists. Just as was the case with Oscar G. Schilke in the experience I related earlier, John Adams' life has been immeasurably enriched by his association with coins and with fellow numismatists.

John Adams and His 1794 Large Cents

Doctor Sheldon was fond of quoting Samuel Hudson Chapman to the effect that, sooner or later, the serious collector would gravitate to copper; once there, it was said, he would probably succumb to 1794. ——John W. Adams

John Weston Adams of Boston, Massachusetts may well be regarded as one of the most knowledgeable numismatists of our day. As a collector, his enchantment with 1794 large cents, an enthusiasm he has shared with many, has added something special to the charm and allure they already possess. At the same time, he can be applauded for the many fine and informative contributions he has made to the numismatic fraternity. Over the years he has written many articles on 1794 large cents and related subjects. In 1982 numismatists were delighted to see the first volume of a projected three-book set, *United States Numismatic*

1794 Cents from the Adams Collection

Sheldon-24

S-26

S-42

S-59

S-60

S-65

S-69

S-70

Several of the many die varieties of 1794 large cents.

Literature. Published by George Frederick Kolbe, the volume, written and researched by John Adams, gave an in-depth presentation of 19th-century auction catalogues and the numismatists who produced them.

A descendant of a Vermont family of loggers and dairy farmers, John was born in Paoli, Pennsylvania on April 2, 1936. Raised by his mother and grandmother, he attended elementary and secondary schools at Paoli and Haverford, respectively. Later, he went on to Princeton and then to Harvard where he received an MBA in 1960. During the past decade he has been a partner in Adams, Harkness & Hill, Boston investment bankers and securities brokers.

When John was queried about the relationship between his vocation and avocation, he said that coins provided him a refreshing change from the intense concentration that his work demanded and also allowed him to engage in the pleasurable pursuits of research and writing. Since he travels much of the time he is able to visit collectors and attend conventions and important auctions. Clearly, John has experienced a certain personal enjoyment and fulfillment from coin collecting in the more than three decades he has been involved in numismatics.

His interest in collecting was sparked by his mother, who had a good eye for collectible items. Although the family was by no means affluent, she was able over the years to assemble a small and aesthetically pleasing group of antiques, silver, furniture, and paintings. Her good eye along with her collection spirit was passed on to John, who at the age of eight, was given a Lincoln cent album by his mother as an encouragement to save money.

He went to the local banks to search through cent rolls for missing dates and mintmarks, his mother encouraging him all the while. One Christmas, his mother gave him 100 Indian cents she had purchased from the famous Philadelphia dealer, David M. Bullowa,[1] for two cents apiece. John became enchanted with Indian cents and during his teenage years, as he could afford to do so, he would take a train to Philadelphia to acquire additional lots of 100.

One day Bullowa offered him two 1858 Flying Eagle cents, the Large and Small Letters varieties, in Proof, at $92.50 for the pair,

---

[1] David Bullowa, who was also associated with the New Netherlands Coin Co. for a time, is remembered today as a leading scholar of his time. Among his efforts was a text on commemorative coins published in 1938.

but the cost was prohibitive to his budget at the time. Bullowa told him that quality was the key and that the coins were rare. Further, he offered to hold the coins until John could save the money necessary for their purchase. A year and a half later John bought the coins and went from that point on to assemble a complete collection of Flying Eagle and Indian cents in Proof grade, always keeping an eye out for overall attractiveness and color characteristics.

His collecting slowed while he attended Princeton, where his studies became increasingly important. Somehow he did find time to assemble a set of 12 different varieties of 1858 cent patterns in copper-nickel metal, thus reconstructing a group of pattern pieces which was popular with numismatists during the formative years of the hobby in America. To help finance his MBA degree at Harvard he later sold the patterns and his Indian cents as well.

In 1966, deciding to seriously collect again, he stopped by Lester Merkin's office while on a business trip to New York City.[1] Lester, in his unique style, suggested to John that he assemble a collection of type coins, attend auctions, and delve into numismatic literature.

The Interest in Large Cents Begins

A few years later, after reading a copy of the *Rare Coin Review*, John called me at my office. I suggested that if he was interested in large cent collecting he would do well to become knowledgeable about the series first—by reading about the pieces and joining a society specializing in early copper coinage.

John ordered an 1811 large cent from me as a beginning, but it turned out that the next 100 large cents he acquired would all be dated 1794! He joined the Early American Coppers Club, which publishes *Penny-Wise*—an informal journal of new discoveries, information on rarity and condition ratings, gossip, and news in the field of copper issues, particularly large cents. By means of letters to the editor and scholarly articles, John became a contributor.

An indication of John's collecting interest was expressed by his first letter to the editor of *Penny-Wise* in 1971:

[1] Lester Merkin, a dedicated numismatist of many years' standing, entered professional numismatics in the 1960s and quickly became known for the excellence of the material he offered at auction and by direct sale and for his reputation as a fine gentleman.

"I very much enjoyed attending the EAC annual meeting in New York. It was a pleasure to be able to get together with fellow collectors on such an informal basis."

At a 1971 convention in Boston, John perceived that grading of 1794 cents was not exactly by the book, as per a letter to the *Penny-Wise* editor: "Fanciers of '94s were not exactly surfeited with choice offerings. The commercial EFs seemed to be getting further down into and, in some cases, all the way out of the VF classification."

His concern with regard to preserving the numismatic tradition is best expressed in a letter published in *Penny-Wise* in 1972 with reference to the collection of large cents housed by the American Numismatic Society in New York City:

"It is unquestionably true that their large cents are not being taken care of, and, as a consequence, are showing noticeable signs of deterioration.... It seems to me that EAC has a moral obligation to do something about the situation. I would happily contribute time to a committee which brushed or otherwise cared for the coins."

The "Starred Reverse" 1794 is Acquired

During the same year John added possibly the most famous individual coin to his collection, certainly the most distinctive of all die varieties, the finest known specimen of the famous Sheldon-48. The editor of *Penny-Wise* did not overlook the purchase:

"A new world's record for the sale of a United States large cent was established when the 'finest known' 1794 S-48 Starred Reverse brought $15,000."

Acquired from Stack's in 1972, this coin was certainly the "star" of the sale. It brought nearly double what *any other coin* in the sale was bid, with an 1879 $4 Stella, the next highest priced coin, fetching $7,850.

With inflation accelerating on a broad front, John expressed the view in print that "prices have reached a level which are not only restrictive to the average collector but which are also unreasonable in the abstract." This was in 1973. He went on to state "as grim as today's inflationary prices may be, there are at least two possibilities for reversing the trend. If a large collection were to be dispersed," he continued, "prices might level off or decrease.

Another option would be for "we wolves [the buyers of coins] to go on strike" and pay only a certain percentage of the then newly established "basal values." Clearly, John was interested in making the coins available to a larger group of collectors. This is perhaps reflective of a certain camaraderie among large cent enthusiasts, a feeling which has resulted numerous times in coins being exchanged or traded at valuations of less than they could have brought if featured in a public auction sale. Indeed, one piece in the Adams Collection was acquired as a gift from a fellow collector.

Later in 1973 John made substantial purchases from the Naftzger Collection, which greatly contributed to the depth of his holdings. Also during 1973 he purchased several important pieces by private treaty from The Johns Hopkins University, owner of the Garrett Collection.

John W. Adams, Author

During the following years he contributed several articles to *Penny-Wise* and edified its readers on such topics as "The American Numismatic Society and Mr. Clapp" and "Heads of 1793," as well as providing information on Cogan, Garrett, and Sheldon.

In 1976 he edited *Monographs on Varieties of United States Large Cents 1793-1794*, of which a reviewer wrote: "These studies are preceded by a fine essay in which John W. Adams discusses the origins of large cent collecting and reviews significant literature for the coppers of 1793 and 1794 in a most interesting manner. John Adams always makes for good reading, and this is no exception."

Also in 1976 John wrote the foreword to a new printing of Attinelli's *Numisgraphics*, which was first published in 1876. He noted: "Near the center of the history-making process were auction sales with their catalogues which served as reference guides to authenticity, rarity, and value. Many individual copies contain the names of buyers, thus establishing the first links in the documentation of pedigree."

His abiding interest in numismatic literature and the information it contained became John's newest specialty. He enjoyed tracing a coin's ownership back to the early numismatists of the 19th century. Subsequently, he contributed articles to *Penny-Wise* concerning early auction catalogues and large cent literature.

Perhaps the *love* he has for his 1794 large cents was best expressed by his printed commentary: "It was not important that the coin was Sheldon-31 or that it graded MS-60, thus placing it tied for second in the Condition Census. It was important that the coin had been owned by Henry Hines or Dr. Beckwith or Capt. Haseltine. Numismatics was not what I could accomplish in a vacuum. Instead, it involved an already-rich tradition of which I was but one link and which it was my trust to preserve."

Continuing his writing efforts, John contributed articles to *Penny-Wise* on "the Starred Reverse," the "Hall-Brand Saga," Hines, Steigerwalt, and, regretfully, obituaries for Dr. William H. Sheldon and Dorothy I. Paschal.[1]

John's own comments are pertinent here:

"Just as the strong allure of 1794 cents has attracted a distinguished group of collectors to the specialty, so has the study of the subject served to weave the successive generations of collectors into a coherent fabric. In the process of publishing their respective works, Maris in 1869, Hays in 1893, Chapman in 1923, and Sheldon in 1949, all assembled the finest specimens in the land. To my way of thinking these special study collections, seemingly assembled once every generation, are especially significant in that they form landmarks along the route of evolution. *I have assiduously sought out these landmarks.*"

The Adams Collection

The conventional standards for measuring a large cent collection are (1) the condition of the coins and (2) the number of varieties represented. The John Adams Collection of large cents was outstanding in both respects. Of the 75 coins contained therein, 55 were included in the Condition Census, with five being finest knowns and another 16 being second finest known or tied for that honor.[2] No fewer than 33 of the 75 coins were Uncirculated or About Uncirculated. As for breadth, 48 of 56 collectable Sheldon varieties were included in the Adams Collection.

However, John Adams did not collect by conventional standards. Although he enjoyed high condition, he traded higher-

---

[1] John W. Adams wrote two important books outside of the large cent field: *United States Numismatic Literature, Volume I, Nineteenth Century Auction Catalogs* (1982) and the companion *Volume II, Twentieth Century Auction Catalogues* (1990), both published by George W. Kolbe.
[2] A Condition Census coin is one which is among the top six finest known examples of its particular variety.

grade pieces for lesser ones on many occasions. While he appreciated rare varieties, he did not retain a complete set of 1794s even though he owned all 56 of the varieties of that year at one time or another.

Adams' overriding purpose was to *collect collectors*. Using 1794 as a unifying theme, he was able to assemble specimens formerly owned by virtually every large cent collector of consequence since the hobby began. To give just a few statistics on this point, I observe the following concerning his collection of 75 examples of 1794 cents offered by my firm in the summer of 1982:

1. In the offering were 32 coins plated in S.H. Chapman's 1923 monograph, more than have been owned by any collector then or since.

2. Of the nine 1794s presently traceable to the pioneering collection of Dr. Edward Maris, four were contained therein.

3. The Adams Collection contained 22 pieces which were plated in the landmark work published by Ed. Frossard and W.W. Hays in 1893.

4. Of the nine cents plated in *both* Hays and Chapman, six were to be found therein.

5. The one and only 1794 pictured in Hays, Gilbert, Chapman, and both editions of Sheldon was, naturally, part of the Adams Collection.

6. Of the eight 1794s plated in the famous Parmelee Sale of 1890, Adams owned five.

7. Of the two 1794s owned by the fabled Dr. Henry Beckwith, both were therein offered.

8. Only two cents have definitely been traced to Captain John Haseltine's personal set of 1794s, and Adams owned the pair.

9. There are four coins known to be the discovery specimens of a given 1794 variety; two of the four are in the collection of the American Numismatic Society and two were offered by us in the 1982 catalogue.

10. The Adams Collection included 13 coins traceable to the Frossard Collection, 17 from the famous Garrett Collection, 14 from Ted Naftzger, 32 from Dr. Sheldon—and the list could go on almost without end. All in all, of the 48 individuals whom Adams would place in a Large Cent Hall of Fame, 44 were represented by coins in his collection.

Part of the fun of collecting "pedigrees" is that it need not cost a lot. To be sure, there were pieces in the Adams Collection which were very valuable. However, there were other coins with a claim on numismatic history that were fully equal but which were priced to fit the budget of almost every collector. All of the coins were destined to bring to their new owners a satisfaction which was perhaps best described in the words of their former owner:

The charisma of the cents of 1794 is based on many factors—the nobility of the basic design, the distinctive features of the different dies, and the aesthetic properties of the copper itself, to name just a few. However, as time passes and the edifice of tradition builds up, a still more compelling dimension of the hobby has arisen. Cherished as they were by their various owners, the coins have woven a fabric of caring people each of whom has seen in these humble tokens of commerce a symbol of something vastly more important. It is difficult to articulate the meaning of the symbol; indeed its significance may have been quite different for each who has shared it. However, the kinship of spirit is a common thread which is understood by all who participate. To own a coin owned by Maris or Hays, Clapp or Sheldon, Hines or Newcomb is to own a piece of history. The owner is at once a recipient of the tradition of the past and a trustee of the treasures of the future.

Investing in Half Cents

Now, on to some practical suggestions for building your own specialized collection. I begin with half cents, the first regular-issue copper series. Minted from 1793 to 1857, half cents comprise a wide variety of dates and types. Pieces were struck for circulation bearing dates from 1793 through 1797, 1800, 1802 to 1811, 1825 to 1829, 1831 to 1836, 1849 to 1851, and 1853 to 1857.

Of the regular-issue dates, 1793, although not a great rarity, is highly desirable and quite expensive, for it is also needed in a general type set of United States coins. It is the only half cent of the Liberty Cap type, Head Facing Left. The 1796 half cent occurs in two varieties, With Pole and Without Pole to Cap, and both are major rarities. 1802 is a scarce date, 1811 is somewhat scarce, and 1831 and 1836 are significant rarities.

Fortunately for the specialist, outstanding reference works concerning half cents are available, most notably Walter Breen's

Encyclopedia of United States Half Cents 1793-1857, a large-format book which contains all you ever wanted to know about half cents—all in all a marvelous compendium of major facts, trivia, and just about everything else Walter Breen could come across on the subject. American Half Cents—The "Little Half Sisters," by Roger S. Cohen, Jr., is likewise available and contains much worthwhile information.

Beyond the standard varieties of half cents made for circulation, a number of Proofs were made. Some were produced in the years dated, and others were made as restrikes. Particularly rare and desirable are Proofs of the years 1831, 1836, 1840 through 1848, and 1852.

If half cents interest you, and you have a good balance in your checkbook, you may wish to embark on building a set of dates and major design types. For starters, the listing of varieties in the Guide Book is worth consulting. Beyond this, you may wish to study the minute die varieties described by Breen and Cohen, although major dates and types seem to be the most popular way to go. Another book, Walter Breen's Complete Encyclopedia of U.S. and Colonial Coins gives major varieties and much information, not only on half cents but on all other series as well, and is highly recommended.

Expect to spend a number of years building your collection. Along the way you will enjoy the thrill of the hunt, for not only are certain pieces hard to find in higher grades, but there are the additional considerations of strike, color, planchet quality, surface appearance, and so on. It may be the case that you will have to look at five or 10 half cents of a given issue to find one that is just right for your own purposes. All of this makes collecting the series a fascinating pursuit.

It is fair to say that relatively few collectors have specialized in half cents over the years. Perhaps this is because the series, in contrast to related large cents, is sprinkled with a number of major rarities, namely the issues of 1796, 1831, 1836, 1840 to 1848, and 1852. By contrast, there are no major rarities among large cent dates, although the varieties of 1793 are expensive, and 1799 is elusive. Perhaps confronted with the prospects of having to obtain a dozen or more half cent rarities for completion of a date set, many have chosen to ignore the series. However, for those interested in investigating the half cent denomination, there are many rewards possible.

Various United States Half Cents

1793

1794

1795 with
"punctuated date"

1802/0
Overdate

1809

1833

1847

1854

I recommend the following grade levels: 1793 to 1797, VF-20 or better. Choose attractive, glossy coins without problems or defects. 1800-1808 EF-40 or better. 1809-1836 MS-60 to MS-63. 1840-1857 MS-60 to MS-64. If you opt to include Proof-only (no related business strikes were made) rarities such as 1831, 1836, 1840-1848, 1849 Small Date, and 1852, I recommend a minimum of Proof-63, with evenly-toned, attractive surfaces.

While the Proofs are certainly impressive to own, I do not expect much market play in them in the next several years. If there were just one Proof among many business strike issues, that one Proof date would emerge as a major rarity that many people would strongly desire. However, there are over a dozen rare Proof-only dates. The task of assembling a complete collection is so daunting that many collectors have not even tried; a situation which has caused a somewhat diminished interest in the series.

Investing in Large Cents

More than any other United States series, large cents have attracted a dedicated, loyal following. The Early American Coppers Club publishes a newsletter, *Penny-Wise*, which is primarily devoted to coppers of the 1793 to 1857 span and which gives information concerning die varieties, rarity, impending auction sales, personal opinions of dealers and collectors, and so on— lots of fascinating reading. Enough has been written about large cents that the collector seeking specialized periodicals and articles could spend several weeks reading about them, and still not cover everything.

Basically, two reference books serve as brilliant beacons to the field: *Penny Whimsy*, by Dr. William H. Sheldon, and *United States Copper Cents 1816-1857*, by Howard R. Newcomb. The Sheldon reference material in particular contains much in the way of "philosophy" and is highly recommended, not only to those with an interest in large cents but to anyone with an interest in numismatics.

Although you may wish to collect large cents by die varieties, as John W. Adams did with cents of 1794, the most popular way is to acquire major dates and types. Again the *Guide Book* listing gives some ideas. As is the case with half cents, you may have to examine five, 10, or more specimens of a given early date in order to find one which is just right for your purposes.

For what my thoughts may be worth, I suggest that you collect issues from 1793 through 1796 Liberty Cap, the early part of the series, in VF-20 or better condition, dates from 1796 Draped Bust through 1814 in EF-40 to AU-55 grade (the rare 1799 and 1804 in F-12 or VF-20), the pieces from 1816 through 1839 in EF-40 to MS-63 grade, and those from 1840 to 1857 from EF-40 to MS-63 preservation.

In general, few people consider large cents to be in the fast track of coin investment,[1] and it is probably true that the best such coins will do is inch along year after year. I doubt if they will be subject to any speculative frenzy or will double in price in a short time. However, it is also correct to say that I am unaware of anyone who has ever formed a high-grade collection of cents, buying with care, who has done other than show a nice profit upon its sale. Such coins offer a nice combination of emotional satisfaction with what in the past has been a solid store of value.

Notwithstanding the preceding, there are several areas within the large cent field which I consider to be sharply undervalued at today's levels. These are: Cents 1821 to 1829 inclusive, EF-40 to MS-64, with all coins to have pleasing, glossy surfaces (no pitted, spotted, irregularly toned, etc. coins); 1830-1839 EF-40 to MS-63; 1839 Braided Hair through 1849, EF-40 to MS-63. These last-named pieces, those from 1839 through 1849, are at once fairly available but scarce today and often trade at the same prices as do much more common cents such as those dated from 1850 through 1856.

While nothing in numismatics is a sure thing, I do know that if someone were to come to my office with a nicely matched set of large cents such as I recommend, I'd be delighted to write out a check for the full 1992 *Guide Book* listing or more—and I would be getting a bargain!

There are many sleepers elsewhere in the series. For example, the *Guide Book* lists the 1817 15-Stars cent at $1,200 in MS-60 grade.[2] Very few such coins exist, and at $1,200 such a piece would be a rare bargain. In 1986, I had the opportunity to view with Kenneth E. Bressett (editor of *A Guide Book of U.S. Coins* and in

[1] For example, David Hall, whose investment writings are well known, has repeatedly exhorted his readers: "Sell all copper." Many investment writers concentrate their efforts on areas in which coins are traded in quantity on Teletype and electronic circuits, and ignore areas such as large cents which involve a degree of searching to find and, upon finding, require a degree of discrimination to separate ugly pieces from attractive ones.

[2] An increase of $500 from the *Guide Book* price noted in the last edition of the present *High Profits From Rare Coin Investment* book.

A Beautiful 1793 Cent

This 1793 cent, die variety Sheldon-3, appeared in the sale of the Garrett Collection, Part I, sold by the author's firm to the order of The Johns Hopkins University. Described as Uncirculated, the piece soared in competition to $115,000, the highest price ever realized for a copper coin of any kind. The figure was not to stand for long, for soon thereafter, we sold a pattern 1792 copper cent for $200,000, setting yet another new copper coin record.

The 1793 chain cent is one of the first official United States coins produced for circulation. Criticism was voiced by newspapers and others. One account said that Miss Liberty on the obverse "appears to be in a fright" and that the chain device on the reverse is "an ill omen for Liberty." After a brief appearance, the chain style was discontinued. Today, 1793 chain cents, which exist in several die varieties, are highly prized by collectors.

recent years a governor of the American Numismatic Association) a beautiful group of United States large cents. Included was an Uncirculated 1817 15-Stars issue. Both of us lingered long with this coin, and spent quite a bit of time talking about it. As Ken and I have seen more than just a few coins in our time, it is significant to mention that we were both excited by a large cent which, in comparison to many other issues, has a fairly nominal catalogue value.

By way of comparison, in the current *Guide Book* an 1879-CC silver dollar also catalogues $1,200 in MS-60 grade. To the casual observer, the 1879-CC might appear to be a coin which is rarer than the 15-Stars 1817 cent. However, *thousands* of such 1879-CC dollars exist,[1] and had one been in the group of coins Ken Bressett and I were viewing, neither one of us would have spent more than a few moments looking at it. However, the 1817 15-Stars cent was different—in Uncirculated grade it is a *rarity*, and I doubt if more than a half dozen exist! I dwell upon this only to demonstrate once again that there are indeed many sleepers in American numismatics. However, some study is needed to locate them, for the identification of such issues is not always obvious.

I highly recommend large cents, not because I think they are the best financial investment in the world, for I do not think they are—but because I believe they offer the opportunity to participate in numismatics in its finest sense: to build a beautiful collection over a period of years, to have fun doing it, to study varieties along the way, and to immerse yourself in a fascinating world of articles and books, all to the accompaniment of the friendship of collectors and dealers also interested in the series. If I could envision a numismatic utopia, it would be the field of coin collecting set up so that there was as much interest in all other series from half cents to double eagles, plus colonial, territorial, and other coins as there is in United States large cents from 1793 to 1857! To give credit where credit is due, much of this enthusiasm can be laid at the doorstep of the Early American Coppers Club and its absorbing newsletter (currently edited by Dr. Harry Salyards), *Penny-Wise*.

One more comment: Slabbed coins are a mixed blessing in the field of large cents. Often grading is very erratic, probably because the experts employed by certain services are more adept

---

[1] The Treasury hoard, which came to light in 1962, contained 4,000 such pieces (mostly in MS-60 grade, but with some in higher grades as well); this figure does not include MS-60 1879-CC dollars from other sources.

Various United States Cents

1793
Chain AMERI.

1797

1812

1817

1837

1851

1857

1865

1913-D

at grading investment-oriented series such as Morgan dollars and are not as experienced with early 19th-century copper. I have seen very wide swings in grading among slabbed cents, and in one instance, a coin was slabbed at a high Mint State level even though on the lower left side of the reverse there were a number of disfiguring scratches (these apparently had been overlooked). On the plus side is that nearly all slabbed cents are not marked with variety attributions, such as by Newcomb numbers, thus there is the possibility of finding a rare die variety priced the same as a common date.

Investing in Small Cents

Building a collection of small cents can offer many opportunities, in my opinion, for the series in general has been out of favor for a long time, and rare issues can be obtained for little more than they would have cost 10 or 20 years ago!

The field includes Flying Eagle cents, made in pattern form with the date 1856, and for circulation in 1857 and 1858; the later Indian cents, including copper-nickel alloy issues from 1859 to 1864 and bronze cents from 1864 to 1909; and Lincoln cents from 1909 to date.

In grades from MS-63 to MS-65, Indian cents in particular are sharply undervalued in my opinion. Putting together a nice set matched for color, and consisting of pieces which have not been cleaned, dipped, or "processed," can be a challenge and might well take several years. And yet, when you encounter the coins they are apt to be relatively inexpensive in comparison to many later series. In general, Indian cents from 1866 through 1878 are scarce, if not rare, in MS-63 to MS-65 condition, and yet current market values do not reflect this. There are many bargains to be had.

I recommend building a set of Flying Eagle and Indian cents from 1856 to 1909, consisting of one of each Philadelphia Mint date and major type, plus the 1908-S and 1909-S. I suggest that you be consistent as to grade. I believe that a nicely matched set of MS-63 coins, MS-64 coins, or, if you can afford it, MS-65 specimens, would be an excellent goal. Be very, very "fussy" about quality. For starters, and for relatively little expense, a collection of later-date Philadelphia Mint coins can be built from 1879 to 1909 inclusive. If you like the challenge, then you can later go on to expand the set to include the earlier and more expensive dates.

Lincoln cents, once the darlings of the numismatic fraternity and number one on the popularity list, have also been out of favor in recent years. I suggest building a set of dates and mintmarks from 1909 onward. You will find that in particular the Denver and San Francisco issues from 1910 through 1926 inclusive are very scarce in MS-63 to MS-65, in terms of coins which have never been cleaned, dipped, or "processed." Many of these are quite scarce, even rare, but numerous bargains abound.

If you want to get a head start on what I believe will be a good area for appreciation down the line, I suggest buying certified MS-64 and MS-65 coins, full *original* red, sharply struck, and of good aesthetic quality. This will involve some "cherrypicking," as for some issues you may have to review a dozen or more coins in order to find one that meets these qualifications. Further, you may have to pay significantly over current market levels to buy it. However, such coins as a class are very elusive.

Let me give an example. Quite a few years ago, in the early 1960s I believe, I purchased a very nice set of Uncirculated Lincoln cents dated from 1909 onward. Upon close examination there were two examples of the 1915-S and none of the ostensibly common 1915-D. Seeking to have a truly complete set, I telephoned and sent letters to several dozen dealers. Finally, after an exasperating and frustrating search, I was able to locate one. Before I began my hunt I thought it would be child's play to buy a dozen or two!

Today the 1915-D catalogues just $100 in MS-63 grade in the *Guide Book*. If you advertised to pay $1,000 each for these, or about 10 times the *Guide Book* value, I doubt if you would be able to buy very many! I'm not suggesting the coin is going to be worth $1,000 in the near future, for I do not believe it will be (in fact, during the past several years the catalogue value has *dropped* from $110 to $100), but I am suggesting this and certain other coins are much rarer than catalogue values indicate. And, so many of these pieces have been cleaned that pristine, untouched coins require a great deal of searching to locate.

Notice that I stated that mintmark varieties were scarce from 1910 to 1926, and that I omitted 1909. The reason for this is that cents of 1909, the first year of issue, were hoarded in large quantities, and more of these exist proportionally than of later dates. Although the 1909-S V.D.B. cent is one of the most famous

Flying Eagle and Indian Cents

Flying Eagle cents (1856-1858) and Indian cents (1859-1909) comprise two of the most popular series with date and mintmark specialists. Actually, Flying Eagle cents were produced for circulation only in two years, 1857 and 1858. The 1856 Flying Eagle cent is a famous pattern rarity and was produced to the extent of fewer than 2,500 pieces.

Indian cents, first minted for circulation in 1859, were produced in several different types and numerous varieties. The 1859 issue is the only year with the Laurel Wreath Reverse. In 1860 the oak wreath and shield was substituted. Cents from 1859 through 1864 were struck on thick copper-nickel planchets. Years ago it was popular to call these "white cents," due to the color. Cents from 1864 through 1909 are on thin bronze planchets. Rare issues among Indian cents include 1864 with L (for J.B. Longacre, the designer) on ribbon, 1871, 1872, 1877 (particularly scarce), and 1909-S.

Lincoln Cents

Lincoln cents were first struck in 1909 to commemorate the 100th anniversary of the president's birth. Certain issues of the first year bear the initials of the designer, V.D.B. (for Victor David Brenner), on the reverse. A controversy arose, and they were soon eliminated. Particularly rare is the 1909 San Francisco Mint issue with the initials. Other scarce Lincoln cents include 1914-D and the 1955 Doubled Die. Many issues, common in worn grades, are very elusive in Uncirculated preservation. This is particularly true of some varieties dated prior to 1934.

issues in the entire series, there are thousands of Uncirculated pieces in existence.

Continuing my earlier example, the 1915-D Lincoln cent, which catalogues at $100 in MS-63, is probably at least *several hundred times rarer* in that grade than is the 1909-S V.D.B. cent which catalogues $700 in the same condition!

The reason for the higher price for the 1909-S V.D.B. is that this issue has a low mintage and is scarce in *lower* grades. In well-worn condition; Good-4, a 1909-S V.D.B. cent catalogues for $225, a reasonable value considering that it is needed for completion of a set and that relatively few are around. The 1915-D Lincoln cent catalogues for 60¢ in the same preservation, also reasonable, for the issue has a high mintage of 22,050,000 and is not particularly rare in low states of preservation. The 1915-D is elusive *only* in Uncirculated preservation, for few collectors thought to save them. It is what is called in the trade a *condition rarity*; it is rare in high grades but is otherwise common. Worn pieces are "a dime a dozen," thus the saying goes. Earlier in this book I discussed the concept that a coin can be rare in one grade and not another, mentioning that the 1936-D Washington quarter is rare in Uncir-culated preservation but common in worn states. The same goes for the 1915-D Lincoln cent (and numerous other pieces).

Sometimes in my discussion in this book here I have di-gressed somewhat, but I feel imparting to you a *concept* is some-times more important than simply listing dates and mintmarks of coins with particular recommendations or ideas. It is important to me that you understand *why* certain issues are priced the way they are, why there are sleepers on the market, and so on. I believe that if you can think for yourself and master the same concepts that guide successful rare coin dealers and seasoned numismatic investors, this is better than simply selling you a book with a listing of current recommendations but with no philosophy. My way is the longer and more difficult path, I realize, but I believe that in the long run you will do better.

Concerning Lincoln cents of dates later than 1926, there are some scarcities, although not major ones, to be encountered up through the early 1930s, after which all of the standard varieties are relatively common, with the exception of the 1955 Doubled Die (which is scarce in all grades and which is quite rare in MS-60 preservation). While one might question the investment wisdom of buying, for example, Lincoln cents of the 1960s, which catalogue just 10¢ each in the current *Guide Book*, as the total cost for these is negligible, I suggest that you get them simply to make your Lincoln cent set complete, but do not buy duplicates.

Lincoln cents after 1926 undoubtedly include some issues which are definitely scarcer than others in brilliant (red), well-struck MS-65 grade, and undoubtedly such coins are very inexpensive now. The problem is that I don't know which issues these are, as I have not studied them. (If a reader would care to share information on this point I shall use it with appropriate credit in a future edition.)

Investing in Two-Cent Pieces

Two-cent pieces, minted from 1864 through 1873, are primarily of interest to the type collector who seeks just one representative example for inclusion in a design set. However, it was popular years ago, when prices were lower than they are today, to collect these by date sequence. Today, few indulge in this, and I do not expect any recurrence of interest in the near future. By default, thus certain scarce and rare issues are in relatively low demand and can be obtained for not much more than basic "type" coins. In MS-63 grades and higher, by far the rarest issue in the series is the 1864 Small Motto, although the 1872 gives it a run for the money.

The current *Guide Book* suggests a price of $900 for an MS-63 1864 Small Motto coin, as compared to $200 for a common Large Motto coin of the same year. It is the case that the Small Motto piece is at least 100 times rarer than the Large Motto, so here is a "sleeper." The only fly in the ointment is that I do not expect a resurgence of collecting by varieties to occur in the near future, so even if you and I recognize that the 1864 Small Motto is undervalued, and while it might be truly delightful to own one (I, for one, would enjoy owning such a piece if I were collecting the series), I cannot hold out any promise of a substantial price increase in the near future. Perhaps this lack of optimism will be compensated by the pleasure of owning something that is rare, in this instance at least 100 times rarer than a common "type" issue of the same year.

A specialized set of two-cent pieces consists of one of each date from 1864 through 1873 inclusive, plus the additional Small Motto issue of 1864. The *Guide Book* lists the 1867 Doubled Die issue, but in practice few people have added this to their want lists. Although the issue is quite rare, I suspect that if you look carefully you might be able to acquire one for a reasonable price.

The so-called "1869/8 overdate" may be a repunched date, rather than an overdate. Opinions are divided on the subject, and noted authority Bill Fivaz, for one, does not believe it is an overdate. The state of the art concerning overdates changes from time to time, and has changed numerous times in the past. For the moment, I would recommend caution before paying a significant premium for one of these, for if it is delisted, as the related "1869/8" Indian cent seems to be (earlier it was listed in the *Guide Book* as an overdate, now there is a qualification to the listing), it will have relatively little additional value.

The most plentiful issues among two-cent pieces are the 1864 Large Motto and 1865, followed in approximate order by 1866, 1867, 1868, and 1869, as reflected by the original mintages. MS-60 and finer specimens are scarce for 1870 and 1871, and for 1872 are quite rare. Proofs exist of all issues. The 1864 Small Motto Proof is a major rarity, and probably fewer than two dozen exist.[1] Several hundred or more exist of other Proof issues from the 1864 Large Motto onward. Of particular interest is the 1873, which comes in two minor varieties, Closed 3 and Open 3—both made only in Proof finish; that is, no examples of this date were minted for circulation. Thus, the 1873 has always been considered a key date.

Proof two-cent pieces, if uncleaned and with unimpaired surfaces, are quite rare. Indeed, they are *very* rare. Of a given several hundred Proof 1865 two-cent pieces examined over a period of years, probably no more than 5% to 10% were in truly choice preservation. The formation of a matched set of Proofs, with unimpaired surfaces, would be a great challenge. Upon sale, I suspect it would bring a premium. However, whether it would be the best investment you could make is a matter of opinion, for I do not look for a significant price movement soon.

To summarize, I view two-cent pieces as an area for the collector, not for the investor, in the present market.

---

[1] There are some deceptive prooflike examples of this issue masquerading as Proofs. Be careful when buying a Proof 1864 Small Motto two-cent piece, if you are offered one.

Investing in U.S. Nickel Coins

Investing In U.S. Nickel 3¢ Coins

Usually classified as "nickel" coins, although they are made of an alloy containing nickel and in actuality have more copper than nickel, are the three-cent pieces of the years 1865 through 1889 and the five-cent pieces from 1866 onward.[1]

Nickel three-cent pieces, first minted in 1865, were produced through 1889. Production was continuous, and it is possible to collect one of each date from 1865 onward. In addition, the year 1887 offers an overdate, 1887/6, thus two varieties of this year can be collected. All of these varieties are available in Proof finish. The *Guide Book* lists 1873 Open 3 (not made in Proof finish) and Closed 3 varieties, but in practice few collectors seek more than one coin of the 1873 date. A basic set typically involves one of each date from 1865 through 1889, plus an additional 1887/6 overdate.

The basic or foundational price structure of these pieces is based upon their necessity for inclusion in type sets. Accordingly, there is little premium placed on Proofs of scarcer dates. It is probably the case that the 1866 Proof, for example, is at least 10 times rarer than an 1883 Proof, and yet the 1883 Proof catalogues for more because the 1866 is commoner as a date *in lower grades*. The 1866 had a total mintage of 4,801,000 coins, including 725 or more Proofs, while the 1883 had a mintage of just 10,609 coins—comprised of 6,609 Proofs plus 4,000 business strikes.

From about 1977 until recently, many of these low-mintage coins were aggressively sold as numismatic investments, for to the outside investor they had the magical appeal of being rare,

---

[1] A trick question at coin club meetings: Which contains the most copper, a 1909 Lincoln cent or a 1909 Liberty Head nickel? The answer: The Liberty nickel, which contains 3.5 grams of copper, as opposed to the cent which contains 2.95 grams of copper. The "nickel" coins are 25% nickel and 75% copper.

which they are in a relative sense. However, during the height of the market in the late 1980s, the price for Proofs, especially for those in the Proof-65 numerical category, went well past $2,000 per coin, a valuation which *collecting* demand could not support. When the market fell in 1990, the price plummeted to less than 25% of its previous high!

Today in the early 1990s I suggest the following: If Proofs appeal to you, form a complete set of Proofs 1865-1889, including the 1887/6 overdate. Cherrypick Proof-63 and Proof-64 coins to obtain pieces with high quality surfaces. Remember that such coins are every bit as nice as those which were certified by the ANA Grading Service as Proof-65 in the early 1980s!

The formation of a set of Proofs can be quite a challenge, for many surviving pieces have been cleaned or have problems of one sort or another. This is particularly true for issues dated before the late 1870s. As a rule, Proofs dated prior to 1877 are much rarer than those dated 1877-1889, with the most elusive Proofs being those of the 1860s.

If you want to buy some selected single Proof dates I recommend the 1865 (quite rare), the 1866 (rare), and the 1887 (the rarest date of the 1880s, a coin of which probably no more than 1,250 Proofs were struck).

I recommend building such a holding for collecting purposes, instead of for investment, for I do not see a price increase in the cards—at least not within the next few years. However, there is no question that in comparison to the price levels of a few years ago, today's market is laden with inexpensive coins.

Investing in Nickel 5¢ Coins—Introduction

Nickel five-cent pieces, minted from 1866 onward, are divided into several designs, including the Shield type made from 1866 through 1883, the Liberty Head type made from 1883 through 1913, the Buffalo style made from 1913 to 1938, and the Jefferson motif produced from 1938 to the present day.

Now, in 1991 as these words are being written, nickels are not particularly active. It is interesting to note that Abe Kosoff did a survey of popular series a few decades ago, and at the time Buffalo nickels were number one on his list. Morgan silver dollars, so popular today, did not even place in the top 10! This illustrates the phenomenon of market cycles, as discussed earlier. I do not believe that Buffalo nickels will ever return to be the most popular series in American numismatics, if for no other reason than there are not enough of them to satisfy such a demand, but it may be the case that their popularity will increase over present levels. As it is, Buffalo nickels in their own way have a strong following.

Jefferson nickels have declined in price and popularity in recent years. Today, in 1991, a set of Uncirculated Jefferson nickels from 1938 onward is cheaper than it was 10 years ago. I expect this will change and that in the future today's price will seem to be a bargain. The pricing structure has been complicated by grading, and it remains to be seen what effect this will have.

Michael Wescott has written a manuscript on the subject of nickel five-cent pieces from 1866 to the present era, and it is anticipated that this will be released by Bowers and Merena Publications this year. This may have a favorable impact on the popularity of nickels in general.

Shield Nickels

When I think of Shield nickels, I think of coins needed for a type set. Shield nickels are of two main types, the style With Rays on the reverse, as minted in 1866 and early 1867, and the second style Without Rays, as made from 1867 through 1883. Most demand over the years has come from collectors desiring an example of each type for inclusion in type sets. There has been relatively little call for scarce dates. In a discussion with Liz Arlin, who manages our Want List Department at Bowers and Merena Galleries, she mentioned she was getting quite a few requests for Shield nickels by date. So, I guess my overall impressions are subject to modification, and there is a resurgence of interest in collecting by date sequence. However, "quite a few" in this context probably means a dozen or so, hardly enough to cause a major move in the nationwide market for the series.

As is true in so many other series, there are a number of sleepers so far as scarce dates are concerned. If you look at the 1992 edition of the *Guide Book*, you will note that in MS-60 grade most issues of the Without Rays style from 1867 through 1883 are priced from $100 to $150. The 1883 catalogues at $100, whereas, for example, the 1871 catalogues for $280, or close to three times as much. However, the 1883 is at least 100 times more common than the 1871.

It may be the case that 50 years from now someone will look through a copy of this book and marvel at the fact that in the early 1990s one could buy scarce and rare dates in many series for scarcely more than "type" prices. Again, I recommend studying the lessons of history. Coin prices do go in cycles, as do collecting fads and areas of popularity. The time to buy most profitably is when a series is quiet. In the present market, when rare pieces are obtainable for little more than the price of common coins in many series, there are some great opportunities for the astute buyer. At the same time, I do not believe that the next two or three years will see a widespread resurgence of interest in the Shield nickel series.

Among Shield nickels of the first type, 1866 and 1867 With Rays, the 1867 is five to 10 times scarcer in all grades. Among Shield nickels of the Without Rays type, from 1867 through 1883, the only dates encountered with some frequency in Uncirculated preservation are 1882 and 1883. All other dates are scarcer, particularly such issues as 1871, 1875, 1879, 1880, and 1881. Although the 1879, 1880, and 1881 are rare in Mint State, Proofs are quite available, and thus there is a lessened demand for Mint State coins in the infrequent occasions when they are offered. The 1883/2 overdate is elusive in all grades, and Uncirculated pieces are quite rare.

If you aspire to collect Shield nickels by date sequence, I recommend MS-63 or finer, or Proof-63 or finer. The Proofs will be much easier to obtain than the business strikes, for the most part, although the 1867 With Rays variety is a rarity in Proof finish. Prices today are in most instances fractions of what they were a few years ago.

Liberty Head Nickels

Liberty Head nickels from 1883 through 1912 were a popular collecting discipline years ago, but today most are bought for type set purposes. The 1913, of which just five are known, is a great rarity and is not normally included as part of a regular set.

A regular set consists of two varieties of 1883, with the word CENTS and without, plus one of each date through 1911, plus three varieties of 1912: the Philadelphia, Denver, and San Francisco issues. The 1912-D and 1912-S nickels represent the first time this denomination was coined at branch mints.

Various Nickel Five-Cent Pieces

Shield type
1866-1867
With Rays

Shield type
1867-1883
Without Rays

Liberty Head type
1883-1912

1913
Buffalo nickel.
Type I reverse

1913-1938
Buffalo nickel.
Type II reverse

Again, most pricing is done on the basis of the demand for type sets, with the result that scarce and rare dates can often be obtained for very little extra. Abe Kosoff told me in the 1960s he spent several *years* searching for an Uncirculated 1891 Liberty nickel, a so-called "common date," in order to fill a client's request. And yet, in the current issue of the *Guide Book* this piece catalogues for just $120 in MS-60 grade, scarcely more than the $75 at which most dates from 1900 through 1912 are listed. In recent times I have handled a number of Mint State 1891 nickels, so perhaps they are more available now than they were years ago.[1]

The formation of a Liberty nickel set in MS-63 to MS-65 grade can be quite a challenge, with such dates as 1885 and 1886 being especially hard to locate. Toward the end of the series, a 1912-S is scarce. Interestingly, all 1912-S nickels are struck from a bulged obverse die, giving each piece a peculiar appearance.

Proofs of Liberty Head nickels exist in approximate proportion to the mintages published in the *Guide Book*. As is the case with other Proof series of the era, finding pieces which have not been cleaned or damaged is not easy, and some patience is required. In my opinion, a date and variety set of Liberty Head nickels makes an interesting display and, at today's prices, affords the opportunity to acquire scarce issues at little more than one would pay for "type" prices. While I do not expect Liberty Head nickels to become among the top 20 most favorite United States series, I cannot help but reflect that MS-63 and Proof-63 examples, if cherrypicked for quality, are bargains at today's low levels. Another appeal is that dates with lower Proof mintages (1907 being the lowest of all Proof mintages) can often be purchased for the same price as dates which are more plentiful.

Buffalo Nickels

Indian Head nickels, popularly called "Buffalo" nickels, minted from 1913 through 1938, have seen a resurgence of interest in recent years, but still they are far from being "hot."

Underpriced, in my opinion, are mintmark issues from 1913 Type II through 1927. Truly MS-63 coins are an excellent value at the current *Guide Book* listing, and a number of them are true

---

[1] The perceived rarity of certain issues sometimes changes. Sometimes coins which a dealer considers to be rare become more plentiful, and vice-versa. In the 1950s and 1960s I saw very few Mint State 1937 3-legged Buffalo nickels, for example. Today in the 1990s I handled several within a span of two or three years.

sleepers. The same goes for MS-64 coins. Do not expect needle-sharp strikes among Denver and San Francisco mint issues, for they don't come that way. Instead, the typical piece is apt to be a bit flat on the center parts of the obverse and reverse; still within a given variety it does pay to look for the best strike you can find. Some knowledge is required to differentiate between a flatness due to striking and a flatness due to wear—so when buying the series, educate yourself in advance, or enlist some expert assistance.

The formation of an Uncirculated set of Buffalo nickels in MS-63 or MS-64 condition will probably take several years. Carefully put together, and with selected coins, I feel it will be a good investment over a period of time. I also like MS-65 coins, but in terms of investment value for the price paid, I like MS-63 and MS-64 better on today's market.

Jefferson Nickels

If you were to have purchased a set of Jefferson nickels 10 or 15 years ago, you would have simply bought a set described as "Brilliant Uncirculated" or something similar. Today, collectors take out their magnifying glasses and endeavor to find out whether a given coin is MS-63, MS-64, MS-65, or some other minute difference. They have found, much to their chagrin, that very few Jefferson nickels can be described as MS-65, simply because these coins were made in large quantities, were handled carelessly at the Mint and in banking channels, and no effort was made to create collectors' items. The typical set of Uncirculated Jefferson nickels, if graded according to the numerical system, is apt to be in the MS-60 to MS-63 range. As collectors have been conditioned to buy MS-65 quality, they reject MS-60 and MS-63 coins as not being of "investment quality." Thus, the demand for Jefferson nickels is not particularly great. Therein may lie an opportunity for the dedicated, patient buyer.

Jefferson nickels are in the doldrums now primarily because of the fact that they are inexpensive, and at the same time MS-65 pieces are scarce, thus few collectors want to "bother" picking over a large number of coins in order to find MS-65 pieces, if the coins themselves are not valuable. Nor do dealers want to spend a great deal of time with such issues as 1946-D, for example, which lists for all of 90¢ in MS-65 grade! A 1958 nickel in MS-65 grade catalogues just 35¢, and yet a sharply struck, aesthetically pleasing coin is a *rarity* (yes, it is).

This presents the obvious possibility that the patient collector seeking MS-65 coins at today's low prices will probably have something really worthwhile in the future. Indeed, if you have the time, patience, and inclination, I feel that building an MS-65 set of Jefferson nickels at today's prices will be a really *outstanding* investment. But, don't expect to have dealers help you—for the price structure is not at the level at which a dealer can afford to give such pieces his attention. Jefferson nickels in MS-65 grade are high on my list of favorites. No, I do not have any MS-65 sets squirrelled away—but if I were investing in coins, instead of dealing in them, you can bet this would be one modern series which would attract my interest.

Before leaving the subject of "nickel" coins, I mention that certain of the clad alloy dimes, quarters, half dollars, and dollars of recent years might be properly grouped under "nickel" or "copper" coins rather than under "silver," but as they are part of denominations which had their inception with silver issues, such clad pieces are listed in the chapter to follow.

Investing in U.S. Silver Coins

One Collector's Specialty

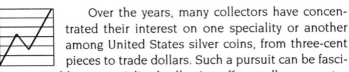

Over the years, many collectors have concentrated their interest on one speciality or another among United States silver coins, from three-cent pieces to trade dollars. Such a pursuit can be fascinating. Building a specialized collection offers endless opportunities for research. Concentrating on a particular area of coinage will enable you to make many interesting discoveries on your own. For one of our auctions I catalogued the celebrated collection of United States half dimes formed by Dr. W.E. Caldwell. A customer and friend for many years, Dr. Caldwell sent me a few paragraphs about his half dimes and the enthusiasm with which he collected them:

"It has been a pleasure to collect the half dimes which you will be selling in your auction. My collecting of this series began quite by accident. I was convalescing from a heart attack when my maid brought in some old coins to see if they were valuable. I laid my paint brushes (my hobby to this point) aside, thank goodness, and borrowed a friend's *Guide Book of United States Coins*.

"I evaluated the small group of miscellaneous coins and bought them. Among these pieces was a well-worn 1837 Liberty Seated half dime which had been holed and plugged. This tiny coin brought back memories of an elderly uncle who gave me a nickel for the local Saturday opera house movies each week when I was a child. I remembered that many of these "nickels" were half dimes. Why not collect half dimes and see how many different dates I could find? An interesting idea!

"Soon I was off and running—buying half dimes wherever I could find them. One can 'buy in haste and repent in leisure,' and after a few months of fast spending I was many dollars wiser. I found it was desirable to buy from reputable dealers, large auction houses, and at major conventions. It seemed that by this method I could be more sure of getting quality coins, even though a higher price might be required. The 'you get what you pay for' adage is certainly true, and I found this out!

"My collection begins with the 1792 half disme, a coin which certainly is one of the most romantic issues in American numismatics. At one time I had a specimen of each and every half dime variety from 1792 to 1873, but later I traded or sold some of the very worn ones in the hope that I would be able to get top-grade pieces later. It turned out that I was able to do this in some instances but not in others. It is very, very difficult to obtain true Uncirculated examples of the 1794 to 1805 years, and had this been an absolute requirement there would have been many dates which I would never have acquired. I feel that all Uncirculated half dimes of this era are grossly undervalued, and that examples in grades close to Uncirculated are of extreme rarity in many instances.

"Among later Liberty Seated half dimes there are many rarities, particularly in the New Orleans Mint pieces. Many if not most New Orleans half dimes are very weakly struck on the reverse, and to find a sharp strike, if indeed this is possible at all, many specimens must be examined. The most underrated seem to be the 1840-O Without Drapery, the 1842-O, and the 1844-O. The 1846 Philadelphia Mint half dime is exceedingly rare in higher grades. Another sleeper is the 1848 Large Date variety in Uncirculated condition. Major rarities are the 1849-O, 1852-O, and 1853-O Without Arrows variety in better grades.

"The 1859 transitional issue with the reverse of 1860 must rate as one of the most important of American coin rarities. During the period I formed my collection, the present specimen, the one you will be auctioning, is the only one I was able to buy, and no others were offered for sale in price lists or auctions.

"I can close my eyes and see all of the half dimes in my collection. I hope that successful bidders on the individual lots will experience the same pleasure I did from these beautiful pieces. While a monetary profit will undoubtedly be realized from the collection, I have profited in what is perhaps an even better way: five years of enjoyable collecting."

When Dr. Caldwell's half dimes were sold, a handsome profit was realized. The sale brought record prices and the results exceeded our expectations. As his own words indicate, an additional "profit," the value of which is impossible to estimate in monetary terms, was derived in collecting pleasure.

In recent years the Liberty Seated Collectors Club, publishers of *The Gobrecht Journal*, has served as the focal point for numismatists interested in Liberty Seated coinage, from half dimes to silver dollars. Joining this organization is highly recommended.

Investing in Silver Three-Cent Pieces

As is the case with bronze two-cent pieces 1864 to 1873, nickel three-cent pieces 1865 to 1889, and a number of other series of the era, the interest in silver three-cent pieces, minted from 1851 through 1873, is primarily on the part of type set collectors.

Silver three-cent pieces are divided into three design types:

1. Type I, minted from 1851 through 1853, has no outline to the star on the obverse and no leaves above or below the numeral on the reverse.

2. Type II, minted from 1854 through 1858, has three lines bordering the star, and leaves above and below the numeral on the reverse.

3. Type III, struck from 1859 through 1873, has two outlines to the stars, and a reverse the same as Type II.

Thus, the type set collector needs to buy three coins in order to have a representation of the major types struck.

The date collector has the opportunity to acquire one specimen from each year from 1851 to 1873, with the addition of the only branch mint coin in the series, the 1851-O (New Orleans), adding interest. Three overdates are listed in the *Guide Book*: 1862/1, which occurs with some frequency, 1863/2, which apparently exists only in Proof state, and 1869/8—the latter variety not being familiar to me. Only time will tell if these overdates will be collected by specialists. For the present, most want lists received at Bowers and Merena Galleries are simply for one of each date, plus, of course, the 1851-O.

If you aspire to collect Uncirculated and Proof coins, you will have no difficulty acquiring examples of 1851, 1852, and 1853. 1851-O is considerably scarcer. Coins in the Type II series will be considerably more difficult to obtain, and in MS-63 or better condition, each issue from 1854 through 1858 is decidedly rare.

Most pieces are poorly struck, the only exception being 1855, the lowest mintage issue of the series, which is occasionally seen sharply defined. You may have to spend many years searching for a sharply struck 1857 and 1858, and even then you might not locate either one. Some compromise is necessary, and while I do not recommend that you buy a "flat" strike, do not be persnickety about wanting only a needle-sharp strike either. Indeed, it was trouble with striking the design features which prompted the type to be discontinued in 1858.

MS-63 or finer specimens of the Type III coins, 1859 onward, are available for the first several years, but issues from 1865 onward are extreme rarities.[1] Proofs are available of various issues from 1859 onward, in proportion to their original mintages. The mintage figures for each can be found in the *Guide Book*.

The traditional way to collect silver three-cent pieces, if you can afford it, is to collect the issues from 1851 through 1858 in MS-63 or better condition, and the issues from 1859 onward in Proof-63 or better state.

I do not look for any great price movement in this series within the next year or two. If the collector community in general becomes more enlightened, and sleepers are recognized for what they are, then I expect that Uncirculated pieces of the Type II design will increase in value. However, this statement is not particularly logical, for there is nothing on the horizon to indicate that the average "collector in the street" is planning to become knowledgeable any time soon, despite my hope that he should be. A lot depends on whether investment writers, numismatic columnists, and others with a wide readership ever become involved in scarce and early issues, and whether or not they call their readers' attention to such things. The almighty vested interest cannot be argued against, and because of this most of what you see in print will be oriented toward coins which are available in quantities—common dates of Morgan silver dollars being a prime example. It is a rare investment writer who will take the time to discuss the striking peculiarities of silver three-cent pieces, for example.

Investing in Half Dimes

The discussion of Dr. W.E. Caldwell's half dime collection in the introduction to this chapter tells of the fascination of this

---

[1] In particular, the dates from 1867 through 1872 are very rare in Uncirculated (business strike) form. Most certified coins I have seen marked "Mint State" have really been Proofs, which *are* available.

Various 19th-Century American Silver Coins

1831 half dime

1814 dime

1830 dime

1838 dime

1878 quarter dollar

1828 half dollar

1866 silver dollar

series. There are no truly "impossible" rarities among half dimes, but the 1802, an American classic, will be very difficult to locate. Indeed, each and every half dime in the early series from 1794 to 1805 can be described as scarce, if not rare. When James F. Ruddy was collecting photographs for his *Photograde* grading book, he found the most difficult design type to acquire over a wide variety of grades was the 1796 to 1797 half dime with Draped Bust obverse and Small Eagle reverse. Dr. James Rosen who has been specializing in coins by design types for many years, told me that in many years of searching he had yet to find a really sharp Extremely Fine half dime of this design, one which meets his exacting requirements. Thus, the 1796 to 1797 half dimes in particular will be a challenge to find, although they are not priced to reflect this.

A number of subspecialties can be made in the half dime series, such as collecting all of the Capped Bust types from 1829 through 1837, a pursuit which can be fascinating and which involves no great rarities. As you can see from the *Guide Book* listings, with the exception of the 1837 with Small 5¢ on the reverse all are priced at about the same level. This does not mean that all are equally easy to find, as you will soon learn when you start seeking them. For investment purposes, I particularly like coins in the higher grade ranges, Extremely Fine upward. If you can afford it, try assembling an MS-63 or better set. On the current market, among Mint State coins I feel that MS-63 pieces, cherrypicked for quality, offer the best value for the money spent.

Liberty Seated half dimes from 1837 through 1873 have attracted the attention of many collectors over the years. Although there are some scattered rarities, most issues are available. A great challenge, in my opinion, would be to assemble a set of the Liberty Seated type with Stars on the Obverse, the design minted from 1838 through 1859. There are enough die varieties to satisfy the most ardent student. However, the challenge lies in finding the coins themselves. MS-60 or better pieces for many issues are extremely rare. Years ago the *Guide Book* used to list them all at nominal prices. Now dashes, indicating extreme rarity, appear for certain varieties in the MS-60 column. The truth is that even more dashes *should* be there! In the meantime, I guarantee if you put together a set of MS-60 or better half dimes of this era, and go about it carefully, you will end up with something truly worthwhile.

If you are buying a single specimen of each half dime variety for a type set, study the certified coin population reports and select varieties which are not among the most common. Many scarce and rare issues can be bought for "type" coin prices, a decided advantage on today's market.

Investing in U.S. Dimes

Relatively little attention was paid to early dimes by die varieties until 1984, when David Davis, Russell J. Logan, Allen F. Lovejoy, John W. McCloskey, and William L. Subjack, members of the John Reich Society (named after an early 19th-century Mint engraver), completed their book, *Early United States Dimes 1796-1837*. This masterful treatise stands today as one of the best studies in print on *any* American numismatic subject. Die varieties of early dimes, 1796 through 1837, are discussed in detail.[1] I highly recommend the volume, which is available wherever numismatic books are sold (or free on loan from the ANA Library).

So far as collecting early dimes goes, if you have a generous budget, it can be a fascinating pursuit. The *Guide Book* lists the basic dates and varieties, although I suggest you ignore certain varieties unless you want to become a specialist. For example, who cares whether an 1823/2 overdate dime has small Es in the legend or large Es? I don't, and I suspect most others don't either.

Liberty Seated Dimes

Collecting Liberty Seated dimes from 1837 to 1891 is an interesting challenge. As is the case with half dimes, numerous unrecognized rarities abound, particularly in the first decade or so of coinage. Most Liberty Seated coins are priced according to the demand from type collectors, leaving many bargains to those who go beyond the type listings. I can give many examples, but just one will suffice. In the *Guide Book*, the 1887 dime is listed at $150 in MS-60 condition. The 1870 dime is listed at $200 in like preservation. The 1887 is at least 10 to 20 times more plentiful!

Barber Dimes

Barber dimes, minted from 1892 through 1916, were often included a few decades ago in general collections by date and

---

[1] Prior to this time the only reference work on dimes was the long out-of-print dime section of Numismatic Gallery's sale of the F.C.C. Boyd Collection ("World's Greatest Collection"). Such varieties were referred to by K (for Abe Kosoff, a principal of Numismatic Gallery) numbers.

Liberty Seated Silver Coins

In 1835 Mint engraver Christian Gobrecht, following a sketch by Thomas Sully, made what is known today as the Liberty Seated motif. First appearing on pattern silver dollars dated 1836, the design featured Miss Liberty in a seated position with a liberty cap and pole cradled by her left arm and with her right hand on a shield.

The design subsequently was adopted for use on circulating silver denominations. Half dimes of this style were made from 1837 through 1873, dimes from 1837 to 1891, 20-cent pieces from 1875 through 1878, quarters from 1838 through 1891, half dollars for the same period, and dollars from 1840 through 1873.

By the time of the 1876 centennial the Liberty Seated design was so ingrained in the minds of the American people that it was used for many other purposes as well, including advertising on packages of firecrackers! By 1891 the design had outlived its usefulness and appreciation, and the dime, quarter, and half dollar styles were changed to Barber's Liberty Head portrait. By that time half dimes and 20-cent pieces were no longer being struck, and the Liberty Seated design for silver dollars had long since been replaced by George T. Morgan's work.

Today Liberty Seated coins of all types are highly prized by numismatists. Proofs of most Philadelphia Mint issues are available from the late 1850s onward. Uncirculated examples are another story entirely. Generally, issues prior to 1860 are very scarce, with certain New Orleans Mint pieces being rarities. There are many elusive issues among circulated pieces as well. Despite their low cost, many Fine, Very Fine, and Extremely Fine Liberty Seated quarters are seldom seen or offered for sale.

mintmark. The great rarity is the 1894-S, of which just a dozen or so are known. Apart from that, all of the others are available, although certain issues such as 1895-O, 1897-O, and, 1901-S are hard to find.

If you have the budget to do it, I believe you would find that assembling a set of branch mints in MS-63 or MS-64 grade, and Philadelphia Mint pieces in Proof-63 or Proof-64 preservation, cherrypicked in each instance for quality would be a challenge and, at the same time, would make a beautiful exhibit. The market remains oriented toward "type" prices, with the result that many scarce and rare issues, particularly mintmark varieties from 1892 through the early years of the 20th century, are severely underpriced. In MS-60 grade an 1895-O Barber dime (catalogue value: $1,660) is at least 250 times rarer than an MS-60 1889-CC Morgan dollar (catalogue value: $6,000). Granted, more people collect Morgan dollars than collect Barber dimes, but should the price differential be *that* great?

Mercury Dimes

Mercury dimes, minted from 1916 to 1945, have always been a favorite series in the numismatic community, and I have every expectation that they will continue to be so. As early issues are expensive in Uncirculated grades, a number of people have put together so-called "short sets," beginning with 1934 and continuing through 1945, or beginning with 1940 or 1941 and continuing through the terminal date.

Perhaps the best way to go is to start with the later dates first, and then if your interest is sustained, work backward to the early series. Particularly desirable are coins with Full Split Bands (often abbreviated as FSB or FB in catalogue listings) on the reverse. Such pieces are scarce for many earlier issues. Among later issues, curiously enough the 1945 Philadelphia issue, quite common in "regular" MS-65 grade, is a great rarity with Full Split Bands. A normal 1945 MS-65 is worth, say, in the $30 range, but an MS-65 with Full Split Bands is worth about $3,000—or 100 times more!

The great classic rarity among Mercury dimes is the 1916-D, of which relatively few MS-65 pieces exist, probably fewer than several hundred. This is quite unusual, for 1916 was the first year of issue, and you would think that many would have been saved. However, that wasn't the case, and top grade 1916-D dimes are and always have been difficult to locate. Truly superb MS-65 pieces are worthwhile acquisitions, in my opinion—if you are lucky enough to find one.

There are a number of sleepers among branch mint coins of the 1917-1927 years, and a study of the frequency of auction appearances and a perusal of grading population reports will reward financially anyone who takes the time to do it, then acts on the information found regarding underpriced issues.

If the subject of Mercury dimes interests you, you may wish to pursue this and other specialized series by reading my book, *United States Dimes, Quarters, and Half Dollars*. A superb biography of the designer, Adolph A. Weinman, by William Gibbs, appeared serially in *Coin World* in the summer of 1991.

Roosevelt Dimes

Roosevelt dimes from 1946 to date are readily available in MS-63 grade, although it will take some patience to put together a complete set, simply because many of them are inexpensive, and dealers do not have the time to fuss with them. Bruce Amspacher wrote in 1986 of his frustrating search to put together an MS-65 set, something which at first he thought would be a snap, but which turned out to be a major challenge. For the investor, some patience in this area will undoubtedly be amply rewarded, for today's Cinderella coins may be tomorrow's princesses. It is like the situation with Jefferson nickels; there are some *rare* coins listed for nominal sums, dealers don't want to bother with them, and a lot of looking is required.

Investing in 20-Cent Pieces

Twenty-cent pieces, minted from 1875 to 1878, comprise just seven different issues: 1875, 1875-CC, 1875-S, 1876, 1876-CC, 1877, and 1878. The 1876-CC, of which fewer than two dozen are known, is a great rarity. The 1877 and 1878, made only in Proof finish, are quite scarce. Traditionally, a "set" of these has consisted of all seven pieces, except the 1876-CC.

A typical way to approach collecting the set is to get the Philadelphia issues in Proof-63 or better condition, and the 1875-CC and 1875-S in MS-63 or better grade. If you can afford it, the 1876-CC, which currently lists at $60,000 for an MS-60 coin in the

The 1827 Original Quarter Dollar

The 1827 original quarter dollar shown above is one of fewer than a dozen specimens known to exist of this rarity. Described as "a Choice Proof in every respect; fully brilliant with just the slightest hint of golden toning. No finer specimen could possibly exist." The piece sold for $190,000 in our sale of the Garrett Collection.

This particular piece traces its pedigree to the Ely, McCoy, and Mickley collections. It is believed to be one of the four specimens obtained by young collector Joseph J. Mickley (then 28 years old) for face value during a visit to the Philadelphia Mint in the year of issue.

Mickley is considered to be the first American numismatist to collect coins by date sequence. His interest was aroused some time around the year 1816 when he sought a cent of the year of his birth, 1799, and had difficulty obtaining one. His interest piqued, Mickley set about acquiring as many pieces as possible.

Guide Book, will be a centerpiece in your collection and a treasure to own.

Most demand for 20-cent pieces in recent times has come from those seeking a single example for a type set. However, now and then someone endeavors to put together a set by varieties. The future price of such a set will depend upon the movement of Liberty Seated coins in general, for I do not look to a focus of particular interest on 20-cent pieces alone, for this series is too restricted. If you are seeking a coin for a type set, you may be able to acquire a scarcer variety—such as 1875, 1875-CC, or 1876—for the same price as the relatively common 1875-S (the issue most often encountered).

Investing in U.S. Quarter Dollars

Quarter dollars from 1796 onward have formed a specialty for a number of numismatists over the years, with the Lahrman, Hawn, Bergen, and other collections creating attention when they were sold. Early quarters of the 1796 to 1828 span are for the most part very rare in higher grades. The assembling of a set in MS-63 to MS-65 condition may well be impossible, unless several decades were devoted to the task, and even then there is no assurance that such issues as 1804 and 1823/2 could be acquired in that state.[1] The 1827, listing at $60,000 in MS-60 grade in the current Guide Book (an erroneous listing, for the issue is known only in Proof state), is a classic American rarity.

Capped Bust quarter dollars in 1831 through 1838 are sometimes collected as a specialty in their own right. They are all priced about the same in the Guide Book, and no particular problem should be encountered in putting together a set. The grade of EF-40 is sharply undervalued, in my opinion, and quality MS-60 coins are a good value as well, but more for inclusion of a single piece in a type set than for the acquisition of several for investment per se.

Liberty Seated Quarters

More so than any other silver series from half dimes to half dollars, early quarter dollars in the Capped Bust and Liberty Seated series are very scarce. Taken as a whole, there are several

---

[1] I am aware of only one 1823/2 quarter dollar in a high grade, a Proof.

decades' worth of coins which are sleepers. Nowhere is this more evident than among Liberty Seated quarters, first minted in 1838, and produced in several type variations through 1891. In particular, Liberty Seated quarters of 1838 through 1852 are seldom seen.[1] I consider nearly all of the different issues in Very Fine, Extremely Fine, and AU conditions to be among the greatest bargains to be found in 19th-century American coinage. In MS-60 through MS-63, coins of selected quality are very scarce. New Orleans issues 1842-O through 1852-O are rarities in Mint State and for the most part are very underpriced. I seriously doubt if you will find many people in the numismatic investment "industry" to agree with this statement, or at least say they agree in print. The reason for this is that few people have a vested interest by having such coins in stock, so why bother writing about them?

The building of a date and mintmark set of Liberty Seated quarters from 1838 to 1891 is possible, with the exception of the 1873-CC Without Arrows, of which just three are confirmed to exist. There will be many challenges along the way, in particular with regard to issues before 1874.

During the past several years, members of the Liberty Seated Coin Club and others have taken a renewed interest in Liberty Seated quarters, thus I imagine that within the next few years the many pricing inequalities now existing in the market will straighten themselves out. In the meantime, if you follow my advice and lay in a stock of early Liberty Seated quarters—if you can find many to acquire—I have every expectation you will do well.

Barber Quarters

Barber quarters minted from 1892 through 1916 are likewise undervalued in many instances. There are three classic issues, 1896-S, 1901-S, and 1913-S. Most other issues are priced according to type, without respect to their actual scarcity. Thus, an 1892-S quarter is listed at $380 in MS-60 grade, whereas a 1908-D, which is dozens of times more plentiful, is listed at $230. As is the case with Barber dimes and also Barber half dollars, there are many, many sleepers to be found, particularly among branch mint coins prior to 1906. In addition, I think all Barber quarters, with the exception of 1896-S, 1901-S, and 1913-S, which are already priced

---

[1] Exceptions in Mint State are 1840-O and 1841-O quarters unearthed a few years ago when excavations were being done at an old bank site in New Orleans. An unstated quantity, probably amounting to several hundred coins, came to light. All were deeply toned.

A Controversial Design

The 1916 Liberty Standing quarter, minted to the extent of just 52,000 pieces, depicts on the obverse the figure of Liberty with an undraped bosom. The design was produced by Hermon A. MacNeil, who used a young Philadelphia girl, Dora Doscher, as a model. Public outcry arose concerning the risque new design, and in a classic case of overcompensation the piece was redesigned in 1917 so that Miss Liberty was wearing a heavy, protective suit of armor!

The 1916 Liberty Standing quarter, one of the scarcest dates in the series, has been a superb investment over the years. The writer recalls that these coins were available for less than $100 each during the early 1950s. Now, four decades later, a sharply struck Choice Uncirculated coin is valued close to $10,000.

at a high level, are undervalued in VF-20, EF-40, and AU-50. If someone came to me with a sack containing dozens of EF-40 Barber quarters, even of the more common dates, I would be delighted to acquire them. In higher grades, MS-63 Barber quarters are considerably scarcer than equivalent Barber dimes, but not as scarce as Barber half dollars. Proofs exist in proportion to their original mintage. Proof-63 or finer coins, without damage, are elusive.

Standing Liberty Quarters

Standing Liberty quarters, minted from 1916 to 1930, have always been popular. The *Guide Book* gives a nice overview of different types and prices. Particularly desirable are issues with the head of Miss Liberty fully struck, with needle-sharp details. Certain issues are very difficult to find in this state, particularly 1926-D, which nearly always is flatly struck. The availability of various issues in various qualities of striking can be learned by reading J.H. Cline's *Standing Liberty Quarters* book.

For the well-financed collector, the formation of a set from 1916 to 1930, in strictly MS-63 or better condition, with decent striking, can be a challenge. When completed, the result will be a beautiful exhibit. In nearly 35 years of dealing in coins, I have never seen more than two or three sets of this quality.[1] So, here is a challenge!

Washington Quarters

Washington quarters from 1932 onward form an interesting collection. Today, prices for many issues are quite reasonable. I recommend MS-63 or better for earlier issues, MS-65 or better for later issues. The keys to the series are 1932-D and 1932-S, both of which I consider to be undervalued in relation to their true potential. Among common later issues, 1968-D and 1969-D, which list at $1 each in MS-65 grade, would be worth putting away, for MS-65 pieces are not particularly plentiful (or at least not in proportion to the mintage), for at the time they were issued collectors viewed clad coins as being undesirable in comparison to the recently discontinued silver issues.

---

[1] The most outstanding collection I have ever seen was that sold by Auctions by Bowers and Merena, Inc. in June 1991 and listed in the Dr. George N. Polis Collection catalogue. The coins averaged better than MS-65!

As is the case with Jefferson nickels and Roosevelt dimes, a study of the availability of modern Washington quarters in selected MS-65 grade will repay the inquirer.

Investing in U.S. Half Dollars

Half dollars, more than other early silver series, have formed a popular collecting area for many numismatists. Issues of the Flowing Hair type, minted in 1794 and 1795, and the very rare Draped Bust obverse, Heraldic Eagle reverse, minted in 1796 and 1797, are desirable and are needed for inclusion in a type set.

Capped Bust Half Dollars

Although some have sought to get one of each date and major variety from 1794 onward, the most popular date to begin a collection with is 1807, the first year of the Capped Bust style with Lettered Edge. This general type, which continues through 1836, can be collected without much difficulty. There are some scarce overdates and varieties, but so far as basic dates are concerned, all are available inexpensively, as the *Guide Book* prices indicate, with the exception of the traditional scarcity, 1815/2. Even this variety is not an insurmountable hurdle, for the current *Guide Book* prices a VF-20 coin at $1,750 and EF-40 for $2,200. Mint State-60 lists for $6,000 but for all practical purposes is unavailable at any price.

Recommendation: Investigate assembling a set of dates and major varieties in MS-60 to MS-63 condition. At today's prices I consider them to be terrific buys. The pieces are truly beautiful, and the main challenge will be in finding the pieces, for varieties before 1820 are apt to be few and far between in the market. In the market there is not much price differential between early Capped Bust half dollars of the years 1807 through about 1820, than of the later series. And yet, issues of the late 1820s and early 1830s are *many times* more plentiful than are, for example, Uncirculated issues of 1807, 1808, 1809, and other early years.

Half dollars of the early era are often collected by die varieties attributed to Overton numbers as described in Al C. Overton's 1967 book (with two subsequent revisions), *Early Half Dollar Die Varieties 1794-1836*. A number of specialists in the series belong to the Bust Half Nut Club.

In December 1836 the Capped Bust design was revised, the diameter was reduced, and pieces appeared with a reeded edge. This general style was made from late in 1836 through 1839-O. Coins in this range are all excellent values, with 1836 in particular being very rare in proportion to its catalogue value (although the catalogue value is hardly inexpensive). The most frequently seen date is 1837.

Liberty Seated Half Dollars

Liberty Seated half dollars from 1839 to 1891 form a challenging collection by date and mintmark. In such grades as VF-20 to EF-40, prices of even rare issues are apt to be quite reasonable. Among Uncirculated coins the same phenomenon seen in other Liberty Seated series is found. Prices are mainly by "type" with the result that scarce and rare dates are relatively inexpensive in comparison.

As an example, in the *Guide Book* an MS-60 1877-S half dollar lists for $375. An MS-60 1840 half dollar lists for $550. The 1840 is at least 100 times rarer! Such issues as 1843, 1843-O, 1844, 1844-O, and 1845 list for $500 to $525 each, or just slightly more than the 1877-S, but each of these earlier issues is many multiples rarer.

Study of the auction appearances of various date and mintmark varieties and their frequency of being graded (as reflected by grading service population reports) will amply repay the collector and will lead to the acquisition of many sleepers. Perhaps more so than at any other time in recent decades, there are some tremendous values to be found among scarce dates and mintmarks in the various early American series.

Barber Half Dollars

Barber half dollars, minted from 1892 to 1915, are undervalued in grades from F-12 through EF-40, in my opinion. Again, most pricing is by "type," with the result that scarce dates and mintmarks can be obtained for little more. As an example, the 1892-O, a rare issue, lists for $950 in MS-60 grade but is several dozen times rarer than 1908-D, which lists for $400. In grades of MS-63 or better, all but a few Barber half dollars are really difficult to find on today's market. Proof-63 or finer coins are likewise elusive. For the collector with a generous budget, the formation of a date and mint set

Different United States Half Dollar Designs

1794-1795
The first United States half dollar: the Flowing Hair type coined in 1794 and 1795.

1796-1797
The Draped Bust type with Small Eagle Reverse was minted in 1796 and 1797. These are very rare.

1801-1807
The Draped Bust type with Heraldic Eagle Reverse was issued from 1801 to 1807.

1807-1836
The Capped Bust type with Lettered Edge was produced from 1807 through 1836.

1836-1837
The Small Capped Bust type with Reeded Edge and with 50 CENTS Reverse was made only for two years.

Different United States Half Dollar Designs

1838-1839
The Small Capped Bust type with HALF DOL. Reverse was struck only in 1838 and 1839.

1839-1866
The Liberty Seated type Without Motto was made from 1839 to 1866, except for several years.

1853
In 1853 the design With Arrows at the date and Rays on the Reverse was used.

1854-1855
During these two years the With Arrows design was used, but Without Rays on the Reverse.

1866-1891
The Liberty Seated type With Motto (IN GOD WE TRUST) was struck during this period.

Different United States Half Dollar Designs

1873-1874
Some varieties of 1873 half dollars and all 1874 halves have arrows at the date.

1892-1915
The Barber half dollar style, designed by Charles E. Barber, was made from 1892 to 1915.

1916-1947
The Liberty Walking half dollar design was used from 1916 to 1947.

1948-1963
From 1948 until 1963 the Franklin half dollar design was produced.

1964 to date
Since 1964, except for the 1776-1976 biecentennial issue (not illustrated), Kennedy half dollars with the Heraldic Eagle Reverse have been made. 1964 issues are of silver; later issues are "clad" metal.

of Barber half dollars can be a very pleasurable and rewarding experience. MS-63 and Proof-63 coins are just as nice as the MS-65 and Proof-65 coins of yesteryear and are available for a fraction of the price.

Liberty Walking Half Dollars

Liberty Walking half dollars minted from 1916 to 1947 have always been popular, due to the beauty of the design. Collectors have approached the field in several ways. As early issues are expensive, some have opted to start their collections with 1934, thus forming a "short set," while others have begun short sets with 1940 or 1941. In general, issues from the 1930s onward are available in MS-63 or better condition, although some searching may be needed to find the mintmark issues with nice striking details.

Among early issues from 1916 through 1929, and especially from about 1918 onward, sharply struck pieces are the exception, not the rule. Such issues as 1923-S, 1927-S, 1928-S, 1929-D, 1929-S are nearly always flatly struck at the center of the obverse. Probably no more than a half dozen sets, if indeed that many, have ever been put together consisting of sharply struck MS-65 Liberty Walking half dollars from 1916 to 1947. If you have the budget, such an effort will reward you.

Recommendation: At today's market levels I really like MS-63, MS-64, and most MS-65 Liberty Walking half dollars of the 1941-1947 late years, which sell for fractions of what they did a few years ago! These coins, if selected with care, are very beautiful to own. Cherrypick for striking quality, and avoid flatly-struck specimens, including 1940-S, 1941-S, and several other mintmark varieties which are usually seen this way. Buy pieces which are brilliant or very lightly toned.

Franklin Half Dollars

Franklin half dollars, first struck in 1948 and last minted in 1963, have varied in popularity over the years. There are no great rarities, although 1949-S is considered to be the key issue. In recent times there has been an interest in collecting them with Full Bell Lines on the reverse. Some issues, common enough without this feature, are quite scarce with the lines present.

As is the case with Jefferson nickels and Roosevelt dimes, the formation of a well-struck MS-65 set of Franklin half dollars is a challenge and will require quite a bit of personal effort, for the market value of the pieces is not sufficiently high that dealers at present spend much time with them. Proofs are available of the years from 1950 through 1963 and make a nice display in their own right.

Kennedy Half Dollars

Kennedy half dollars, produced from 1964 to date, are attractive in design and make a nice collection. None is rare, although several common issues can be considered scarce in MS-65 grade within the context of the series.

The best known scarce variety is the 1970-D, which was sold only in mint sets distributed to collectors.

Investing in U.S. Silver Dollars

Introduction

 Silver dollars are among the most popular coins on the numismatic scene today. These massive silver coins have a long and romantic history. Many were minted from Comstock Lode bullion and have a great historical association with the "Wild West." Added to this is the appeal that many 19th-century issues can be obtained in Uncirculated condition for low cost. For those who like to gamble, or who like a bit of speculation with their numismatic activities, Morgan dollars have had enough ups and downs to do a roller coaster justice. Scarcely a year goes by without one promotion or another taking place, often characterized by a sharp rise in prices then a fall. Usually such promotions have been limited to common issues—issues which exist in large quantities and which therefore are susceptible to mass merchandising.

I was a bit amused in 1986 when I received a flyer from a well-known investment writer. Like many if not most people writing on the subject of coin investments, he was willing to back up his recommendations with an ample supply of the recommended coins for sale. In this instance, he urged readers to respond right away, for he had *only* 100,000 pieces available!

Early Silver Dollars

Silver dollars were first minted in 1794. Early issues are dated from 1794 to 1804, and all are rare. Two of these, the first date and the last, are major rarities. An Uncirculated 1794 was sold by Superior Galleries for $127,500 in 1974. In the same year, my firm offered an 1804 silver dollar for $200,000. This latter price was eclipsed in 1981 when my company sold the Garrett 1804 silver dollar for $400,000 to the firm of Pullen & Hanks, who later sold it to Sam Colavita for an advance over that. Later, the piece changed hands several times, including at auction for $187,000 in 1986, later to be advertised for $225,000 by Dan Drykerman. The $400,000 price for the Garrett coin was realized at the height of the market, and after that time a number of major rarities sold for less. However, by the early 1990s the market value had increased to beyond the $400,000 Garrett Collection price. A superb Proof example, the Dexter Collection specimen, was sold by dealer Ed Milas for a record $990,000 in 1989.

Dates for other early dollars, from 1795 through 1803, are valued from several hundred dollars up to many thousands of dollars, depending on their variety and condition.

Gobrecht Silver Dollars

Then comes a long gap from 1805 through 1835 with no silver dollar issues. Dollars were again made in 1836, 1838, and 1839—the illustrious and stunningly beautiful issues by Mint engraver Christian Gobrecht.[1] These pieces, all of which are very rare, have the Liberty Seated design on the obverse and an eagle in flight on the reverse.

Robert W. Julian has published data showing that Gobrecht silver dollars minted from December 1836 to March 1837, although earlier considered as patterns, were placed into circulation by the Treasury Department, as were certain pieces dated 1839. Thus these should be included as regular issues. Gobrecht dollars of the 1836 to 1839 years have always been popular with collectors.

Liberty Seated Silver Dollars

From 1840 to 1873, silver dollars were made utilizing the Liberty Seated obverse design, an adaptation of the Gobrecht patterns, but with a reverse depicting a perched rather than a flying eagle. Silver dollar coinage was then suspended in 1873, to be resumed (with a different design) in 1878.

Twenty-five years ago, few people collected Liberty Seated dollars. In popular parlance, the series was "dead." Since then, a great interest has developed, much of which has been caused by the enthusiasm generated by the Liberty Seated Collectors Club,

---

[1] *The Gobrecht Journal*, issued regularly by the Liberty Seated Collectors Club, is named after him.

and today several hundred people are pursuing the formation of sets by date and mint variety.

There are many sleepers among Liberty Seated silver dollars. 1840, the first year of issue, catalogues for $1,600 in MS-60 grade, and yet probably no more than a few dozen of them exist. An idea of the rarity of Uncirculated Liberty Seated dollars dated in the 1840s is gained by the interesting fact that the 1991 edition of *Auction Prices Realized*, issued by Krause Publications, and covering auction results achieved by leading United States companies in the year 1990, lists not a single business strike example of *any* issue from 1840 to 1849 which crossed the auction block in 1990 in a grade better than MS-60! That's right—no MS-63 or MS-65 coins of *any* date appeared! In MS-60 grade, offerings were sparse.

Building a set of Liberty Seated dollars offers many interesting opportunities, and even with the increased interest in recent times, there are many sleepers to be considered. Many great rarities list for ridiculously low prices. For example, if you can find an Uncirculated 1859-S dollar for the *Guide Book* price of $3,500 you should run, not walk, to buy it!

Among worn Liberty Seated dollars, in the auction market during the entire year of 1990, listed in circulated grades from VG to AU, the following selected numbers reflect that there are numerous rarities: 1840 (13 circulated coins offered at auction in 1990), 1845 (6), 1846-O (8), 1850-O (3), 1852 (1), 1854 (3), 1855 (5), 1856 (2), 1857 (none), 1858 (7 Proofs, listed here for comparison), 1860 (4), 1861 (none), 1862 (4), 1863 (2), 1864 (6), 1865 (6), 1866 (4), 1866 (1), 1867 (1), 1868 (4), 1869 (4), 1871-CC (3), 1872-S (1), 1873 (1), and 1873-CC (4).

While traditional investment advisors might reel in horror to learn that I recommend that worn coins can have investment potential, I believe that figures just quoted speak for themselves; there are really some bargains out there!

The key, of course, is *knowledge*. Anyone looking at the *Guide Book*, but having no knowledge of the actual rarity of such pieces, would probably give a big yawn. However, after studying actual appearances of coins on the market, my recommendation should make sense to you.

Liberty Seated dollars offer many opportunities to the astute buyer, and I recommend highly the many sleepers therein.

Morgan Silver Dollars

Following a suspension of dollar mintage after 1873, the production of the series resumed in 1878. A new design, by George T. Morgan, made its appearance. This motif was continued until it was replaced by the Peace design in 1921.

In 1878 the silver mining interests in the western part of the United States were responsible for the Bland-Allison Act. This legislation provided for the coinage of immense quantities of silver bullion into silver coins, thus providing a ready market— sort of an early-day price support—for silver. The largest silver coin then being minted was the silver dollar, thus it was decided to use this denomination to convert bulk silver into coin of the realm.

The result was the minting of hundreds of millions of silver dollars. More silver dollars (over 22 million) were minted in the first year of the Morgan design, 1878, than in all other previous years (1794 to 1873) of silver dollar coinage combined! In the following years hundreds of millions more were minted. There was no commercial need for such a huge quantity of dollars, thus nearly all of them went from coinage presses into $1,000 mint bags and then right into Treasury vaults for storage. In 1918 the Pittman Act caused 270,232,722 silver dollars to be melted. But still there were hundreds of millions left; more than enough to go around.

Peace Silver Dollars

From 1921 through 1935 nearly 200 million Peace-type silver dollars were minted, thus adding to the somewhat depleted (but still healthy) Treasury holdings.

No silver dollars were minted after 1935 (until the Eisenhower dollar in 1971, by which time only special pieces made for collectors actually contained silver; after this era a more appropriate term would be *metal* dollars). Eisenhower dollars were made from 1971 through 1978, followed by the ill-fated but quite interesting Susan B. Anthony dollars from 1979 to 1981.

The Treasury Hoard

The appeal of owning a bright Uncirculated silver dollar from the 19th century has interested many individuals. During the first

Morgan Silver Dollars

Peace Silver Dollars

half of the present century a steady stream of these flowed out of the Treasury vaults. In addition, silver dollars were a popular medium of exchange in Nevada and certain other western states.

By the late 1950s word had spread among the public that these "treasures" could be had for face value. While many pieces obtainable at banks were of common dates, occasionally a sharp-eyed teller or numismatist would be rewarded with a coin bearing a Carson City mintmark or with a rare date. Interest increased. Beginning in autumn 1962 a veritable race commenced. Long lines formed at various Federal Reserve and bank outlets as people eagerly purchased silver dollars from years earlier, paying just face value for them. The appeal of the situation was enhanced by reports of finding 1898-O, 1903-O, 1904-O, and other scarce and rare dates among common issues. My *Adventures with Rare Coins* book goes into the subject in detail.

When the "Great Treasury Raid," as some writers have called it, was nearly over, the Treasury decided to stop selling these old coins. At this point there were slightly over 3 million pieces left, mostly scarce issues made during the 19th century at Carson City, Nevada. After much discussion, the General Services Administration offered these for sale in a series of widely publicized auctions which began in 1972 and ended with a final sellout in 1980.

Predictions were aplenty that with so many silver dollars held by the public and by collectors, prices would fall sharply and stay depressed. In actuality, just the opposite happened. Although untold millions of silver dollars were now held by numismatists and others, the number of people interested increased so much that after 1962, demand for silver dollars was greater than ever. The General Services Administration's auction campaign to sell Carson City dollars was conducted with posters, leaflets, and advertising in banks, post offices, and elsewhere—and served to create more interest.

Today in 1991, nearly all silver dollars are higher priced now than they were in 1962, and most of them are many multiples higher in price.

The silver dollar situation has been a real windfall for collectors. In 1991 you could buy a basic Uncirculated Morgan dollar of a common date the 1878 to 1904 type for less than $20, and a 1921 Morgan dollar in MS-60 preservation was less than $15. Most collectors prefer higher grades, such as MS-63 or better, for the common dates, but still the entry-level prices of less than $20 are appealing to newcomers and help pave the way for a more refined interest in the series.

Morgan dollars today are one of the most plentiful of all early coin issues. This appealing situation has created tens of thousands of collectors of this denomination. Indeed, many collectors and investors have made a specialty of silver dollars alone.

Misleading Advertisements

As silver dollars are available in quantity, a number of promotion minded outfits have run advertisements in popular magazines, large metropolitan newspapers, and other places, offering these pieces for sale at "special" prices. And, these prices are sometimes indeed *special*: two or three times what the same coins would cost if bought from a knowledgeable professional dealer! The coin hobby papers have run a number of exposés of these practices. While I agree that the advertisements are misleading, at the same time the popular publications carrying the advertisements have advertising rates running into many thousands of dollars. While certain silver dollars may have been sold for two or three times the going price, a substantial part of these profits probably went to pay advertising bills!

Anyway, such advertisements have served to heighten public interest in coins. Hopefully, many silver dollar purchasers who paid high prices later learned about the community of rare coin collectors and dealers and were able to make subsequent acquisitions at more reasonable levels.

The Silver Dollar Minting Process

Uncirculated silver dollars and most other coins occur with varying degrees of bagmarks. The minting process included the following steps, among others: dollars were struck at high speed on production presses. Following striking, they were ejected into a chute and dumped into a collecting box, mingled with hundreds of other coins. As the collection box became full, the dollars were then dumped into a large receiving bin. By this point the average piece had a liberal number of nicks!

From that point the dollars were run through sorting, weighing, and counting devices, then put into cloth bags of 1,000 coins.

The bags were tossed onto carts and heaped with additional bags. From that point the typical bag went into storage in the vault of the Mint. As a result, piles of silver dollar bags stacked eight to 10 feet high were lined up. You can well imagine that the dollars at the bottom of the pile received even more abrasions! From time to time stored dollars were transferred to different Treasury or Federal Reserve facilities. Each time the administration of a given set of Treasury officials ended, the bags had to be counted by hand, involving more moving and damage.

By 1962, when most Uncirculated Morgan and Peace dollars of earlier dates were released, the typical coin had been bandied about many times, and yet it had not seen circulation. It is further interesting to note that it was the practice at the Philadelphia Mint during the early part of the present century to bounce silver dollars off the surface of a heavy iron table to see if they had the proper sonority or "ring."

No thought was given to preserving silver dollars for future collectors! The Treasury Department had one objective in mind: to coin as many silver dollars as possible. It is not that the Treasury wanted to do this. The action was necessitated by the Bland-Allison Act of 1878, as well as subsequent legislation which in effect was a bail-out for western silver mining interests who wanted an additional market for the metal which at that time was selling for depressed prices. Thus, as noted earlier in the text, hundreds of millions of silver dollars, unwanted and unneeded by the public, piled up in Treasury vaults.

Prooflike Coins

As can be imagined from the coining and handling process, silver dollars which qualify as MS-65 or better are in many instances scarce. Some pieces were struck from dies with a high degree of mirrorlike surface and are known as "prooflike" by collectors today. Although Wayne Miller (for one) has suggested a definition for such terms as prooflike (abbreviated PL), deep prooflike (DPL), and deep mirror prooflike (DMPL), in practice slabbed coins designated as DMPL, for example, are apt to vary widely. Some indeed have deep mirrorlike surfaces, but others are more frosty than prooflike. In addition, the prooflike surface of any of these coins serves to accentuate any contact marks the coins have received. In general, I do not recommend such coins for investment purposes. While an MS-65 DMPL (if it is really deep mirror prooflike) can be quite desirable and beautiful, MS-63 coins with such surfaces are apt to appear heavily bagmarked and unattractive from an aesthetic viewpoint.

Investment Aspects of Morgan Dollars

Among Morgan silver dollars from 1878 to 1921 there are many price inconsistencies. In the early 1980s, a vast quantity of 1881-S Morgan dollars came to light in the holdings of a Chicago bank. Immediately, this issue was promoted, and by 1985 to 1986 prices for MS-65 coins had crossed the $600 mark, finally achieving a high "bid" price of $825. Today, hand-picked, selected examples of such coins sell for less than 25% of the high water mark price.

There is nothing at all wrong with 1881-S silver dollars. They are fine and dandy, and every collection of Morgan dollars should include *one*. It has been fun watching the various promotions this particular issue has been subjected to over the years.

Among Morgan dollars released in large quantities during the Treasury dispersal in the early 1960s were 1879-S, 1880-S, 1881-S, 1884-O, and 1885-O, after which come several dozen other issues in large numbers. If one were to make a list of the 20 or 30 most common Morgan dollars and then survey investment literature published in the past 20 years, one would find that far more space had been given to these common issues than to rare issues. There are many scarce and rare issues which have been overlooked.

Although there are a number of exceptions, in general Morgan silver dollars of the 1890s are as a class scarcer than those of the 1880s. MS-65 examples of such issues as 1890-CC, 1891, 1891-CC, 1891-S, 1892, 1892-CC, 1892-O, 1892-S, 1893, 1893-CC, 1893-O, 1893-S (a classic rarity of the series), 1894, 1894-O, 1894-S, 1895 (available only in Proof preservation), 1895-O, 1895-S, 1896-O, 1896-S, and 1897-O are quite elusive in relation to the demand for them.

Figuring out which dates of Morgan dollars are scarce in MS-65 grade and which aren't is not an easy task, for prior to 1985, many coins were called MS-65 by dealers and by the American Numismatic Association Grading Service which by today's stricter grading interpretations would be called MS-60 to MS-63.[1]

---

[1] As noted earlier in the present text, the American Numismatic Association Board of Governors issued an announcement in early 1986 to the effect that coins certified by the ANA Grading Service as MS-65 in the early 1980s were in many instances MS-60 to MS-63 by new official interpretations.

The number of coins which have been certified in MS-65 grade by various grading services in recent years may provide some clues—actually, probably the best clue— to the relative rarity of certain issues, and population reports published by NGC and PCGS are recommended for study in this regard.

Morgan Dollar Recommendations

In the field of Morgan dollars, I recommend building a *collection* of as many date and mintmark varieties as possible. If you can afford it, by all means go for MS-65. However, the completion of a set in this preservation involves over a million dollars, so it is not for the faint-hearted!

A more practical route is to opt for MS-63 coins in most instances. If money is no object, go for a mixture of MS-63 and MS-64. Both the MS-63 and MS-64 grades offer some outstanding values.

Cherrypicking Investment Coins

If you want to cherrypick some issues for investment only (not as part of a collection), make a list of the nearly 100 different standard date and mintmark varieties (no overdates, unusual varieties of CC coins of 1880, etc.) of Morgan dollars, ranking them in order in MS-63 price from the cheapest to the most expensive. Delete the 30 cheapest varieties and the 25 most expensive. This will leave you with over 40 middle-range coins. Buy as many as you can of each of these middle-range coins, up to 20 coins per variety. Salt them away for a few years. I believe that this formula, if followed, will yield an above average return in comparison to the price movement of the Morgan dollar series as a whole.

I also like MS-64 in this regard, and although I prefer MS-63 in terms of value received, you might pick up some MS-64 coins also.

Additional Morgan Dollar Comments

What about common issues of silver dollars? So far as the investment outlook for something like a plentiful 1881-S silver dollar in MS-63 grade, its price movement will depend upon the movement of Morgan dollars in general. It is not rare, thus it will never be a key issue. On the other hand, if the series in general moves upward, as it has done in recent decades, this issue (and other common issues) should move upward with it.

There are a number of sleepers to be found among certain issues, and studying the availability of such can pinpoint some buying opportunities.

At present I am researching the field, with the view of publishing the findings in a specialized book on silver dollars as part of the "Action Guide" series of books within the next few years. In the meantime, checking grading service population reports, auction prices realized lists, and sale offerings can be useful. The 1991 edition of *Auction Prices Realized*, containing auction results for 1990, published by Krause Publications, will be a valuable tool.

Expected to be published in the near future are several important reference book on the subject by various authors. A manuscript by Robert W. Julian, with annotations by Walter H. Breen and comments by me, is being prepared for publication in 1992. John Highfill, long the sponsor and guiding light of the National Silver Dollar Roundtable, has gathered articles on the denomination for publication in an anthology said to comprise nearly 1,000 pages. A new edition of the *Comprehensive Catalogue and Encyclopedia of U.S. Morgan and Peace Silver Dollars*, by Leroy C. Van Allen and A. George Mallis, last published in 1976, is also in the works. Each of these will increase interest in the field.

A Question of Value

Scarce and rare Morgan dollars, such as those I have mentioned from the 1890s as well as the middle price range issues, are expensive, but the price multiples these sell for in comparison to common issues (such as 1881-S) do not reflect their true rarity; in proportion, if an 1881-S MS-63 Morgan dollar is worth, for purposes of argument, $35 (although the price may be higher or lower by the time you read this), then an 1892-O (current value in the $225 range in MS-63 grade) should be worth several thousand dollars, as it is 100 or more times rare than an 1881-S. An MS-63 1896-O dollar (value now about $4,000) is at least 1,000 times rarer than an MS-63 1881-S. I could cite many other examples.

Before buying Morgan dollars of any kind, acquaint yourself with the series, familiarize yourself with grading, and learn as much as you can. A very small difference in grade can make a very large difference in price, as a perusal of catalogue values indicate.

Among slabbed coins there are many inconsistencies, some of which can lead to profit for you.

If you examine, for example, a 10 slabbed 1893-CC dollars marked MS-63, you will soon find that some are much nicer than others. Another party might grade the same coins as MS-62, MS-62, MS-62, MS-63, MS-63, MS-63, MS-63, MS-63, MS-64, and MS-64. Obviously, the two coins in the group which seem to be of MS-64 quality are a lot better buy than the ones which are MS-62.

Not all groups of Morgan dollars will show differences, but enough do that it was brought out in testimony before the Federal Trade Commission that some 35% of the coins resubmitted to a certain grading service received a different grade the second time around.

There is also the aspect of striking sharpness to consider. Some issues, particularly certain New Orleans varieties, often are shallowly struck at the center of the reverse and obverse. Morgan dollars of 1921 of all mints, but particularly 1921-S, are typically poorly struck. When buying 1921-S dollars in any grade, be patient and select choice ones.

One MS-65 or 16 MS-64s for the Same Price?

Consider the price of the 1921-S dollar in high grades in the July 12, 1991 issue of *The Coin Dealer Newsletter*: MS-63 $39, MS-64 $190, MS-65 $3,100. Anyone buying an MS-65 coin of this variety had better be *very careful*, for reasons that the prices make obvious. Such situations prompt me again and again to suggest that for purposes of potential appreciation, cherrypicked MS-63 and MS-64 coins are much better buys than MS-65 coins for many multiples of the MS-63 or MS-64 prices.

Using the above example, you can buy 16(!) MS-64 1921-S dollars for the price of a single MS-65. Moreover, chances are good that one or more of your MS-64 coins will be fully equal to what some sellers or certification services designate as MS-65. How can you lose by buying MS-64s? Of course, you have no need for 16 specimens, but you can use the left-over money to add other varieties to your collection.

The market for Morgan (and Peace) dollars has been subject to many cycles and price fluctuations in recent decades, not to overlook market promotions. I caution you against investing heavily in a single date or mintmark variety. If you decide to collect silver dollars, and certainly this is an interesting and highly recommended pursuit, then by all means spread your investment over a number of different issues.

Investing in Peace Dollars

Peace silver dollars, minted from 1921 to 1935, represent an interesting field on their own. In general, Peace dollars are much harder to find in higher grades than are Morgan dollars. The reason for this is that the design, except for the high relief 1921, is flat, and with little in the way of protective design elements, small nicks and marks are apt to be highlighted.

Forming an MS-63 set of Peace dollars from 1921 to 1935 is no easy task, despite the modest values, and forming an MS-65 set is a major challenge! Again, grading interpretations have changed dramatically in recent times, and whereas coins which met the MS-65 qualification of the American Numismatic Association were quite plentiful in the 1970s, when grading was "looser," by the strict interpretations of today, MS-65 coins of certain issues are few and far between. I've always liked Peace dollars, but for some reason they have never had the "play" that Morgan dollars have. In the meantime, the series represents an interesting design and a worthwhile collection.

Comments on Anthony and Eisenhower Dollars

Eisenhower dollars, not properly called *silver* dollars except for some special issues made for collectors, were produced from 1971 to 1978. In general, Proof pieces are obtainable in Proof-65 or better grade, but circulation strikes are apt to be scarce if you are fussy about nicks and marks. Many issues in strict MS-65 preservation are scarcer than catalogue values indicate.

Susan B. Anthony dollars, made from 1979 to 1981, are available and form a nice mini-collection of pieces from our own era. The business strikes of 1981 all have low mintages, thus these stand out as being more desirable than the rest. Such varieties as the Filled S and Clear S issues of 1979-S are so much piffle, so far as I am concerned—but let collectors collect whatever they want; who am I to argue? However, from my viewpoint it would be a waste of money to pay a premium of 10 times over the regular price to buy 1979-S Proof Anthony dollars with a Clear S mintmark.

Investing in U.S. Trade Dollars

Trade dollars are often collected along with silver dollars. Minted in quantity from 1873 to 1878, trade dollars were produced to create a circulating bullion-type coin for the Orient, where merchants wanted payment in coins, not bank drafts or currency.

The trade dollar, weighing 420 grains, is slightly heavier than the silver dollar and was produced in order to compete with Mexican dollars, which were preferred by Oriental merchants at the time (for Mexican dollars were slightly heavier than regular-issue United States silver dollars). Most trade dollars were minted on the West Coast at San Francisco, with additional large mintages from time to time at Carson City, as these mints were closest to the Orient.

Among business strikes, nearly all issues from 1873 through 1878 are scarce or rare in MS-64 and MS-65 preservation, with exceptions being 1876-S, 1877, 1877-S, and 1878-S. Particularly rare are 1877-CC and 1878-CC. Probably no more than a half dozen MS-65 1878-CC trade dollars exist.

Proofs were made of all dates from 1873 through 1883. Interestingly, Proof-63 or better specimens are significantly scarcer for dates from 1873 through 1877 than for the later dates from 1878 through 1883. The reason for this is that trade dollars were not esteemed by collectors during the time of issue, but numismatists had to buy Proof examples in order to get the other silver Proof coins of the era, for silver coins were sold only in sets. The trade dollars were often picked out and "spent." Beginning in 1878, and continuing through 1883, no business strikes were made at the Philadelphia Mint. Collectors realized that the Proofs of these issues might be desirable due to the low overall mintage for the dates, thus the spending stopped and most were saved.

Trade dollars of 1884 and 1885 were made privately at the Mint. Little is known concerning their history. It is traditionally stated that just 10 1884 trade dollars and just five 1885 trade dollars were minted. Each is a classic rarity.

If you have the budget to afford it, building a set of Philadelphia Mint trade dollars in Proof-63 or better grade from 1873 through 1883, plus the branch mint issues in MS-63 or better grade, forms an interesting challenge and, when completed, a beautiful collection. Prices on the present market are in some instances fractions of what they were a year or two ago.

Investing in U.S. Commemoratives

Introduction

 According to what you read in most places, American commemorative coins were first produced in 1892, in which year specially designed half dollars were struck for distribution at the World's Columbian Exposition (which actually took place a year later, in 1893).

Actually, the earliest official commemorative of which we have definite record is the 1848 quarter eagle with CAL. counterstamped on the reverse; an issue made specifically for those desiring to acquire a souvenir coin made from California metal. However, "tradition," that arbiter of numismatic tastes, has dictated that the 1848 CAL. not be considered a commemorative but, instead, just a variety of quarter eagle (and thus of primary interest to quarter eagle specialists).[1]

In 1991 my book, *Commemorative Coins of the United States: A Complete Encyclopedia*, was published. I refer you to a copy of that work (available from numismatic booksellers, or free on loan from the ANA Library). I give extensive market and investment data for each and every issue from the 19th century to date.

I like commemoratives. Each type has its own story to tell. "No nation has surpassed our own country when it comes to commemorative coins, in this we have reason to be proud," notes *A Guide Book of United States Coins*. "The unique position occupied by commemoratives in United States coinage is largely due to the

---

[1] Another candidate for an early commemorative may be a certain counterstamp applied on United States large cents and other coins in 1824. One side of the counterstamp depicts a portrait of President Washington, while the other shows the head of Lafayette. F.G. Duffield, writing in *The Numismatist* in August 1921, gave two versions concerning the origin of the counterstamp. The first was that the pieces were made at the Philadelphia Mint, by overstamping coins of recent date, after which time they were distributed as souvenirs during Lafayette's visit to the United States in 1824 and 1825. The second version is that the counterstamps were applied privately, and that bystanders threw the coins in the path of Lafayette as he appeared in parades. I personally find it difficult to envision anyone throwing coins away in 1824, but that's how the story goes.

fact that with few exceptions they are the only coins that have a real historical significance. The progress and advances of people in the New World are presented in an interesting and instructive manner on commemorative issues. Such a record of facts artistically presented on our gold and silver memorial issues appeals strongly to the collector who favors the historical side of numismatics."

In the present book I give some basic guidelines for building a nice collection of commemoratives with potential price appreciation in mind:

Commemorative Silver Coins

Commemorative half dollars of the early series were made in different designs from 1892 to 1954, beginning with the Columbian half dollar of the former date. After 1954 there was a long lapse, until the 1982 Washington commemoratives, followed by the 1984 Olympics coins, the 1986 Statue of Liberty issues (including the first nickel clad half dollar), and 1987 Constitution pieces, on down to the latest 1991 Mount Rushmore, Korean War Anniversary, and USO Anniversary issues.

The 1776-1976 bicentennial coins were commemoratives of a sort, but as most were placed into circulation, and as they took the place of regular issues at the time, they are not considered to be a part of the commemorative series.

From the 1892 Columbian half dollar down to coins minted in our own time, there exists a fascinating array of pieces with interesting designs, great historical significance, and high numismatic interest.

Most commemorative coins have been of the half dollar denomination. From 1892 to 1954 there were 48 different major design types issued. If all date and mintmark varieties are considered, then there are 142 different varieties.

Some commemorative half dollars, the 1946 Iowa Centennial issue for example, were issued in just one type or variety. Others were issued in many varieties. As an example of the latter I mention the Arkansas centennial pieces issued each year from 1935 to 1939 inclusive (although, strictly speaking, only 1936 was the centennial year), and at three mints (Philadelphia, Denver, and San Francisco) each year. Thus, a complete set of Arkansas

United States Commemorative Coins

1900 Lafayette silver dollar

1893 Isabella quarter

From 1892 to 1954, and beginning again in 1982, commemorative silver coins were issued in a wide variety of designs. With the exception of the 1893 Isabella quarter dollar and the 1900 Lafayette silver dollar, all United States commemorative coins of the 1892 to 1954 early period are half dollars. The 1928 Hawaiian, 1937 Antietam, and 1927 Vermont issues, three of 48 major designs produced during the early years, are shown on this page—together with the 1893 Isabella quarter and the 1900 Lafayette silver dollar.

1928 Hawaiian half dollar

Events commemorated on coins range from the significant to the obscure. In the former category are the 1892 and 1893 Columbian Exposition, 1935 Connecticut Tercentenary (300th anniversary), 1946 Iowa statehood centennial, and the 1915 Panama-Pacific International Exposition. Among the lesser events from a national viewpoint are the 1936 300th anniversary of York County in Maine, the 1786-1936 anniversary of the Lynchburg, Virginia city charger, and the 150th anniversary of the founding of the city of Hudson in New York state.

1937 Antietam half dollar

1927 Vermont half dollar

half dollar varieties consists of three coins from each of five years, for a total of 15 pieces.

There are two main ways to collect half dollars of the 1892 to 1954 era: a type set of 48 pieces or a complete variety set of 142 pieces. Which to choose depends upon your budget, for a complete variety set is substantially more expensive than a type set. Over the years, all commemorative half dollars have been excellent investments. However, as mentioned earlier in this book, commemoratives have been subject to speculation from time to time, and market cycles have also had an influence, with resultant ups and downs in prices. The long-term trend, however, has been upward.

Two early silver commemorative coins of special interest are the 1893 Isabella quarter dollar and the 1900 Lafayette dollar, for they represent unusual denominations apart from the half dollar series.

Commemorative Gold Coins

Nine different varieties of commemorative gold dollars were issued. Events memorialized include the 1922 Grant Memorial, 1915 Panama-Pacific International Exposition, 1903 Louisiana Purchase Exposition, and the 1904-1905 Lewis and Clark Exposition, as well as others.

All commemorative gold dollars are scarce today. The rarity of such pieces depends not so much on the mintage as the method of distribution. Hence, 1904-1905 Lewis and Clark issues are much rarer than 1916-1917 McKinley issues, although approximately equal numbers were issued of each design type.

The reason is that most of the Lewis and Clark pieces were sold as souvenirs at the Exposition, and thus were acquired by the public. In the intervening years many have been lost, damaged, or destroyed. By contrast, most of the 1916 and 1917 McKinley pieces were sold to coin dealers and collectors who saved them carefully. In MS-65 preservation, the 1904-1905 Lewis and Clark gold dollars are at least 20 times rarer than 1916 McKinley pieces, although catalogue values do not reflect this! (On their own, 1917 McKinley dollars are two to three times rarer than those dated 1916, but popular references do not reflect this, either.)

Commemorative quarter eagles ($2.50 gold pieces) were issued on two occasions: for the 1915 Panama-Pacific Interna-

Commemorative Gold Coins

Obverse, $50 round   Reverse, $50 octagonal

From 1903 to 1926 13 different commemorative gold designs were produced. Nine were gold dollars, two were quarter eagles, and two were massive $50 pieces. The latter, produced in round and octagonal formats, were struck for the Panama-Pacific International Exposition held in San Francisco in 1915 and are great rarities today.

tional Exposition and for the 1926 Sesquicentennial (150 years of American independence) celebration.

Most spectacular of all commemoratives are the massive $50 gold pieces issued in 1915 and sold at the Panama-Pacific International Exposition. There were 483 pieces of the round shape and 645 of the octagonal format sold. Today these coins are highly desired by numismatists, and the appearance of an MS-63 or better specimen in an auction sale or other offering is an outstanding event. By 1991 a complete Panama-Pacific set of commemoratives, including the two $50 gold pieces, was valued in the $75,000 range in MS-63 grade, and at a high point in the market a year or so ago a dealer paid $250,000 for an MS-65 set!

Availability in Certain Grades

I recommend that all commemoratives that you buy for investment be in MS-63 or better condition. While circulated pieces may go up in value, MS-63 to MS-65 pieces will probably always be in the greatest demand. And, perhaps more than other American series dated prior to a few decades ago (with the possible exception of Morgan and Peace dollars), Uncirculated pieces are readily available. In fact, for some commemorative issues, a *worn* piece would be a major rarity!

As strange as it may seem, commemorative half dollars with the lowest mintages are not necessarily the hardest to find in MS-63 or better grade. The original method of distribution furnishes the key to the availability of high-grade coins today. Issues that went primarily to the public instead of to numismatists tend to show damage and signs of mishandling when seen today. Among the scarcer half dollars from the viewpoint of MS-64 and MS-65 specimens are the Alabama, California Jubilee, surprisingly the 1892 and 1893 Columbian issues (scarce in comparison to their large mintages), Grant, Hawaiian (a combination of low mintage plus distribution emphasis to people who were not numismatists), Maine, Missouri, Monroe, Panama-Pacific, and Sesquicentennial of American Independence.

It is probably the case that only a few hundred MS-65 1921 Alabama or Missouri half dollars exist today! How can this be? After all, thousands of these coins were sold to collectors. The answer is that at the Mint itself, these coins were handled carelessly. They were then shipped mixed together in cloth bags, thus by the actual time of distribution most coins were MS-63 or less! In fact, today even MS-63 examples of these two issues are scarce. Most known pieces are AU-50 to MS-60. A number of other illustrations could be mentioned.

Contrast that to the 1938 New Rochelle half dollar. These were handled carefully, thus most known examples are in MS-63 or better condition. A worn piece would be a major rarity. Of course, a worn piece would not be worth nearly as much as an Uncirculated coin, for even if it is rare, not many people would want it.

To the older issues can be added modern commemoratives from the 1982 Washington pieces to date. All of the modern issues are readily available in gem Uncirculated and Proof as issued.

Commemorative Recommendations

As a beginning on a silver commemorative collection with investment in mind, I recommend building a type set of half dollars of the 1892 to 1954 designs, 48 different pieces, plus the 1893 Isabella quarter and 1900 Lafayette dollar. As a condition objective, stick to MS-63 or better. I like MS-63 and MS-64 in the present market and feel that some MS-65 pieces still have some adjustments in store, although all are selling for much less now in the summer of 1991 than they were from one to four years ago.

In a recent edition of this book, written before the run-up in prices in the late 1980s, I wrote the following:

"If you want to invest in a few extra pieces—now we are getting into the subject of hoarding—sleepers in MS-65 grade include just about any coin issued prior to the 1930s. Such a common issue as the 1923-S Monroe is *very rare* in MS-65 preservation. While there are thousands and thousands of these in the hands of numismatists, very few merit the MS-65 designation. Stated another way, if you accumulate a dozen 1938 New Rochelle half dollars in MS-65 grade, you may have something worthwhile, but if you could accumulate a dozen MS-65 1921 Alabama half dollars (of either variety minted of the coin) or a dozen MS-65 1921 Missouri half dollars (of either variety), or a dozen MS-65 1923-S Monroe halves, then you would have accomplished something truly remarkable. How all this will translate into investment dollars in your pocket remains to be seen, for the age of enlightenment so far as the true recognition of numismatic rarities has yet to come. This is precisely the reason why you can make some excellent buys *now*. A recurring theme throughout the book is that there are many sleepers awaiting those caring to seek them out, but little investment literature will mention them, simply because few have a vested interest."

Now, in the summer of 1991, I feel that the preceding recommendation is no longer valid, for prices today are much higher. Now, an MS-65 1923-S Monroe sells for nearly 10 times the price of an MS-64! As stated, I now prefer MS-63 and MS-64 coins for the value they offer. Of course, if money is no object, then MS-65 or even finder commemoratives are very pleasing to own, so do not let me dissuade you. However, I feel that MS-63 and MS-64 coins will be better from an investment viewpoint.

As the Treasury Department and Congress seem to be agreeable to issuing more commemoratives in the future, this should make the traditional early series of the 1892 to 1954 years even more desirable in comparison, for the earlier issues are much rarer than the pieces produced in modern times.

Don't overlook the *fun* aspect of learning about commemoratives and becoming involved in the series. Membership in the Society for U.S. Commemorative Coins, which publishes *The Commemorative Trail*, is very worthwhile. While putting the finishing touches on my *Commemorative Coins of the United States: A Complete Encyclopedia* in 1990 and early 1991 I often exchanged fascinating letters a couple of pages or more in length with such fellow enthusiasts as Helen L. Carmody and Bill Fivaz. There is a certain quintessential feeling among collectors, an electricity if you will. Enjoyment is yours free for the taking as part of your participation as a commemorative collector.

I hasten to mention the Bowers and Merena Commemorative Coin Club, a commemorative coin-of-the-month (more or less) group which Bowers and Merena Galleries formed in 1991, and which has been quite popular with buyers who like the idea of building a commemorative collection with automatic shipments.

Of course, there are many other ways to buy as well. No matter how you buy, or from whom, it will pay you to be fussy about quality.

Investing in U.S. Gold Coins

Introduction to Gold Coins

 Gold has always held a fascination for mankind. From ancient times to the present, gold has had an allure, a romance unmatched by any other metal. Throughout history the highest-valued coins of the realm have been struck in gold. In recent centuries this precious metal has been the foundation of the world's monetary system. Paper money currency systems come and go, but gold holds its value.

In the late 1970s and in the 1980s, a number of "hard money" economists warned of the inadvisability of placing faith in paper money. While the amount of paper money in circulation around the world is so great that it is unlikely gold coins will ever make a widespread comeback as monetary units, still gold is used as an international yardstick against which paper currency is measured. In the United States and elsewhere, a number of people derive a measure of security by holding gold bullion-type coins.

Gold coins have a special charm: they represent the world's most famous, most desired metal in a convenient and artistic form. One can only read about the bars of gold in Fort Knox or in the Bank of England, but one can actually *hold* and *own* a gold coin.

Paper francs and marks and cruzieros and dollars and pounds may rise and fall in value. The holder of German paper marks during the early 1920s found that a bushel basket of currency would not buy a loaf of bread. The holder of United States Gold Certificates, "guaranteed in gold" obligations of the United States government, and other pieces of paper, found that they were just that: pieces of paper—when the United States government decided to dishonor and renege upon all of its gold obligations in 1933 and 1934. Most other countries have experienced similar situations.

Aware of the stability of gold, especially as measured against the uncertain value of paper money, many governments have tried to legislate against the ownership of gold. Did you know, for example, that in the United States, a country renowned for its freedoms, it was illegal until December 31, 1974 to own a small bar of gold metal? To buy or sell such a thing without a special license could have resulted in a prison term, a Kafkaesque situation in retrospect from the view of the 1990s. Fortunately in most world areas it is not illegal to own coins. Therein lies an opportunity.

There are two basic reasons to collect or invest in gold coins. The first is investment from a numismatic viewpoint. A date set or type set of gold coins can be formed with emphasis on pieces of historical or numismatic interest. The second is investment from a metallic or intrinsic value viewpoint. Purchasers buying from a metallic viewpoint do not care about the numismatic aspects. Instead, the price of gold on world markets is what affects the price of their investment.

In recent decades both types of investors have done well, but the market has been characterized by wide fluctuations in price and demand. Investors who have emphasized gold coins *of numismatic importance* have done quite well for the most part.

Gold Coins in American History

Throughout colonial times, gold coins of other countries, particularly of Spanish-American countries and Great Britain, circulated in America and were used in large commercial transactions.

The first United States gold coins were minted in 1795 and consisted of pieces of the $5 and $10 denominations. From then until gold coins were last minted in 1933, hundreds of millions of individual pieces were produced. If you are interested in learning about United States gold coins in depth, you may enjoy reading a copy of my book, United States Gold Coins: An Illustrated History. Separate chapters are devoted to each gold denomination. Detailed information is given concerning rarity of individual issues, background, how gold coins are minted, and other facets.

I was very pleased to learn that on September 8, 1986, in his talk at the momentous ceremony of the first striking of new United States bullion coins, Secretary of the Treasury James A. Baker, III, began his talk with a quotation from this particular book:

"It is a pleasure to be with you all today. The writer Q. David Bowers has called gold 'that precious, rare, beautiful, glamorous, and nearly indestructible element.' Because it has such qualities, gold has long been a source of fascination and an object of financial security. The metal which brings us here today has its roots far back in the mists of time.

"Ancient Egypt, for example, was sustained by its gold mines in the Nubian Desert. And, according to one scholar, the Greek myth of the Argonauts' search for the Golden Fleece 'probably has its origin in a raid upon miners who were using sheepskins to catch fragments of gold, just as some modern gold washing has employed blankets.'

"Centuries later, of course, the American hemisphere attracted many who had hopes of finding gold. 'El Dorado' the Spanish called it, as they sought the legendary Seven Cities filled with precious metals. The cities had supposedly been built by seven bishops who fled from invaders of the Iberian Peninsula in A.D. 734.

"And, later, in the United States, prospectors 'rushed' to far-flung parts of the wilderness to dig dangerous mines or wade through icy mountain creeks. Though some gold towns became ghost towns, many gold hunters settled down in thriving permanent communities in California, Colorado, and Alaska...."

U.S. Denominations

Among United States coins, standard gold denominations are: $1, $2.50, $3, $5, $10, and $20. When the American monetary system was established, the basic coin value was established as the "eagle" or $10 gold coin, first minted in 1795. It had been intended to produce gold coins as early as 1793, but surety bonds were required of certain Mint officials before they could strike pieces in this precious metal, and the requirements were not fulfilled until 1795. Later, in 1850 when $20 gold coins were first made for circulation, they were called "double eagles." Today, numismatists adhere to these same terms. The $2.50 is called a "quarter eagle" and the $5 a "half eagle." There are no special terms for the $1 and $3 issues, apart from "gold dollar" and "three-dollar gold piece."

In 1879 and 1880 a number of pattern $4 gold coins were produced. One 1879 issue was minted to the extent of an estimated 600 or so pieces (a rather large issue for a pattern coin) so specimens would be available for congressmen, newspaper editors, and other influential people. $4 gold pieces, called "stellas" (from the five-pointed star on the reverse), are numismatic prizes today. A Proof-65 example of the "common" 1879 issue, the variety with Miss Liberty in a flowing hair style, brings over $50,000 today, and rarer varieties of 1879 and 1880 sell for into six figures.

$50 gold coins were produced as patterns by the Philadelphia Mint in 1877. A few years ago Ray Merena did a survey, subsequently published in *Coin World*, in which he asked professional numismatists which coins on a theoretical basis would bring the most money if offered at auction. The 1877 $50 pieces were at the head of the list. There is an interesting and rather complicated story involving these two pieces, and how they escaped from the Mint, were sold to collector William H. Woodin, and subsequently returned; all of this is related in my *Coins and Collectors* book.

In 1915 the San Francisco Mint struck a small number of $50 pieces, some of round shape and others octagonal, as commemoratives to be sold at the Panama-Pacific International Exposition held that year. The coins were offered at twice face value, or $100 each. Today each coin, if in MS-63 grade, is worth in the $30,000 range. A complete set of five Panama-Pacific International Exposition commemorative coins, consisting of two $50 pieces, a $2.50 issue, the $1 gold and the half dollar, in MS-63 grade, brings in the $75,000 range, as noted earlier in my discussion of commemoratives.

Used For Large Transactions

During the early years of our republic, gold coins were used in settlement of large transactions, particularly in distant places. Prior to 1861 the American currency system was hectic, and few people placed any trust in the millions of notes issued by private banks. Gold was *the* store of value.

Following the establishment in 1861 of the United States paper money system as we know it, the public became more and more confident in paper money (often called "fiat currency," for its value depends upon faith of the government issuing it rather than any intrinsic value), and dependence on gold coins declined. Gold coins were rarely seen in circulation after about 1880. However, the quantities of gold coins minted actually increased after 1880,

United States Gold Coin Type Set

$1 gold Type I

$1 gold Type II

$1 gold Type III

$2½ gold Liberty Head

$2½ gold Indian

$3 gold

$5 gold Liberty Head

$5 gold Indian

$10 gold Liberty Head

$10 gold Indian

$20 gold Liberty Head

$20 gold Saint-Gaudens

On this page are shown gold coins included in a type set of major designs from the middle 19th century through the early 20th century.

continuing through the 1920s. Gold pieces were minted by the millions. Most were stored in Treasury or bank vaults or were shipped overseas in settlement of international transactions.

As an example, in the 20th century, in the year 1928 there were 8,816,000 $20 gold pieces struck! In face value this amounted to $176,320,000. During the same year the total combined face value of the coins commonly used in circulation—pieces from half cents through silver dollars (although silver dollars were not used actively)—amounted to just $11,261,732—a fraction of the 1928 $20 coinage.

What Happened To the Gold Coins?

What happened to all of the 1928 $20 pieces and the hundreds of millions of other gold coins minted over the years? Most gold coins of the early era of United States mintage, the years from 1795 through July 1834, were melted down around the latter year when the intrinsic value of gold coins exceeded their face value. The situation became so acute that the Act of August 31, 1834 was passed in order to reduce the weight of gold coins so that they could once again circulate. For this reason, all coins of the early, heavier standard employed from 1795 through July 1834 are rare today, and some are extremely rare.

Except for losses due to casualty and recall by the government of early issues (such as the obsolete $1 and $3 denominations), most gold coins minted from 1834 through 1933 were still in existence by the latter year. In 1933 President Franklin Roosevelt decreed that gold coins would no longer be minted, and the ownership of gold coins by the public (but not including numismatists) was made illegal.

Gold coins held by the Treasury, by banks, and by the public were called in and were melted into gold bullion. Once this had been accomplished, the United States government raised the price of gold bullion from $20.67 an ounce to $35.00—thus making a fantastic (and, some said, unconscionable) profit at the expense of the citizens and banks who received only face value for their coins. Immediately a typical common $20 gold piece, worth just $20 early in 1933, became worth $35!

During the late 19th and early 20th centuries tremendous quantities of American gold coins, particularly of the $5, $10, and $20 denominations, were shipped overseas in settlement of

The CAL. Quarter Eagle—America's First Commemorative

Made from California gold and specifically identified as such on the coin, the 1848 CAL. $2.50 gold piece is perhaps the most historically significant of all United States territorial-related gold coins. Certainly no gold coin bearing the imprimatur of the U.S. Mint has a closer connection with the famed Gold Rush.

When gold was first discovered at Sutter's Mill in California, samples were rushed to the U.S. Mint for testing and assay. A letter to Dr. R.M. Patterson (director of the U.S. Mint in Philadelphia) from Secretary of War W.L. Marcy read in part: "If the metal is found to be pure gold, as I doubt not that it will be, I request you to reserve enough of it for two medals ordered by Congress and not yet completed, and the remainder, with the exception of one or two small bars, I wish to have coined and sent with the bars to this department. As many may wish to procure specimens of coin made of California gold, by exchanging other coin for it, I would suggest that it be made into quarter eagles with a distinguishing mark on each."

The distinguishing mark, was, of course, "CAL." above the eagle on the reverse. Thus one of America's most romantic and famous rarities was created. Although it has not been extensively publicized as such, the coin is the first commemorative issue produced by the U.S. Mint.

Shown above is a Choice Uncirculated piece from the Robert Marks Collection.

international transactions. When the Executive Gold Order of 1933 was declared, foreign governments gave no thought to returning their $20 gold pieces and other gold coins to the United States government in exchange for "greenbacks." If anything, they held on to their gold coins even more tightly!

Foreign Banks a Source for U.S. Gold Coins

This had a very fortunate sequel. When collecting gold coins became popular, Switzerland became the number one source for gold coins in quantities. From deep within Swiss bank vaults came millions of American gold coins, many of them in Uncirculated condition! It is from Swiss banks and other overseas sources that most so-called "common date" gold coins have been acquired in recent years. Although Swiss holdings have included some rarities as well, most classic rarities remained in coin collections in America (there was no requirement to turn the rarities into the government for melting in 1933).

In the 1891-1991 ANA Centennial Convention Auction Sale we included a consignment of U.S. gold coins from the central bank of a prominent world country (not Switzerland), which had consigned the treasure trove to us.

In the late 1980s we sold on behalf of a leading international financial institution vast quantities of $5, $10, and $20 U.S. gold coins from several world banks.

Thus, the gold coins available for collecting and investment today are comprised of a combination of rarities from old-time collections plus other issues, usually of the $5, $10, and $20 denominations, which have been imported from Switzerland and other countries in relatively recent times. Now, in the early 1990s, most if not all overseas hoards of American coins have been picked over very thoroughly, with the result that prices for United States coins purchased in foreign lands are sometimes higher than they are here in America! Then there is the problem of counterfeit gold coins, discussed earlier in the present book. Many overseas banks seem to have a generous supply of these for sale to tourists!

Collecting U.S. Gold Coins

Regular-issue United States gold coins can be collected in a number of ways. Such pieces can form a type set as discussed

The 1879 Coiled Hair $4 Stella

    This Choice Proof example of the rare 1879 pattern Stella with coiled hair (another design was made with long flowing tresses for Miss Liberty) was auctioned by the author's firm.

    The $4 gold piece derives its popular name of *Stella* from the five-pointed star on the reverse. The design was inspired by a suggestion from the Hon. John A. Kasson, who served as United States minister to Austria. Prior to his appointment abroad, he had been the chairman of the Committee of Coinage, Weights, and Measures and developed his interest in the United States monetary system. Kasson believed an American $4 piece would be useful in Europe where it would have approximately the same value as the Spanish 20 pesetas, the Italian 20 lire, the Dutch eight florins, and the French 20 francs. Patterns for the Stella were produced by Charles E. Barber, who submitted the Flowing Hair design, and George T. Morgan, who created the Coiled Hair design. Mint records indicate a mintage of 415 pieces of the Flowing Hair design in 1879, and 15 pieces dated 1880; of the rarer Coiled Hair design, 10 were made of each date. In actuality, a few more pieces are known, indicating that the official records were not complete. It is estimated that the production of 1879 Flowing Hair $4 pieces was slightly over 600 coins, and probably about 15 to 20 were made of each of the later varieties.

earlier in my chapter on the subject. This is one of the most interesting ways to form a holding of gold coins, and it is highly recommended.

Gold coins can also be collected by date and mintmark sequence. My firm has helped a number of clients build sets of $20 pieces from 1850 through the last collectible date in the series, 1932; sets of gold dollars from 1849 through 1889; sets of $3 pieces from 1854 through 1889; and so on. Building these sets is always a challenge, and to the best of my knowledge, without exception, each collection produced a handsome profit for the client who purchased it and held it for the long term.

One of our clients, an eastern numismatist, became interested in the $3 denomination and purchased many varieties from us, including a superb Proof of the highly-prized 1875 rarity. Upon completing his set, he turned to the collecting of pattern coins of the $3 denomination, and over the years he has built a fine specialized holding of these.

United States gold coins have done extremely well as an investment over the years. For example, an 1851 gold dollar, in what is now called MS-63 grade, valued at $7.50 in 1948 catalogues for $450 in the 1992 edition of the *Guide Book*, although it is an indication of fluctuating values to note that in the 1988 edition the same coin catalogued for $1,000. The 1851 gold dollar is scarce in MS-60 grade, but is hardly a rarity. In the late 1980s it and many other common, semi-scarce, and scarce gold coins rose dramatically in value. Since then the prices of many have subsided. Holding their values better have been important rarities and key dates.

Spectacular has been the performance of an 1855 gold dollar, an example of the scarce so-called "Type II" design minted in 1854 and 1855. An Uncirculated 1855 gold dollar catalogued $12.50 in 1946. In the 1992 catalogue, the same coin is listed at $3,000—for just MS-60. An MS-63 coin is worth thousands of dollars more.

An 1807 Uncirculated $2.50 piece went from $100 to $16,000 (again in *only* MS-60 grade). A 1907 MCMVII $20 High Relief in Uncirculated preservation went from $120 to $6,500 (in MS-60 preservation), and so on. Gold coins of exceptional numismatic value have indeed been spectacular investments!

Gold coins of high intrinsic value but of moderate scarcity also did well, but not as well as their rarer brothers. For example,

1861 Philadelphia Mint Paquet Reverse $20

The MS-67 Philadelphia Mint Paquet Reverse $20 sold for $660,000 in the Norweb III auction by Auctions by Bowers and Merena in November 1988. A segment of the description read as follows:

"A virtually flawless coin. . . . The obverse and reverse are sharply and deeply struck, exceedingly well detailed in all areas, and are lustrous with a satinlike frost. . . . Irrespective of a variety, here is one of the finest extant Liberty Head double eagle of *any* issue.

"It is believed that just two specimens are known to exist. The present coin from the Norweb Collection, has reposed there ever since August 16, 1954, when it was acquired from John J. Ford, Jr. of the New Netherlands Coin Company. Immediately before then, the coin had been sold as part of the Palace Collection of King Farouk of Egypt, and was acquired at that sale by New Netherlands Coin Company through the agency of David Spink of Spink & Son, Ltd."

In 1991 the coin was the subject of a special study by Michael Hodder published in *The American Numismatic Association Centennial Anthology*.

an Uncirculated 1828 $20 gold piece, a so-called "common date" (and a piece I mentioned a few paragraphs earlier), went from a $70 catalogue value in 1946 to $500, for a gain of 614%, not bad on an absolute basis, but a slow performer by numismatic investment standards.

Gold Coins Overlooked by Early Numismatists

Collecting gold coins by dates and mintmarks was not popular until well into the present century. In 1909, when Edgar H. Adams wrote his *Official Premium List of United States, Private and Territorial Gold Coins*, he noted that scarce issues were obtainable for face value:

"Many rare gold coins are circulated throughout the United States, unappreciated in passing for only their face value, that would be highly prized by collectors. These coins embrace many of the issues of the United States prior to 1860, with their various mint letters.

"With the regular United States coins, there is no reason why a careful watch of all the gold coins in circulation should not result in the uncovering of some of the great rarities that now command the highest premiums.

"A collector who devotes his attention to the accumulation of the gold pieces is not satisfied that he has a complete representation of every coin issued under the United States authority unless his cabinet contains specimens of each denomination, of each year, and bearing the mint letter of every one of the mints."

Adams went on to describe $1 pieces, early $2.50 issues, $3 pieces, and early varieties of $5 coins. Little attention was paid to $2.50 and $5 pieces after 1860. Eagles or $10 pieces received a similar treatment. Varieties were described from 1795 to 1804, after which the comment appeared, "Very few of the $10 pieces issued after 1804 bear a premium.... Nearly all of the eagles issued from 1838 up to 1907 are omitted, and bearing as a rule such small premiums, if any, that mention of them is scarcely worthwhile."

Adams had a similar comment concerning the $20 pieces: "Not many of the double eagles command a premium, for the reason that there are only a few collectors who gather the denomination."

$20 Gold Double Eagles

MCMVII (1907) High Relief $20 gold. This design by Augustus Saint-Gaudens, the noted sculptor, is one of America's most artistic. Just 11,250 of these beautiful coins were minted. Later issues have the date in regular (Arabic) figures.

An 1850 $20 of the 1849-1866 type without motto; and an 1873-CC (Carson City) $20 of the 1866-1876 type with IN GOD WE TRUST and TWENTY D.

An 1884-CC $20 of the 1877-1907 type with TWENTY DOLLARS on reverse; and a 1925-D $20 of the 1907-1933 Saint-Gaudens type in shallow relief.

This lack of attention to quarter eagles, half eagles, and double eagles after 1850 or 1860 was to have profound repercussions on the collectors in later years. By the early 1940s, when collecting these larger denominations by date and mintmark became extremely popular, numismatists realized that even so-called common dates were in some instances great rarities in Uncirculated grade, for no one had bothered to save them.

Sleepers Among Gold Coins

There are many other rarities awaiting discovery. If you study the *Guide Book* listings of gold coins you will find that numerous $5, $10, and $20 pieces in the 1850s, 1860s, and 1870s are catalogued in Uncirculated grade. And yet, certain of these pieces either are unknown in Uncirculated grade or are so rare that spans of many years may lapse between offerings.

There is indeed the distinct possibility that you, if you study the field, can purchase coins which can be sold for 10 or 20 times the catalogue listings! The key to this, of course, is knowledge. If you have the knowledge that a piece is rare and the seller does not, you can earn thousands of dollars in profit. At the Eliasberg United States Gold Coin Collection Sale held in 1982, several different half eagles of the 1890s, cataloguing $250 each (in MS-60 grade) sold for over $10,000 each in MS-65 to MS-67 grade! One brought over 50 times MS-60 catalogue value!

If the thrill of the chase excites you, there are many opportunities among American gold coins from dollars to double eagles.

Charlotte and Dahlonega Gold

In general, Charlotte and Dahlonega $1, $2.50, $3, and $5 pieces are weakly struck or have other imperfections. Offhand, you might say that this situation is unfavorable and that Proof Philadelphia Mint coins of the period would be better or more interesting to collect for they more closely approach perfection. However, there is something about Charlotte and Dahlonega issues which stimulates the imagination.

If you survey sale prices and find that the best example offered in recent years of a given issue is Extremely Fine-40, then an AU-50 or AU-55 coin will be viewed as a great prize. If you could simply write out a check and buy a complete run in flawless Uncirculated grade there would be no challenge.

Indeed, you may wish to endeavor to assemble a complete set of Charlotte or Dahlonega coins. The goal is achievable, and the challenge is tremendous. In 1987, Dr. Richard A. Bagg of our staff appraised a complete collection of Charlotte Mint gold coins, primarily in grades of Extremely Fine and AU, and the total valuation was in the $100,000 range—not exactly peanuts, but not a fortune either. I mention this to give you an indication of value.

Dr. William H. Sheldon gives the analogy that while it is theoretically possible to shoot a round of golf with 18 strokes, in practice no one has ever done it. The challenge is trying to go from, say, 95 to 85 and then from 85 to 80. Thus it is with coins. While no collector will ever assemble an Uncirculated set of Charlotte and Dahlonega mint gold pieces, trying to obtain specimens in higher grades, perhaps including a few scattered Uncirculated issues, can be a lot of fun.

Romantic Ties to History

Certain gold coins have incredibly romantic ties to history. The 1848 quarter eagle variety with CAL. on the reverse was minted from gold sent from California to the Philadelphia Mint, as one of the first samples proving the discovery which subsequently led to the Gold Rush. The 1861-D gold dollar was struck illegally at the Dahlonega Mint after Confederate troops seized the facility. The MCMVII $20 was the result of President Theodore Roosevelt's personal interest in American coinage. And, numerous other romantic and historical examples could be cited.

Opportunities

In my opinion, gold coins in higher grades offer some really tremendous opportunities. Although Walter H. Breen, David Akers, Dr. Richard A. Bagg, and certain others have done a good deal of research in the field, there is still more to be done. In any event, the rarity of issues in higher grades, particularly Uncirculated pieces of the $5, $10, and $20 denominations prior to about 1880, has not "sunk in" with the average dealer or collector. There are numerous pieces listed for nominal prices in the *Guide Book* which are *extreme rarities* in Uncirculated grade.

It is not a reasonable expectation to put together an Uncirculated set of Coronet type half eagles from 1839 to 1908, for example, for even though the *Guide Book* lists most of the different varieties in MS-60 preservation, in practice, a lifetime of collecting would not bring you certain issues in this grade! And, this is true even if your checkbook has an unlimited balance.

To be more practical about it, I suggest that you read the published works of Walter H. Breen, David Akers, and others, determine which pieces among the higher denominations ($5, $10, $20) are rarities in higher grades, make up a "want list" of these, and then keep it on hand should stray pieces be offered from time to time for reasonable prices.

Recall the comments I gave earlier concerning the unappreciated rarity of certain Liberty Seated silver dollars, some of which were so elusive that from none to only a half dozen or so circulated specimens appeared on the auction market in a given year. Information is available via published auction reports, grading service population reports, and elsewhere to trace the availability of 19th-century gold coins. I recommend as a fertile field for research the area of Coronet or Liberty Head $5, $10, and $20 coins before 1880. Study the field and make purchases accordingly, and you are virtually guaranteed to make a profit.

There are numerous pieces, particularly among those dated prior to 1880, for which you could double or triple your money right now if you could buy them for the *Guide Book* listings! As is true of so many of the "sleepers" of which I have written, you will have to think independently in this regard, for coin investment advisory firms have few if any of these in stock.

However, history has vividly shown that those investors who think independently often do spectacularly well!

Territorial Gold Coins

Related to regular United States gold issues are "territorial" or "pioneer" pieces. Throughout American history there have been a number of important gold discoveries. These were made at locations distant from United States mints at the time. Coins were minted in these areas, often by private assayers and bankers who produced coins from newly found metal.

Christopher Bechtler and August Bechtler operated a private mint at Rutherfordton, North Carolina, during the early 19th century. All of the Bechtler issues are scarce and in great demand today.

Territorial Gold Coins

Undated (circa 1849) $16 gold ingot of Moffat & Co.

1852/1 overdate $10 issued by Augustus Humbert in San Francisco. Note the prominent die break on the reverse.

1854 Kellogg & Co. $20

1855 Wass, Molitor & Co. $50, the finest known specimen.

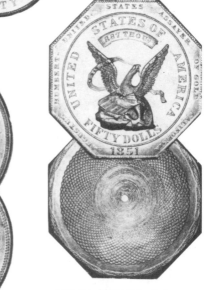

1851 Proof $50 originally from the personal holdings of Augustus Humbert. This piece was auctioned by the author's firm for $500,000 in 1979, the second highest world record price for a territorial gold coin at the time.

In 1849, $5 and $10 gold pieces were issued by the Oregon Exchange Company. These coins, extremely rare today, depict a beaver on the obverse and were made from gold brought to the Oregon Territory.

In Salt Lake City, Utah, the Mormons produced gold coins from 1849 through 1860, in denominations of $2.50, $5, $10, and $20.

In Colorado during the 1860s several firms produced gold coins. The most famous of these was Clark, Gruber & Co., some of whose $10 and $20 coins depicted Pikes Peak on the obverse, although the mountain in question was shown in the form of a cone quite unlike the rather amorphous real Pikes Peak.

Most spectacular of all territorial or pioneer gold coins are the issues produced in California following the discovery of gold there in January 1848. Large $50 gold pieces, first made in 1851, mostly of octagonal shape, were popularly designated as "slugs," supposedly because several of these made an ideal weapon when wrapped in a handkerchief! These massive gold coins are extremely rare today. The rarity, romantic appeal, and historical association of these pieces combine to make $50 California gold coins among the most desirable of all American issues.

The *Central America* Treasure Ship

In the late 1980s the numismatic world was electrified when it was announced that a group of Columbus, Ohio entrepreneurs, headed by Tommy Thompson, Bob Evans, and Barry Schatz, had discovered the wreck of the ship *Central America*, which went down to the bottom of the Atlantic Ocean in a storm in 1857, carrying with it thousands of United States and territorial gold coins, including several thousand Mint State 1857-S $20 pieces being shipped from the San Francisco Mint to the New York Assay Office. As of the summer of 1991, recovery of the treasure is still underway. Numismatists will be in for a treat when the coins, ingots, and related items are eventually sold into the market.

Over the years selected territorial gold coins have been excellent investments. For the collector or investor who can afford them (for even the most "common" issues are apt to cost hundreds of dollars each, and rarities sell for many thousands of dollars), these issues combine investment and romance in a very desirable way.

Territorial Gold Coins

1860 Clark, Gruber & Co.
copper pattern

1860 Clark, Gruber & Co. $10
Regular gold issue

1849 Moffat & Co. $5 gold.

Exceedingly rare 1849 $10 issued by
the Cincinnati Mining & Trading Co.

1855 $50 of Kellogg & Co.

Completion will never be achieved in the territorial gold field, for so many pieces are of such great rarity that decades can pass between offerings. However, a representative grouping of Clark, Gruber, & Co. issues from Colorado, Mormon issues from Utah, Bechtler coins, and various California pieces can be obtained in the range of $500 to $2,000 per coin.

Gold Coins of the World

When the United States ceased producing gold issues for circulation in 1933, many other countries still adhered to the time-honored tradition of minting gold coins. Certain countries still produce gold coins today, although this production is mainly for special issues (such as bullion trading coins and commemoratives), rather than for pieces which find wide use as a circulating medium.

There are several ways to invest in and collect gold coins of the world. The standard reference on the series, *Gold Coins of the World*, by Robert Friedberg, provides a guide to the general types minted from AD 600 to the present. For date and mintmark varieties it is necessary to consult specialized books pertaining to individual countries. *The Standard Catalog of World Coins*, by Chester Krause and Clifford Mishler, is a very valuable reference for gold issues of the past two centuries.

Collecting one gold coin from as many different countries as possible is a popular method of collecting and investing. As might be expected, this interest has sharply focused demand on certain gold coins from obscure countries—the 10-mark and 20-mark 1895 gold coins of German New Guinea being excellent examples. In Uncirculated grade each of the coins brings thousands of dollars—simply because these two issues are the only gold coins ever produced for this country (which was in existence under that name only from 1894 until the end of World War I).

It is interesting to note that Newfoundland, a province of Canada, circulated its own gold coins from 1865 through 1888 inclusive, These pieces were of the unusual denomination of $2. Eight different varieties were produced during that span of years.

Likewise popular are Canadian $5 gold pieces minted from 1912 to 1914, $10 gold pieces minted during the same years, and a series of gold sovereigns (of the same approximate size as the $5 gold piece but of different design) minted from 1908 through 1919.

Very popular with collectors in the United States from about the 1960s until 1986 (when the U.S. first issued its own bullion coins) were the large and very impressive-appearing Mexican 50-peso gold pieces minted with dates from 1921 through 1947 inclusive. A complete date collection of these pieces, each of which is larger than a United States $20 gold piece, comprises issues of the years 1921 through 1931 inclusive and 1943 through 1947 inclusive—16 different dates in all. These are still highly desired today, but the demand is less than it was 10 years ago.

The area of dates and mintmarks among world gold coins has not been fully researched, and new discoveries are constantly being made as collector interest in world gold coins increases. An interesting example of this was Lot No. 1939 in our sale of the Matt Rothert Collection in November 1973.

This coin, a part of the collection acquired over a long period of years by Mr. Rothert, was described as: "1915 P.V.G. 1 Libra. Friedberg No. 73; Harris 60. Rare, possibly unique specimen of this date with initials P.V.G. Harris lists this date as 'rare' and notes that it is unconfirmed, meaning that no specimens were known to him at the time of his compilation. Such an opportunity will elicit spirited bidding competition. Choice Brilliant Uncirculated condition."

The coin sold for $875. The point of all this? Mr. Rothert acquired it years earlier as a "common" $5-size gold coin of Peru and paid probably $15 to $30 for it! The coin was a wonderful investment for Mr. Rothert. Chances are good that it will be a wonderful investment for its subsequent owner, too—for who can argue that $875 is "too high" for a coin of which perhaps one or just a few specimens are known?

Restrikes and Counterfeits

While there are many investment possibilities among world gold coins, care should be exercised in the purchase of them, for many have been restruck or unofficially produced. To fill the demand for British sovereigns, French napoleons, and even United States $20 gold pieces, private "mints" in Lebanon, Italy, and elsewhere have produced a flood of coins.

Even government mints sometimes restrike their own coins. For example, in 1980 the Bank of Mexico ran many full-page color advertisements in United States publications selling restrikes of

1947-dated 50-peso pieces and other issues. The Vienna Mint in Austria has long restruck many of its gold issues, the 1915-dated 4-ducat piece being an outstanding example. If you purchase such pieces for their bullion or melt-down value, all is well and good. But, from a *numismatic* viewpoint such pieces are of questionable value, simply because they have been restruck by the zillions.

When buying gold coins, or any rarities for that matter, it makes good sense to buy from an established rare coin dealer with impeccable professional credentials. For example, dealer members of the Professional Numismatists Guild and the International Association of Professional Numismatists guarantee the authenticity of the items they sell.

There are *many* tales of "clever" investors who have paid cash on the barrelhead to buy krugerrands, common-date American double eagles, and other issues, only to find out later that the pieces are forgeries. By all means, buy from a recognized dealer and, as noted, get a receipt for your coins which states that authenticity is guaranteed.

Investing in Common-Date Gold Coins

All gold coins are basically scarce by comparison to smaller denominations of a given country. However, there are some which are known as "common gold" issues, simply because the coins, while scarce in a relative sense, are common within their own series. For example, the 1928 $20 United States gold piece, to use my earlier illustration again, is a common date. The price movement of such a coin tends to be more influenced by the current world market price of gold bullion than by numismatic considerations.

The 1928 $20 gold piece (or any United States $20) contains .9675 ounce of gold. Thus, in July 1991 when gold was selling for about $365 per ounce (as these words were written), such a coin had a melt-down value of about $353.

Popular with investors who desire a high metallic value are the following world gold coin issues: Austria 4 ducats (.443 oz. pure gold), Austria 100 corona (.980 oz.), Belgium 20 francs (.187 oz.), Canada "maple leaf" (1 oz.), Colombia 5 pesos (.235 oz.), France 20 francs (.187 oz.), England 1 pound or sovereign (.235 oz.), Hungary 20 krona (.196 oz.), Mexico 50 pesos (1.206 oz.), Mexico 10 pesos (.241 oz.), Mexico 5 pesos (.121 oz.), Mexico 2 1/2 pesos (.060 oz.), Mexico 2 pesos (.048 oz.), Netherlands 10 guilders (.195 oz.), Peru 1 libra (.235 oz.), Russia 5 rubles (.124 oz.), South Africa krugerrand (1 oz.—the krugerrand is also available in fractional parts), Switzerland 20 francs (.187 oz.), United States $20 (.967 oz.), United States $10 (.484 oz.), and United States $5 (.242 oz.).

Many of these issues, particularly older dates, sell at a premium of 10% to 25% or more above intrinsic value. Currently minted pieces typically sell for close to bullion value. In recent times the IRS and the government have discussed common-date bullion-type gold coins and, in fact, by early 1985 reporting requirements were in place involving krugerrands and certain other bullion-type world gold coins, but not United States issues.

Prices of common-date world gold coins move in relation to the price of gold bullion and also in relation to international monetary and political crises. The previously mentioned common 1928 Uncirculated $20 gold piece has on its own been a fine investment, but not a notable one. As noted, the best investment rewards have gone to numismatically rare gold coins, of which the 1928 $20 is not one.

In the past, investment in common date gold coins has appealed mainly to the investor interested in hedging against the depreciation of the United States dollar and, at the same time, taking advantage of the price rise in gold bullion. It is abundantly evident that the price rises over the years are very modest in comparison to the profits from *numismatically rare* pieces. But nevertheless there has been an attractive profit.

My recommendations are as follows, if you wish to invest in common gold coins:

(1) If you are mainly interested in hedging against the value of the dollar and if you are interested in the price fluctuation of gold bullion, then common date gold coins provide an interesting way of participating in this. I think the best profits are to be found with *numismatically rare* coins, but I also realize that it is natural for an investor to want to diversify. Bear in mind that the values for common date gold coins have tended to fluctuate (move up and down) whereas the values of numismatically rare gold coins have a reasonably steady trend upward. If you want to invest in gold metal, then common date gold coins are ideal for this.

(2) If you invest in common date coins and are interested in those of earlier dates (as opposed to modern bullion-type issues),

I recommend paying a small premium to buy Uncirculated pieces. Most sales of common date gold coins are by "sales organizations," not established rare coin dealers, and their customers for the most part don't know about coin grading. This is an advantage for you, for it means that Uncirculated pieces can be obtained for little more than it takes to buy worn coins. By buying Uncirculated coins you will then have two future markets: the common date gold coin market and also to a slight degree the numismatic market. This gives you a double market for just slightly added cost.

Bullion-Type Coins

In relatively recent times various countries have produced issues specifically designed for the gold investor. For example, the krugerrands produced by the Union of South Africa are available in 1-ounce and fractional denominations. These pieces are simply bullion issues, not coins intended to be spent as currency in South Africa. As they contain an ounce of gold, holders of these coins can easily check the position of their investment by checking newspapers for the daily spot gold figures. This is much less complicated, for example, than owning a Mexican 50-peso piece of 1.206 ounce weight—for which it would be necessary to perform mathematical calculations to determine the value at any given time.

The "maple leaf," issued by Canada in recent years, has likewise been popular. A few years ago, the United States Treasury Department issued a series of Fine Arts commemorative medallions of half-ounce and ounce weights, depicting American luminaries such as John Wayne, Willa Cather, Mark Twain, and others. However, these failed to capture the fancy of gold investors.

U.S. Bullion-Type Gold "Eagles"

In 1986, the United States Treasury Department commenced the issuance of gold bullion-type coins, called "eagles," with the highest denomination being $50. Other denominations included $5, $10, and $25. These "denominations" were placed on the pieces to give them coin status; there was no intention that they serve in the channels of commerce for $5, $10, etc. In all instances the gold bullion content at the time of issue was multiples of the "face value."

Gold eagles (and related one-ounce silver eagles as well) were made as a defensive move, to capture the business of collectors and investors who were spending money on South African krugerrands, Canadian maple leaf issues, and other current bullion coins of the world.

The initial interest in these eagles was nothing short of spectacular, and hundreds of millions of dollars' worth of pieces were sold. The government proclaimed the business strike issues to be of "investment grade," one of several instances in which government officials or departments officially recommended coins as an investment. (Normally, the investment aspect isn't mentioned; the Mint simply produces coins, and the Treasury Department sells them, without any investment hype.)

After an initial surge of interest, orders subsided, and the sharp premiums given to gold eagles at or near the time of issue were lost, as pieces began to trade close to the bullion value.

At this point I insert another caveat into the text of this book: In general, when a new numismatic issue is released, if you can acquire it from the government at the issue price, fine and dandy, but it is usually the situation that as soon as the first pieces become available in the numismatic marketplace, a significant premium is charged by dealers for them. Typically, this premium lasts for only a short time, until the Mint makes enough deliveries that everyone who wants an example will have one. Then the premium diminishes, and those who bought at an inflated price are apt to suffer a loss. In 1986 this happened with Statue of Liberty commemorative sets and bullion gold coins, for example.

As is the case with one-ounce South African krugerrands and the Canadian maple leaf issues, you can check the bullion value quickly in a newspaper, without having to undergo computations (except for fractional denominations, which have to be calculated separately). Thus, if you have a 1-ounce "$50" United States gold bullion coin, and gold is trading for $365 per ounce, you have a coin with an intrinsic value of $365—quite simple to figure out. To buy such a coin you will have to pay a premium or handling charge, however, and to sell such a piece you will have to pay a fee. However, the price will continue to approximate the bullion value and to be predicated upon this value.

Summary

There are two main areas of interest to the investor in gold coins.

(1) Historically, rare gold coins have furnished the best investment return. This is the field I recommend. Scarce and rare gold dollars, $2.50 pieces, $3 gold, etc., including pieces from the Charlotte and Dahlonega mints, have been in demand in recent decades and have appreciated attractively for their owners. Important and challenging collections can be built in different areas of gold coins.

There are many undervalued coins, "sleepers," to be found among U.S. gold coins. It is my opinion that many of these are to be found in the area of Coronet or Liberty Head gold coins before 1880. Research involving market appearances can help identify which issues bear low catalogue values but which are very rare.

(2) Common-date gold coins and bullion-type gold coins move mainly in response to the fluctuating world market price of gold bullion. These are quasi-numismatic in nature and appeal mainly to those who want gold in quantity as a hedge against possible monetary or world disorder. Generally, the long-term investment return on such pieces has been less than that posted for scarce and rare U.S. gold coins. I do not recommend this field, but I realize that there is widespread interest in it, thus I have given observations which should be of use to anyone interested.

Investing in
Paper Money

Introduction

 United States paper money is a large and interesting field. While a couple decades ago paper money was mainly in the realm of the specialist and information was hard to obtain, today interest is widespread.

The market for many currency notes peaked in the late 1970s, with the result that now, in the early 1990s, there are many excellent values to be found. To overlook currency as a collecting and investing opportunity would be to miss one of the most fascinating areas of American numismatics.

Collecting paper money requires study beforehand. In particular, be forewarned that there are no universally accepted standards of grading, although most sellers use the same terms. While some prefer the "Uncirculated" term for an unused note, more popular is "New." The latter can be divided into several refinements, in ascending quality as follows: New, Choice New, and Gem New. Lesser-quality, worn notes are designated by such terms as Good, Very Good, Fine, Very Fine, and Extremely Fine. *The Currency Dealer Newsletter*, a monthly publication, gives some guidelines for these.

It is a popular practice to "wash" or "launder" notes to restore brightness and crispness to notes that would otherwise be called Extremely Fine. Sometimes washed notes have been offered as New. This aspect is very tricky, and I suggest that you study currency grading and quality carefully before entering the field in a big way.

I discuss individual categories of currency specialities in the pages to follow.

Colonial Currency

This field comprises notes issued by the 13 colonies and by other authorities, including the Continental Congress, during the American colonial period and the early years of independence. The standard reference work in the field is *The Early Paper Money of America* by noted numismatic scholar Eric P. Newman.

Unusual designs and mottos appear on many of the notes and add a dimension of interest. Numerous notes have important historical significance as well, with some of them being signed by individuals who also affixed their signature to the Declaration of Independence.

As Eric P. Newman relates, among the more interesting inscriptions are examples such as *Come Over & Help Us* (found on a 1690 Massachusetts note), *Quaerenda Pecunia Primumest* ("The search for money comes first," on a North Carolina issue), *Misera Omni Servatus* ("Slavery of all kinds is wretched," on a South Carolina note), and *Libertas Carior Aura* ("Freedom is more precious than gold," on a Georgia issue). Another piece of Georgia currency shows two floating jugs representing America and England with the inscription *Si Coloigimus Frangimur* ("If we collide we break").

Early currency comes in a wide variety of values and denominations. Continental currency payable in Spanish milled dollars was authorized by the Continental Congress in Philadelphia beginning May 10, 1775, and continuing through 1779. The first issue consisted of values of the denominations $1, $2, $3, $4, $5, $6, $7, $8, $20, and $30. Later issues were to go as high as $80. The fledgling United States government paper money issue did not get off to a good start, and holders of Continental currency subsequently found the notes were nearly valueless. By late 1787, $1 in coins would purchase $250 in Continental currency notes! The term "not worth a continental" became a synonym for worthlessness.

The various colonies and states along the Atlantic Seaboard issued notes on different occasions. For example, Connecticut notes are dated from July 12, 1709, through July 1, 1780. In keeping with the connection with England during most of the period, notes were payable in pounds (£), shillings (s), and pence (d).

Sometimes notes would be issued for a special situation. On January 6, 1776, New York City issued £3,000 value of promissory notes for the Water Works. Denominations were comprised of 2, 4, and 8 shillings.

The values of Continental, state, and related issues vary according to a number of factors, including rarity, condition, design, and historical significance. As examples, Vermont notes are expensive for relatively few were issued in comparison to those of New York, New Jersey, and certain other states. A typical Vermont note in just Fair grade is priced at $1,000 in the Newman reference, while a Good specimen is $2,000 and a Very Good note is $3,000. By contrast, a variety of New Jersey 30-shilling note dated April 8, 1762, is priced at $10 Fair, $25 Good, and $50 Very Good. Many Continental currency notes are even less expensive.

Hundreds of different people signed early notes, with over 260 signing Continental currency issues alone. Of special value are the state and Continental notes signed by those who also signed the Declaration of Independence: Abraham Clark, George Clymer, William Ellery, Lyman Hall, John Hart, Frances Hopkinson, Philip Livingston, Arthur Middleton, John Morton, George Walton, and James Wilson.

From a pure investment viewpoint it is difficult for me to recommend early notes, as a high degree of interest and scholarship is required to collect them intelligently. However, if history is your forte, certainly these notes are among the most significant in American numismatics. Like so many other specialized fields, a collection formed with care over a period of years will probably yield an attractive profit upon its sale.

Broken Bank Notes

During the late 18th and early 19th centuries many varieties of currency were issued by private banks, various states, merchants and manufacturers, and others in need of a medium of exchange. Often such notes were redeemable only by the bank or business which issued them.

The term "broken bank notes" is used today to cover the field, the term being derived from the fact that many of these early banks and businesses went broke, especially in the Panic of 1837, and their currency issues became worthless. Today, such issues are avidly sought after by collectors. Many interesting varieties, some of which are extremely ornate and artistic, can be purchased from

$10 to $30 each, although some scarce varieties are apt to cost $50 to $100 or more.

Most collectors choose a specialty within the field, such as endeavoring to collect as many notes as possible of the interesting $3 denomination, or trying to assemble as many pieces of currency as possible from a specific area such as the state of New Jersey or the city of New York.

Confederate and Southern States Currency

Issues of the Confederate States of America and of the related Southern states have formed an interesting specialty for many collectors. Many different notes, including extreme rarities, are available for low cost. *Confederate and Southern States Currency*, by Grover C. Criswell, is the main reference.

In anticipation of a price rise, which many thought would occur during the Civil War centennial, interest in Confederate notes multiplied during the 1950s. When the centennial came about in early 1961, there were more sellers than buyers, for the market had peaked in 1959-1960. Since that time Confederate currency has found a fluctuating and indefinite market.

This is not as it should be, for there are many interesting varieties, a close link with history, and a fairly comprehensive collection can be assembled for low cost. Perhaps it is time for a renewal of interest in the area. In combination with a love for southern history and the Confederacy, such a collection would make a fascinating possession. Carefully purchased and held for an appropriate length of time, an attractive profit may be realized when your collection is sold.

United States Notes

Early United States issues such as those released by the Continental congress and the Bank of the United States were repudiated, and while they are of interest to the collector, they are no longer of interest to the government!

In 1861 the first Demand Notes were issued, marking the beginning of United States currency still legal tender today. These notes are so-called because they carry the notation, "The United States promise to pay to the bearer —Dollars on demand."

The Beautiful "Educational" Notes of 1896

$1 "Educational" Silver Certificate of 1896. The scene depicts "History Instructing Youth."

$2 "Educational" Silver Certificate of 1896 depicting "Science Presenting Steam and Electricity to Commerce and Manufacture."

$5 "Educational" Silver Certificate of 1896 illustrating electricity as the dominant force in the world.

From that time onward many different types of notes have been issued. Silver Certificates and Gold Certificates were backed by the respective metals mentioned (this backing has since been repudiated by the United States government). Compound Interest Treasury Notes, Interest Bearing Notes, Refunding Certificates, Treasury or Coin Notes, and all others were all produced in a wide variety of designs and denominations.

From 1863 to 1929 many National Banks in America issued distinctive notes: regular United States currency designs (of legal tender value anywhere in the U.S.A.) but with the name of the issuing bank imprinted. Today these are avidly collected, and many varieties have great value. This is especially true in New (the currency equivalent of "Uncirculated") condition. It is popular to collect these from a specific geographical area, such as the state of Pennsylvania.

From 1861 to 1928 currency was of a size considerably larger than used today. The IBM data-processing cardboard card, first made in the early 1920s and kept in use through the 1960s, was made the size of the paper money of the era so people would find them easy to use. Until the 1970s, when computers began storing information on chips and disks, IBM cards were very much a part of the American business community. Now these cards, like large-size currency, are relics of the past.

In years gone by many very beautiful currency designs were produced. The high point was reached with the Silver Certificates, Series of 1896. The $1 note portrays an allegorical scene of "History Instructing Youth," the $2 note, a scene of "Science Presenting Steam and Electricity to Commerce and Manufacture," and the $5 note (the largest in the 1896 series), an untitled scene showing the Goddess of Electricity as the dominant force in the world. Other magnificent designs are found throughout the series of large-size notes. Perhaps someday the Treasury will think again in terms of artistry in addition to utility. Really, the two can make a perfect combination.

In recent decades there has been an increased interest in small-size notes issued from 1928 to date. Most popular have been the lower denominations, particularly the $1 varieties. There are some very scarce issues, the note of the Series of 1928-E being the most famous.

Popular varieties include notes with the HAWAII overprint (made during World War II for circulation in Hawaii; if Hawaii had fallen into the hands of the Japanese, then the notes with this overprint would have been repudiated), notes with "R" and "S" red overprinted letters (to differentiate "regular" and "synthetic" paper used during a currency experiment), star notes, interesting serial numbers, and others.

In recent years currency notes have been identified by origin from the 12 different Federal Reserve banks, thus resulting in 12 varieties available for collecting each time there is a signature change or a new design feature. Beginning in 1981, the Bureau of Engraving and Printing made available to collectors uncut sheets of $1 and $2 notes, the first time these had been generally available to numismatists in over two decades.

Fractional currency, issued as a replacement for coins which were withdrawn from circulation during and after the Civil War, was printed in denominations of three cents to 50 cents and is very popular today. The ultimate display item in this field is the Fractional Currency Shield, a framed display of several dozen specimen or proof one-sided notes pasted on a shield-shaped design background, issued by the Treasury Department to banks in the late 1860s. A nice-quality Fractional Currency Shield sells in the range of $5,000 or more. The standard Shield has a printed gray background. Rarer varieties are printed in pink, green, or purple.

Encased postage stamps date from the Civil War and are of interest to paper money collectors as well as those specializing in coins and tokens. Several dozen varieties were issued by various merchants and others. Denominations produced ranged from 1¢ to 90¢, the higher values being by far the rarer.

There are several excellent reference books available in the field of United States currency. These include *Paper Money of the United States* by Robert Friedberg and *The Comprehensive Catalog of U.S. Paper Money* by Gene Hessler. The Society of Paper Money Collectors provides an international forum for collectors and investors interested in all fields of paper money.

In my opinion, regular-issue United States paper money from 1861 to date offers attractive investment opportunities. I recommend acquiring United States notes in strictly New condition, without folds, soiling, or other evidence of wear. Be careful about

Popular United States Paper Money Varieties

This design of National Currency is known as the "Lazy 2" variety, for the 2 is lying on its side. In high grades these are very scarce.

$5 note featuring a Sioux Indian chief. This beautiful design has always been a paper money collectors' favorite.

The "numismatic reverse" of a $5 note of 1886. Illustrated are five silver dollars of that year. In the past there have been many stunningly beautiful currency designs.

grading, and know your seller. Most popular today, and probably most popular in the future, are the issues of the lower denominations: $1, $2, $5, and $10—particularly the scarce "types" as opposed to rare signature combinations.

Beauty is always attractive, and such splendid designs as the 1896 "Educational" Silver Certificates, the 1886 $5 note showing Morgan silver dollars on the reverse, the 1901 $10 "bison" note, and others, will probably always be popular.

The field of United States paper money has had its ups and downs. In the 1970s the area was fairly serene. In 1974, when the first edition of the present book was published, I recommended as a good buy a complete set of $1, $2, and $5 1896 "Educational" Silver Certificates at $1,000, the value at the time. I commented at the time that this $1,000 set "would double in value within five years."

My prediction proved to be conservative, very conservative. Within five years it was selling for nearly 10 times that amount, and in 1980, at the height of a bull market in currency, a dealer friend told me he paid over $12,000 for a set which my firm had sold to a client for $1,000 six years earlier!

The market peak of 1978-1980 was caused in part by a number of speculators and investors "discovering" currency and wildly buying almost anything that was rectangular and crisp. Collectors sat on the sidelines, and investors bought from other investors, prices went up, and everyone was happy. Happy until investors stopped buying. Then prices came down. In 1991 a Choice New set of "Educational" notes was valued at around $7,000 to $9,000, a drop from the 1980 price, but still an attractive appreciation from years earlier.

Currency is a permanent part of the collecting spectrum. Today's prices are considerably more attractive than they were a few years ago. At the same time there are problems with grading, and, as mentioned earlier, many notes are misrepresented. It has been popular to "starch" notes to make them crisp. In one instance my firm sold a rare $20 note in Very Fine grade. Lo and behold! Soon thereafter the same note, identifiable by its serial number,[1] appeared in a competitor's auction marked as "Crisp New!" The note had been "processed" by washing and starching. Fortunately, an expert can tell the difference. An ultraviolet light, when beamed

---

[1] In a computerized data base maintained by specialist Martin Gengerke.

on a note, will cause a starched note to fluoresce and point out the deception, although this test is not always definitive.

I personally am very enthusiastic about the future of notes as an investment and feel that large profits will be made by those who buy carefully. But, be sure to buy carefully. This is very, very important. For starters, join the Society of Paper Money Collectors and buy the Friedberg and Hessler books. Do this, and assimilate what you read, and you may develop an interest in the field. With interest comes knowledge, and with knowledge comes success.

Off the
Beaten Path

Introduction

 In addition to the standard series of United States coins there are many other numismatic specialties which have attracted collectors and investors in the past. Some of these areas, which are off the beaten path, have done as well as or better than certain standard series!

For example, the field of colonial coins does not come to mind when one thinks of investment, but the fact remains that colonial coins have offered some of the best investment profits to be found anywhere. United States pattern coins are another similar case. Specialists in this field have seen prices double, triple, then increase again during recent decades.

Generally, investment in a specialized field such as tokens, patterns, colonials, paper money, and other series, some of which are called "exonumia" (or "out of numismatics"), requires more persistence and care than does investment in standard series. However, if you are willing to take this extra time (or have a trusted dealer do it for you), the financial and intellectual rewards can be very great. I recommend consideration of such diverse fields if you can meet the following criteria:

1. A basic *numismatic* interest (in addition to your investment interest) is helpful and desirable. Most diverse fields of collecting have a high degree of history, romance, and numismatic interest attached to them—and an understanding of this, or a willingness to learn, aids in evaluating which pieces are the best buys, why certain items sell for more than others, and so on. This "requirement" is a plus factor, I might say—for in my opinion, some of the most fascinating items in all of numismatics are in these fields.

Early Colonial Coins of Massachusetts

"NE" shilling. First made in 1652, the earliest Massachusetts silver shillings are simple planchets with "NE" stamped on one side and "XII" (for 12 pence or one shilling) on the reverse.

Willow Tree shilling. The squiggles and curlicues of this early design have been likened to a willow tree. Made for a limited time, Willow Tree shillings are rare.

An attractive 1652 Oak Tree shilling. Following the original "NE" (for "New England") coinage, Massachusetts silver coins were made with willow, oak, and then pine tree motifs. Most specimens in existence today are of the pine tree style.

1652-dated Pine Tree shilling. Much has been written of these romantic silver pieces in history and fiction.

Left: This Pine Tree shilling, a specimen from the George A. Merriweather Collection Sale, was once bent. In colonial times a bent coin was said to ward off witches, and many Pine Tree shillings are seen today with evidence of this long-ago practice. Attractive specimens of the Pine Tree shilling can be obtained in the $1,000 to $3,000 range.

2. Patience is required. Actually, two types of patience are required. First, you will find that tokens, colonial coins, patterns, rare issues of paper money, and so on are often out of the field of experience of the average coin dealer, thus your inquiry might be met with some careless comment such as "I don't know anything about pattern coins, and I never stock them." Of course, this is the dealer's loss! Persistence is needed to seek out pieces for purchase. Fortunately, nearly all of the larger numismatic firms maintain stocks (although usually not large ones, due to the rarity of the material) and have such pieces in their auction sales. The second type of patience involves price movements. Prices of most of these pieces do not change on a month-to-month basis. In fact, perhaps several years will go by without a price movement. Then there will be a sudden movement—historically upward. Then comes a period of unchanged prices.

It is my recommendation that all coin investment be considered a long-term (five to 10 years or more) investment, for shorter-term investments make money only for dealers—and making money for *you* is what interests you most! With paper money, colonials, and other diverse fields, long-term thinking is essential. However, without exception to my knowledge, any of my customers who built a nice collection within various "off the beaten track" series five to 10 years or more ago can make a tremendous profit by selling today.

3. Working hand-in-hand with a professional dealer is a "must" in these fields. Without great study it is difficult for the individual investor to keep abreast of all of the varieties and their prices, which items are significant and which aren't, and other developments. A trusted dealer is a priceless asset in this regard. The door swings both ways, and you are an asset to the dealer as well—simply because the chances are good that you will give him your "want list" for the pieces you need, or you will give him an order to buy general or selected pieces for your account.

Investing in Colonial Coins

The coins of colonial and early America, discussed as a background to the regular United States coins earlier in this book, provide a fertile field for the investor. In recent decades most collectors have placed an emphasis on regular United States Mint issues produced from 1793 to the present time. Somewhat neglected have been earlier pieces such as the circa 1785-1788

State Copper Coins of the 1785-1788 Era

This 1785 Vermont copper coin shows the sun peeping over a forested ridge, with a plow below—motifs representative of the Green Mountain State. The reverse reads "STELLA QUARTA DECIMA" — "The 14th star"—anticipating Vermont's status as the 14th state in the Union.

1787 Nova Eborac coin of New York.

1787 Connecticut copper coin. Called the "Laughing Head" variety by collectors, the portrait on the obverse bears a silly grin! Many fascinating varieties await the collector of early Connecticut coins.

1785 Connecticut copper coin. The obverse is that of a laureated warrior, a classical design. The reverse bears the Latin legend "INDE ET LIB," an abbreviation for "independence and liberty."

1787 New Jersey copper coin. New Jersey issued coins from 1786 through 1788.

1787 Massachusetts copper cent. Coinage of such pieces was abandoned when the state government learned that each coin cost twice face value to produce!

copper coins of Vermont, Connecticut, Massachusetts, and New Jersey, the 1652-dated silver coins of the Massachusetts Bay Colony, coins of the 1790s honoring President George Washington, and related issues.

The result is that many of these early coins can be bought for fractions of the prices of later American coins of comparable rarity. As these words are being written, there are many wonderful opportunities in the field of colonial pieces. A number of the prominent personalities in the market are no longer alive—such luminaries as Richard Picker, Ted Craige, and John Roper—with the result that competition for rarities is not as intense.

It is my belief that in future years the colonial field will have *many* rarities in the $5,000 to $50,000 range, although today there are relatively few pieces which sell for that much. It would not surprise me to see several issues sell for well over $100,000. To be sure, there are a few early American rarities which bear high price tags at the present time, being an outstanding example. However, by and large most colonial, state, and related pieces are severely underpriced compared to their later American counterparts.

If they rise in value a few years from now, that will not be the time to buy them. The time to consider them is now! Indeed, our March 1987 auction of the Taylor Collection, featuring colonial coins, was one of the most spectacular sales of the year—an indication of the pent-up demand for quality colonial coins. The colonial coins offered as part of our Norweb Collection, Part I, in October 1987 likewise broke many records, as did the outstanding coins in our March 1990 auction presentation of pieces from the Boyd, Brand, and Ryder collections.

Colonial coins have done well in the past. A 1652 Pine Tree shilling, a coin valued at $27.50 in 1946, was worth 40 times that price in 1991. A 1786 Vermont copper coin of the "Baby Head" variety was valued at $10 in Fine grade in 1946. In 1991 such a piece is valued at $800 in the *Guide Book*, but a specimen was likely to cost you even more due to its rarity. A 1787 Massachusetts half cent that was valued at $4.50 in 1946 would have cost you 40 times or more that figure in 1991.

The procession of the value of the 1776 Continental dollar in pewter metal, in Fine grade, is likewise interesting: 1946 $45, 1950 $45, 1955 $65, 1960 $125, 1965 $325, 1970 $400, 1975 $3,000, 1980 $2,250, 1990 $2,750, 1991 $3,000. Per these figures, the coin hit a high point circa 1975 and has traded lower since.

Colonial and Early American Coins

The Continental Currency coin of 1776 features on the obverse a sundial and two mottos, "Fugio" ("I fly"—referring to time) and "Mind Your Business." The reverse shows an endless chain of 13 links. each one bearing the name of one of the 13 colonies.

1787 Fugio cent. Issued by a private contractor under authority of the United States government, the Fugio cent is one of the first official coins of our country.

1787 Immunis Columbia cent. Columbia, emblematic of the new American nation, was immune to the world's misfortunes.

1794 Franklin Press token depicts an early wooden hand press.

1723 Rosa Americana twopence. Made in England, this coin was intended for circulation in America (then an English possession). The reverse inscriptions translate to "The American Rose; the Useful with the Sweet."

My recommendation is to build a type set of state coins as a beginning. At the start you can ignore the rarities. For example, a type set of Vermont coppers, issued from 1785 to 1788, would consist of the following designs:

1. 1785-1786 type with sun peeking over forested ridge

2. 1786 Baby Head type

3. 1786 Bust Left type

4. 1787-1788 Bust Right type

5. 1787 Type with BRITANNIA reverse

If you study the field you will learn that the 1787 BRITANNIA variety is a *counterfeit*, but is not undesirable in this context, as illogical as this statement may seem as you read it! When you study Vermont coins you will learn the reason why. The 1785 Immune Columbia Vermont issue, which is a rarity, is an interesting issue which you may wish to add to a basic type set but which is expensive (over $1,000). Interestingly, the Immune Columbia issue always comes weakly struck and on undersized planchets! However, it is precisely such crude characteristics that make the piece fascinating.

The field of colonial coins offers many opportunities for the buyer who desires a generous measure of numismatic and American history. For several thousand dollars you can make an attractive beginning in a basic collection of colonial and state coins. A publication, *The Colonial Newsletter*, published by James C. Spilman, is worth subscribing to and offers much interesting research information.

Investing in Tokens

The field of tokens offers many opportunities. In this field, investment is a secondary consideration, with collecting enjoyment coming first. However, astute numismatists who have put together token collections have nearly always—perhaps absolutely always—found that their collections can be sold at a profit if held for a suitable length of time.

Popular with collectors are such issues as Hard Times tokens issued privately in the United States from 1833 through 1844, Civil War tokens of the 1860s, as well as a wide variety of other issues.

In recent times, specialized token series have been in demand. One numismatist may aspire to own as many different

Numismatic Americana

Davis' Dining Saloon 30c
$209 (two pieces)

Silver business card
About Uncirculated, $247.50

1923 Token struck in gold
Choice About Uncirculated, $550

1884 U.S. Assay medal
Choice Proof, $660

HK-unlisted So-called dollar
$209

Wisconsin Civil War store card
Rarity-8, $198

1837 Low-128 Hard Times token
Rarity-5, $2,145

1933 HK-820 Montana dollar   Uncirculated, $297

Diverse items from the Russell B. Patterson Collection Sale conducted by
Auctions by Bowers and Merena, Inc. in 1985.

Token Recalls the Elegance of a Bygone Age

From shortly before the turn of the century until it was destroyed in a spectacular blaze in 1907, San Francisco's famous French chateau-style Cliff House was one of that city's foremost attractions. Built by Adolph Sutro, who earned his fortune in Nevada's Comstock Lode, the Cliff House and the adjacent Sutro Museum exhibited all sorts of interesting things—including a huge "orchestrion," or automatic orchestra operated by paper rolls. When a dime or a dime-size token was put into the slot of this marvelous device, a symphony concert filled the air! The author, a collector of orchestrions as well as tokens pertaining to them, considers this little dime-size "Good for 10c trade—Drop in Orchestrian" token to be a real prize, although its numismatic value is only about $25. This crude (note that "orchestrion" is misspelled as "orchestrian") little token has its own fascinating story to tell—as do thousands of other early coins and tokens. For those with an inquiring mind, such pieces can be wonderful keys to history. A whole book could be written about the Cliff House and Adolph Sutro, for example!

The 1792 Birch Cent

Photo enlarged two diameters.

Shown above—enlarged two diameters—is Lot 2349 from the Garrett Collection Sale, which realized $200,000. The piece, described as Choice Uncirculated with ample original mint red, is believed to be the finest known example of this rarity.

This is one of several different patterns prepared in 1792 for use at the Philadelphia Mint. A notation with the above specimen showed that it originally came from David Rittenhouse, who was the first director of the Mint. A more significant pedigree could not be imagined!

The obverse bears a female head, the representation of Liberty, facing to the right with the signature of the engraver, BIRCH, on the back of the neck truncation. The date 1792 is immediately below. Surrounding is the inscription LIBERTY PARENT OF SCIENCE & INDUSTRY. The reverse displays a wreath and inscriptions. Concerning the obverse motto, Professor Montroville W. Dickeson noted over a century ago: "[Our founding fathers were motivated] to proclaim upon their currency that has since been exemplified, that *Liberty is the parent of science and industry.* For if science does not particularly flourish under a free government, then freedom of thought is at least essential to its progress, and liberty is the very breath of industry."

circus-related items as possible, while another may find saloon tokens to be attractive, while a third may be after pieces issued in the Territory of Arizona before it became a state. Many other examples could be cited.

A good way to investigate tokens is to purchase the illustrious (and quite inexpensive) series of studies on the subject by Russell Rulau. Issued by Krause Publications, these are available from numismatic booksellers or can be borrowed free from the ANA Library. In addition, I recommend that you obtain current issues of the TAMS *Journal* issued by the Token and Medal Society. Another group, the American Token Collectors Organization (ATCO), produces a magazine listing many items for sale.

Investing in Pattern Coins

From 1792 through the 20th century many varieties of pattern coins were distributed to government officials, collectors, and others. These coins, comprising over 1,500 distinct varieties in all, are avidly collected today.

In 1961 my firm purchased and resold the fabulous collection of United States pattern coins formed by Maj. Lenox R. Lohr, who was once in charge of the Columbia Broadcasting System and, later, of Chicago's Museum of Science and Industry. This collection, containing nearly every variety of pattern coin known to exist (over 1,500 different issues), was the largest such group ever to be priced and offered for sale. Included were seven different patterns of the year 1792 (several of which were the only known specimens of their kind), $4 "Stellas" of 1879 and 1880, many different Gobrecht silver dollars of 1836 to 1839, and others—all in dazzling array. Retail prices of that day seem like incredible bargains now. It would be my guess that if my firm had sold the Lohr Collection intact to an investor, that same investor would have seen his investment increase in value more than 20 or 30 times since then! This estimate is probably on the low side, for in 1991 when Auctions by Bowers and Merena, Inc. offered several dozen patterns for sale that had been purchased from the Lohr Collection 30 years earlier in 1961, the consignor saw numerous items bring from 50 to 100 times the original cost!

The collector and investor willing to take the time to learn about patterns will find this a fertile field for investment. The standard reference book on the subject is *United States Patterns*, by

Beautiful United States Pattern Coins

This beautiful 1872 pattern $20 gold piece is struck in aluminum! It is from the great Terrell Collection auction sale.

An attractive pattern silver dollar of 1880. Over the years many different designs were tried.

The Amazonian pattern silver dollar of 1872 is considered to be one of the most beautiful of all American coins. This specimen was a highlight of the fabulous collection formed by Mr. Armand Champa and auctioned by the author's firm.

Along the right-hand margin are several varieties of pattern one-cent pieces minted in 1858. Over a dozen different designs and die combinations were issued that year.

1877 Pattern Half Dollars—"What Might Have Been"

Regular issue 1877 half dollar of the type struck for circulation.

To the right are four of over a dozen different pattern half dollar designs issued in 1877. To collectors, patterns tell "what might have been"—but wasn't. The study of pattern coins is fascinating. For the investor in patterns, there is a great opportunity. Many outstanding rarities—coins of which just a few specimens are known to exist—can be obtained for relatively low sums in comparison to regular-issue United States coins.

Over the years the author's firm has bought and sold many of the finest pattern coin collections ever formed. The coins shown here are from the Armand Champa Collection. Earlier the Maj. Lenox R. Lohr Collection, a group of over 1,500 coins, was purchased and resold. This was the largest collection of United States pattern coins ever to be priced and offered for sale. Second only to the Lohr Collection in scope among pattern offerings on the market in recent years was the Garrett Collection, also sold by the author's firm.

Dr. J. Hewitt Judd and Abe Kosoff, now out of print but available from sellers and auctioneers of numismatic literature. Andrew W. Pollock III is presently conducting research in the field which, when published, will provide a new text on the series.

The Judd-Kosoff book plus auction catalogues of leading numismatic firms combine to provide a reasonable amount of pricing information. The several dealers who specialize in patterns can also be of great help to you. Many pattern coins reached a high level of price and interest in the 1979 to 1980 era, particularly during our sale of the Garrett Collection. After that time, some prices subsided, only to regain strength and reach high levels in recent years. Still, I feel that there are selected good values to be found in the present market. History shows that over a long period of time the prices of patterns have trended upward.

I recommend that patterns be obtained in grades of Proof-63 or finer (most patterns were originally issued with Proof surfaces). As the field is a rather technical one, I recommend that investment in patterns only be considered after you gain several years or more of experience in the field of regular United States coins, and after you spend time studying auction appearances and price movements of patterns. This is not a field for amateurs, as nearly all patterns cost over $1,000 each, and prices often vary widely from seller to seller.

Investing in Numismatic Books

"Investing" in numismatic books has a double meaning. Books are a tremendous investment in *knowledge*. In fact, on a dollar-for-dollar basis, books can be one of the best investments you can make.

But numismatic books can also be a rewarding financial investment as well. As is the case with tokens and other exonumia, I would not recommend investing in books for the sake of pure investment. The market is rather restricted, and the profit margin made by dealers is greater than it is for regular issue coins. Still, several people with whom I am acquainted have done quite well by acquiring classic auction catalogues, old reference books, and other numismatic publications.

Investing in
Coins of the World

Introduction

Coins of the world—coins of countries other than the United States—have always been popular with collectors. While most collectors and investors begin their interest with United States issues, often coins of other countries will subsequently attract their interest.

The scope of world coins is as unlimited as the world itself. Perhaps indicative of this are the figures given in the front of the *Standard Catalog of World Coins,* by Chester Krause and Clifford Mishler. This book, which *only* covers coins from approximately 1801 to the present time, features pieces from nearly 300 different countries, including tens of thousands of coins listed by individual dates. A recent edition noted on the cover that it included 43,223 photographs! When you consider that the years from 1801 to date comprise but a fraction of the world's total coinage, you can see that the field is virtually endless!

No one has ever attempted to collect one of each and every date and mintmark from every country in the world. To do this would require several lifetimes, not to mention King Midas' treasury! Not even Virgil M. Brand, who at the time of his death in 1926 had amassed approximately 350,000 coins, medals, and tokens, including duplicates, came close to completion. Thus, collectors and investors tend to specialize.

Crowns or Silver Dollars of the World

One popular specialty is to collect dollar-size coins of the world—coins generally known as "crowns." Most countries issued such pieces. These can be gathered in a number of ways. Obtaining a silver dollar-size coin from each of as many different countries as possible is an interesting challenge. Did you realize, for

Interesting Silver Crowns of the World

AUSTRIA
1698
taler of
Leopold
"the
Hogmouth"

GERMANY
1772
taler
from
Frankfurt

FRANCE
1811
5 francs
of Napoleon

GERMANY
1913
pattern
5 marks
of Bavaria

Interesting Silver Crowns of the World

GUATEMALA
1824
8 reales

SWITZERLAND
1812
40 batzen
of Vaud

MEXICO
1738
8 reales
"Pillar
dollar"

JAPAN
1882
1 yen

example, that Hawaii was once an independent country (Kingdom of Hawaii) and issued its own coinage, including silver dollars? An 1883 Hawaiian silver dollar in MS-65 condition can be obtained for several thousand dollars. How has such a coin performed as an investment? The answer: In 1991 a specimen in MS-63 to MS-65 grade was valued in the range of $5,000 to $10,000. In 1971 we were selling these for about $400 each, and in the early 1960s my firm offered them in the $150 to $200 range. They have been a wonderful investment for those who have owned them.

Just as is true in the United States series, certain coins of the world are rare and others are common. As an investor you will be mainly interested in coins of proven scarcity and rarity in fields which are popular or which may become popular in the future. Thus, the 1883 Hawaiian dollar has been an excellent investment, for it is a "key" item—the only silver dollar-size coin ever officially issued by the Kingdom of Hawaii.

Popular with many collectors and investors are many of the silver dollar issues of our neighbor to the north, Canada. In 1935 the Canadian government commenced issuing an illustrious series of silver dollars. These large and impressive coins have been used over the years to commemorate various historical events. The standard silver dollar design portrays the British monarch (King George V in 1935 and 1936, King George VI from 1937 to 1952, and Queen Elizabeth II from 1953 onward) on the obverse and an Indian and a fur trapper in a canoe on the reverse. Interspersed among regular issues have been many commemoratives and other special designs.

Crowns of Great Britain have always been popular with collectors and investors. Scarcer issues have appreciated in value dramatically over the years. The series of British crowns is a long and illustrious one. The earliest issue to bear a date was struck in the year 1551. Since then many different varieties have been produced. Most bear the portrait of the reigning king or queen on the obverse. The reverse usually depicts a heraldic motif or an allegorical scene (such as the popular St. George and the dragon design).

In particular demand by collectors are the issues of the 19th and 20th centuries, beginning with the first crown of Queen Victoria, a coin issued in 1839. In 1847 a particularly beautiful design, the "Gothic crown," was produced. The obverse and reverse of this piece have the legend in ornate Gothic-style letters.

Crowns of Great Britain

Over the centuries Great Britain has produced many beautiful crowns. The approximate size of a silver dollar, these coins are favorites with collectors. On this page are shown several interesting varieties:

1703 issue with "VIGO" below the portrait of Queen Anne. This romantic coin was struck from Spanish silver treasure captured by the British naval forces in the harbor of Vigo, Spain. This crown commemorates the event.

1845 crown depicting Queen Victoria (who ascended to the throne in 1837) as a young girl. Crowns of this design were first minted in 1839.

The beautiful "Gothic" crown was minted in 1846, 1847, and 1853. Most specimens are of the 1847 date. The one illustrated here is the exceedingly rare 1846 from the Terrell Collection auction sale.

Only 932 specimens were minted of the rare 1934 crown—making it one of the world's greatest modern scarcities.

Examples of this design were struck, although in severely restricted numbers, in 1846 and 1853 as well. Today the Gothic crown is a favorite with collectors. As is the case with most other British crowns, Gothic crowns have been an excellent investment. A piece which cost $20 to $30 in the early 1960s sells for over $2,000 today!

Among 20th-century crowns, the issues of King George V have always been popular. These were produced from 1927 through 1936, but only in small numbers—with the exception of the 1935 Jubilee commemorative. The rarest issue, 1934, is a coin of which only 932 pieces were minted!

The field of crowns or silver dollar-size coins of the world offers as many variations in design and craftsmanship as there are individual countries. Many small countries, now part of larger countries or otherwise lost to modern political geography, are remembered by coins.

Take for example German New Guinea. This country became part of the German colonial empire in 1894. It was ruled under German auspices until the end of World War I, at which time it was turned over to Australia for administration and guidance. German New Guinea issued coins only in 1894 and 1895. One of these, the 5-mark piece, is of crown or silver dollar-size. The obverse depicts a beautiful bird of paradise in resplendent glory. The scarcity and beauty of this coin, combined with the fact that it is the only crown-size coin of this former country, have made the 1894 crown a "blue chip" with collectors and investors for many decades. Coins like this will always be in demand.

Likewise renowned for its beauty and rarity is the splendid 1925 one-quetzal crown of Guatemala. This lovely coin depicts a quetzal bird on the obverse and reverse. It has always been an important coin, and over the years choice specimens have been worthwhile investments.

Mexico, our neighbor to the south, has issued crown-size coins for many years. The sheer variety and number of dates and mintmarks issued exceed our own United States silver dollar coins. Fourteen different mints, each with its own distinctive mintmark, produced coins in Mexico over a period of time, often using silver from local or regional mines. In addition, there were many unofficial issues produced by revolutionaries and insurgents, especially during the period 1910-1917.

In early times the Mexican monetary system was the same as the Spanish and was divided into the real—with multiples and fractions. A real was one-eighth of a dollar, or 12 1/2 cents. Real pieces were known as "bits." Our present term "two bits" is from the days in America when 2-real or two-bit coins were in circulation (a two-bit piece being worth 25 cents). The dollar-size Mexican coins of the 1700s and 1800s were of the 8-real denomination. Known also as "pillar dollars," early issues of the 8-real denomination have been featured in many stories of pirate and treasure lore. Such coins were legal tender in the United States until 1857.

In later years the peso was adopted as the standard for a silver dollar-size coin. Many interesting varieties, including some with commemorative motifs, have been produced in recent decades. Mexican currency has depreciated over the years so far as face value is concerned. When a silver dollar-size coin was made in 1968 to commemorate the XIX Olympics it bore a value not of 1 peso but of 25 pesos! When the author visited Mexico in 1991, local shops at the border noted that one United States dollar was worth 3,000 Mexican pesos, a vivid example of continuing depreciation of the value of Mexico's standard currency unit.

The country of Switzerland has produced many magnificent crown-size coins in recent centuries. Perhaps the most famous of these are the so-called "shooting talers"—dollar-size coins used to commemorate shooting festivals held by sportsmen in that alpine land. A few examples are the coins issued for the 1842 festival in Chur, Switzerland, the 1855 festival in Solothurn, the 1857 festival in Bern, the 1859 event in Zurich, and the 1876 gathering in Lausanne. There are many other issues as well.

In recent years a number of countries have capitalized on collector interest for crown-size coins and have produced pieces in large quantities for sale to numismatists. Often these have been sold at a high premium above their intrinsic value. In other instances, the pieces have been given a high face value but represent a true production cost of much less. The hope is, of course, that buyers will not go to the country issuing the coins, often an obscure place, and redeem them. So great have the abuses been in this area that many numismatists refuse to buy certain new issues at the time of release, knowing they can buy them cheaper later! Certain pieces which are legal tender but which are made primarily for sale to collectors, just as some countries issued commemorative stamps just for collectors, have been designated as "non-circulating legal tender" (NCLT) issues and are described that way in the Krause-Mishler catalogue and elsewhere. Many such pieces are fascinating to collect, but it is important to be aware of promotional aspects, to be careful of the price you pay, and to realize that it may be decades before there is a broad-based numismatic demand for them.

By comparison to many modern issues, the surviving quantities of early crown issues of the years prior to about 1940, particularly those in better grades of condition, are very small. The earlier pieces have been excellent investments in the past, and with a worldwide interest in coin collecting I believe they will be excellent investments in the future. As guidelines, I recommend that you select pieces of better grades, emphasize "type" pieces (as opposed to rare sub-varieties), and diversify your investment among at least several different countries.

Minor Coins of the World

Classified as "minor coins" are the pieces of less than crown or dollar size. Such coins circulated as small change within the currency system of a given country. Just as American numismatists collect Lincoln cents and Jefferson nickels by date and mintmark varieties, collectors of other countries often aspire to complete date and mint sets of centimes, kroner, centavos, and other minor denominations, often struck in bronze, nickel, aluminum, and other non-precious metals. Prior to about the 1960s, most countries utilized silver for denominations other than the very lowest ones.

Due to the vast number of issues produced in past centuries, the market for rare dates and mintmarks is usually confined to numismatists within that country. To be sure, there are some exceptions: American numismatists are avid collectors of Canadian, British, and Mexican coins by dates and mintmarks, for example. However, it is true to say that the main market for centime pieces by date and mint is with French numismatists, the main market for pfennigs by date and mint is with German collectors, and so on.

Often the number of varieties can be quite extensive. For example, German mints since 1850 comprise nearly a dozen locations, as indicated by the following mintmarks: A for Berlin, B for Hannover (until 1878), B for Vienna (1938 to 1945 only), C for Frankfurt, D for Munich, E for Dresden, F for Stuttgart, G for

Interesting Minor (less than crown size) Coins of the World

Great Britain: Very rare pattern 1937-dated coins of King Edward VIII. Shown are the penny, shilling, farthing (1/4 penny), sixpence, and half crown. A crown-size piece (not illustrated) accompanied the group.

German East Africa: 1890 1 rupie in silver.

Mexico: 1736 two-real or "two-bit" piece in silver. Pillar design.

Hong Kong: Bronze cent of 1941. Very rare issue. Only a few were released.

German New Guinea: 1894 1 mark with the bird of paradise motif.

Karlsruhe, H for Darmstadt, and J for Hamburg. Considering all of these mints, the number of coins produced is simply tremendous. To cite but a random example, the collector of one-mark coins (a mark is a silver coin about the size of a United States quarter dollar) would for the year 1874 have the following varieties to gather: 1874-A, 1874-B, 1874-C, 1874-D, 1874-E, 1874-F, 1874-G, and 1874-H!

Often a mint produced coins for many different countries. Perhaps the world's most prolific mint in terms of internationality was the Heaton Mint in Birmingham, England. This mint produced coins, usually designated by an "H" mintmark, for many different countries throughout the British Empire, including dozens of Canadian issues. The Heaton Mint, privately owned, also produced many pieces for Great Britain, especially during times when the facilities of the Royal Mint were extremely busy.

Another interesting private mint in England was the curiously named King's Norton Mint, which produced English pennies during the years of 1918 and 1919. These coins, designated as 1918-KN and 1919-KN, were made in relatively small quantities and are highly desired by collectors today.

In 1904 a tiny coin appeared in Panama; a coin scarcely the size of an aspirin tablet and with a value of 2 1/2 centesimos. Made of silver, this coin is affectionately known as the "Panama pill." The curiosity value of this piece has made it a favorite with collectors. This illustrates another point: often items with a "story" or with come particularly unusual feature are in great demand by collectors.

Throughout the panorama of world coins there are many pieces with interesting stories. Such historical associations often make pieces popular with collectors, even though the same collectors would not otherwise seek these coins.

Interesting examples include the 1929 one-puffin and half-puffin issues of the island of Lundy. In 1925 Martin Coles Harmon, a businessman from London, purchased this small island situated off the coast of the southern part of England. In 1929 he produced these small coins as souvenirs and for circulation in his private empire. Created mainly as a curiosity, the pieces depicted the puffin, a bird indigenous to that lonely isle. In April 1930 the British government fined Harman for producing coins in contravention of the Coinage Act of 1850. This did not prevent coins from reaching numismatists, and today these coins are avidly sought by collectors.

Investment in minor coins presents some questions to ponder: Will the collecting of minor coins by date and mintmark varieties ever be popular with collectors who reside within that particular country? Are the pieces relatively immune to the effects of restriking and counterfeiting (does the country have stringent laws against this)? Are the coins attractively designed and of pleasing appearance?

If the preceding questions can be answered in the affirmative, then chances are that a given coin will be a good investment—providing it is a scarce issue and is not high priced at the present time. Attractive profits have been made by many of our clients who have correctly anticipated that certain countries of the world—particularly Canada, Great Britain, France, Germany, Japan, Switzerland, and the Scandinavian countries—would develop numismatists within their borders who would collect their own country's coinage by dates and mintmarks. The market for such specialized collecting is still in its infancy, and there are many attractive profits still to be made.

There is no single source where you can find complete information about coins of the world from ancient times to the present. Even a beginning library on the subject would fill a bookshelf. About $100 to $200 will buy you most of the popular reference books. In addition, such periodical publications as *Coin World* and *Numismatic News* and the specialized (coins of the world only; United States coins are not featured) *World Coin News*, to mention just three of several news sources printed in America, have offerings, information, and other news about coins of the world. Many fine catalogues are available from dealers.

A word of caution: The best way to buy foreign minor coins is from a specialist or auction house which regularly sells coins of the world. In recent times (1990 and 1991) a number of investment-oriented firms have bought up world coins for cheap prices, have had them certified and put in plastic slabs, and have marketed them to buyers in the United States as "good investments" at prices far in excess of what similarly-graded coins would have cost if ordered from a world coin professional numismatist. For starters, check to see if the seller is a member in good standing of the International Association of Professional Numismatists (IAPN), the leading worldwide dealers' organization.

Coins of the world offer many attractive opportunities. Some study is required, and a bit of intellectual curiosity will do no harm either! The standard of living is rising around the world, and with it is coming a growing interest in coin collecting. Buying coins today to satisfy the demand of tomorrow can be quite rewarding!

Ancient Coins

Among the most interesting of all coins in numismatics are bronze, silver, and gold coins issued by Greece and Rome during their height of glory. Cleopatra, the Caesars, Mark Antony, and many other personalities are depicted on such issues. It is interesting to note that today the visages of certain ancient emperors are known only by their portraits on coins; no other forms of art have survived.

As an investment, ancient coins have many advantages. First, there is truly a worldwide market for them. Silver coins of Rhodes, an island in the Aegean Sea, are just as avidly collected by numismatists in Switzerland as they are by collectors in the United States, England, or Australia. Ancient pieces have a close link to history. Personalities are depicted and numerous events are commemorated. By means of changing denominations and alloys the monetary systems of ancient times can be studied as can the rise and fall of empires.

While there are many classic rarities, and while ancient gold coins are mainly of interest to the wealthy who can afford them, still there are numerous inexpensive issues. Today certain bronze coins have retail values in the $5 to $10 range, certainly affordable by any standard.

In the past a carefully formed collection of ancient coins has proven to be a good investment over a long period of years. However, the field is mined with clever forgeries, and often prices can be erratic with one seller charging twice or three times the price another asks.

Before venturing into ancient coins as an investment, I strongly recommend that you buy reference books, examine first hand pieces in museums and collections, and become acquainted with experts. This will necessarily take some time to do, perhaps a year or two as a beginning. Do this and you will be rewarded with a virtually limitless field for study, exploration, and research. And, your collection, if selected carefully, should do well for you.

Postscript

 It is my hope that the preceding pages have been of value to you. If you've read what I have had to say, you are now in a position to take advantage of the knowledge which has made untold millions of dollars for the customers of my firm.

It is a great feeling to make money for others—it is like doing a favor for a fine friend. It is my sincere wish that this book will be your guide for making lots of money. Follow the precepts I have outlined, and the book should literally be worth its weight in gold to you.

Writing in the February-March 1959 issue of *Empire Topics*, I said: "Our outlook on the coin market for 1959? With the possible exception [of very modern issues] most United States coins should continue their steady appreciation in value. This will be particularly true of early material in choice condition...." In that issue of nearly 30 years ago my firm offered for sale many different choice early coins. Without exception, each and every Uncirculated or Proof coin has *multiplied* in value.

When I wrote the first edition of this book in 1974, I reprinted the previous paragraphs, noting that "1959 is not today, you might say—and this is true. However, the principles which guided successful coin investment in 1959 and have resulted in fortunes being made for our customers since then are still in effect today."

How true these words were! Now, in 1991, 1974 seems like "ancient history." If you had followed the advice given in the first edition of this book and had spent $100,000 or so in coins, chances are you would be a millionaire today! This book was not secretly distributed. Indeed, it was widely advertised in *Coin World*, *Numismatic News*, and elsewhere. Many people purchased the book.

Some used it. Some did not. I feel sorry for those who relegated it to disuse on the shelf.

On the other hand, I appreciate very much the many comments received from buyers who did use the book. While my profit is not any greater with the person who used the book as opposed to the person who did not, my satisfaction is immeasurable when I help someone make a large sum of money. As noted earlier, this is one of the greatest feelings anyone can experience!

Today you might take the attitude that the opportunities which existed in 1974—or 1959—are gone forever, as indeed they are. By the same reasoning, you can look at *The Wall Street Journal* and wish that you had bought certain stocks 10, 20, or 30 years ago. Today is today, the present is what we have to deal with. Read this book carefully—indeed at this point you may have already contemplated every paragraph—and then act just as carefully using your knowledge. I am not aware of even a single person—no, not even one—who has purchased this book in the past, who has followed its advice carefully, and who has done other than make a profit after following the advice given. Now, you might be the exception, but I doubt it. I believe that a "treasure for the future" is awaiting *you*. Let this book be your passport to building a truly fine numismatic *collection*—which both you and I hope will also be a great investment over a period of time.

Q. David Bowers

APPENDICES

SOME FACTS AND FIGURES

INDEX

125,000			$122,400
120,000			
115,000			
110,000	**Performance Comparison ***		
105,000	**Of 127 Selected Rare Coins**		
100,000	1946-1991		
95,000			
90,000			
85,000			
80,000			
75,000			
70,000			
65,000			
60,000			
55,000			
50,000			
45,000			
40,000			
35,000			
30,000		$25,914	
25,000			
20,000			
15,000			
10,000	$8,985		
5,000			
0			

$1,000 Purchasing Power	5% Savings Account	S & P 500 Stock Index	Selected Rare Coins

This graph compares price performance of 127 scarce and rare coins (individually enumerated on the pages to follow). These coins are not necessarily representative of the coin market as a whole, nor are they representative of any selected aspect of it. Rather, they are the author's idea of typical coins which may have been selected by a discriminating buyer. It is important to remember that past performance is no guarantee or indication of the future.

Coins listing at $4,712 in 1946 increased to $576,746 by 1991. In other words, each $1,000 in 1946 increased to $122,400 replacement value 45 years later!

*Computations reflect price data from 1992-dated edition of A Guide Book of United States Coins, reflecting 1991 prices in comparison with the Standard &Poor's 500 Stock Composite Index and the return on a 5% savings account as of July 18, 1991.

Selected Coin Prices 1946-1991

1652 Pine Tree Shilling Grade: Fine	1786 Vermont Baby Head Grade: Fine	1855 Half Cent Grade: Uncirculated
1946 .... $27.50	1946 .... $10	1946 .... $4.50
1950 .... $30	1950 .... $12.50	1950 .... $5
1955 .... $37.50	1955 .... $15	1955 .... $8
1960 .... $65	1960 .... $45	1960 .... $14
1965 .... $165	1965 .... $90	1965 .... $47.50
1970 .... $265	1970 .... $175	1970 .... $67.50
1975 .... $475	1975 .... $500	1975 .... $200
1980 .... $1200	1980 .... $600	1980 .... $350
1985 .... $700	1985 .... $550	1985 .... $300
1990 .... $1100	1990 .... $800	1990 .... $275
1991 .... $1100	1991 .... $800	1991 .... $225
Increase: 3,900%	**Increase: 7,900%**	**Increase: 4,900%**

Beginning on this page I give the price histories of selected United States coins, including regular copper, silver, and gold issues, plus colonials and commemoratives. I have included a number of major scarcities and rarities for two reasons: (1) These are numismatic classics of the past and should continue to be numismatic classics of the future, and (2) I have owned specimens of these coins in the past and have recommended them to clients over the years.

The prices given are from A *Guide Book of United States Coins* and are used with permission of the Western Publishing Company. As the "cover date" of each issue is one year in advance of the publication date, my 1991 prices are from the 1992 edition (published in the summer of 1991). Really choice examples of scarcities and rarities have often sold for over catalogue prices in the past. If anything, certain 1991 figures are conservative for better graded coins.

In some instances I have given the price movement of the same coin in different grades; in Uncirculated and Proof grades, for example. Taken as a whole, prices of choice rare coins have advanced steadily over the years. However, individual coin prices move upward or downward at varying rates. For this reason, I have always recommended diversification across many different coin issues. The figures given start with 1946, the first year that the *Guide Book* was published, and then beginning in 1950 continue at five-year intervals, plus the edition of the most recent year, 1991, making this a 45-year study of rare coin prices.

For eight issues of coins in the following study (1795 half dime, 1797 15-stars half dime, 1800 half dime, 1796 dime, 1805 half dollar, 1795 Flowing Hair dollar 1796 silver dollar and 1796 $2\frac{1}{2}$ gold), Uncirculated prices were estimated to reflect values in 1946, as in the first edition of the *Guide Book* they were priced only in Fine or Very Fine grade. Beginning with 1950 the actual *Guide Book* prices are used.

1854 Cent
Grade: Uncirculated

1946	$3.50
1950	$4
1955	$5.50
1960	$11
1965	$40
1970	$62.50
1975	$165
1980	$200
1985	$275
1990	$210
1991	$210

Increase: 5,900%

1859 Cent
Grade: Uncirculated

1946	$4.50
1950	$5.50
1955	$10
1960	$35
1965	$90
1970	$82.50
1975	$385
1980	$375
1985	$300
1990	$200
1991	$175

Increase: 3,788%

1859 Cent
Grade: Proof

1946	$10
1950	$11
1955	$13.50
1960	$80
1965	$600
1970	$600
1975	$750
1980	$1000
1985	$1500
1990	$1300
1991	$1000

Increase: 9,900%

1906 Cent
Grade: Uncirculated

1946	$1
1950	75¢
1955	$1.50
1960	$4.25
1965	$12.50
1970	$9.25
1975	$25
1980	$32.50
1985	$32.50
1990	$30
1991	$25

Increase: 2,400%

1865 2¢ Piece
Grade: Uncirculated

1946	$1
1950	$1
1955	$3.50
1960	$8.50
1965	$22.50
1970	$27.50
1975	$135
1980	$200
1985	$175
1990	$135
1991	$100

Increase: 9,900%

1865 Nickel 3¢ Piece
Grade: Uncirculated

1946	$1.35
1950	$1.25
1955	$2.50
1960	$5
1965	$13
1970	$17.50
1975	$80
1980	$200
1985	$125
1990	$85
1991	$75

Increase: 5,455%

1882 Nickel 5¢
Grade: Proof

1946	$4
1950	$4
1955	$8
1960	$16.50
1965	$56
1970	$70
1975	$135
1980	$800
1985	$675
1990	$500
1991	$400

Increase: 9,900%

1910 Nickel 5¢
Grade: Proof

1946	$3.50
1950	$3.75
1955	$7.50
1960	$17.50
1965	$47.50
1970	$55
1975	$110
1980	$325
1985	$525
1990	$375
1991	$200

Increase: 5,614%

1913 TI Buffalo 5¢
Grade: Uncirculated

1946	75¢
1950	75¢
1955	$1.50
1960	$3.50
1965	$9
1970	$11
1975	$25
1980	$60
1985	$75
1990	$80
1991	$50

Increase: 6,566%

1852 Silver 3¢ Piece
Grade: Uncirculated

1946	$3.25
1950	$3.50
1955	$5.50
1960	$10.50
1965	$27.50
1970	$50
1975	$137.50
1980	$400
1985	$270
1990	$200
1991	$175

Increase: 5,285%

1858 Silver 3¢ Piece
Grade: Uncirculated

1946	$2.50
1950	$2.75
1955	$7
1960	$14
1965	$50
1970	$85
1975	$490
1980	$800
1985	$450
1990	$325
1991	$300

Increase: 11,900%

1859 Silver 3¢ Piece
Grade: Uncirculated

1946	$3
1950	$3
1955	$9
1960	$15
1965	$32
1970	$55
1975	$150
1980	$400
1985	$275
1990	$200
1991	$175

Increase: 5,733%

1795 Half Dime
Grade: Uncirculated

1946	$30
1950	$45
1955	$65
1960	$200
1965	$750
1970	$950
1975	$2475
1980	$6000
1985	$8000
1990	$6750
1991	$5500

Increase: 12,122%

1797 15-Star ½ 10¢
Grade: Uncirculated

1946	$56
1950	$80
1955	$120
1960	$215
1965	$1000
1970	$1325
1975	$3800
1980	$6250
1985	$7500
1990	$7500
1991	$6500

Increase: 11,507%

1800 Half Dime
Grade: Fine

1946	$12.50
1950	$15
1955	$25
1960	$70
1965	$240
1970	$300
1975	$350
1980	$650
1985	$1000
1990	$900
1991	$900

Increase: 7,100%

1800 Half Dime
Grade: Uncirculated

1946	$42
1950	$50
1955	$80
1960	$215
1965	$900
1970	$1150
1975	$3650
1980	$6000
1985	$7000
1990	$7000
1991	$6000

Increase: 14,186%

1862 Half Dime
Grade: Uncirculated

1946	$1.50
1950	$1.25
1955	$3.50
1960	$6.50
1965	$20
1970	$40
1975	$150
1980	$375
1985	$275
1990	$175
1991	$175

Increase: 11,567%

1832 Half Dime
Grade: Uncirculated

1946	$2.25
1950	$2.50
1955	$5.50
1960	$10
1965	$50
1970	$82.50
1975	$325
1980	$550
1985	$600
1990	$400
1991	$425

Increase: 18,789%

1842 Half Dime
Grade: Uncirculated

1946	$2.50
1950	$2.50
1955	$5
1960	$11
1965	$27.50
1970	$40
1975	$200
1980	$450
1985	$325
1990	$250
1991	$250

Increase: 9,900%

1862 Half Dime
Grade: Proof

1946	$5
1950	$4.50
1955	$10
1960	$24
1965	$60
1970	$90
1975	$165
1980	$550
1985	$850
1990	$750
1991	$750

Increase: 14,900%

1837 No Stars ½ 10¢
Grade: Uncirculated

1946	$4.50
1950	$8
1955	$20
1960	$65
1965	$225
1970	$275
1975	$600
1980	$1200
1985	$800
1990	$600
1991	$600

Increase: 13,233%

1853 Arrows ½ 10¢
Grade: Uncirculated

1946	$1.25
1950	$1.50
1955	$5
1960	$10.50
1965	$33.50
1970	$60
1975	$260
1980	$625
1985	$350
1990	$250
1991	$225

Increase: 17,900%

1796 Dime
Grade: Uncirculated

1946	$109
1950	$125
1955	$175
1960	$485
1965	$2000
1970	$2450
1975	$5200
1980	$9000
1985	$10,000
1990	$10,000
1991	$10,000

Increase: 9,074%

1807 Dime
Grade: Uncirculated

1946	$25
1950	$30
1955	$47.50
1960	$95
1965	$550
1970	$700
1975	$2000
1980	$5250
1985	$5000
1990	$4500
1991	$4700

Increase: 18,700%

1827 Dime
Grade: Uncirculated

1946	$7.50
1950	$8.50
1955	$12.50
1960	$27.50
1965	$125
1970	$180
1975	$2000
1980	$2100
1985	$1350
1990	$1250
1991	$1000

Increase: 13,233%

1832 Dime
Grade: Uncirculated

1946	$3
1950	$3
1955	$6
1960	$12.50
1965	$70
1970	$145
1975	$800
1980	$1600
1985	$775
1990	$800
1991	$750

Increase: 24,900%

1837 No Stars Dime
Grade: Uncirculated

1946	$12.50
1950	$15
1955	$32.50
1960	$87.50
1965	$240
1970	$350
1975	$1250
1980	$2100
1985	$1100
1990	$900
1991	$950

Increase: 7,500%

1853 Arrows Dime
Grade: Uncirculated

1946	$1.75
1950	$2.50
1955	$5.50
1960	$10
1965	$30
1970	$60
1975	$350
1980	$750
1985	$350
1990	$350
1991	$300

Increase: 17,043%

1863 Dime
Grade: Uncirculated

1946	$2.50
1950	$7.50
1955	$12.50
1960	$24
1965	$55
1970	$90
1975	$400
1980	$1100
1985	$800
1990	$1000
1991	$1000

Increase: 39,900%

1863 Dime
Grade: Proof

1946	$6.50
1950	$7.50
1955	$15
1960	$47.50
1965	$85
1970	$120
1975	$250
1980	$600
1985	$1100
1990	$1000
1991	$1000

Increase: 15,285%

1874 Dime
Grade: Fine

1946	75¢
1950	$1
1955	$4
1960	$9.50
1965	$19
1970	$19
1975	$27.50
1980	$27.50
1985	$18.50
1990	$16
1991	$16

Increase: 2,033%

1874 Dime
Grade: Uncirculated

1946	$2
1950	$3.50
1955	$14
1960	$40
1965	$95
1970	$155
1975	$400
1980	$1100
1985	$750
1990	$700
1991	$600

Increase: 29,900%

1874 Dime
Grade: Proof

1946	$4
1950	$5
1955	$22.50
1960	$70
1965	$225
1970	$300
1975	$475
1980	$1300
1985	$2200
1990	$2000
1991	$1800

Increase: 44,900%

1901 Dime
Grade: Proof

1946	$4
1950	$4
1955	$7.50
1960	$30
1965	$60
1970	$95
1975	$175
1980	$600
1985	$825
1990	$950
1991	$750

Increase: 18,650%

1942 Dime
Grade: Proof

1946	$1.25
1950	$1
1955	$3.25
1960	$5
1965	$22.50
1970	$20
1975	$55
1980	$425
1985	$500
1990	$700
1991	$550

Increase: 43,900%

1875-S 20¢ Piece
Grade: Uncirculated

1946	$4
1950	$6
1955	$17.50
1960	$35
1965	$90
1970	$175
1975	$700
1980	$1100
1985	$1000
1990	$800
1991	$700

Increase: 17,400%

1876 20¢ Piece
Grade: Proof

1946	$17.50
1950	$20
1955	$35
1960	$70
1965	$210
1970	$275
1975	$850
1980	$1800
1985	$2700
1990	$2700
1991	$2400

Increase: 13,614%

1796 Quarter
Grade: Fine

1946	$65
1950	$75
1955	$150
1960	$750
1965	$2000
1970	$2150
1975	$2500
1980	$3750
1985	$4300
1990	$5500
1991	$7000

Increase: 10,669%

1796 Quarter
Grade: Uncirculated

1946	$100
1950	$175
1955	$325
1960	$1450
1965	$4250
1970	$5750
1975	$12,000
1980	$23,000
1985	$22,000
1990	$30,000
1991	$30,000

Increase: 29,900%

1806 Quarter
Grade: Fine

1946 .... $5
1950 .... $8
1955 .... $17.50
1960 .... $37.50
1965 .... $110
1970 .... $125
1975 .... $175
1980 .... $325
1985 .... $500
1990 .... $500
1991 .... $425

Increase: 8,400%

1806 Quarter
Grade: Uncirculated

1946 .... $25
1950 .... $35
1955 .... $65
1960 .... $175
1965 .... $640
1970 .... $850
1975 .... $2250
1980 .... $7000
1985 .... $6750
1990 .... $7000
1991 .... $5000

Increase: 19,900%

1818 Quarter
Grade: Uncirculated

1946 .... $15
1950 .... $15
1955 .... $30
1960 .... $70
1965 .... $245
1970 .... $450
1975 .... $2000
1980 .... $3100
1985 .... $2100
1990 .... $2300
1991 .... $2400

Increase: 15,900%

1832 Quarter
Grade: Uncirculated

1946 .... $5.50
1950 .... $5
1955 .... $12.50
1960 .... $23
1965 .... $100
1970 .... $300
1975 .... $1400
1980 .... $1900
1985 .... $1100
1990 .... $1100
1991 .... $1000

Increase: 18,082%

1839 Quarter
Grade: Uncirculated

1946 .... $6.50
1950 .... $7.50
1955 .... $13.50
1960 .... $22.50
1965 .... $75
1970 .... $110
1975 .... $1250
1980 .... $2600
1985 .... $1800
1990 .... $1800
1991 .... $1700

Increase: 26,054%

1853 A&R Quarter
Grade: Uncirculated

1946 .... $3.50
1950 .... $5
1955 .... $11
1960 .... $25
1965 .... $65
1970 .... $350
1975 .... $950
1980 .... $1600
1985 .... $1000
1990 .... $1100
1991 .... $900

Increase: 25,614%

1861 Quarter
Grade: Uncirculated

1946 .... $1.75
1950 .... $2.25
1955 .... $4.50
1960 .... $9
1965 .... $25
1970 .... $47.50
1975 .... $325
1980 .... $750
1985 .... $450
1990 .... $400
1991 .... $350

Increase: 19,900%

1861 Quarter
Grade: Proof

1946	$10
1950	$10
1955	$12
1960	$40
1965	$95
1970	$140
1975	$400
1980	$800
1985	$1000
1990	$1300
1991	$1400

Increase: 13,900%

1874 Quarter
Grade: Uncirculated

1946	$3
1950	$4.50
1955	$20
1960	$60
1965	$150
1970	$200
1975	$475
1980	$1300
1985	$1000
1990	$1000
1991	$1000

Increase: 33,233%

1878 Quarter
Grade: Proof

1946	$5
1950	$5.50
1955	$7.50
1960	$24
1965	$57.50
1970	$80
1975	$325
1980	$625
1985	$950
1990	$1000
1991	$1000

Increase: 19,900%

1874 Quarter
Grade: Proof

1946	$7.50
1950	$8
1955	$30
1960	$100
1965	$250
1970	$325
1975	$550
1980	$1500
1985	$2300
1990	$2300
1991	$2000

Increase: 26,567%

1882 Quarter
Grade: Uncirculated

1946	$2.50
1950	$5
1955	$10
1960	$19
1965	$47.50
1970	$85
1975	$350
1980	$1000
1985	$650
1990	$650
1991	$650

Increase: 25,900%

1874 Quarter
Grade: Fine

1946	$1
1950	$1.50
1955	$7.50
1960	$17.50
1965	$28
1970	$28
1975	$40
1980	$30
1985	$20
1990	$22
1991	$25

Increase: 2,400%

1878 Quarter
Grade: Uncirculated

1946	$1.75
1950	$2.50
1955	$5
1960	$6.50
1965	$20
1970	$47.50
1975	$250
1980	$700
1985	$375
1990	$375
1991	$300

Increase: 17,043%

1882 Quarter
Grade: Proof

1946	$5
1950	$6.50
1955	$12.50
1960	$30
1965	$70
1970	$100
1975	$350
1980	$675
1985	$1100
1990	$1200
1991	$1200

Increase: 23,900%

1908 Quarter
Grade: Uncirculated

1946	$3.50
1950	$3.50
1955	$6.50
1960	$10.50
1965	$25
1970	$42.50
1975	$190
1980	$385
1985	$300
1990	$250
1991	$210

Increase: 5,900%

1908 Quarter
Grade: Proof

1946	$6
1950	$6.50
1955	$11
1960	$47.50
1965	$82.50
1970	$120
1975	$300
1980	$600
1985	$900
1990	$1200
1991	$1000

Increase: 16,567%

1917 TI Quarter
Grade: Uncirculated

1946	$2.75
1950	$2.75
1955	$5.50
1960	$10
1965	$36
1970	$47.50
1975	$175
1980	$275
1985	$250
1990	$500
1991	$350

Increase: 12,627%

1918/7-S Quarter
Grade: Uncirculated

1946	$150
1950	$150
1955	$250
1960	$700
1965	$2900
1970	$3250
1975	$4500
1980	$6250
1985	$15,000
1990	$15,000
1991	$25,000

Increase: 16,566%

1929 Quarter
Grade: Uncirculated

1946	$1.50
1950	$2.50
1955	$4.50
1960	$7.50
1965	$22.50
1970	$35
1975	$75
1980	$150
1985	$185
1990	$350
1991	$200

Increase: 13,233%

1932 Quarter
Grade: Uncirculated

1946	$1.35
1950	$1.75
1955	$3
1960	$6
1965	$12
1970	$15
1975	$30
1980	$35
1985	$60
1990	$60
1991	$60

Increase: 4,344%

1797 Half Dollar
Grade: Fine

1946	$200
1950	$225
1955	$325
1960	$675
1965	$2700
1970	$3800
1975	$4500
1980	$8500
1985	$15,000
1990	$17,000
1991	$17,000

Increase: 8,400%

1805 Half Dollar
Grade: Uncirculated

1946	$21
1950	$22.50
1955	$35
1960	$90
1965	$450
1970	$650
1975	$2000
1980	$8000
1985	$5500
1990	$5500
1991	$5500

Increase: 26,090%

1815/2 Half Dollar
Grade: Uncirculated

1946	$45
1950	$65
1955	$90
1960	$240
1965	$600
1970	$875
1975	$2250
1980	$3000
1985	$5000
1990	$6000
1991	$6000

Increase: 13,233%

1833 Half Dollar
Grade: Uncirculated

1946	$3.50
1950	$3.75
1955	$6
1960	$15
1965	$25
1970	$65
1975	$350
1980	$650
1985	$750
1990	$900
1991	$900

Increase: 25,614%

1837 Half Dollar
Grade: Uncirculated

1946	$6
1950	$6.50
1955	$12.50
1960	$45
1965	$95
1970	$190
1975	$550
1980	$1500
1985	$900
1990	$1100
1991	$1100

Increase: 18,233%

1838 Half Dollar
Grade: Uncirculated

1946	$5
1950	$6.50
1955	$15
1960	$45
1965	$85
1970	$175
1975	$600
1980	$1500
1985	$900
1990	$1100
1991	$1200

Increase: 23,900%

1844 Half Dollar
Grade: Uncirculated

1946	$8
1950	$7.50
1955	$10
1960	$21
1965	$45
1970	$70
1975	$325
1980	$775
1985	$575
1990	$550
1991	$500

Increase: 6,150%

1853 Half Dollar
Grade: Uncirculated

1946	$6.50
1950	$8
1955	$17.50
1960	$42.50
1965	$90
1970	$450
1975	$1500
1980	$4000
1985	$2000
1990	$2000
1991	$1800

Increase: 27,592%

1854 Half Dollar
Grade: Uncirculated

1946	$3
1950	$4
1955	$8.50
1960	$19
1965	$45
1970	$100
1975	$500
1980	$1200
1985	$900
1990	$850
1991	$700

Increase: 23,233%

**1863 Half Dollar
Grade: Uncirculated**

1946 .... $5
1950 .... $4.50
1955 .... $6.50
1960 .... $13
1965 .... $35
1970 .... $65
1975 .... $350
1980 .... $850
1985 .... $700
1990 .... $700
1991 .... $700

Increase: 13,900%

**1863 Half Dollar
Grade: Proof**

1946 .... $12
1950 .... $11
1955 .... $20
1960 .... $70
1965 .... $115
1970 .... $165
1975 .... $425
1980 .... $800
1985 .... $1300
1990 .... $1500
1991 .... $1500

Increase: 12,400%

**1874 Half Dollar
Grade: Uncirculated**

1946 .... $3.75
1950 .... $6
1955 .... $20
1960 .... $75
1965 .... $165
1970 .... $250
1975 .... $550
1980 .... $1700
1985 .... $1000
1990 .... $900
1991 .... $900

Increase: 23,900%

**1874 Half Dollar
Grade: Proof**

1946 .... $10
1950 .... $13.50
1955 .... $37.50
1960 .... $140
1965 .... $300
1970 .... $450
1975 .... $650
1980 .... $2000
1985 .... $2500
1990 .... $2300
1991 .... $2500

Increase: 24,900%

**1876-CC Half Dollar
Grade: Uncirculated**

1946 .... $6
1950 .... $5
1955 .... $9
1960 .... $22.50
1965 .... $45
1970 .... $65
1975 .... $350
1980 .... $800
1985 .... $625
1990 .... $600
1991 .... $600

Increase: 9,900%

**1877 Half Dollar
Grade: Uncirculated**

1946 .... $3
1950 .... $4
1955 .... $5.50
1960 .... $11
1965 .... $25
1970 .... $57.50
1975 .... $325
1980 .... $650
1985 .... $475
1990 .... $400
1991 .... $375

Increase: 12,400%

**1877 Half Dollar
Grade: Proof**

1946 .... $9
1950 .... $15
1955 .... $22.50
1960 .... $65
1965 .... $125
1970 .... $180
1975 .... $385
1980 .... $700
1985 .... $1200
1990 .... $1300
1991 .... $1300

Increase: 14,344%

**1886 Half Dollar
Grade: Uncirculated**

1946 .... $6.50
1950 .... $7.50
1955 .... $17.50
1960 .... $46
1965 .... $100
1970 .... $115
1975 .... $450
1980 .... $900
1985 .... $950
1990 .... $1000
1991 .... $1000

Increase: 15,285%

1903 Half Dollar
Grade: Proof

1946	$8.50
1950	$10
1955	$16
1960	$60
1965	$105
1970	$145
1975	$500
1980	$900
1985	$1500
1990	$1500
1991	$1300

Increase: 15,194%

1942 Half Dollar
Grade: Proof

1946	$2.50
1950	$2.50
1955	$8
1960	$11
1965	$50
1970	$55
1975	$110
1980	$875
1985	$950
1990	$1350
1991	$1050

Increase: 41,900%

1886 Half Dollar
Grade: Proof

1946	$12
1950	$12.50
1955	$47.50
1960	$100
1965	$135
1970	$160
1975	$385
1980	$700
1985	$1400
1990	$1500
1991	$1500

Increase: 12,400%

1916 Half Dollar
Grade: Uncirculated

1946	$5
1950	$5.50
1955	$17.50
1960	$25
1965	$55
1970	$110
1975	$210
1980	$400
1985	$450
1990	$375
1991	$225

Increase: 4,400%

1795 Flowing Hair $1
Grade: Fine

1946	$20
1950	$25
1955	$37.50
1960	$75
1965	$220
1970	$300
1975	$500
1980	$850
1985	$1800
1990	$1400
1991	$1000

Increase: 4,900%

1903 Half Dollar
Grade: Uncirculated

1946	$3.50
1950	$4
1955	$10
1960	$18.50
1965	$57.50
1970	$100
1975	$400
1980	$775
1985	$575
1990	$500
1991	$400

Increase: 11,329%

1795 Flowing Hair $1
Grade: Uncirculated

1946	$131
1950	$150
1955	$160
1960	$400
1965	$1100
1970	$1600
1975	$12,500
1980	$18,000
1985	$30,000
1990	$25,000
1991	$20,000

Increase: 15,167%

1796 Silver Dollar
Grade: Uncirculated

1946	$78
1950	$125
1955	$140
1960	$275
1965	$950
1970	$1600
1975	$7000
1980	$13,000
1985	$12,500
1990	$15,000
1991	$14,000

Increase: 17,849%

1847 Silver Dollar
Grade: Uncirculated

1946	$10
1950	$15
1955	$27.50
1960	$50
1965	$75
1970	$175
1975	$600
1980	$1000
1985	$950
1990	$1300
1991	$1300

Increase: 12,900%

1863 Silver Dollar
Grade: Uncirculated

1946	$12.50
1950	$13.50
1955	$30
1960	$65
1965	$110
1970	$245
1975	$600
1980	$1200
1985	$1700
1990	$2000
1991	$2000

Increase: 15,900%

1863 Silver Dollar
Grade: Proof

1946	$22.50
1950	$25
1955	$45
1960	$110
1965	$200
1970	$425
1975	$1000
1980	$2000
1985	$2500
1990	$4000
1991	$3750

Increase: 16,567%

1870 Silver Dollar
Grade: Uncirculated

1946	$7.50
1950	$11
1955	$20
1960	$36
1965	$50
1970	$125
1975	$575
1980	$800
1985	$1200
1990	$1600
1991	$1500

Increase: 19,900%

1870 Silver Dollar
Grade: Proof

1946	$14
1950	$20
1955	$30
1960	$60
1965	$170
1970	$325
1975	$1000
1980	$2000
1985	$2400
1990	$3500
1991	$3100

Increase: 22,043%

1879 Silver Dollar
Grade: Proof

1946	$10
1950	$10
1955	$17.50
1960	$60
1965	$150
1970	$220
1975	$500
1980	$1500
1985	$2000
1990	$3000
1991	$2500

Increase: 24,900%

1895 Silver Dollar
Grade: Proof

1946	$35
1950	$85
1955	$300
1960	$700
1965	$4500
1970	$4750
1975	$8000
1980	$20,000
1985	$13,500
1990	$14,000
1991	$14,000

Increase: 39,900%

1934-S Silver Dollar
Grade: Uncirculated

1946	$4
1950	$15
1955	$32.50
1960	$60
1965	$300
1970	$275
1975	$800
1980	$2500
1985	$2000
1990	$4800
1991	$3000

Increase: 74,900%

1878-S Trade Dollar
Grade: Uncirculated

1946	$4
1950	$6
1955	$13.50
1960	$20
1965	$35
1970	$100
1975	$400
1980	$650
1985	$725
1990	$725
1991	$600

Increase: 14,900%

1879 Trade Dollar
Grade: Proof

1946	$11
1950	$15
1955	$27.50
1960	$60
1965	$275
1970	$375
1975	$1150
1980	$2000
1985	$2750
1990	$3300
1991	$2600

Increase: 23,536%

1851 Gold Dollar
Grade: Uncirculated

1946	$7.50
1950	$7.50
1955	$14
1960	$35
1965	$45
1970	$75
1975	$300
1980	$850
1985	$750
1990	$600
1991	$450

Increase: 5,900%

1855 Gold Dollar
Grade: Uncirculated

1946	$12.50
1950	$12.50
1955	$20
1960	$65
1965	$275
1970	$450
1975	$2000
1980	$5000
1985	$3500
1990	$4500
1991	$3000

Increase: 23,900%

1862 Gold Dollar
Grade: Uncirculated

1946	$7
1950	$9
1955	$14
1960	$37.50
1965	$60
1970	$85
1975	$300
1980	$800
1985	$700
1990	$550
1991	$400

Increase: 5,614%

1875 Gold Dollar
Grade: Proof

1946	$300
1950	$275
1955	$325
1960	$550
1965	$2750
1970	$3700
1975	$10,000
1980	$20,000
1985	$25,000
1990	$25,000
1991	$25,000

Increase: 8,233%

1796 NS $2½ Gold
Grade: Uncirculated

1946	$300
1950	$300
1955	$450
1960	$1750
1965	$7250
1970	$7750
1975	$19,000
1980	$35,000
1985	$45,000
1990	$45,000
1991	$50,000

Increase: 16,567%

1808 $2¹/₂ Gold
Grade: Uncirculated

1946 .... $250
1950 .... $275
1955 .... $375
1960 .... $1750
1965 .... $6500
1970 .... $7000
1975 .... $18,000
1980 .... $40,000
1985 .... $50,000
1990 .... $47,500
1991 .... $50,000

Increase: 19,900%

1831 $2¹/₂ Gold
Grade: Uncirculated

1946 .... $75
1950 .... $75
1955 .... $80
1960 .... $190
1965 .... $950
1970 .... $1100
1975 .... $5500
1980 .... $10,000
1985 .... $13,000
1990 .... $13,500
1991 .... $12,000

Increase: 15,900%

1836 $2¹/₂ Gold
Grade: Uncirculated

1946 .... $18
1950 .... $17.50
1955 .... $17.50
1960 .... $35
1965 .... $120
1970 .... $200
1975 .... $1400
1980 .... $4000
1985 .... $2000
1990 .... $2400
1991 .... $2400

Increase: 13,233%

1848 CAL. $2¹/₂ Gold
Grade: Uncirculated

1946 .... $200
1950 .... $250
1955 .... $300
1960 .... $750
1965 .... $5500
1970 .... $6000
1975 .... $11,500
1980 .... $30,000
1985 .... $30,000
1990 .... $30,000
1991 .... $30,000

Increase: 14,900%

1908 $2¹/₂ Gold
Grade: Uncirculated

1946 .... $10
1950 .... $8
1955 .... $11
1960 .... $25
1965 .... $35
1970 .... $75
1975 .... $200
1980 .... $500
1985 .... $350
1990 .... $375
1991 .... $275

Increase: 2,650%

1854 $3 Gold
Grade: Uncirculated

1946 .... $22.50
1950 .... $27.50
1955 .... $45
1960 .... $140
1965 .... $275
1970 .... $350
1975 .... $1650
1980 .... $3500
1985 .... $3500
1990 .... $3200
1991 .... $2500

Increase: 11,011%

1879 Flowing Hair $4
Grade: Proof

1946 .... $550
1950 .... $500
1955 .... $950
1960 .... $2900
1965 .... $6000
1970 .... $6000
1975 .... $20,000
1980 .... $35,000
1985 .... $55,000
1990 .... $35,000
1991 .... $28,000

Increase: 4,991%

1795 $5 Gold
Grade: Uncirculated

1946 .... $150
1950 .... $150
1955 .... $250
1960 .... $500
1965 .... $2000
1970 .... $2500
1975 .... $8500
1980 .... $17,500
1985 .... $27,500
1990 .... $32,000
1991 .... $25,000

Increase: 16,567%

1805 $5 Gold
Grade: Uncirculated

1946	$60
1950	$50
1955	$82.50
1960	$160
1965	$700
1970	$750
1975	$2700
1980	$5000
1985	$10,000
1990	$9500
1991	$8000

Increase: 13,233%

1795 $10 Gold
Grade: Uncirculated

1946	$200
1950	$200
1955	$300
1960	$600
1965	$2500
1970	$3000
1975	$12,000
1980	$27,500
1985	$30,000
1990	$32,000
1991	$28,500

Increase: 14,150%

1808 $5 Gold
Grade: Fine

1946	$30
1950	$35
1955	$47.50
1960	$75
1965	$340
1970	$375
1975	$625
1980	$800
1985	$1100
1990	$1100
1991	$1100

Increase: 3,567%

1835 $5 Gold
Grade: Uncirculated

1946	$30
1950	$25
1955	$27.50
1960	$45
1965	$140
1970	$200
1975	$1100
1980	$5000
1985	$2500
1990	$2500
1991	$2500

Increase: 8,233%

1799 $10 Gold
Grade: Fine

1946	$75
1950	$65
1955	$80
1960	$175
1965	$475
1970	$550
1975	$1000
1980	$1500
1985	$2250
1990	$2250
1991	$2250

Increase: 2,900%

1808 $5 Gold
Grade: Uncirculated

1946	$55
1950	$47.50
1955	$75
1960	$150
1965	$575
1970	$625
1975	$2350
1980	$4500
1985	$9500
1990	$8000
1991	$7000

Increase: 12,627%

1908 $5 Gold
Grade: Uncirculated

1946	$17.50
1950	$13.50
1955	$20
1960	$22.50
1965	$35
1970	$80
1975	$125
1980	$800
1985	$900
1990	$650
1991	$400

Increase: 2,186%

1799 $10 Gold
Grade: Uncirculated

1946	$100
1950	$90
1955	$130
1960	$300
1965	$1050
1970	$1200
1975	$4500
1980	$8000
1985	$13,000
1990	$15,000
1991	$10,000

Increase: 9,900%

1911 $10 Gold
Grade: Uncirculated

1946	$37.50
1950	$35
1955	$35
1960	$35
1965	$50
1970	$90
1975	$285
1980	$1000
1985	$800
1990	$550
1991	$500

Increase: 1,233%

1907 MCMVII $20
Grade: Uncirculated

1946	$120
1950	$110
1955	$145
1960	$350
1965	$850
1970	$950
1975	$4400
1980	$10,000
1985	$9400
1990	$8500
1991	$6500

Increase: 5,317%

1928 $20 Gold
Grade: Uncirculated

1946	$70
1950	$60
1955	$55
1960	$55
1965	$80
1970	$85
1975	$340
1980	$850
1985	$775
1990	$575
1991	$500

Increase: 614%

1893 Isabella Quarter
Grade: Uncirculated

1946	$9.50
1950	$9.50
1955	$30
1960	$39
1965	$100
1970	$85
1975	$180
1980	$550
1985	$550
1990	$425
1991	$400

Increase: 4,110%

1915-S Pan-Pac ½ $1
Grade: Uncirculated

1946	$17.50
1950	$20
1955	$45
1960	$55
1965	$120
1970	$90
1975	$325
1980	$925
1985	$550
1990	$400
1991	$300

Increase: 1,614%

1928 Hawaiian ½ $1
Grade: Uncirculated

1946	$30
1950	$32.50
1955	$110
1960	$165
1965	$650
1970	$465
1975	$1000
1980	$1650
1985	$850
1990	$850
1991	$700

Increase: 2,233%

1900 Lafayette Dollar
Grade: Uncirculated

1946	$12.50
1950	$15
1955	$42.50
1960	$50
1965	$160
1970	$180
1975	$530
1980	$1900
1985	$1000
1990	$800
1991	$650

Increase: 5,100%

1915-S Pan-Pac $50
(Octagonal) Unc.

1946	$500
1950	$515
1955	$1150
1960	$2100
1965	$4750
1970	$4250
1975	$13,000
1980	$14,000
1985	$25,000
1990	$25,000
1991	$23,000

Increase: 4,500%

Index

E

Early American Cents: 127, 145

Early American Coppers Club: 278, 286, 289

Early Coins of America: 274

Early Half Dollar Die Varieties 1794-1836: 320

Early Paper Money of America: 376

Early United States Dimes 1796-1837: 311

Eliasberg Collection of United States Gold Coins: 22, 85, 169, 247, 274, 362

Eliasberg, Louis: 38, 40, 247

Elizabeth II of England: 402

Empire Coin Co., Inc: 35

Empire Investors Report: 76, 173, 262

Empire Topics: 363

Encyclopedia of United States Half Cents 1793-1857: 284

Eric P. Newman: 376

Evans, Bob: 366

Executive Gold Order of 1933: 356

exonumia: 385

F

Fazzari, F. Michael: 156

Federal Trade Commission: 16, 18, 62, 88, 90, 97, 145, 338

Fine Arts commemorative medallions: 372

Fivaz, Bill: 296, 348

Flynn, Joe: 205

Foley, Kevin: 144

Forecaster, The: 205, 262

Ford, John J. Jr.: 65, 130, 198

Forman, Harry: 76

Fort Knox: 349

Fractional Currency Shield: 381

Franklin, Benjamin: 48, 272

Friedberg, Robert: 368, 381

Frossard, Ed.: 49, 50

Fuld, Dr. George J.: 215

G

Gale, A.W.: 130, 131, 138

Garbaro, Frank: 259

Gengerke, Martin: 383

George I of England: 211

George V of England: 404

George VI of England: 402

Gettys, Loyd: 149

Gibbs, William: 314

Gobrecht, Christian: 328

Gobrecht Journal: 307

Gobrecht silver dollars: 328

Gold Certificates: 380

Gold Coins of the World, by Robert Friedberg: 368

Gold Rush: 23, 263, 363

Gothic crown: 404

Green, Col. E.H.R.: 55

Green, Hetty: 55

Guide Book of United States Coins: 28, 41, 68, 76, 126, 131, 132, 134, 143, 150, 170, 179, 224, 228, 230, 241, 248-250, 260, 265, 266, 284, 286, 287, 289, 292, 295-297, 299, 302, 305, 307, 308, 310, 311, 316, 319-321, 329, 341, 358, 362-364, 389, Garrett Collection: 45, 141, 142, 169, 170, 193, 214, 274, 328, 398

Garrett, John Work: 55

Garrett, T. Harrison: 27, 49, 55, 274

Garroway, Dave: 35

Gasparro, Frank: 259

Guttag Brothers: 65

H

half cents: 283

half dimes: 308

half dollars: 320

half dollars, Barber: 321

half dollars, Capped Bust: 320

half dollars, Franklin: 325

half dollars, Kennedy: 326

half dollars, Liberty Seated: 321

half dollars, Walking Liberty: 325

Hall, David: 287

Hancock, Virgil: 202

Hanks, Larry: 141

Hard Times tokens: 129, 274, 391

Harmon, Martin Coles: 408

Haseltine, Capt. John: 50, 281

Hawaiian Sesquicentennial half dollar: 23

Hawn, Reed: 141

Hayes, Jimmy, Collection: 250

Healey, Kelly: 16

Heath, Dr. George F.: 50

Heaton, Augustus G.: 50

Heaton Mint: 408

Hessler, Gene: 381

Hewitt, Lee: 203

Higgy Collection: 68

High Profits From Rare Coin Investment: 177

Highfill, John: 337

Higley, John: 214

Hines, Henry: 281

History of United States Coinage, The: 49, 215, 274

Hudson half dollars: 56

Hydeman, Edward: 38

Hydeman, Edwin: 37

I

Iacocca, Mike: 259

Internal Revenue Service: 269

International Association of Professional Numismatists: 269, 370, 409

Isabella quarter: 51

J

J.W. Scott & Co.: 51

James, Inc.: 70

Janeway, Eliot: 188

Jarvis, James: 214